# PRAXIS

# ELEMENTARY EDUCATION:
# MULTIPLE SUBJECTS (5001)

By: Sharon Wynne, M.S.

*XAMonline, INC.*

*Boston*

To obtain permission(s) to use the material from this work for any purpose including workshops or seminars, please submit a written request to:

XAMonline, Inc.
21 Orient Avenue
Melrose, MA 02176
Toll Free 1-800-509-4128
Email: info@xamonline.com
Web: www.xamonline.com
Fax: 1-617-583-5552

Library of Congress Cataloging-in-Publication Data

Wynne, Sharon A.
    PRAXIS Elementary Education: Multiple Subjects (5001) / Sharon A. Wynne. 2st ed
    ISBN 978-1-60787-3594
    1. Elementary Education 5001
    2. Study Guides
    3. PRAXIS
    4. Teachers' Certification & Licensure
    5. Careers

**Disclaimer:**

The opinions expressed in this publication are the sole works of XAMonline and were created independently from the National Education Association, Educational Testing Service, or any State Department of Education, National Evaluation Systems or other testing affiliates.

Between the time of publication and printing, state specific standards as well as testing formats and Web site information may change and therefore would not be included in part or in whole within this product. Sample test questions are developed by XAMonline and reflect content similar to that on real tests; however, they are not former test questions. XAMonline assembles content that aligns with state standards but makes no claims nor guarantees teacher candidates a passing score. Numerical scores are determined by testing companies such as NES or ETS and then are compared with individual state standards. A passing score varies from state to state.

Printed in the United States of America                                          œ-1

PRAXIS Elementary Education: Multiple Subjects (5001)
ISBN: 978-1-60787-3594

# PRAXIS
# ELEMENTARY EDUCATION: MULTIPLE SUBJECTS (5001)

# SECTION 1

## ABOUT XAMONLINE

### XAMonline—A Specialty Teacher Certification Company

Created in 1996, XAMonline was the first company to publish study guides for state-specific teacher certification examinations. Founder Sharon Wynne found it frustrating that materials were not available for teacher certification preparation and decided to create the first single, state-specific guide. XAMonline has grown into a company of over 1,800 contributors and writers and offers over 300 titles for the entire PRAXIS series and every state examination. No matter what state you plan on teaching in, XAMonline has a unique teacher certification study guide just for you.

### XAMonline—Value and Innovation

We are committed to providing value and innovation. Our print-on-demand technology allows us to be the first in the market to reflect changes in test standards and user feedback as they occur. Our guides are written by experienced teachers who are experts in their fields. And our content reflects the highest standards of quality. Comprehensive practice tests with varied levels of rigor means that your study experience will closely match the actual in-test experience.

To date, XAMonline has helped nearly 600,000 teachers pass their certification or licensing exams. Our commitment to preparation exceeds simply providing the proper material for study—it extends to helping teachers **gain mastery** of the subject matter, giving them the **tools** to become the most effective classroom leaders possible, and ushering today's students toward a **successful future**.

# SECTION 2

## ABOUT THIS STUDY GUIDE

### Purpose of This Guide

Is there a little voice inside of you saying, "Am I ready?" Our goal is to replace that little voice and remove all doubt with a new voice that says, "I AM READY. **Bring it on!**" by offering the highest quality of teacher certification study guides.

## Organization of Content

You will see that while every test may start with overlapping general topics, each is very unique in the skills they wish to test. Only XAMonline presents custom content that analyzes deeper than a title, a subarea, or an objective. Only XAMonline presents content and sample test assessments along with **focus statements**, the deepest-level rationale and interpretation of the skills that are unique to the exam.

### Title and field number of test

→Each exam has its own name and number. XAMonline's guides are written to give you the content you need to know for the specific exam you are taking. You can be confident when you buy our guide that it contains the information you need to study for the specific test you are taking.

#### Subareas

→These are the major content categories found on the exam. XAMonline's guides are written to cover all of the subareas found in the test frameworks developed for the exam.

##### Objectives

→These are standards that are unique to the exam and represent the main subcategories of the subareas/content categories. XAMonline's guides are written to address every specific objective required to pass the exam.

###### Focus statements

→These are examples and interpretations of the objectives. You find them in parenthesis directly following the objective. They provide detailed examples of the range, type, and level of content that appear on the test questions. **Only XAMonline's guides drill down to this level.**

## How Do We Compare with Our Competitors?

XAMonline—drills down to the focus statement level.
CliffsNotes and REA—organized at the objective level
Kaplan—provides only links to content
MoMedia—content not specific to the state test

Each subarea is divided into manageable sections that cover the specific skill areas. Explanations are easy to understand and thorough. You'll find that every test answer contains a rejoinder so if you need a refresher or further review after taking the test, you'll know exactly to which section you must return.

## How to Use This Book

Our informal polls show that most people begin studying up to eight weeks prior to the test date, so start early. Then ask yourself some questions: How much do you really know? Are you coming to the test straight from your teacher-education program or are you having to review subjects you haven't considered in ten years? Either way, take a **diagnostic or assessment test** first. Also, spend time on sample tests so that you become accustomed to the way the actual test will appear.

This guide comes with an online diagnostic test of 30 questions found online at *www.XAMonline.com*. It is a little boot camp to get you up for the task and reveal things about your compendium of knowledge in general. Although this guide is structured to follow the order of the test, you are not required to study in that order. By finding a time-management and study plan that fits your life you will be more effective. The results of your diagnostic or self-assessment test can be a guide for how to manage your time and point you toward an area that needs more attention.

| Week | Activity |
|---|---|
| 8 weeks prior to test | Take a diagnostic test found at www.XAMonline.com |
| 6-3 weeks prior to test | For each of these four weeks, choose a content area to study. You don't have to go in the order of the book. It may be that you start with the content that needs the most review. Alternately, you may want to ease yourself into plan by starting with the most familiar material. |
| 2 weeks prior to test | Take the sample test, score it, and create a review plan for the final week before the test. |
| 1 week prior to test | Following your plan (which will likely be aligned with the areas that need the most review) go back and study the sections that align with the questions you may have gotten wrong. Then go back and study the sections related to the questions you answered correctly. If need be, create flashcards and drill yourself on any area that you makes you anxious. |

# SECTION 3
## ABOUT THE PRAXIS EXAMS

### What Is PRAXIS?

PRAXIS II tests measure the knowledge of specific content areas in K–12 education. The test is a way of insuring that educators are prepared to not only teach in a particular subject area, but also have the necessary teaching skills to be effective. The Educational Testing Service administers the test in most states and has worked with the states to develop the material so that it is appropriate for state standards.

### PRAXIS Points

1. The PRAXIS Series comprises more than 140 different tests in over seventy different subject areas.

2. Over 90% of the PRAXIS tests measure subject area knowledge.

3. The purpose of the test is to measure whether the teacher candidate possesses a sufficient level of knowledge and skills to perform job duties effectively and responsibly.

4. Your state sets the acceptable passing score.

5. Any candidate, whether from a traditional teaching-preparation path or an alternative route, can seek to enter the teaching profession by taking a PRAXIS test.

6. PRAXIS tests are updated regularly to ensure current content.

Often **your own state's requirements** determine whether or not you should take any particular test. The most reliable source of information regarding this is either your state's Department of Education or the Educational Testing Service. Either resource should also have a complete list of testing centers and dates. Test dates vary by subject area and not all test dates necessarily include your particular test, so be sure to check carefully.

If you are in a teacher-education program, check with the Education Department or the Certification Officer for specific information for testing and testing timelines. The Certification Office should have most of the information you need.

If you choose an alternative route to certification you can either rely on our Web site at *www.XAMonline.com* or on the resources provided by an alternative certification program. Many states now have specific agencies devoted to alternative certification and there are some national organizations as well:

*National Center for Education Information*
*http://www.ncei.com/Alt-Teacher-Cert.htm*

*National Associate for Alternative Certification*
*http://www.alt-teachercert.org/index.asp*

## Interpreting Test Results

Contrary to what you may have heard, the results of a PRAXIS test are not based on time. More accurately, you will be scored on the raw number of points you earn in relation to the raw number of points available. Each question is worth one raw point. It is likely to your benefit to complete as many questions in the time allotted, but it will not necessarily work to your advantage if you hurry through the test.

Follow the guidelines provided by ETS for interpreting your score. The web site offers a sample test score sheet and clearly explains how the scores are scaled and what to expect if you have an essay portion on your test.

Scores are usually available by phone within a month of the test date and scores will be sent to your chosen institution(s) within six weeks. Additionally, ETS now makes online, downloadable reports available for 45 days from the reporting date.

It is **critical** that you be aware of your own state's passing score. Your raw score may qualify you to teach in some states, but not all. ETS administers the test and assigns a score, but the states make their own interpretations and, in some cases, consider combined scores if you are testing in more than one area.

## What's on the Test?

PRAXIS tests vary from subject to subject and sometimes even within subject area. The PRAXIS Elementary Education: Multiple Subjects (5001)is a computer-delivered test. The test lasts for 3.5 hours (4 hours if the four subject areas are taken separately) and consists of approximately 210 multiple-choice questions. The use of scientific or four-function calculators is permitted for this test. The breakdown of the questions is as follows:

| Category | Approximate Number of Questions | Time |
|---|---|---|
| **Elementary Education (5031)** | | |
| I: Reading/Language Arts (5032) | 80 | 90 minutes |

*Table continued on next page*

| Category | Approximate Number of Questions | Time |
|---|---|---|
| II:  Mathematics (5033) | 50 | 65 minutes |
| III: Social Studies (5034) | 55 | 50 minutes |
| IV: Science (5035) | 50 | 50 minutes |

## Question Types

You're probably thinking, enough already, I want to study! Indulge us a little longer while we explain that there is actually more than one type of multiple-choice question. You can thank us later after you realize how well prepared you are for your exam.

1. **Complete the Statement.** The name says it all. In this question type you'll be asked to choose the correct completion of a given statement. For example:

> The Dolch Basic Sight Words consist of a relatively short list of words that children should be able to:
>
> A. Sound out
>
> B. Know the meaning of
>
> C. Recognize on sight
>
> D. Use in a sentence

The correct answer is C. In order to check your answer, test out the statement by adding the choices to the end of it.

2. **Which of the Following.** One way to test your answer choice for this type of question is to replace the phrase "which of the following" with your selection. Use this example:

> Which of the following words is one of the twelve most frequently used in children's reading texts:
>
> A. There
>
> B. This
>
> C. The
>
> D. An

Don't look! Test your answer. _____ is one of the twelve most frequently used in children's reading texts. Did you guess C? Then you guessed correctly.

3. **Roman Numeral Choices.** This question type is used when there is more than one possible correct answer. For example:

> Which of the following two arguments accurately supports the use of cooperative learning as an effective method of instruction?
> I.   Cooperative learning groups facilitate healthy competition between individuals in the group.
> II.  Cooperative learning groups allow academic achievers to carry or cover for academic underachievers.
> III. Cooperative learning groups make each student in the group accountable for the success of the group.
> IV.  Cooperative learning groups make it possible for students to reward other group members for achieving.
>
> A. I and II
>
> B. II and III
>
> C. I and III
>
> D. III and IV

Notice that the question states there are **two** possible answers. It's best to read all the possibilities first before looking at the answer choices. In this case, the correct answer is D.

4. **Negative Questions.** This type of question contains words such as "not," "least," and "except." Each correct answer will be the statement that does **not** fit the situation described in the question. Such as:

> Multicultural education is **not**
>
> A. An idea or concept
>
> B. A "tack-on" to the school curriculum
>
> C. An educational reform movement
>
> D. A process

Think to yourself that the statement could be anything but the correct answer. This question form is more open to interpretation than other types, so read carefully and don't forget that you're answering a negative statement.

5. **Questions that Include Graphs, Tables, or Reading Passages.** As always, read the question carefully. It likely asks for a very specific answer and not a broad interpretation of the visual. Here is a simple (though not statistically accurate) example of a graph question:

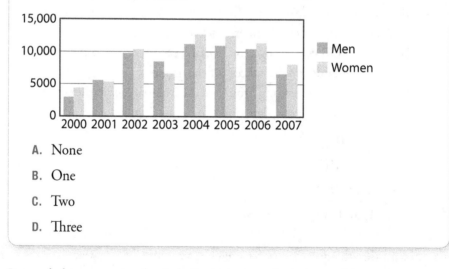

> In the following graph in how many years did more men take the NYSTCE exam than women?
>
> A. None
>
> B. One
>
> C. Two
>
> D. Three

It may help you to simply circle the two years that answer the question. Make sure you've read the question thoroughly and once you've made your determination, double check your work. The correct answer is C.

# SECTION 4
## HELPFUL HINTS

## Study Tips

1. **You are what you eat.** Certain foods aid the learning process by releasing natural memory enhancers called CCKs (cholecystokinin) composed of tryptophan, choline, and phenylalanine. All of these chemicals enhance the neurotransmitters associated with memory and certain foods release memory enhancing chemicals. A light meal or snacks of one of the following foods fall into this category:

   - Milk
   - Rice
   - Eggs
   - Fish
   - Nuts and seeds
   - Oats
   - Turkey

   The better the connections, the more you comprehend!

2. **See the forest for the trees.** In other words, get the concept before you look at the details. One way to do this is to take notes as you read, paraphrasing or summarizing in your own words. Putting the concept in terms that are comfortable and familiar may increase retention.

3. **Question authority.** Ask why, why, why? Pull apart written material paragraph by paragraph and don't forget the captions under the illustrations. For example, if a heading reads *Stream Erosion* put it in the form of a question (Why do streams erode? What is stream erosion?) then find the answer within the material. If you train your mind to think in this manner you will learn more and prepare yourself for answering test questions.

4. **Play mind games.** Using your brain for reading or puzzles keeps it flexible. Even with a limited amount of time your brain can take in data (much like a computer) and store it for later use. In ten minutes you can: read two paragraphs (at least), quiz yourself with flash cards, or review notes. Even if you don't fully understand something on the first pass, your mind stores it for recall, which is why frequent reading or review increases chances of retention and comprehension.

5. **The pen is mightier than the sword.** Learn to take great notes. A by-product of our modern culture is that we have grown accustomed to getting our information in short doses. We've subconsciously trained ourselves to assimilate information into neat little packages. Messy notes fragment the flow of information. Your notes can be much clearer with proper formatting. *The Cornell Method* is one such format. This method was popularized in *How to Study in College*, Ninth Edition, by Walter Pauk. You can benefit from the method without purchasing an additional book by simply looking up the method online. Below is a sample of how *The Cornell Method* can be adapted for use with this guide.

| ← 2½" → Cue Column | ← 6" → Note Taking Column |
|---|---|
| | 1. Record: During your reading, use the note-taking column to record important points. |
| | 2. Questions: As soon as you finish a section, formulate questions based on the notes in the right-hand column. Writing questions helps to clarify meanings, reveal relationships, establish community, and strengthen memory. Also, the writing of questions sets the state for exam study later. |
| | 3. Recite: Cover the note-taking column with a sheet of paper. Then, looking at the questions or cue-words in the question and cue column only, say aloud, in your own words, the answers to the questions, facts, or ideas indicated by the cue words. |
| | 4. Reflect: Reflect on the material by asking yourself questions. |
| | 5. Review: Spend at least ten minutes every week reviewing all your previous notes. Doing so helps you retain ideas and topics for the exam. |
| ↑ 2" ↓ | **Summary** After reading, use this space to summarize the notes from each page. |

*Adapted from **How to Study in College**, Ninth Edition, by Walter Pauk, ©2008 Wadsworth*

6. **Place yourself in exile and set the mood.** Set aside a particular place and time to study that best suits your personal needs and biorhythms. If you're a night person, burn the midnight oil. If you're a morning person set yourself up with some coffee and get to it. Make your study time and place as free from distraction as possible and surround yourself with what you need, be it silence or music. Studies have shown that music can aid in concentration, absorption, and retrieval of information. Not all music, though. Classical music is said to work best

7. **Get pointed in the right direction.** Use arrows to point to important passages or pieces of information. It's easier to read than a page full of yellow highlights. Highlighting can be used sparingly, but add an arrow to the margin to call attention to it.

8. **Check your budget.** You should at least review all the content material before your test, but allocate the most amount of time to the areas that need the most refreshing. It sounds obvious, but it's easy to forget. You can use the study rubric above to balance your study budget.

> *The proctor will write the start time where it can be seen and then, later, provide the time remaining, typically fifteen minutes before the end of the test.*

## Testing Tips

1. **Get smart, play dumb.** Sometimes a question is just a question. No one is out to trick you, so don't assume that the test writer is looking for something other than what was asked. Stick to the question as written and don't overanalyze.

2. **Do a double take.** Read test questions and answer choices at least twice because it's easy to miss something, to transpose a word or some letters. If you have no idea what the correct answer is, skip it and come back later if there's time. If you're still clueless, it's okay to guess. Remember, you're scored on the number of questions you answer correctly and you're not penalized for wrong answers. The worst case scenario is that you miss a point from a good guess.

3. **Turn it on its ear.** The syntax of a question can often provide a clue, so make things interesting and turn the question into a statement to see if it changes the meaning or relates better (or worse) to the answer choices.

4. **Get out your magnifying glass.** Look for hidden clues in the questions because it's difficult to write a multiple-choice question without giving away part of the answer in the options presented. In most questions you can readily eliminate one or two potential answers, increasing your chances of answering correctly to 50/50, which will help out if you've skipped a question and gone back to it (see tip #2).

5. **Call it intuition.** Often your first instinct is correct. If you've been studying the content you've likely absorbed something and have subconsciously retained the knowledge. On questions you're not sure about trust your instincts because a first impression is usually correct.

6. **Graffiti.** Sometimes it's a good idea to mark your answers directly on the test booklet and go back to fill in the optical scan sheet later. You don't get extra points for perfectly blackened ovals. If you choose to manage your test this way, be sure not to mismark your answers when you transcribe to the scan sheet.

7. **Become a clock-watcher.** You have a set amount of time to answer the questions. Don't get bogged down laboring over a question you're not sure about when there are ten others you could answer more readily. If you choose to follow the advice of tip #6, be sure you leave time near the end to go back and fill in the scan sheet.

## Do the Drill

No matter how prepared you feel it's sometimes a good idea to apply Murphy's Law. So the following tips might seem silly, mundane, or obvious, but we're including them anyway.

1. **Remember, you are what you eat, so bring a snack.** Choose from the list of energizing foods that appear earlier in the introduction.

2. **You're not too sexy for your test.** Wear comfortable clothes. You'll be distracted if your belt is too tight or if you're too cold or too hot.

3. **Lie to yourself.** Even if you think you're a prompt person, pretend you're not and leave plenty of time to get to the testing center. Map it out ahead of time and do a dry run if you have to. There's no need to add road rage to your list of anxieties.

4. **Bring sharp number 2 pencils.** It may seem impossible to forget this need from your school days, but you might. And make sure the erasers are intact, too.

5. **No ticket, no test.** Bring your admission ticket as well as **two** forms of identification, including one with a picture and signature. You will not be admitted to the test without these things.

6. **You can't take it with you.** Leave any study aids, dictionaries, notebooks, computers, and the like at home. Certain tests **do** allow a scientific or four-function calculator, so check ahead of time to see if your test does.

7. **Prepare for the desert.** Any time spent on a bathroom break **cannot** be made up later, so use your judgment on the amount you eat or drink.

8. **Quiet, Please!** Keeping your own time is a good idea, but not with a timepiece that has a loud ticker. If you use a watch, take it off and place it nearby but not so that it distracts you. And **silence your cell phone**.

To the best of our ability, we have compiled the content you need to know in this book and in the accompanying online resources. The rest is up to you. You can use the study and testing tips or you can follow your own methods. Either way, you can be confident that there aren't any missing pieces of information and there shouldn't be any surprises in the content on the test.

If you have questions about test fees, registration, electronic testing, or other content verification issues please visit *www.ets.org*.

Good luck!

*Sharon Wynne*
*Founder, XAMonline*

# Table of Contents

# COMPETENCY 002

# DOMAIN II
## MATHEMATICS (5003) .................................................. 79

## COMPETENCY 003
### NUMBERS AND OPERATIONS

# COMPETENCY 004

# COMPETENCY 005
## GEOMETRY AND MEASUREMENT, DATA, STATISTICS, AND PROBABILITY ...................................130

# DOMAIN III
## SOCIAL STUDIES (5004) ..................................................... 163

# DOMAIN IV
## SCIENCE (5005) ................................................................ 225

# SAMPLE TEST

# DOMAIN I
# READING AND LANGUAGE ARTS (5002)

# PERSONALIZED STUDY PLAN

| PAGE | COMPETENCY AND SKILL | KNOWN MATERIAL/ SKIP IT | BRIEFLY REVIEW eSTICKYNOTES | MAKE eFLASHCARDS | TAKE ADDITIONAL SAMPLE TESTS |
|---|---|---|---|---|---|
| 7 | **001: Reading** | ☐ | ☐ | ☐ | ☐ |
| | 1.1: Understands the role of phonological awareness in literacy development | ☐ | ☐ | ☐ | ☐ |
| | 1.1a: Explains the importance of phonological awareness as a foundational skill for literacy development | ☐ | ☐ | ☐ | ☐ |
| | 1.1b: Identifies and provides examples of phonemes, syllables, onsets, rimes | ☐ | ☐ | ☐ | ☐ |
| | 1.1c: Identifies and provides examples of blending, segmenting, substituting, and deleting phonemes, syllables, onsets, rimes | ☐ | ☐ | ☐ | ☐ |
| | 1.2: Understands the role of phonics and word analysis in literacy development | ☐ | ☐ | ☐ | ☐ |
| | 1.2a: Explains the importance of phonics and word analysis in literacy development | ☐ | ☐ | ☐ | ☐ |
| | 1.2b: Distinguishes among common letter sound correspondences and spelling conventions | ☐ | ☐ | ☐ | ☐ |
| | 1.2c: Distinguishes high-frequency sight words from decodable words appropriate for particular grades | ☐ | ☐ | ☐ | ☐ |
| | 1.2d: Identifies roots and affixes to decode unfamiliar words | ☐ | ☐ | ☐ | ☐ |
| | 1.2e: Recognizes various stages of language acquisition (*e.g., WIDA taxonomy*) | ☐ | ☐ | ☐ | ☐ |
| | 1.2f: Delineates common phonics and word recognition approaches for ELLs (*pedagogy*) | ☐ | ☐ | ☐ | ☐ |
| | 1.2g: Differentiates syllabication patterns (*e.g. open, closed, CVe*) | ☐ | ☐ | ☐ | ☐ |
| | 1.3: Understands the role of fluency in literacy development | ☐ | ☐ | ☐ | ☐ |
| | 1.3a: Defines fluency and related terms (*e.g., accuracy, rate, prosody*) | ☐ | ☐ | ☐ | ☐ |
| | 1.3b: Explains the impact of fluency on comprehension | ☐ | ☐ | ☐ | ☐ |
| | **Literature and informational texts** | | | | |
| | 1.4: Understands how to use key ideas and details to comprehend literature and informational text | ☐ | ☐ | ☐ | ☐ |
| | 1.4a: Identifies key details, moral, and/or theme of a literary text, citing specific textual evidence | ☐ | ☐ | ☐ | ☐ |
| | 1.4b: Identifies the key details and/or central idea of an informational text, citing specific textual information | ☐ | ☐ | ☐ | ☐ |
| | 1.4c: Makes inferences from a text and supports them with appropriate evidence | ☐ | ☐ | ☐ | ☐ |
| | 1.4d: Summarizes information from a text | ☐ | ☐ | ☐ | ☐ |
| | 1.4e: Analyzes the characters, setting, and plot of a literary text | ☐ | ☐ | ☐ | ☐ |
| | 1.4f: Analyzes the relationships among individuals, events, ideas, and concepts in an informational text | ☐ | ☐ | ☐ | ☐ |
| | 1.5: Understands how to use key ideas and details to comprehend literature and informational text | ☐ | ☐ | ☐ | ☐ |
| | 1.5a: Identifies structural elements of literature across genres (*e.g., cast of characters and stage directions in drama, rhyme, and meter in poetry*) | ☐ | ☐ | ☐ | ☐ |

# PERSONALIZED STUDY PLAN

| PAGE | COMPETENCY AND SKILL | KNOWN MATERIAL/ SKIP IT | BRIEFLY REVIEW eSTICKYNOTES | MAKE eFLASHCARDS | TAKE ADDITIONAL SAMPLE TESTS |
|---|---|---|---|---|---|
| | 1.5b: Uses text features (e.g., headings, sidebars, hyperlinks) to locate information in a print or digital informational text | ☐ | ☐ | ☐ | ☐ |
| | 1.5c: Identifies organizational structures of informational text (e.g., cause/effect, problem/solution) | ☐ | ☐ | ☐ | ☐ |
| | 1.5d: Identifies how structural elements contribute to the development of a literary text as a whole | ☐ | ☐ | ☐ | ☐ |
| | 1.6: Understands the concept of point of view using evidence from the text | ☐ | ☐ | ☐ | ☐ |
| | 1.6a: Identifies author's point of view in various genres and supports conclusions with evidence from text | ☐ | ☐ | ☐ | ☐ |
| | 1.6b: Compares multiple accounts of the same event or topic to identify similarities or differences in point of view | ☐ | ☐ | ☐ | ☐ |
| | 1.6c: Identifies how point of view impacts the overall structure of a literary or informational text | ☐ | ☐ | ☐ | ☐ |
| | 1.7: Understands how to integrate and compare written, visual, and oral information from texts and multimedia sources | ☐ | ☐ | ☐ | ☐ |
| | 1.7a: Explains how visual and oral elements enhance the meaning and effect of a literary text (e.g., picture book, graphic novel, multimedia presentation of a folktale) | ☐ | ☐ | ☐ | ☐ |
| | 1.7b: Compares the written version of a literary text with an oral, staged, or filmed version | ☐ | ☐ | ☐ | ☐ |
| | 1.7c: Compares two or more literary texts that address the same theme | ☐ | ☐ | ☐ | ☐ |
| | 1.7d: Compares two or more informational texts that address the same topic | ☐ | ☐ | ☐ | ☐ |
| | 1.7e: Interprets visual and multimedia elements in literary and informational texts | ☐ | ☐ | ☐ | ☐ |
| | 1.7f: Evaluates key themes in a text and supports them with reasons and evidence from the text | ☐ | ☐ | ☐ | ☐ |
| | 1.8: Knows the role of text complexity in reading development | ☐ | ☐ | ☐ | ☐ |
| | 1.8a: Explains the three factors (i.e., quantitative, qualitative, and reader and task) that measure text complexity | ☐ | ☐ | ☐ | ☐ |
| | 1.8b: Identifies the key features of text-leveling systems | ☐ | ☐ | ☐ | ☐ |
| 46 | **002: Writing, speaking, and listening** | ☐ | ☐ | ☐ | ☐ |
| | **Writing** | ☐ | ☐ | ☐ | ☐ |
| | 2.1: Understands the characteristics of common types of writing | ☐ | ☐ | ☐ | ☐ |
| | 2.1a: Distinguishes among common types of writing (e.g., opinion/argument, informative/explanatory, narrative) | ☐ | ☐ | ☐ | ☐ |
| | 2.1b: Identifies the purpose, key components, and sub-genres (e.g., speeches, advertisements, narrative poems) of each common type of writing | ☐ | ☐ | ☐ | ☐ |
| | 2.1c: Evaluates the effectiveness of writing samples of each type | ☐ | ☐ | ☐ | ☐ |

# PERSONALIZED STUDY PLAN

| PAGE | COMPETENCY AND SKILL | KNOWN MATERIAL/ SKIP IT | BRIEFLY REVIEW eSTICKYNOTES | MAKE eFLASHCARDS | TAKE ADDITIONAL SAMPLE TESTS |
|---|---|---|---|---|---|
| 2.2: | Understands the characteristics of effective writing | ☐ | ☐ | ☐ | ☐ |
| 2.2a: | Evaluates the appropriateness of a particular piece of writing for a specific task, purpose, and audience | ☐ | ☐ | ☐ | ☐ |
| 2.2b: | Evaluates the development, organization, or style of a piece of writing | ☐ | ☐ | ☐ | ☐ |
| 2.2c: | Identifies appropriate revisions to strengthen a piece of writing | ☐ | ☐ | ☐ | ☐ |
| 2.2d: | Writes clearly and coherently | ☐ | ☐ | ☐ | ☐ |
| 2.2e: | Identifies interrelationships among planning, revising, and editing in the process of writing | ☐ | ☐ | ☐ | ☐ |
| 2.3: | Knows the developmental stages of writing (e.g., picture, scribble) | ☐ | ☐ | ☐ | ☐ |
| 2.3a: | Identifies grade-appropriate continuum of student writing | ☐ | ☐ | ☐ | ☐ |
| 2.4: | Knows the importance of digital tools for producing and publishing writing and for interacting with others | ☐ | ☐ | ☐ | ☐ |
| 2.4a: | Identifies characteristics and purposes of a variety of digital tools for producing and publishing writing | ☐ | ☐ | ☐ | ☐ |
| 2.4b: | Identifies the purposes of a variety of digital tools for interacting with others | ☐ | ☐ | ☐ | ☐ |
| 2.5: | Knows the research process | ☐ | ☐ | ☐ | ☐ |
| 2.5a: | Identifies the steps in the research process | ☐ | ☐ | ☐ | ☐ |
| 2.5b: | Distinguishes between primary and secondary sources and their uses | ☐ | ☐ | ☐ | ☐ |
| 2.5c: | Distinguishes between reliable and unreliable sources | ☐ | ☐ | ☐ | ☐ |
| 2.5d: | Distinguishes between paraphrasing and plagiarizing | ☐ | ☐ | ☐ | ☐ |
| 2.5e: | Knows how to locate credible print and digital sources, locate information within the sources, and cite the sources | ☐ | ☐ | ☐ | ☐ |
| | **Language** | ☐ | ☐ | ☐ | ☐ |
| 2.6: | Knows the conventions of standard English grammar, usage, mechanics, and spelling when writing, speaking, reading, and listening | ☐ | ☐ | ☐ | ☐ |
| 2.6a: | Explains the function of different parts of speech | ☐ | ☐ | ☐ | ☐ |
| 2.6b: | Corrects errors in usage, mechanics, and spelling | ☐ | ☐ | ☐ | ☐ |
| 2.6c: | Identifies examples of different sentence types (e.g., simple, compound, compound-complex) | ☐ | ☐ | ☐ | ☐ |
| 2.6d: | Identifies how varieties of English (e.g., dialects, registers) used in stories, dramas, or poems support the overall meaning | ☐ | ☐ | ☐ | ☐ |
| 2.7: | Understands how to determine the meaning of words and phrases | ☐ | ☐ | ☐ | ☐ |
| 2.7a: | Determines the literal meaning of unknown words and phrases from context, syntax, and/or knowledge of roots and affixes | ☐ | ☐ | ☐ | ☐ |
| 2.7b: | Identifies types of figurative language | ☐ | ☐ | ☐ | ☐ |

# PERSONALIZED STUDY PLAN

| PAGE | COMPETENCY AND SKILL | KNOWN MATERIAL/ SKIP IT | BRIEFLY REVIEW eSTICKYNOTES | MAKE eFLASHCARDS | TAKE ADDITIONAL SAMPLE TESTS |
|---|---|---|---|---|---|
| 2.7c: | Interprets figurative language | ☐ | ☐ | ☐ | ☐ |
| 2.7d: | Analyzes the relationship between word choice and tone in a text | ☐ | ☐ | ☐ | ☐ |
| 2.8: | Understands the characteristics of conversational, academic, and domain-specific language | ☐ | ☐ | ☐ | ☐ |
| 2.8a: | Differentiates among the three tiers of vocabulary | ☐ | ☐ | ☐ | ☐ |
| 2.8b: | Identifies relevant features of language such as word choice, order, and punctuation | ☐ | ☐ | ☐ | ☐ |
| | **Speaking and listening** | ☐ | ☐ | ☐ | ☐ |
| 2.9: | Knows the characteristics of effective collaboration to promote comprehension | ☐ | ☐ | ☐ | ☐ |
| 2.9a: | Identitifies techniques to communicate for a variety of purposes with diverse partners | ☐ | ☐ | ☐ | ☐ |
| 2.9b: | Identifies the characteristics of active listening | ☐ | ☐ | ☐ | ☐ |
| 2.10: | Knows the characteristics of engaging oral presentations | ☐ | ☐ | ☐ | ☐ |
| 2.10a: | Identifies elements of engaging oral presentations *(e.g., volume, articulation, awareness of audience)* | ☐ | ☐ | ☐ | ☐ |

# COMPETENCY 001
## READING

## Foundational Skills

During the preschool years, children acquire cognitive skills in oral language that they apply later on to reading comprehension. Reading aloud to young children is one of the most important things that an adult can do because they are teaching children how to monitor, question, predict, and confirm what they hear in stories. Reid (1988) described three metalinguistic abilities that young children acquire through early involvement in reading activities:

1. **Word consciousness:** Children who have access to books can first understand the story through the pictures. Gradually, they begin to understand the connection between the spoken words and the printed words. The beginning of letter and word discrimination begins in the early years.

2. **Language and conventions of print:** During this early stage, children learn how to hold a book, where to begin to read, left-to-right tracking, and how to continue from one line to another.

3. **Functions of print:** Children discover that print can be used for a variety of purposes and functions, including entertainment and information.

The typical variation in literacy that children bring to reading can make teaching more difficult. Often a teacher has to choose between focusing on the learning needs of a few students at the expense of the group or focusing on the group at the risk of leaving some students behind academically. This situation is particularly critical for diverse learners who have had less experience with reading.

> Reading aloud to young children is one of the most important things that an adult can do because they are teaching children how to monitor, question, predict, and confirm what they hear in stories.

| KEY CONCEPTS | |
|---|---|
| Experiences with print (through reading and writing) help preschool children develop an understanding of the conventions, purpose, and functions of print. | Children learn about print from a variety of sources, and in the process, they come to realize that print carries a story. They also learn how text is structured visually (for example, in English, the text begins at the top of the page, moves from left to right, and carries over to the next page when the page is turned). Although knowledge of print conventions enables children to understand the physical structure of language, the conceptual knowledge that printed words convey a message also helps children bridge the gap between oral and written language. |

*Table continued on next page*

| | |
|---|---|
| Phonological awareness and letter recognition contribute to initial reading acquisition by helping children develop efficient word recognition strategies (for example, detecting pronunciations and storing associations in memory). | Phonological awareness and knowledge of print-speech relations play an important role in facilitating reading acquisition. Therefore, phonological awareness instruction should be an integral component of early reading programs. Within the emergent literacy research, viewpoints diverge on whether acquisition of phonological awareness and letter recognition are preconditions of literacy acquisition or whether they develop interdependently with literacy activities such as story reading and writing. |
| Story reading affects children's knowledge about, strategies for, and attitudes toward reading. | Of all the strategies intended to promote growth in literacy acquisition, none is as commonly practiced, nor as strongly supported across the emergent literacy literature, as story reading. Children in different social and cultural groups have varying degrees of access to story reading. For example, it is not unusual for a teacher to have students who have experienced thousands of hours of story-reading time along with other students who have had little or no such exposure. |

According to leading theorists, comprehension for balanced literacy is a strategic process. The reader interacts with the text and brings his or her prior knowledge and experience to it. Writing complements reading and is a mutually integrative and supportive parallel process. Hence, dividing literacy learning into reading workshops and writing workshops, using the same anchor readings or books for both, is particularly effective in teaching students.

Consider the sentence:

> The test booklet was white with black print, but very scary looking.

According to the idea of constructing meaning as one reads the sentence above, readers' personal schemata (generic information stored in the mind) of tests will be activated by the author's idea that tests are scary. Readers will remember emotions they experienced during testing themselves and use this information to comprehend the author's statement. Therefore, the ultimate meaning a reader derives from the page results from the interaction of the reader's own experiences with the ideas the author presents. The reader constructs a meaning that reflects the author's intent as well as the reader's response to that intent.

Remember, also, that readings are generally fairly lengthy passages, consisting of paragraphs, which in turn consist of more than one sentence. With each successive sentence, and every new paragraph, the reader refocuses. The schemata are reconsidered, and a new meaning is constructed.

The purpose of reading is to convert visual images (letters and words) into a message. Pronouncing the words is not enough; the reader must be able to extract the meaning of the text. When people read, they utilize four sources of background information to comprehend the meaning behind the literal text:

1. **Word knowledge:** This is information about words and letters. One's knowledge of word meanings is **lexical knowledge**—a sort of dictionary. Knowledge of spelling patterns and pronunciations is **orthographic knowledge**. Poor readers do not develop a high level of automaticity in using orthographic knowledge to identify words and decode unfamiliar words.

2. **Syntax and contextual information:** When children encounter unknown words in a sentence, they rely on their background knowledge to choose a word that makes sense. Errors of younger children, therefore, are often substitutions of words in the same syntactic class. Poor readers often fail to make use of context clues to help them identify words or activate the background knowledge that would help them with comprehension. Poor readers also process sentences word by word, instead of by "chunking" phrases and clauses. This tendency results in a slow pace that focuses on decoding rather than comprehension. Poor readers also have problems answering *wh-* questions (who, what, where, when, why?) as a result of these problems with syntax.

3. **Semantic knowledge:** This encompasses the reader's background knowledge of a topic, which is combined with the text information as the reader tries to comprehend the material. New information is compared with the background information and incorporated into the reader's schema. Poor readers have problems using their background knowledge, especially with passages that require inference or cause-and-effect thinking.

4. **Text organization:** Good readers are able to differentiate types of text structure (for example, story narrative, exposition, compare-contrast, or time sequence). They use their knowledge of text to build expectations and to construct a framework of ideas on which to build meaning. Poor readers may not be able to differentiate types of text and may miss important ideas. They may also miss important ideas and details by concentrating on lesser or irrelevant details.

Research on reading development has yielded information on the behaviors and habits of good readers versus poor readers. Some of the characteristics of good readers are:

- They think about the information they will read in the text, formulate questions they predict will be answered in the text, and confirm those predictions from the information in the text

- When faced with unfamiliar words, they attempt to pronounce them using analogies to familiar words

- Before reading, they establish a purpose for reading, anticipate possible text structure, choose a reading strategy, and make predictions about what will be in the reading

- As they read, they test and confirm their predictions, go back when something does not make sense, and make new predictions

### SKILL 1.1 Understands the role of phonological awareness in literacy development

**PHONEMIC AWARENESS:** the acknowledgement of sounds and words, for example, a child's realization that some words rhyme

**PHONEMIC AWARENESS** is the acknowledgement of sounds and words, for example, a child's realization that some words rhyme. Onset and rhyme, for example, are skills that might help students learn that the sound of the first letter *b* in the word *bad* can be changed with the sound *d* to make it *dad*. The key in phonemic awareness is that when you teach it to children, it can be taught with the students' eyes closed. In other words, it's all about sounds, not ascribing written letters to sounds.

*To be phonemically aware means that the reader and listener can recognize and manipulate specific sounds in spoken words.*

To be phonemically aware means that the reader and listener can recognize and manipulate specific sounds in spoken words. The majority of phonemic awareness tasks, activities, and exercises are oral.

**PHONEMES:** the smallest unit of language capable of conveying distinction in meaning

Because the ability to distinguish between individual sounds, or **PHONEMES**, within words is a prerequisite to associating sounds with letters and manipulating sounds to blend words—a fancy way of saying "reading," teaching phonemic awareness is crucial to emergent literacy (early childhood K–2 reading instruction). Children need a strong background in phonemic awareness for phonics instruction (sound–spelling relationship–printed materials) to be effective.

## SKILL 1.1a Explains the importance of phonological awareness as a foundational skill for literacy development

PHONOLOGICAL AWARENESS is the ability of the reader to recognize the sounds of spoken language. This recognition includes how these sounds can be blended together, segmented (divided up), and manipulated (switched around). This type of awareness then leads to phonics, which is a method of teaching children to read. It helps them to "sound out" words.

Development of phonological skills may begin during the pre-K years. Indeed, by the age of five, a child who has been exposed to rhyme can typically recognize another rhyme. Such a child can demonstrate phonological awareness by filling in the missing rhyming word in a familiar rhyme or rhymed picture book. It isn't unheard of for children to surprise their parents by filling in missing rhymes in a familiar nursery rhyme book at the age of four or even earlier.

Children acquire phonological awareness when they are taught the sounds made by the letters, the sounds made by various combinations of letters, and the ability to recognize individual sounds in words.

> **PHONOLOGICAL AWARENESS:** the ability of the reader to recognize the sounds of spoken language

## SKILL 1.1b Identifies and provides examples of phonemes, syllables, onsets, rimes

Phonological awareness involves the recognition that spoken words are composed of a set of smaller units such as onsets and rimes, syllables, and sounds.

Onset-Rime Blending—Everything before the vowel and RIME (the vowel and everything after it). For example, the word "sleep" can be broken into /sl/ and /eep/. Word families are built using rimes. The /eep/ word family would include jeep, keep, and weep.

Words are comprised of individual phonemes (sounds) that can be blended. Theorist Marilyn Jager Adams who researches early reading has outlined five basic types of phonemic awareness tasks:

Task 1 Ability to hear rhymes and alliteration.
For example, the children would listen to a poem, rhyming picture book or song and identify the rhyming words heard which the teacher might then record or list on chart.

Task 2 Ability to do oddity tasks (recognize the member of a set that is different [odd] among the group). For example, children might look at pictures of grass, a garden and a rose, answering, Which one starts with a different sound?

Task 3 The ability to orally blend words and split syllables.
For example, the children can say the first sound of a word and then the rest of the word and put it together as a single word.

Task 4 The ability to orally segment words.
For example, the ability to count sounds. The child would be asked to count or clap the sounds in "hamburger."

Task 5 The ability to do phonics manipulation tasks.
For example, replace the "r" sound in rose with a "p" sound.

---

**SKILL 1.1c** **Identifies and provides examples of blending, segmenting, substituting, and deleting phonemes, syllables, onsets, rimes**

Phonological awareness skills include:

- Rhyming (similar sounds) and syllabification (breaking words down into single syllables).

- Blending sounds into words (such as pic-tur-bo-k).

- Identifying beginning or initial phonemes and ending or final phonemes in short, one-syllable words.

- Breaking words down into sounds (also called "segmenting" words) For example, identifying the initial and final sounds in the word /moo/.

- Removing phonemes and substituting others. An example includes replacing the /b/ in /bat/ with an /m/ becomes /mat/.

- Recognizing small words contained in bigger words by removing starting sounds (*hear* to *ear*).

- Identifying patterns, sounds, letter-sound association.

*See also Skill 1.1b*

## SKILL 1.2 Understands the role of phonics and word analysis in literacy development

WORD ANALYSIS (also called phonics or decoding) is the process readers use to figure out unfamiliar words based on written patterns. WORD RECOGNITION is the process of automatically determining the pronunciation and some degree of the meaning of an unknown word. In other words, fluent readers recognize most written words easily and correctly, without consciously decoding or breaking them down. DECODING involves changing communication signals into messages. Reading comprehension requires that the reader learn the code in which a message is written and be able to decode it to get the message. ENCODING involves changing a message into symbols. Examples include encoding oral language into writing (spelling), encoding an idea into words, or encoding a mathematical or physical idea into appropriate mathematical symbols.

Although effective reading comprehension requires identifying words automatically, children do not have to be able to identify every single word or know the exact meaning of every word in a text to understand it. In fact, children can read a work with a high level of comprehension even if they do not fully know as many as 15 percent of the words in that text. Children develop the ability to decode and recognize words automatically. They can then extend their ability to decode to multisyllabic words.

**WORD ANALYSIS:** the process readers use to figure out unfamiliar words based on written patterns

**WORD RECOGNITION:** the process of automatically determining the pronunciation and some degree of the meaning of an unknown word

**DECODING:** changing communication signals into messages

**ENCODING:** changing a message into symbols

## SKILL 1.2a Explains the importance of phonics and word analysis in literacy development

PHONICS must be taught with the students' eyes open. Phonics is the connection between the sounds and letters on a page. Students should be able to hear and see the connection between sounds and letters in order to analyze the word as a whole. In other words, students learning phonics might see the word *bad* and sound each letter out slowly until they recognize that they just said the word. As students' skills advance, they will gain the ability to identify common letter sound correspondences, associating each letter with the appropriate sound.

**PHONICS:** method of teaching reading and spelling based on a phonetic interpretation of ordinary spelling

Effective spelling strategies should emphasize the following principles:

- Knowledge of patterns, sounds, letter-sound association, syllables
- Memorizing sight words
- Writing those words correctly many times
- Incorporating the words in personal writing

> **SKILL** Distinguishes among common letter sound correspondences and
> **1.2b** spelling conventions

*See Skill 1.2a*

> **SKILL** Distinguishes high-frequency sight words from decodable words
> **1.2c** appropriate for particular grades

**HIGH-FREQUENCY WORDS:** the words most often used in the English language

**SIGH WORDS:** words that the reader learns to read spontaneously, either because of frequency or lack of conformity to orthographic rules

**HIGH-FREQUENCY WORDS** are the words most often used in the English language. **SIGHT WORDS** include words that the reader learns to read spontaneously, either because of frequency or lack of conformity to orthographic rules. As students continue to expand upon their knowledge of sight words, they ultimately build their vocabulary. When vocabulary items are derived from content learning materials, the learner will be better equipped to deal with specific reading matter in content areas.

- Vocabulary tasks should be restructured as necessary. It is important to be certain that students fully understand what is asked of them in the context of reading rather than to focus only on the words to be learned.

- Vocabulary learning is effective when it entails active engagement in learning tasks.

- Computer technology can be used effectively to help teach vocabulary.

- Vocabulary can be acquired through incidental learning. Much of a student's vocabulary will have to be learned in the course of doing things rather than through explicit vocabulary learning. Repetition, richness of context, and motivation may also add to the efficacy of incidental learning of vocabulary

- Dependence on a single vocabulary instruction method will not result in optimal learning. A variety of methods can be used effectively with emphasis on multimedia, richness of context, and repeated exposure to vocabulary words.

*The National Reading Panel found that one critical feature of effective classrooms involves utilizing lessons and activities through which students apply their vocabulary knowledge and strategies to reading and writing.*

- The National Reading Panel found that one critical feature of effective classrooms involves utilizing lessons and activities through which students apply their vocabulary knowledge and strategies to reading and writing. Included in the activities were discussions that allowed teachers and students to talk about words, their features, and strategies for understanding unfamiliar words.

- There are many methods for directly and explicitly teaching words. The panel identified twenty-one methods that have been found effective in research projects. Many emphasize the underlying concept of a word and its connections to other words using graphics such as semantic mapping and diagrams.

- The **keyword method** uses words and illustrations that highlight salient features of meaning. The visualization or drawing of a picture either by the student or the teacher was found to be effective. Many words cannot be learned in this way, so effective classrooms provide multiple ways for students to learn and interact with words. The panel also found that computer-assisted activities can have a positive role in the development of vocabulary.

## SKILL 1.2d Identifies roots and affixes to decode unfamiliar words

Building upon phonics, spelling assists students in learning to identify root words and affixes. For example, a student might recognize the root /multi/ in the word /multiple/ and remember that this implies the word means plural. The affix /ing/ in the word /singing/ will assist the student in breaking down the word to learn that it's an action word.

Students decode by applying their knowledge of sound correspondence to accurately pronounce written words. Spelling instruction should include learning the words that are misspelled in daily writing, generalizing spelling knowledge, and mastering objectives in progressive phases of development.

The developmental stages of spelling are:

1. **Pre-phonemic spelling:** Children know that letters stand for a message but they do not know the relationship between spelling and pronunciation.

2. **Early phonemic spelling:** Children are beginning to understand spelling. They usually write the first letter correctly, with the rest of the word comprising consonants or long vowels.

3. **Letter-name spelling:** Children spell some words consistently and correctly. They are developing a sight vocabulary and a stable understanding of letters as representations of sounds. Long vowels are usually used accurately, but silent vowels are omitted. They spell unknown words by attempting to match the name of the letter to the sound.

4. **Transitional spelling:** Children typically enter this phase in late elementary school. They master short vowel sounds and know some spelling rules. They are developing a sense of correct and incorrect spellings.

5. **Derivational spelling:** This stage is usually reached between high school and adulthood. This is the stage when spelling rules are being mastered.

## SKILL 1.2e Recognizes various stages of language acquisition *(e.g., WIDA taxonomy)*

The World-Class Instructional Design and Assessment (WIDA) Consortium has developed new standards and assessment metrics for English language proficiency, specifically in grades K–12. The new standards focus on levels of language acquisition for English Language Learners (ELL) that are considered necessary for academic success. The theoretical foundation within the WIDA standards creates a framework for teachers to support students in achieving alongside native English speaking peers.

The five critical components within the standards framework include:

1. Can Do Philosophy

2. Guiding Principles of Language Development

3. Age-appropriate Academic Language in Sociocultural Contexts

4. Performance Definitions

5. Strands of Model Performance Indicators

The WIDA English Language Development (ELD) Standards represent the social, instructional, and academic language that students need to engage with peers, educators, and the curriculum in schools.

The current ELD Standards include:

1. English language learners communicate for social and instructional purposes within the school setting.

2. English language learners communicate information, ideas and concepts necessary for academic success in the content area of Language Arts.

3. English language learners communicate information, ideas and concepts necessary for academic success in the content area of mathematics.

4. English language learners communicate information, ideas and concepts necessary for academic success in the content area of science.

5. English language learners communicate information, ideas and concepts necessary for academic success in the content area of social studies.

## SKILL 1.2f Delineates common phonics and word recognition approaches for ELLs *(pedagogy)*

Building (*pedagogy*) off of teaching phonics—the ability to recognize sounds, letters, and words by hearing—word recognition includes the ability to recognize written words and sounds. Because sounds and letters that have never been seen or heard before may come as a challenge to English language learners, teachers must provide ample opportunities for decoding and interpreting the language. There are a variety of teaching strategies that can assist students in understanding the relationship between written letters and their sound.

A few approaches include:

- Use vocabulary lists with images to represent vocabulary words.

- Write new definitions on the board and draw a picture next to the word.

- Create a word wall with new words and associated images.

- Introduce new words using a story or song to put them in context.

- Use a listening activity to have students write what they heard.

- Have students read their writing out loud to a partner.

- Read a passage aloud and have students follow along with a written version.

- Provide a more hands-on approach by reading aloud and having students raise their hands when they recognize target words as they follow along in their books.

*See also Skill 1.1*

SKILL **Differentiates syllabication patterns** *(e.g. open, closed, CVe)*
1.2g

Decoding [*Skill 1.2d*] plays a large role in assisting students to break down words into manageable units. The smallest unit in pronunciation is a syllable. The syllable generally contains one vowel sound and one or more consonants. For example, /mom/ contains one syllable that consists of two consonants and a vowel sound. The word /brother/ contains two syllables, /bro/ and /ther/, with one vowel sound in each part. Students are often first introduced to monosyllabic words and advance to words with multiple syllables as their reading skills progress. By identifying syllables, they gain the ability to break larger words into manageable parts. Students may simply identify each sound by including dots over each sound or write each sound out separately to create a visual of the breakdown.

The six types of syllable patterns include:

1. **Open:** Ends with a single vowel, typically a long vowel. (so, she, spy)

2. **Closed:** Vowel followed by a consonant. This is the most common. (bad, big, is)

3. **Vowel Team:** Two or more letters create one vowel sound. (meat, south, plain)

4. **R-controlled:** Vowel is followed by an /r/. (four, far, bur-ger)

5. **Vowel-silent e:** Also referred to as vowel-consonant e. The first vowel becomes long and the e is silent. (fame, ape, pride)

6. **Consonant + le:** Consonant followed by /le/. (sam-ple, puz-zle, ta-ble)

SKILL **Understands the role of fluency in literacy development**
1.3

When students work on fluency, they practice reading connected pieces of text. In other words, instead of looking at a word as just a word, they might read a sentence straight through. In order for a student to comprehend what they are reading, they would need to be able to successfully piece words together in a sentence quickly. If a student is not fluent in reading, they would sound each letter or word out slowly and pay more attention to the phonics of each word. On the other hand, a fluent reader might read a sentence out loud using appropriate intonations.

*Fluency in reading depends on automatic word identification, which helps the student achieve comprehension of the material.*

## SKILL 1.3a Defines fluency and related terms (e.g., accuracy, rate, prosody)

Fluency in reading depends on automatic word identification, which helps the student achieve comprehension of the material. Even slight difficulties in word identification can significantly increase the time it takes a student to read material, may require the student to reread some passages, and reduces the level of comprehension expected. If the student experiences reading as a constant struggle or an arduous chore, then he or she will avoid reading whenever possible and consider it a negative experience. Obviously, the ability to read for comprehension, and learning in general, will suffer if students are not assured that all aspects of reading fluency are skills that can be readily acquired with the appropriate effort.

Automatic reading (or **AUTOMATICITY**) involves the development of strong orthographic representations, which allows fast and accurate identification of whole words made up of specific letter patterns. Most young students move easily from the use of alphabetic strategies to the use of orthographic representations, which can be accessed automatically. Initially, word identification is based on the application of phonic word-accessibility strategies (letter-sound associations). These strategies are in turn based on the development of phonemic awareness, which is necessary to learn how to relate speech to print.

**PROSODY** concerns versification of text and involves such matters as which syllable of a word is accented. In terms of fluency, it is that aspect which translates reading into the same experience as listening in the reader's mind. It involves intonation and rhythm through such devices as syllable accent and punctuation.

The student's development of the elements necessary to automaticity continually moves through stages. Another important stage involves the automatic recognition of single graphemes as a critical first step to the development of the letter patterns that make up words or word parts. English orthography consists of four basic word types:

1. Regular, for reading and spelling (e.g., *cat, print*)

2. Regular, for reading but not for spelling (e.g., *float, brain*—could be spelled *flote* or *brane*, respectively)

3. Rule based (e.g., *canning*—doubling rule; *faking*—drop *e* rule)

4. Irregular (e.g., *beauty*)

Students must be taught to recognize all four types of words automatically in order to be effective readers. Repeated practice in pattern recognition is often necessary. True automaticity should be linked with prosody and anticipation

> **AUTOMATICITY:** automatic reading involves the development of strong orthographic representations, which allows fast and accurate identification of whole words made up of specific letter patterns

> **PROSODY:** concerns versification of text and involves such matters as which syllable of a word is accented

to acquire full fluency. Such things as which syllable is accented and how word structure can be predictive are necessary to true automaticity and essential to complete fluency.

A student whose reading rate is slow, or halting and inconsistent, is exhibiting a lack of reading fluency. Some students develop accurate word pronunciation skills but read at a slow rate. They have not moved to the phase where decoding is automatic, and their limited fluency may affect performance in the following ways:

- They read less text than their peers and have less time to remember, review, or comprehend the text

- They expend more cognitive energy than their peers trying to identify individual words

- They may be less able to retain text in their memories and less likely to integrate those segments with other parts of the text

Reading fluency and comprehension involve three cueing methods: orthographic awareness, semantic cueing, and syntactic cueing. Also, sight-word and high-frequency word skills contribute to reading fluency. Teachers need to be aware of how to assess and teach those skills to enhance reading fluency.

## SKILL 1.3b Explains the impact of fluency on comprehension

Fluency is an important skill because it helps readers develop from word recognition to comprehension. When readers don't have to spend time focusing on reading individual words, they can group words together to form ideas, which leads to comprehension.

Not only can they grasp the main idea of the text, but they can make connections between the text and their prior knowledge and events in their own lives.

Fluency is a skill that is developed over time with repeated practice, exposure to literature and opportunities to read for various purposes. Early readers read words rather than phrases and sentences and the act of reading often appears to be laborious rather than enjoyable. Fluency changes over time as readers are exposed to more difficult texts.

The most fluent readers at one level may read slowly when they are first introduced to a more difficult text because they need time for comprehension.

When students work on fluency, they practice reading connected pieces of text. In other words, instead of looking at a word as just a word, they might read a sentence straight through. In order for a student to comprehend what she is reading, she would need to be able to "fluently" piece words together in a sentence quickly. If a student is not fluent in reading, she would sound each letter or word out slowly and pay more attention to the phonics of each word. A fluent reader, on the other hand, might read a sentence out loud using appropriate intonations. Fluency in reading depends on automatic word identification, which helps the student achieve comprehension of the material seamlessly. Even slight difficulties in word identification can significantly increase the time it takes a student to read material, require the student to reread some passages, and reduce the level of anticipated comprehension. If the student perceives reading as a constant struggle, intimidating task, or a strenuous chore, then he or she will avoid reading whenever possible and consider it a negative experience. Obviously, the ability to read for comprehension, and learning in general, will suffer if students are not assured that all aspects of reading fluency are skills that can be readily acquired with the appropriate amount of effort.

Fluency requires more than just a repertoire of recognizable words, however; expression is also part of fluency. To read fluently with expression a reader must be able to break the text into meaningful phrases and clauses. Some techniques to use when teaching students to read fluently include:

- Repeated reading of the same text
- Oral reading practice using audiotapes
- Providing models of what fluent reading looks and sounds like
- Reading to students
- Choral reading
- Partner reading
- Readers' theater

# Literature and informational texts

> **SKILL** Understands how to use key ideas and details to comprehend
> **1.4** literature and informational text

Beginning readers must learn to recognize the conventions that create meaning and expectations in the text. For beginning readers, these literal skills include deciphering the words, punctuation, and grammar in a text. When readers achieve comprehension, they create meaning from a text. Comprehension occurs when they are able to make predictions, select main ideas, and establish significant and supporting details of the story.

A successful program of comprehension instruction should include four components:

1. Large amounts of time for actual text reading

2. Teacher-directed instruction in comprehension strategies

3. Opportunities for peer and collaborative learning

4. Occasions for students to talk to a teacher and one another about their responses to reading

> *Teachers can improve children's comprehension skills by providing them with opportunities and guidance in making text selections.*

Teachers can improve children's comprehension skills by providing them with opportunities and guidance in making text selections. Student choice is related to interest and motivation, both of which are related directly to learning. Teachers can encourage the rereading of texts, which, research suggests, leads to greater fluency and comprehension. Teachers can also allow time for students to read with another student, pairing students of different abilities. This provides regular opportunities for readers to discuss their reading with the teacher and with one another. Teachers can also employ guided practice strategies in which they provide feedback to the students, gradually giving them more and more responsibility for evaluating their own performances.

## Bloom's Taxonomy

> *Learn more about Bloom's Taxonomy:*
>
> *http://faculty.washington.edu/ krumme/guides/bloom1.html*

Reading comprehension skills such as generating and answering literal, inferential, and interpretive questions to demonstrate understanding of what is read in complex text are often found in the various levels of Bloom's Taxonomy. These levels, in ascending order of sophistication, are:

1. Knowledge
2. Comprehension
3. Application
4. Analysis
5. Synthesis
6. Evaluation

Higher-order cognitive questions are defined as those that ask the student to mentally manipulate bits of information previously learned in order to support an answer with logically reasoned evidence. Higher-order cognitive questions are also called open-ended, interpretive, evaluative, and inferential questions. Lower-order cognitive questions are those that ask the student merely to recall literally the material previously read or taught by the teacher.

Students often misrepresent the differences between FICTION and NONFICTION. They mistakenly believe that stories are always examples of fiction. The simple truth is that stories are both fiction and nonfiction. The primary difference is that fiction is imaginary, and nonfiction is generally true (or an opinion). It is harder for students to understand that nonfiction encompasses an enormous range of material, from textbooks to true stories and newspaper articles to speeches. Fiction, on the other hand, is a fairly simple concept—imaginary stories, novels, and the like. But it is also important for students to understand that most fiction throughout history has been based on true events. In other words, authors use their own life experiences to help them create works of fiction.

> **FICTION:** works that are made up by the author, or are not true

> **NONFICTION:** written accounts of real people, places, objects, or events

The artistry in telling a story to convey a point is important in understanding fiction. When students see that an author's choice in a work of fiction is for the sole purpose of conveying a viewpoint, they can make better sense of the specific details.

Realizing what is truth and what is perspective is important in understanding nonfiction. Often, a nonfiction writer will present an opinion, and that opinion is quite different from a truth. Knowing the difference between the two is crucial.

> *Realizing what is truth and what is perspective is important in understanding nonfiction.*

## SKILL 1.4a Identifies key details, moral, and/or theme of a literary text, citing specific textual evidence

In comparing fiction to nonfiction, students need to learn about the conventions of each genre. In fiction, students can generally expect to find plot, characters, setting, and themes. In nonfiction, students may find a plot, characters, settings, and themes, but they will also find interpretations, opinions, theories, research, and other elements. The more fanciful or unrealistic a text or story is, the more likely it is fiction. By citing specific textual information and pointing out patterns of key details, students can begin to distinguish fiction from nonfiction.

SKILL
1.4b **Identifies the key details and/or central idea of an informational text, citing specific textual information**

Nonfiction comes in a variety of styles. While many students simplify nonfiction as being true (as opposed to fiction, which is make-believe), nonfiction is much deeper than that. Students should be exposed to all of the various types of nonfiction.

| TYPES OF NONFICTION | |
|---|---|
| Informational Texts | These types of books explain concepts or phenomena. An informational text might explain the history of a state or the idea of photosynthesis. These types of text are usually based on research. |
| Newspaper Articles | These short texts rely completely on factual information and are presented in a very straightforward, sometimes choppy manner. The purpose of these texts is to present information to readers in a quick and efficient manner. |
| Essays | Usually, essays take an opinion (whether it is about a concept, a work of literature, a person, or an event) and describe how the opinion was arrived at or why the opinion is a good one. |
| Biographies | These texts describe the lives of individuals. They are usually based on extensive research. |
| Memoirs | in a way, a memoir is like an autobiography, but memoirs tend to be based on a specific idea, concept, issue, or event in life. For example, most presidents of the United States write memoirs about their time in office. |
| Letters | When letters are read and analyzed in the classroom, students are generally studying the writer's style or the writer's true opinions and feelings about certain events. Often, students will find letters of famous individuals in history reprinted in textbooks. |
| Journals | Like letters, journals present personal ideas. When available (most people rarely want their journals published), they give students the opportunity to see peoples' thought processes about various events or issues. |

## Children's Literature

Children's literature is a genre of its own. Although it can share some of the characteristics of adult literature, it emerged as a distinct and independent form in the second half of the seventeenth century. *The Visible World in Pictures* by John Amos Comenius, a Czech educator, was one of the first printed works in existence as well as the first picture book. After its publication, educators acknowledged for the first time that children are different from adults in many respects.

*Modern educators acknowledge that introducing elementary students to a wide range of reading experiences plays an important role in their mental, social, and psychological development.*

Modern educators acknowledge that introducing elementary students to a wide range of reading experiences plays an important role in their mental, social, and psychological development.

## COMMON FORMS OF CHILDREN'S LITERATURE

| | |
|---|---|
| **Traditional Literature** | Traditional literature opens up a world where right wins out over wrong, hard work and perseverance are rewarded, and helpless victims find vindication. These are worthwhile values that children identify with even as early as kindergarten.<br><br>In traditional literature, children are introduced to fanciful beings, humans with exaggerated powers, talking animals, and heroes that will inspire them. For younger elementary children, these stories in Big Book format are ideal for providing predictable and repetitive elements that are easily grasped. |
| **Folktales/ Fairy Tales** | Adventures of animals or humans and the supernatural typically characterize these stories. The hero is usually on a quest aided by other-worldly helpers. More often than not, the story focuses on good and evil and reward and punishment. Some examples of folktales and fairy tales include: "The Three Bears," "Little Red Riding Hood," "Snow White," "Sleeping Beauty," "Puss in Boots," "Rapunzel," and "Rumpelstiltskin." |
| **Picture Books** | Designed primarily for preschool children, these books tell their story with the illustrations as well as with text. The text is often limited, but can be essential. Picture books are often a child's first introduction to books and print. |
| **Fables** | Animals that act like humans are featured in these stories; the animals usually reveal human foibles or teach a lesson. Example: *Aesop's Fables*. |
| **Myths** | These stories about events from the earliest times, such as the origin of the world, are often considered true in various societies. |
| **Legends** | These are similar to myths except that they are usually about events that occurred more recently. Example: Arthurian legends. |
| **Tall Tales** | These are purposely exaggerated accounts of individuals with superhuman strength. Examples: Paul Bunyan, John Henry, and Pecos Bill. |
| **Modern Realistic Fiction** | These stories are about real problems that real children face. By finding that their hopes and fears are shared by others, young children can find insight into their own problems. Young readers also tend to experience a broadening of interests as the result of this kind of reading. It is good for them to know that a child can be brave and intelligent and solve difficult problems. |
| **Historical Fiction** | This type of literature provides the opportunity to introduce younger children to history in a beneficial way. *Rifles for Watie* is an example of historical fiction. Presented in a historically accurate setting, it's about a sixteen-year-old boy who serves in the Union army. He experiences great hardships but discovers that his enemy is an admirable human being. |
| **Biography** | Reading about inventors, explorers, scientists, political and religious leaders, social reformers, artists, sports figures, doctors, teachers, writers, and war heroes helps children see that one person can make a difference. It also opens new vistas for children to consider when they choose a future occupation. |
| **Informational Books** | These are ways for children to learn more about something they are interested in or something that they know little about. Encyclopedias are good resources, of course, but a book like *Polar Wildlife* by Kamini Khanduri also shows pictures and facts that will capture the imaginations of young children. |

## Preadolescent and Adolescent Literature

The social changes post–World War II significantly affected adolescent literature. The civil rights movement, feminism, the protests of the Vietnam War era, and issues surrounding homelessness, neglect, teen pregnancy, drugs, and violence bred a new vein of contemporary fiction that helps adolescents understand and cope with the world they live in.

Popular books for preadolescents often focus on establishing relationships with members of the opposite sex (Sweet Valley High series) and learning to cope with changing bodies, personalities, or life situations (Judy Blume's *Are You There, God? It's Me, Margaret*).

Adolescents are typically interested in the fantasy and science fiction genres as well as popular juvenile fiction. Even today, middle school students still read the Little House on the Prairie series and the mysteries of the Hardy Boys and Nancy Drew. Teens also value adult literature, such as the works of Emily and Charlotte Brontë, Willa Cather, Jack London, William Shakespeare, and Mark Twain as much as those of the more modern Piers Anthony, S. E. Hinton, Madeleine L'Engle, Stephen King, and J. R. R. Tolkien.

> **SKILL 1.4c** **Makes inferences from a text and supports them with appropriate evidence**

*See Skill 1.4a*

**Inference** is a process that involves a reader making a reasonable judgment based on the information given. Children are engaged using the evidence found in a text to literally construct meaning. In addition to using specific evidence that clearly defines a situation (observation), children must analyze passages and use their best judgment to determine what they believe is happening.

By learning to infer while reading, students will pick up on implications in passages. This is a skill that can begin as early as preschool and has the ability to be applied across disciples throughout an entire K–12 curriculum.

For example, a preschool teacher might close a book a few pages in and ask a few questions. This is not only a strategy to check for comprehension, but also a way to quickly see how students are using inference. In a secondary setting, graphic organizers can help students align their inferences with appropriate evidence from the text that they are reading. This strategy can be used before, during or after finishing up with a reading. By having students engage with the text throughout the reading process to provide inferences, they must use active learning. This not only draws students deeper into the reading process, it also assists them in internalizing the content. Each student will have an individualized reading experience and collecting thoughts on graphic organizers allows them to explain what they were thinking at the time and what part of the text led them to make this particular conclusion. It's particularly helpful if the graphic organizer has a column for the student to write down the exact quote and page number to reference when describing their thoughts.

## SKILL 1.4d  Summarizes information from a text

Identifying key points in a reading will assist students in formulating a personal summary. By organizing the main ideas and providing an overview of what has been learned, students can summarize information from a text. Often times, students will want to repeat back to you everything that's happened in the passage that they're reading, so one great first step is to teach students how to draw the main idea from a paragraph. As they move on to larger passages, they can report back one or two of the biggest points that were made, and slowly they will gain the ability to determine a brief summary of what they have just read. If you are reading aloud to them, you could take a quick break during or after the reading to check for understanding and ask students to provide their own summary of the reading.

Other students may agree on the points that their peers made, and they may also have another suggestion to add in to piggy back off of the information that was already shared.

Another way to get students thinking about how to shorten everything they remember to simply providing a summary is to ask them to imagine they are telling a story about what they had just read to a parent or friend. If they asked you what had happened in the book *Charlotte's Web,* you wouldn't be able to remember *everything* that you read. You would simply explain the main characters and the critical parts of the story.

**Analyzes the characters, setting, and plot of a literary text**

When analyzing a literary text, it's important to play close attention to the separate elements, such as characters, setting, and plot. While each of these elements stands alone, the storyline is made up of a collaboration amongst the three. Characters can represent humans, animals, and even ghosts. Asking students "who" is in the story can assist them in quickly identifying the characters. For example, although the *Wizard of Oz* includes a variety of fictional character types, a student should not have any issues in determining the main characters when asked who the story was about.

The setting assists in setting the mood for the story. This includes not only the physical Location but also the time period in which it takes place. For example, a story that's set in the Wild West might include a few pages of back story to detail the extremities of the setting. This assists students in understanding the type of environment that the characters lived in and may also set them up in picking up on the plot line.

The main events in a story make up the plot. Typically, a plot includes an introduction (this could overlap with a description of the setting and/or characters), rising action (which ultimately leads to conflict), a climax (the most critical part of the story), falling action, and a conclusion.

When aiding students in understanding the plot, you can ask them for the main ideas. Pulling together two or three main events will help students in realizing where the climax occurred and they can build on that knowledge to fill in the other elements associated with plot. Graphic organizers are extremely helpful in creating a visual of the plot line.

SKILL
1.4f **Analyzes the relationships among individuals, events, ideas, and concepts in an informational text**

Learning how to analyze characters and plot (Skill 1.4e) will assist students in understanding relationships among individuals, events, ideas, and concepts. Many of these relationships will be intertwined throughout a text.

Because informational texts are based on non-fiction, there will not be characters, but the skill of analyzing characters will assist students in determining whom the most important individuals are in that particular piece. Individuals may have relationships with one another, such as a family member to another family member, a romantic relationship, a friendship, or even a work relationship. Breaking down the basic plot and questioning the "why" as to they these individuals have an overlap will assist in analyzing their relationship.

The relationship of an event can be closely tied to the setting, which would most likely include a time period and significant details as to why that individual would be impacted. This also ties in with the ideas that the individual may generate throughout the event, and ideas and concepts that may be inspired by a given event.

Unlike a literary text, informational texts do not include a well-defined plot line. Passages and key ideas are often written in chronological order, another reason why setting is such a critical element to analyze. Students should also be taught to keep in mind the perspective of the author. For example, a bias may be uncovered in a text, and students may be able to point out fabricated information that could alter the way they view the relationships that are described.

| SKILL 1.5 | Understands how to use key ideas and details to comprehend literature and informational text |
|---|---|

*See Skill 1.4*

| SKILL 1.5a | Identifies structural elements of literature across genres *(e.g., cast of characters and stage directions in drama, rhyme, and meter in poetry)* |
|---|---|

## Drama

Drama comes from the Greek word *dran*, meaning "to do." Therefore, drama is the acting out of a written story. Theater itself involves various elements, such as speech, gesture, dance, music, sound, and spectacle. This art form combines many of the arts into a single live performance.

Drama can involve a range of "enactments" of text or spontaneous role portrayal. Traditionally, plays (comedy, modern, or tragedy) are performed in three to five acts. Traditionalists and neoclassicists adhere to Aristotle's unities of time, place, and action. Plot development is advanced through dialogue. Literary devices include asides, soliloquies, and the chorus, which represents public opinion. Considered by many to be the greatest of all dramatists/playwrights is William Shakespeare. Other dramaturges include Ibsen, Williams, Miller, Shaw, Stoppard, Racine, Moliére, Sophocles, Aeschylus, Euripides, and Aristophanes.

It is important to expose children to character development through stories, role playing, and modeling through various teacher-guided experiences. Some experiences that are age-appropriate for the early-childhood level include puppet theater, paper dolls, character sketches, storytelling, and the retelling of stories in a student's own words. There are many plays written for children as well as adaptations of plays suitable for classroom production. Many students find a "dramatic read-aloud" of stories they are reading enhances their interest and comprehension.

- **Acting:** Acting requires the student to demonstrate the ability to effectively communicate using speech, movement, rhythm, and sensory awareness.

- **Directing:** Direction requires the management skills to produce and perform an onstage activity. This requires guiding and inspiring students as well as script and stage supervision.

- **Designing:** Designing involves creating and initiating the onsite management of the art of acting.

- **Scriptwriting:** Scriptwriting demands that a leader be able to produce original material and stage an entire production through the writing and designing of a story that has performance value.

Students can engage in acting, directing, designing, or scriptwriting in response to stories they have read or written. Acting out parts of stories can be very engaging for some students and enhance comprehension, vocabulary development, and interest in language arts.

## Poetry

People read poetry for many reasons, which are often the very same reasons poets give for writing it. Just the feeling and sounds of the words that the artistic hands and mind of a poet turn into a delightful experience is a good reason to read a poem. Good poetry constantly surprises.

The major purpose a poet has for creating his or her works of art is the sharing of an experience, a feeling, or an emotion; this is also the reason a reader turns to poetry rather than prose. Reading poetry is often a search for variety, joy, and satisfaction.

There is another important reason that poets create and that readers are drawn to their poems: Poets are interpreters of life. They feel deeply the things that others feel or even things that may be overlooked by others. Poets also have the skill and inspiration to recreate those feelings and interpret them in such a way that understanding and insight may come from the experience. They often bring understanding to life's big (or even not-so-big) questions.

Children can respond to poetry at very early ages. Elementary students are at the stage where the sounds of unusual words intrigue and entertain them. They are also very open to emotional meanings of passages. Teaching poetry to fifth graders can be an important introduction to seeking meaning in literature. If a fifth grader enjoys reading poetry both silently and aloud, he or she may form a habit that will last a lifetime.

When we speak of structure with regard to poetry, we usually mean one of three things:

1. The pattern of the sound and rhythm

2. The visible shape it takes

3. Rhyme and free verse

## The pattern of the sound and rhythm

It helps to know the background of this peculiarity of poetry. History was passed down in oral form almost exclusively until the invention of the printing press; it was often set to music. A rhymed story is much easier to commit to memory, and adding a tune makes it even easier to remember. Therefore, it is not surprising that much of the earliest literature—epics, odes, and so on, are rhymed and were probably sung.

When we speak of the pattern of sound and rhythm, we are referring to two things: verse form and stanza form. The verse form is the rhythmic pattern of a single verse. An example is any meter; blank verse, for instance, is iambic pentameter. A stanza is a group of a certain number of verses (lines) with a rhyme scheme. If the poem is written, there is usually white space between the verses (although a short poem may consist of only one stanza). If the poem is spoken, there is a pause between stanzas.

## The visible shape it takes

In the seventeenth century, some poets shaped their poems on the page to reflect the theme. A good example of this is George Herbert's "Easter Wings." Since that time, poets have occasionally played with this device; however, it is generally viewed as nothing more than a demonstration of ingenuity. The rhythm, effect, and meaning are often sacrificed by being forced into the visual contours of the poem's shape.

## Rhyme and free verse

Poets also use devices that underscore the meanings of their poems to establish form. One such common device is alliteration. When the poem is read (as poetry

> Teaching poetry to fifth graders can be an important introduction to seeking meaning in literature.

is usually intended to be), the repetition of a sound may not only underscore the meaning, but also add pleasure to the reading.

Following a strict rhyming pattern can add intensity to the meaning of the poem in the hands of a skilled and creative poet. On the other hand, the meaning can be drowned out by the steady beat-beat-beat of it. Shakespeare skillfully used the regularity of rhyme in his poetry, breaking the rhythm at certain points to effectively underscore a point. For example, in Sonnet 130, "My mistress' eyes are nothing like the sun," the rhythm is primarily iambic pentameter. It lulls the reader (or listener) to accept that the poet is following the standard conventions for love poetry, which in that day reliably used rhyme and, more often than not, iambic pentameter to express feelings of romantic love along conventional lines. However, in Sonnet 130, the last two lines sharply break from the monotonous pattern, forcing the reader or speaker to pause:

> And yet, by heaven, I think my love as rare
> As any she belied with false compare.

Shakespeare's purpose is clear: He is not writing a conventional love poem; the object of his love is not the red-and-white conventional woman written about in other poems of the period. This is a good example of a poet using form to underscore meaning.

Poets eventually began to feel constricted by rhyming conventions and began to break away and make new rules for poetry. When poetry was only rhymed, it was easy to define it. When free verse, or poetry written in a flexible form, came upon the scene in France in the 1880s, it quickly began to influence English-language poets such as T. S. Eliot, whose memorable poem, "The Wasteland," had an alarming but desolate message for the modern world. It is impossible to imagine that "The Wasteland" could have been written in the soothing, lulling rhymed verse of previous periods.

Those who first began writing in free verse in English were responding to the influence of the French *vers libre*. However, it should be noted that free verse could also be loosely applied to the poetry of Walt Whitman, writing in the mid-nineteenth century, as can be seen in the first stanza of "Song of Myself."

> I celebrate myself, and sing myself,
> And what I assume you shall assume,
> For every atom belonging to me as good belongs to you.

When poetry was no longer defined as a piece of writing arranged in verses that had a rhyme-scheme of some sort, distinguishing poetry from prose became a point of discussion. Merriam-Webster's *Encyclopedia of Literature* defines poetry as "writing that formulates a concentrated imaginative awareness of experience in language chosen and arranged to create a specific emotional response through its meaning, sound and rhythm."

A poet chooses the form of poetry deliberately, based upon the emotional response he or she hopes to evoke and the meaning he or she wishes to convey. Robert Frost, a twentieth-century poet who chose to use conventional rhyming verse to make his point, is a memorable and often-quoted modern poet. Who can forget his closing lines in "Stopping by Woods"?

*And miles to go before I sleep,*
*And miles to go before I sleep.*

## Literary Techniques

There are a number of literary techniques that make an appearance in poetry of all forms. It is important to understand the different mechanisms that poets use in order to fully understand the meaning of a poem.

| LITERARY TECHNIQUES USED IN POETRY | |
| --- | --- |
| Slant Rhyme | This occurs when a rhyme is not exact; often, the final consonant sounds are the same but the vowels are different. It occurs frequently in Irish, Welsh, and Icelandic verse. Examples include *green* and *gone*, *that* and *hit*, and *ill* and *shell*. |
| Alliteration | Alliteration occurs when the initial sounds of a word, beginning with either a consonant or a vowel, are repeated in close succession. Examples include *Athena and Apollo*, *Nate never knows*, and *people who pen poetry*.<br><br>The function of alliteration, like rhyme, might be to accentuate the beauty of language in a given context, or to unite words or concepts through a kind of repetition. Alliteration, like rhyme, can follow specific patterns. Sometimes the similar-sounding consonants aren't always the initial ones (although they are generally the stressed syllables). Alliteration is less common than rhyme, but because it is less common, it can call attention to a word or line in a poem that might not have the same emphasis otherwise. |

*Table continued on next page*

| Assonance | As alliteration typically occurs at the beginning of a word, and rhyme occurs at the end, assonance takes the middle territory. Assonance occurs when the vowel sound in a word matches the sound in a nearby word, but the surrounding consonant sounds are different. *Tune* and *June* are rhymes; *tune* and *food* are assonant. The function of assonance is frequently the same as end rhyme or alliteration: All serve to give a sense of continuity or fluidity to the verse. Assonance is often especially effective when rhyme is absent, as it gives the poet more flexibility and it is not typically used as part of a predetermined pattern. Like alliteration, it does not determine the structure or form of a poem; rather, it is ornamental. |
|---|---|
| Onomatopoeia | These are words used to evoke meaning by their sounds. The early Batman television series used *pow*, *zap*, *whop*, *zonk*, and *eek* in an onomatopoetic way. |
| Rhythm | In poetry, rhythm refers to the recurrence of stresses at equal intervals. A stress (accent) is a greater amount of force given to one syllable in speaking than that given to another. For example, we put the stress on the first syllable of such words as *father*, *mother*, *daughter*, and *children*. The unstressed or unaccented syllable is sometimes called a slack syllable. All English words carry at least one stress (except articles and some prepositions such as *by*, *from*, and *at*). Indicating where stresses occur is called scansion, or scanning. Very little is gained in understanding a poem or in making a statement about it by merely scanning it. The pattern of the rhythm—the meter—should be analyzed in terms of its overall relationship to the message and impression of the poem. |

---

**SKILL** **Uses text features** *(e.g., headings, sidebars, hyperlinks)* **to locate information**
**1.5b** **in a print or digital informational text**

---

Text features have an organizational function that allows for ease of reading informational texts. They break information into manageable, organized categories (such as chapters or sections) to assist the reader in accessing information. Typically, a table of contents in a text will assist you in locating specific sections of information. This is also the case for digital versions, but the function CTRL+F on a keyboard allows for the easiest location of specific information.

A heading, or title, is often found at the top page of a text, regardless of print or digital format. A varied font or style (such as bold and italics) can be used to make this information stand out to the reader. Used as an organizational tool to break larger informational texts into categorized information, the heading serves as a main point for the information that follows.

**SIDEBARS: bits of critical information found alongside a larger passage**

SIDEBARS pull main points, ideas, and critical information from a large text to a small, manageable summary. These can be formatted in sentences, bullet points, or even simple definitions. You may have noticed there are sidebars on nearly every page of this text. When skimming pages, you may simply read the sidebar to get a gist of the information, or you may use the sidebars to determine which portion of the page that is most essential to read it its entirety.

When reading informational texts in digital form, hyperlinks may assist in finding information quickly. They can serve as links within the document- for example, hyperlinks can be incorporated into a table of contents to quickly bring you to the section that you desire. They may also be used to bring the reader to images, data points, charts, and graphs located within the document. You may also see hyperlinks used to bring the reader to an outside source which reaffirms information in the text, such as "for more information, read the following *New York Times* article from November 11th, 1958."

## SKILL 1.5c Identifies organizational structures of informational text *(e.g., cause/ effect, problem/solution)*

Often times, informational texts flow in a way that easily connects each section to the next. This can be done chronologically, through cause and effect, and problems with solutions.

Informational texts, such as biographies or autobiographies, are organized in chronological order. Facts are laid out starting with the beginning point in history and information is built on each section. Headings may read as time periods (1800–1887) or significant points in a person's life, such as the "I have a dream" speech that Martin Luther King gave in 1968.

Cause and effect is a strategy used to organize information in a way that demonstrates an outcome. In history texts, such as a book describing the Boston Tea Party, information is laid out in a way that shows the cause for an outcome. The outcome is not always predictable. Information is normally included to give the context of the situation and details are provided to elaborate on what happened following the outcome.

When organized in problem and solution manner, information is laid out sequentially. For example, a science text may provide a brief description of a problem that occurred and then an invention that was created to eradicate the problem. The solution will not always be predictable nor positive. For example, a war may be listed as a solution to ongoing turmoil across two nations. The outcome of the war will then tie in with cause and effect.

## SKILL 1.5d  Identifies how structural elements contribute to the development of a literary text as a whole

When developing a literary text, an author will begin with an outline, similar to a blueprint, of how they envision the information to be organized. They may use a concept map, list potential headings, or simple categories, to begin developing a plan for how their text will be written.

As content is written, an author may decide on more details, such as sidebars (*see Skill 1.5b*) and, if digital, what information they'd like to hyperlink (*see Skill 1.5b*). When considering a maximum word count, an author may go back and delete images or combine sections, eliminating headings to maximize the content that he or she is trying to produce. These structural elements contribute to the organization of the content throughout the entire development process.

## SKILL 1.6  Understands the concept of point of view using evidence from the text

Using clues such as the words "I," "he," and "they," a reader can pull evidence from a text to determine which point of view the story is being told from.

The following pronouns align with first, second, and third person point of view:

| POINT OF VIEW | | |
|---|---|---|
| Pronoun | Point of View | Example |
| I, me | First | "I enjoyed the beach." |
| You | Second | "It's clear you would want to visit." |
| He, they | Third | "He visits every summer." |

## SKILL 1.6a Identifies author's point of view in various genres and supports conclusions with evidence from text

An author's personal relationship with the content, or point of view, may impact the way information is written. Even if based on factual information, this may create a bias and sway information to match the opinion of the person creating the content.

A controversial topic, such as the Civil War, may tell a very different story when told by a slave compared to a slave owner. Different perspectives will alter the information in a way that may seem factual, with an attempt to get the reader to believe or agree with their side of the story.

Another more modern example could include the concept of pesticides on farming and the impact of GMO on the average American's health. A large pro-GMO company may write an informational packet to show various data points and their perspective that demonstrates this is the most "efficient" way to farm. An organic farmer may produce a similar information packet with graphs to show the incline of organic farming and its impact on producing a healthier America. Evidence can be pulled from the material by locating trigger words such as "I" or "We." Looking at these examples, it's easy to identify the bias in each:

*We believe this is the healthiest option and the future of farming for the United States.*

*We have information that shows this is the most effective farming method for our country.*

## SKILL 1.6b Compares multiple accounts of the same event or topic to identify similarities or differences in point of view

*See Skill 1.6a*

## SKILL 1.6c Identifies how point of view impacts the overall structure of a literary or informational text

When structuring a text, whether literary or informational, point of view can have a great deal of impact on how information is organized. Personal emotions may be used to open up a writing passage, or they may be used after setting the scene for the reader.

Point of view may also have an impact on the layout of the plot. Because a point of view can alter the perception of a setting, key events, and most important part of a story, it has potential to inject bias into how the information can be portrayed.

*See also Skill 1.6e*

**SKILL 1.7** **Understands how to integrate and compare written, visual, and oral information from texts and multimedia sources**

Texts no longer simply include the written word. Graphics, such as images, charts, maps, drawings, diagrams, and designs are now common additions and add to the overall meaning of the work. They enhance the meaning, engage the reader, and demonstrate simple examples and comparisons in which the text details.

When selecting materials to enhance content, you'll want to keep the overall format in mind. You do not want your additions to overwhelm the page, nor take away from the meaning of the text. Similar to the small points on the sides of the pages of this book, you want to draw the reader's attention to the main points and use added materials to heighten the understanding of the reader.

**SKILL 1.7a** **Explains how visual and oral elements enhance the meaning and effect of a literary text** *(e.g., picture book, graphic novel, multimedia presentation of a folktale)*

Visual elements not only demonstrate what the text attempts to achieve, they also bring the words to life. For example, if a history text included a few passages about a migration and the distance that it took, a few images could bring the reader in to a deeper understanding. Images might include a map of the region(s) from the given time period, a map demonstrating the geographic features, and a map of the region(s) in present day.

In an English class, students will experience visual and oral elements as enhancements while reading picture books, graphic novels, in addition to while listening to poetry readings, and watching peer presentations in class. Picture books and graphic novels will have very few words included, with the interpretation of the imagery in the images playing a huge part. Students may begin to learn how to read through the interpretation of the images, and later in life use these skills to further understand difficult texts. Abstract meanings and content that is difficult to connect to, such as something from a different time period, may have more meaning when a visual or oral element is added.

By listening to a poetry reading, students will better understand the intention of the writer. Listening to pauses, emphasized words, and the speed of the reading will assist students in their interpretation of the meaning.

During in-class presentations, students should be taught to include oral and visual elements to enhance the content that they are sharing with their peers. For example, PowerPoint slides could include a graph to demonstrate data points, images to show what an author looked like during the time period in which the text was written, or even a brief video clip of an interview of the author.

## SKILL 1.7b Compares the written version of a literary text with an oral, staged, or filmed version

Literary texts will be interpreted differently from reader to reader. Students will connect with different elements in the text, both large and small. This also goes for people that have made visual and oral representations of the text.

When reading the original text, students should pay close attention to the language that is used. They may underline vocabulary words that are significant to the time period and meaning, in addition to sentences and passages that contribute to the outcome of the story. When watching or listening to another version, students may hear these words or passages, assisting in their understanding of the connection between the two.

In your future classroom, students may have the ability to compare a book to a movie, such as *Hamlet* and "The Lion King." They will be able to break down common themes, characters, climaxes, and details that both overlap and contradict one another. This could also include a play based on this story, and interpretive dance, or even a dramatic reading. Students could complete individual comparisons or work in small groups to create a visual or chart that demonstrates what they believe are the most significant overlaps and differences.

### SKILL 1.7c — Compares two or more literary texts that address the same theme

**Themes** are main ideas that an author conveys in a literary text. They are not always explicitly written within the text, and it is common for the reader to make an interpretation on what they believe best defines the theme within the text. When teaching the idea of themes, it may be helpful for students the grasp their understanding by reading a few literary texts that share a common theme. They may read two stories and create a visual, such as a graphic organizer or Venn diagram, to demonstrate similarities and differences.

A simple theme that students may learn in an early grade could be "treat others the way you want to be treated." This theme may apply to a children's book in which the main character is a bully and the story ends in the bully being punished or receiving similar treatment of the poor behavior they demonstrated. This could then tie in to a Shakespearean text, a slave narrative, and even a text based on popular culture. Students will learn to deconstruct the meaning in order to determine the theme, and by using close reading strategies, skills in identifying and analyzing themes will assist students in reading texts throughout their schooling.

### SKILL 1.7d — Compares two or more informational texts that address the same topic

Similar to learning to compare common themes, analyzing differences in topics for informational texts will be applicable for years. A topic could include a person or an object, such as Edgar Allen Poe, or a classic automobile. When breaking down differences and similarities, graphic organizers can be very helpful to create a visual representation. Students could include main ideas and the page number that they found the information on to better support their claims.

Informational texts will demonstrate similar factual information but varied interpretations for information that is not based on truth. For example, if a text was written about the life of George Washington, perspectives will vary greatly if one was written by the child of a slave and another version was written by a Caucasian relative of George Washington. Facts that will remain the same could include the day he was born, the day he was elected president, information about his death, and the location of his residence. Information that may vary from version to version could include his personality, the way he treated his slaves, his sense of fashion, and even his eating and drinking habits. One text may describe him to be an extremely generous family man with a background in going out of his way for others, while another could include gruesome details about his temper or poor treatment of the staff that worked and lived on his property. By analyzing the author, time period in which the text was written, and the connection between the author and the content, students will have a greater ability to compare two texts that address the same topic.

## SKILL 1.7e Interprets visual and multimedia elements in literary and informational texts

Along with the rise in digital literacy, modern texts and eBooks include a large number of visual and multimedia elements to enhance the content. It's critical for students to take the time to look over added elements and interpret their meaning and connection to the text.

Within informational texts, images to demonstrate time periods may be included to better demonstrate garb, location, food, animals, and housing. Through interpretation, students may find they are able to comprehend the text and the intended meaning of the author better than if the content simply included text.

Literary texts may include visuals to better describe abstract meanings, fairytales, and characters that may be difficult to interpret in writing. Thinking of *The Lord of the Rings* and *Harry Potter,* images would be a great way to enhance the story and provide a connection from the content to the intended meaning of the author.

*See also Skill 1.7a*

## SKILL 1.7f Evaluates key themes in a text and supports them with reasons and evidence from the text

The theme is the main element in which the entire story revolves around. Key themes are often the main ideas of a story, although not stated explicitly. Many details are places in the story intentionally to teach the reader what the author intended the theme to be. While identifying key themes, it's important to use evidence from the text to make a stronger analysis of the significance it has on the story.

Themes may be as simple as war, love, or friendship and they could include a deeper meaning such as people get what they deserve. Students may have different interpretations as to what the key themes are, so it's crucial to teach them to analyze their reasoning behind their selection. They could use a chart, such as the one below, to include evidence from the text to support their claim. This also includes a spot for students to explain what the theme means to them.

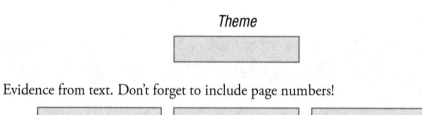

*Theme*

Evidence from text. Don't forget to include page numbers!

What does this theme mean to you? Why is this theme important?

*See also Skill 1.7c*

---

**SKILL 1.8** **Knows the role of text complexity in reading development**

Text complexity is broken down into three components: quantitative, qualitative, and reader and task. Reading development, including experience in reading a variety of genres, will play a large role in a student's ability to comprehend each factor of text complexity.

## Quantitative*

- Text cohesion
- Word length
- Readability
- Sentence length
- Word frequency
- Total word count

*Often measured by computer software

## Qualitative*

- Levels of meaning
- Levels of purpose
- Clarity of language
- Predictability
- Structure
- Familiarity with topic
- Appropriate age level/maturity level

*Cannot be measured by computer software

## Reader and task*

- Student motivation
- Interest level
- Background knowledge
- Purpose of task
- Level of rigor in questions being asked

*Must be measured by teacher

---

**SKILL 1.8a** Explains the three factors (i.e., quantitative, qualitative, and reader and task) that measure text complexity

*See Skills 1.8 and 1.8b*

## SKILL 1.8b  Identifies the key features of text-leveling systems

**Text-leveling** is a strategy that can be used for both literary and informational texts. Leveling is when series of texts are arranged from easiest to most difficult; a variety of factors impacts how this arrangement is determined.

**Quantitative** (most commonly determined by computer algorithms) and **qualitative** (factors selected by teachers) are both key factors in determining the level of a text. These factors, which make up text complexity, will play a large role in labeling an appropriate text level. Unlike systems that may break texts up by grade level, text levels could include benchmarks and numbers that all tie to a common grade. A student entering the fourth grade may be paired up with a text level 4.2, while their peer with advanced reading skills could be matched with a 4.7. As the student that received the 4.2 text advances, he or she will continue to advance up the leveling system.

The **Lexile Framework** is a common measure used to determine reading level. Scores vary over one thousand points, and students will be placed on a scale from beginning reader to advanced reader. Once teachers and students are aware of a Lexile level, the appropriate level of text within a leveling system can be matched.

Text-leveling can also be used for English Language Learning (ELL) development. The range of levels may be broken down by proficiency, with beginner at the very bottom, and fluent as the most advanced level. The texts may share common topics, themes, and information, but the rigor and layout will vary greatly.

# COMPETENCY 002
## WRITING, SPEAKING, AND LISTENING

## Writing

There are four main types of writing, each with different uses and purposes. The four types of writing are Persuasive, Narrative, Expository and Descriptive.

> *The four types of writing are Persuasive, Narrative, Expository and Descriptive.*

### Persuasive Writing

Persuasive writing is writing in which the author takes a definitive stance on an issue or subject, and supports that stance through rational written arguments that intend on influencing the reader to agree with the author's perspective. Persuasive writing can be seen as a form of written debate where to author is trying to "win over" their audience.

### Narrative Writing

Narrative writing tells a story about an event or experience that happened to the author. The story can be factual/non-fiction or imaginary/fiction. The story line of narrative writing should provide insight into the relatable experience of the author or protagonist.

## Expository Writing

**Expository writing** is factual and specific with the objective of informing the reader of information pertaining to the specific topic of the writing. Examples of expository writing can include recipes, instructional manuals, and encyclopedias.

## Descriptive Writing

Often, but not always used within expository writing, **descriptive writing** looks to explain concepts, ideas, or subjects in as much detail as possible. Authors of descriptive writing have the objective of providing as clear a picture to the reader as possible and can go into intricate details of topics being covered.

---

**SKILL 2.1b** **Identifies the purpose, key components, and sub-genres** *(e.g., speeches, advertisements, narrative poems)* **of each common type of writing**

*See Skill 2.1a*

---

**SKILL 2.1c** **Evaluates the effectiveness of writing samples of each type**

*See Skill 2.1a*

---

**SKILL 2.2** **Understands the characteristics of effective writing**

*Effective writing should leave the reader with a clear understanding of the author's point of view, topic discussed, or narrative insight.*

Effective writing should leave the reader with a clear understanding of the author's point of view, topic discussed, or narrative insight. Different types of writing should be used in different situations, depending on the purpose of the writing and the intended audience. In all types and purposes of writing, the author should be careful to avoid errors in spelling, grammar and structure that can be distracting to the reader and take away from the authors objective outcomes. Effective writing has a clear objective, is written to the desired audience, and is free of distractions.

## SKILL Evaluates the appropriateness of a particular piece of writing for a
## 2.2a specific task, purpose, and audience

The purpose of a piece of writing should dictate the type of writing being used. For example, descriptive writing is ideal for developing a detailed instruction manual for new employees to learn how to master their new job responsibilities. A new employee would need clear concise information to be able to easily learn how to complete their responsibilities.

However, if an author wanted to impart important life lessons on the values of sharing, friendship and caring for others, a narrative story could be more impactful based on the desired outcome. In every situation, an author must analyze the purpose of their writing and their intended audience to determine the most appropriate form of writing for the task.

*The purpose of a piece of writing should dictate the type of writing being used.*

## SKILL Evaluates the development, organization, or style of a piece of
## 2.2b writing

In addition to the types of writing being used, authors will also demonstrate different styles and ways of organizing their content. Style and organization help deliver the author's content more effectively and allows them to further align their content with their target audience.

Organization is how the author orders the topics and moves from topic to topic in a seamless transition. Smooth organization of content can help the reader better retain the information and develop a fuller concept of the author's main ideas.

Style is the author's voice and in some ways, the personality they give to their writing. Authors can write in a formal or informal style, they could very descriptive adjectives, or could be more conversational.

*Style and organization help deliver the author's content more effectively and allows them to further align their content with their target audience.*

## SKILL Identifies appropriate revisions to strengthen a piece of writing
## 2.2c

Authors of all types of writing revise their work multiple times throughout the drafting process before finalizing their work. Identification of appropriate revisions give the author the opportunity to review their work as though they were the reader, through their reader's eyes.

Authors should envision themselves as their reader with special attention to the type of writing being used, organization of topics and ideas, and the style being used to engage the reader. At this point in the revision process, the author should take the opportunity to make changes to structure, style and content in order to ensure their writing will have the desired impact on the reader.

## SKILL 2.2d Writes clearly and coherently

Clarity and coherency describe how easily the reader is able to synthesize the concepts, ideas, and story line of the author's writing. During the revision process it is important for the author to analyze the clarity and coherency of their writing at regular intervals. These two elements contribute greatly to the "flow" of the writing and are imperative to ensuring the writing has the desired outcome on the reader. If ideas and content are not presented in a clear and coherent manner, the reader can become disengaged, and the writing can lose its effectiveness.

*See also Skill 2.6*

## SKILL 2.2e Identifies interrelationships among planning, revising, and editing in the process of writing

As can be seen from the sections above, writing is a process, a series of steps that need to be taken to ensure the content will have the desired impact on the reader and will be free from distractions and errors. These steps include planning, drafting, revising and editing. All these steps are interconnected and build upon each other in each subsequent step in the process.

## Planning

PLANNING is the first step in the process and where the authors identifies the purpose/goal of the writing. This is also where to author will identify what type of writing will be used and who will be the target audience. This is the brain storming phase and where the author will develop their vision for the writing.

## Drafting

DRAFTING is when the author puts their vision into the first version, or draft of their writing. The first draft, known as the "rough draft" is not checked for spelling, grammar, or organization. It is the initial thoughts written down by the author in a "rough" form. In subsequent drafts, an author will continue to revise and reorganize the document through the readers prospective and aligning with the objectives of the writing. Some authors may go through 3 to 5 or even more drafts, however many are necessary until they are satisfied with the final copy.

> DRAFTING: when the author puts their vision into the first version, or draft of their writing

## Editing

EDITING is the final step, after the final content has been developed and the piece is virtually complete. Editing is when the author, or another individual reviews the document for any potential spelling or grammatical errors that could distract the reader from the content of the writing.

> EDITING: the final step, after the final content has been developed and the piece is virtually complete

---

**SKILL 2.3** **Knows the developmental stages of writing** (e.g., picture, scribble)

---

Students will being their first stages of writing development as early as pre-k classes. It may seem like gibberish at the time, but scribbling on paper is the first stage. Simple marks on a paper, regardless of the comprehensiveness, is a start to creating words and phrases.

Next, students will begin drawing letter-like symbols, such as crosses and letters that overlap, followed by strings of the same letter. Typically aligned with an image, the next step will include students producing one letter at a time, such as "b" for "bird."

As rigor increases, students will advance to have the ability to fill in the blank to include missing letters. These could be at the beginning, middle, or end of a word. Following successful fill in the blank exercises, students should develop the ability to attempt to write on their own. The last phase will include proper spelling and comprehensible phrases.

Young children develop writing in stages just as they do reading. As with reading, writing development is not a linear progression, but rather an overlapping one. Though many label the scribbling that children start out with as prewriting, it is actually one of the stages of writing development.

| THREE CUEING SYSTEMS | |
|---|---|
| **Orthographic Awareness** | The ability to perceive and recall letter strings and word forms as well as the retrieval of letters and words. Sight-word vocabulary for both reading and spelling depends on this skill.<br><br>A weakness in orthographic awareness results in slow reading rates and problems with spelling. This, in turn, affects reading comprehension and writing fluency. |
| **Syntactic Cueing** | Evaluating a word for its part of speech and its place in the sentence. For example, the reader determines whether the word is a noun, verb, adjective, or other part of speech. If it is an adjective, the reader determines which word it modifies. If it is a pronoun, the reader must decide which noun it takes the place of. Syntactic cueing directly affects reading comprehension. |
| **Semantic Cueing** | Determining the meaning of a word, phrase, or sentence and determining what the passage is about. |

Each writing stage has unique characteristics involving the areas of spelling, penmanship, print/mechanics concepts, and content. The following table explains the requisite skill for each stage and area.

| | Spelling | Penmanship | Print/Mechanics Concepts | Content |
|---|---|---|---|---|
| **Role-Play Writer** | Scribbles and uses writing-like behavior; scribbles to represent word; no phonetic association | Develops pencil position and traces words and letters | Develops awareness of environmental print | Uses pictures and scribble writing |
| **Emergent Writer** | Writes initial consonants; correlates some letter/sounds; each syllable has a letter | Can write on line; incorrectly mixes upper- and lowercase letters | Makes some letters and words; attempts to write name | Copies words and uses pattern sentences |
| **Developing Writer** | Left/right correspondence; invented spelling with initial/final consonants; few vowels | Correctly uses upper- and lowercase letters | Directional writing and one-to-one writing/ reading words; writes word patterns | Uses invented spelling and simple sentences |
| **Beginning Writer** | Correct spelling for most words; uses resources and decoding for spelling | Sentence structure; only focuses on one writing component at a time, i.e., spelling or punctuation | Chooses personally significant topics for writing assignments | Organizes paragraphs using complete sentences |
| **Expanding Writer** | Edits for mechanics during and after writing | Varies writing components based on writing task | Uses organization and variety of word choices | Writes in a variety of formats: poetry, stories, reports |

## SKILL 2.3a  Identifies grade-appropriate continuum of student writing

The quality of writing, including the development of style, structure, and writing type will vary greatly depending on the grade level of the author. For this reason, instructors should develop a continuum of grading scales to ensure that student are only being held responsible for the level of work they can reasonably be expected to complete based on their grade level and previous academic preparation.

Often times, these levels will vary greatly within students of the same class. It is important for instructors to establish this continuum as well as appropriate grading practices and policies to effectively evaluate students based on these scales.

> The quality of writing, including the development of style, structure, and writing type will vary greatly depending on the grade level of the author.

## SKILL 2.4  Knows the importance of digital tools for producing and publishing writing and for interacting with others

The internet has developed a number of tools that can assist in the production of student writing. Tools vary from automated citation software, to sophisticated research assistance, document sharing/collaboration, to automatic plagiarism detection programs.

Students should be encouraged to use the appropriate tools in instances when it may assist in the quality of their writing style and content. Instructors should create opportunities early in the semester to familiarize students with useful tools, and also caution against detracting tools that may encourage short-cuts and/or plagiarism.

## SKILL 2.4a  Identifies characteristics and purposes of a variety of digital tools for producing and publishing writing

**Digital resources** can be classified into one of three categories, sharing tools, research tools, or development tools. Sharing tools, are those which allow student to collaborate with others, or share their work with others to receive feedback and make edits to their work. Research tools, are those that allow a student to conduct research on a topic in order to develop content for their writing. Development tools are those that assist a student in the actual writing process and developing the content for their paper.

## SKILL 2.4b  Identifies the purposes of a variety of digital tools for interacting with others

The digital age has created numerous ways for students to collaborate, interact, and engage with each other through various online tools. Some of these tools include Google docs, Microsoft one drive, Twitter, YouTube, and Facebook. Although many of these tools have historically been developed and used for social interactions, instructors can find ways to utilize them within the content of course material. As previously stated, it is important to illustrate the appropriate and inappropriate ways to utilize these tools early in the class to ensure that students are utilizing the tools in the most appropriate and educational ways.

## SKILL 2.5  Knows the research process

Research is a critical part in the writing process, especially when developing works of non-fiction. Knowing how to conduct sounds research is one of the first steps in ensuring a quality piece of non-fiction.

## SKILL 2.5a  Identifies the steps in the research process

The research process begins with a research questions. A research questions should identify the purpose of the writing, and seek to provide the rationale for the writing being produced. All additional research should be based around finding an answer to the research question.

In addition to identifying the primary research questions, authors should also establish a concrete "thesis." A **RESEARCH THESIS** is the author's presumption of what the reasonable answer to the research question is.

A thesis can be proven or disproven based on the results of the subsequent research, however it is very important for an author to identify their thesis prior to conducting their research. The thesis serves the purpose of identifying any potential author bias, and serves as a baseline for discovery throughout the research process.

**RESEARCH THESIS:** the author's presumption of what the reasonable answer to the research question is

The third step in the research process is identifying sources of information to assist in answering the research questions. Identification of sources provides the heart of any good writing, but there are varying degrees of quality and reliability when it comes to sources of information.

## SKILL 2.5b Distinguishes between primary and secondary sources and their uses

Sources can be "Primary" or "Secondary." **"Primary" resources** are the most reliable, and represent original, factual information directly related to the research questions. Examples of primary sources can include, original texts, research, or artifacts. Primary sources can be seen as firsthand information, meaning that it came directly from the sources with direct knowledge of the events or facts that are in questions.

*Sources can be "Primary" or "Secondary."*

**Secondary information**, although often times still relevant, is not considered "first hand" information. It is considered quality information but that has been received from an outside source. An example of secondary information would be an article about a topic written by an author based on their research. Said author may not have firsthand experience with the content of their paper, but have collected research from first hand sources to produce the paper. This paper would be considered a secondary source because it comes from an author, not the primary subject matter.

## SKILL 2.5c Distinguishes between reliable and unreliable sources

Both primary and secondary sources can have varying levels of reliability. Naturally, secondary sources are more at risk of marginal reliability, but even primary sources need to be carefully analyzed for reliability. In today's digital world, it is easy for an infinite number of authors to publish information that appears to be factual regardless of whether or not they have completed accurate research, or contain any validity to their work.

Instructors should take advantage of early opportunities to discuss with their students the difference between sources and ways to establish the validity of published writing. Some of these include, identification of the author, potential motivations of the author, sources of primary information cited by the author, and any potential opinions, or bias contained within the source.

## SKILL 2.5d  Distinguishes between paraphrasing and plagiarizing

A challenge for many student can be learning how to appropriately use sources of information without committing plagiarism. Plagiarism is the act of passing off another authors work as your own, without giving them credit for their work.

A challenge for many student can be learning how to appropriately use sources of information without committing plagiarism. Plagiarism is the act of passing off another authors work as your own, without giving them credit for their work. When drawing from a source, students need clear direction on the difference between using a source in their writing, and passing off a source as if it where your own original thought.

Although this can be a challenging line for student to draw, instructors can use practice exercises and specific examples of each to best articulate the difference between citation and plagiarism. There are also a number of plagiarism-detection technology tools that may assist students in realizing where citations are necessary. Modeling the proper use of these tools will assist students in learning how and when to cite information that they are using in their written assignments.

## SKILL 2.5e  Knows how to locate credible print and digital sources, locate information within the sources, and cite the sources

The most credible sources can be found in published, peer reviewed academic journals. Academic journals are peer-reviewed to ensure the validity of the content, and certify the sources are reliable. Print sources are most reliable when located in the non-fiction section of the library, and when they can be identified as having come from a primary source. Credible sources are usually developed by non-profit organizations, college and universities, or academics who do not produce the work for the primary objective of earning a profit.

Appropriate citation of sources is an author's way of giving credit to the original author when using their work, or conclusion they draw within their writing. Citation can take many forms but is usually either completed in the Modern Language Association (MLA) or the American Psychological Association (APA) format.

Each style has subtle difference but each include an in text citation, citing the source at the time their work is presented in the authors writing, and on a works cited page at the end of the writing. The work cited page will usually include the author of the source, where the source can be found, the type of source, year it was published, and who published the information. By completing this type of citation, an author's work can be cross referenced to ensure validity, and further strengthen the argument of the writer.

# Language

## SKILL Knows the conventions of standard English grammar, usage, 2.6 mechanics, and spelling when writing, speaking, reading, and listening

Conventions for language that appear in print have developed over several centuries; they change somewhat from generation to generation but compared to the use of language in electronic media, they are fairly static. On the other hand, language use in radio and television has undergone rapid changes. Listening to a radio show from the thirties is a step back in time. The intonation had its own peculiar qualities. Even in its own time, it would not have been recognized as a conversation between two people.

Listening to President Franklin Delano Roosevelt's "fireside chats" also takes us back in time, not only because of the content of the speeches, but also in the way they were delivered. Declamation is a good term for the radio presentation style of that day, and, to some extent, even the style of public speeches. Declamation was notable for rhetorical effect or display. Television followed in the style of the radio shows. It was declamatory in nature and sounded more like an announcement than a conversation. Listening to early television news shows—broadcasters such as Edward R. Murrow, for example—reminds us instantly of an earlier time.

Radio and television speech nowadays is much more conversational in tone. In fact, on many of the news shows, two or more newspeople carry on a conversation before, after, and between the news stories. This would have seemed peculiar to earlier listeners.

Because so many aspects of language change while others stay the same, teachers must be familiar with the proper rules and conventions of punctuation, capitalization, and spelling in the modern oral and written language. Competency exams are designed to ensure this by testing the ability to apply advanced language skills.

To aid in meeting the expectations of the competency exams, a limited number of the more frustrating rules are presented here. Rules should be applied according to the American style of English (that is, spelling theater instead of theatre and placing terminal marks of punctuation almost exclusively within other marks of punctuation). The most common conventions are discussed below.

*Conventions for language that appear in print have developed over several centuries; they change somewhat from generation to generation but compared to the use of language in electronic media, they are fairly static.*

*Because so many aspects of language change while others stay the same, teachers must be familiar with the proper rules and conventions of punctuation, capitalization, and spelling in the modern oral and written language.*

## Syntax

SYNTAX refers to the rules or patterned relationships that correctly create phrases and sentences from words. When readers develop an understanding of syntax, they begin to understand the structure of how sentences are built, and eventually the beginning of grammar.

Example: *"I am going to the movies."*

*This statement is syntactically and grammatically correct.*

Example: *"They am going to the movies."*

*This statement is syntactically correct since all the words are in their correct place, but it is grammatically incorrect with the use of the word "They" rather than "I."*

## Spelling

Concentration in this section will be on spelling plurals and possessives. The multiplicity and complexity of spelling rules based on phonics, letter doubling, and exceptions to rules that are not mastered by adulthood should be replaced by a good dictionary. As spelling mastery is also difficult for adolescents, the recommendation is the same: Learning the use of a dictionary and thesaurus will be a more rewarding use of time.

Most plurals of nouns that end in hard consonant sounds followed by a silent *e* are made by adding *s*. Some words ending in vowels also only add an *s*.

*fingers, numerals, banks, bugs, riots, homes, gates, radios, bananas*

For nouns that end in the soft consonant sounds *s, j, x, z, ch*, and *sh*, add *es* to make them plural. Some nouns ending in *o* also add *es*.

*dresses, waxes, churches, brushes, tomatoes, potatoes*

Nouns ending in *y* preceded by a vowel are pluralized by just adding *s*.

*boys, alleys*

For nouns ending in *y* preceded by a consonant, change the *y* to *i* and add *es* to make them plural.

*babies, corollaries, frugalities, poppies*

Some noun plurals are formed irregularly or remain the same.

*sheep, deer, children, leaves, oxen*

Some nouns derived from foreign words, especially Latin, may make their plurals in two different ways. Sometimes, the meanings are the same; other times, the two plurals are used in slightly different contexts. It is always wise to consult the dictionary.

> appendices, appendixes          criterion, criteria
>
> indexes, indices                crisis, crises

Make the plurals of closed (solid) compound words in the usual way except for words ending in *ful*, which make their plurals on the root word.

> timelines, hairpins, cupsful

Make the plurals of open or hyphenated compounds by adding the change in inflection to the word that changes in number.

> fathers-in-law, courts-martial, masters of art, doctors of medicine

Make the plurals of letters, numbers, and abbreviations by adding *s*.

> fives and tens, IBMs, 1990s, ps and qs

## Sentence Completeness

Avoid fragments and run-on sentences. Recognizing sentence elements necessary to make a complete thought, properly using independent and dependent clauses, and using proper punctuation will correct such errors.

## Capitalization

Capitalize all proper names of persons (including specific organizations or agencies of government); places (countries, states, cities, parks, and specific geographical areas); things (political parties, structures, historical and cultural terms, and calendar and time designations); and religious terms (any deity, revered person or group, sacred writings).

> Percy Bysshe Shelley, Argentina, Mount Rainier National Park, Grand Canyon, League of Nations, Sears Tower, Birmingham, Lyric Theater, Americans, Midwesterners, Democrats, Renaissance, Boy Scouts of America, Easter, God, Bible, Dead Sea Scrolls, Koran

Capitalize proper adjectives and titles used with proper names.

> California gold rush, President John Adams, French fries, Homeric epic, Romanesque architecture, Senator John Glenn

**Note:** Some words that represent titles and offices are not capitalized unless used with a proper name.

| Capitalized | Not Capitalized |
| --- | --- |
| Congressman McKay | the congressman from Florida |
| Commander Alger | commander of the Pacific Fleet |
| Queen Elizabeth | the queen of England |

Capitalize all main words in titles of works of literature, art, and music.

*(See "Italics" in the "Punctuation" section)*

## Punctuation

In a quoted statement that is either declarative or imperative, place the period inside the closing quotation marks.

*"The airplane crashed on the runway during takeoff."*

If the quotation is followed by other words in the sentence, place a comma inside the closing quotations marks and a period at the end of the sentence.

*"The airplane crashed on the runway during takeoff," said the announcer.*

In most instances in which a quoted title or expression occurs at the end of a sentence, the period is placed before either the single or double quotation marks.

*"The middle school readers were unprepared to understand Bryant's poem 'Thanatopsis.'"*

*Early book-length adventure stories like Don Quixote and The Three Musketeers were known as "picaresque novels."*

There is an instance in which the final quotation mark would precede the period: If the content of the sentence were about a speech or quote, and the meaning would be obscured by the placement of the period.

*The first thing out of his mouth was "Hi, I'm home."*

but

*The first line of his speech began "I arrived home to an empty house".*

In sentences that are interrogatory or exclamatory, the question mark or exclamation point should be positioned outside the closing quotation marks if the quote itself is a statement or command or cited title.

Who decided to lead us in the recitation of the "Pledge of Allegiance"?

Why was Tillie shaking as she began her recitation, "Once upon a midnight dreary..."?

I was embarrassed when Mrs. White said, "Your slip is showing"!

In sentences that are declarative but the quotation is a question or an exclamation, place the question mark or exclamation point inside the quotation marks.

The hall monitor yelled, "Fire! Fire!"

"Fire! Fire!" yelled the hall monitor.

Cory shrieked, "Is there a mouse in the room?" (In this instance, the question supersedes the exclamation.)

## Commas

Separate two or more coordinate adjectives that modify the same word and three or more nouns, phrases, or clauses in a list.

It was a dank, dark day.

Maggie's hair was dull, dirty, and lice-ridden.

Dickens portrayed the Artful Dodger as a skillful pickpocket, loyal follower of Fagin, and defender of Oliver Twist.

Ellen daydreamed about getting out of the rain, taking a shower, and eating a hot dinner.

In Elizabethan England, Ben Johnson wrote comedy, Christopher Marlowe wrote tragedies, and William Shakespeare composed both.

Use commas to separate antithetical or complementary expressions from the rest of the sentence.

The veterinarian, not his assistant, would perform the delicate surgery.

The more he knew about her, the less he wished he had known.

Randy hopes to, and probably will, get an appointment to the Naval Academy.

His thorough, though esoteric, scientific research could not easily be understood by high school students.

## Semicolons

Use semicolons to separate independent clauses when the second clause is introduced by a transitional adverb. (These clauses may also be written as separate sentences, preferably by placing the adverb within the second sentence.)

> *The Elizabethans modified the rhyme scheme of the sonnet; thus, it was called the English sonnet.*
>
> **or**
>
> *The Elizabethans modified the rhyme scheme of the sonnet. Thus, it was called the English sonnet.*

Use semicolons to separate items in a series that are long and complex or have internal punctuation.

> *The Italian Renaissance produced masters in the fine arts: Dante Alighieri, author of the ; Leonardo da Vinci, painter of ; and Donatello, sculptor of the , the four saints.*
>
> *The leading scorers in the WNBA were Zheng Haixia, averaging 23.9 points per game; Lisa Leslie, 22; and Cynthia Cooper, 19.5.*

## Colons

Place a colon at the beginning of a list of items. (Note its use in the sentence about Renaissance Italians in the previous section.)

> *The teacher directed us to compare Faulkner's three symbolic novels:* **Absalom, Absalom**; **As I Lay Dying**; *and* **Light in August**.

Do not use a colon if the list is preceded by a verb.

> *Three of Faulkner's symbolic novels are* **Absalom, Absalom**; **As I Lay Dying**; *and* **Light in August**.

## Subject-Verb Agreement

A verb should always agree in number with its subject. Making them agree relies on the ability to properly identify the subject.

> *One of the boys was playing too rough.*
>
> *No one in the class, not the teacher nor the students, was listening to the message from the intercom.*
>
> *The candidates, including a grandmother and a teenager, are debating some controversial issues.*

If two singular subjects are connected by *and*, the verb must be plural.

> *A man **and** his dog <u>were jogging</u> on the beach.*

If two singular subjects are connected by *or* or *nor*, a singular verb is required.

> *Neither Dot **nor** Joyce <u>has missed</u> a day of school this year.*
> *Either Fran **or** Paul <u>is</u> missing.*

If one singular subject and one plural subject are connected by *or* or *nor*, the verb agrees with the subject nearest to the verb.

> *Neither the coach **nor** the players were able to sleep on the bus.*

If the subject is a collective noun, its sense of number in the sentence determines the verb: singular if the noun represents a group or unit, and plural if the noun represents individuals.

> <u>*The House of Representatives has adjourned*</u> *for the holidays.*
> <u>*The House of Representatives have failed to reach agreement*</u> *on the subject of adjournment.*

## Verbs (Tense)

Present tense is used to express that which is currently happening or is always true.

> *Randy is playing the piano.*
> *Randy plays the piano like a pro.*

Past tense is used to express action that occurred in a past time.

> *Randy learned to play the piano when he was six years old.*

Future tense is used to express action or a condition of future time.

> *Randy will probably earn a music scholarship.*

Present perfect tense is used to express action or a condition that started in the past and is continued to or completed in the present.

> *Randy has practiced piano every day for the last ten years.*
> *Randy has never been bored with practice.*

Past perfect tense expresses action or a condition that occurred as a precedent to some other action or condition.

> *Randy had considered playing clarinet before he discovered the piano.*

Future perfect tense expresses action that started in the past or the present and will conclude at some time in the future.

> *By the time he goes to college, Randy will have been an accomplished pianist for more than half of his life.*

## Verbs (Mood)

Indicative mood is used to make unconditional statements; subjunctive mood is used for conditional clauses or wish statements that pose untrue conditions. Verbs in subjunctive mood are plural with both singular and plural subjects.

> *If I were a bird, I would fly.*
>
> *I wish I were as rich as Donald Trump.*

## Conjugation of verbs

The conjugation of verbs follows the patterns used in the discussion of tense above. However, the most frequent problems in verb use stem from the improper formation of past and past participial forms.

> **Regular verb:** *believe, believed, (have) believed*
>
> **Irregular verbs:** *run, ran, run; sit, sat, sat; teach, taught, taught*

Other problems stem from the use of verbs that are the same in some tenses but have different forms and different meanings in other tenses.

> *I lie on the ground. I lay on the ground yesterday. I have lain down.*
>
> *I lay the blanket on the bed. I laid the blanket there yesterday. I have laid the blanket every night.*
>
> *The sun rises. The sun rose. The sun has risen. He raises the flag. He raised the flag. He had raised the flag.*
>
> *I sit on the porch. I sat on the porch. I have sat in the porch swing.*
>
> *I set the plate on the table. I set the plate there yesterday. I had set the table before dinner.*

Two other common verb problems stem from misusing the preposition *of* for the verb auxiliary *have* and misusing the verb ought (now rare).

> *Incorrect:*     *I should of gone to bed.*
>
> *Correct:*       *I should have gone to bed.*
>
> *Incorrect:*     *He hadn't ought to get so angry.*
>
> *Correct:*       *He ought not to get so angry.*

## Pronouns

A pronoun used as a subject of predicate nominative is in nominative case.

> She was the drum majorette. The lead trombonists were Joe and he. The band director accepted whoever could march in step.

A pronoun used as a direct object, indirect object, or object of a preposition is in objective case.

> The teacher praised him. She gave him an A on the test. Her praise of him was appreciated. The students whom she did not praise will work harder next time.

Some common pronoun errors occur from the misuse of reflexive pronouns:

| | |
|---|---|
| Singular: | myself, yourself, herself, himself, itself |
| Plural: | ourselves, yourselves, themselves |
| Incorrect: | Jack cut hisself shaving. |
| Correct: | Jack cut himself shaving. |
| Incorrect: | They backed theirselves into a corner. |
| Correct: | They backed themselves into a corner. |

## Adjectives

An adjective should agree with its antecedent in number.

> Those apples are rotten. This one is ripe. These peaches are hard.

Comparative adjectives end in *-er* and superlatives in *-est*, with some exceptions like *worse* and *worst*. Some adjectives that cannot easily make comparative inflections are preceded by *more* and *most*.

> Mrs. Carmichael is the better of the two basketball coaches.
>
> That is the hastiest excuse you have ever contrived.

Avoid double comparisons.

| | |
|---|---|
| Incorrect: | This is the worstest headache I ever had. |
| Correct: | This is the worst headache I ever had. |

When comparing one thing to others in a group, exclude the thing under comparison from the rest of the group.

> Incorrect: *Joey is larger than any baby I have ever seen. (Since you have seen him, he cannot be larger than himself.)*
>
> Correct: *Joey is larger than <u>any other</u> baby I have ever seen.*

Include all the words necessary to make a comparison clear in meaning.

> *I am as tall as my mother. I am as tall as she (is).*
>
> *My cats are better behaved than those of my neighbor.*

---

**SKILL Explains the function of different parts of speech
2.6a**

*See Skill 2.6*

---

**SKILL Corrects errors in usage, mechanics, and spelling
2.6b**

*See Skill 2.6*

---

**SKILL Identifies examples of different sentence types** *(e.g., simple, compound,
2.6c compound-complex)*

## Types of Sentences

Sentences are made up of two parts: the subject and the predicate. The **subject** is the "do-er" of an action or the element that is being joined. Any adjectives describing this do-er or element are also part of the subject. The **predicate** is made up of the verb and any other adverbs, adjectives, pronouns, or clauses that describe the action of the sentence.

A **simple sentence** contains one independent clause (which contains one subject and one predicate).

In the following examples, the subject is underlined once and the predicate is underlined twice.

> *The dancer bowed.*
>
> *Nathan skied down the hill.*

A **compound sentence** is made up of two independent clauses that are joined by a conjunction, a correlative conjunction (e.g., *either-or, neither-nor*), or a semicolon. Both of these independent clauses are able to stand on their own, but for sentence variety, authors will often combine two independent clauses.

In the following examples, the subjects of each independent clause are underlined once, and the predicates of each independent clause are underlined twice. The conjunction is in bold.

> *Samantha ate the cookie,* **and** *she drank her milk.*
>
> *Mark is excellent with computers; he has worked with them for years.*
>
> **Either** *Terry runs the project* **or** *I will not participate.*

A **complex sentence** is made up of one independent clause and at least one dependent clause. In the following examples, the subjects of each clause are underlined once, and the predicates are underlined twice. The independent clause is in plain text, and the dependent clause is in italics.

> *When Jody saw how clean the house was,* she was *happy.*
>
> Brian loves *taking diving lessons, which he has done for years.*

## SKILL 2.6d Identifies how varieties of English *(e.g., dialects, registers)* used in stories, dramas, or poems support the overall meaning

In the analysis process for a text, readers should be aware of the particular setting that is being portrayed. Both geographical regions and the physical setting, whether formal or informal, can play a large role in the semantics of the content.

**Dialect** includes vocabulary that is specific to a region. This can vary extensively even within the same language. For example, language in the Northeastern region of the United States may say "soda," while natives to the South could call it "pop." Although both regions speak English, there are a number of words that vary between the two. This can be applied on a global level. While reading, getting to know the background of the author, or the setting that the author is attempting to portray, will assist in identifying and decoding various dialects.

> Register is a variation in language depending on the formality and intention for a conversation.

**Register** is a variation in language depending on the formality and intention for a conversation. This van be widely applied, from a comparison in how you would deliver information to your best friend compared to someone highly respected, to the "baby talk" that you may convey while speaking with a pet or a young child. Although the meaning will not change greatly, the discourse and delivery of the information will vary. While reading, there are a number of details to keep in mind to assist in deconstructing the register: relationships that characters have, the formality of the setting, the time period, the age of the characters, and the intention for the conversation.

---

**SKILL 2.7**    **Understands how to determine the meaning of words and phrases**

---

*See also Skill 1.4*

## Decoding, Word Recognition, and Spelling

> **WORD ANALYSIS:** the process readers use to figure out unfamiliar words based on written patterns

> **WORD RECOGNITION:** the process of automatically determining the pronunciation and some degree of the meaning of an unknown word

> **DECODING:** changing communication signals into messages

> **ENCODING:** changing a message into symbols

**WORD ANALYSIS** (also called phonics or decoding) is the process readers use to figure out unfamiliar words based on written patterns. **WORD RECOGNITION** is the process of automatically determining the pronunciation and some degree of the meaning of an unknown word. In other words, fluent readers recognize most written words easily and correctly, without consciously decoding or breaking them down.

**DECODING** involves changing communication signals into messages. Reading comprehension requires that the reader learn the code in which a message is written and be able to decode it to get the message. **ENCODING** involves changing a message into symbols. Examples include encoding oral language into writing (spelling), encoding an idea into words, or encoding a mathematical or physical idea into appropriate mathematical symbols.

Although effective reading comprehension requires identifying words automatically, children do not have to be able to identify every single word or know the exact meaning of every word in a text to understand it. In fact, children can read a work with a high level of comprehension even if they do not fully know as many as 15 percent of the words in that text. Children develop the ability to decode and recognize words automatically. They can then extend their ability to decode to multisyllabic words.

**SKILL 2.7a   Determines the literal meaning of unknown words and phrases from context, syntax, and/or knowledge of roots and affixes**

Knowledge of how words are built can help students with basic and more advanced decoding. A root word is the primary base of a word. A prefix is the affix (a morpheme that attaches to a base word) that is placed at the start of a root word, but can't make a word on its own. Examples of prefixes include *re-*, *pre-*, and *un-*. A suffix follows the root word to which it attaches and appears at the end of the word. Examples of suffixes include *-s*, *-es*, *-ed*, *-ly*, and *-tion*. In the word *unlikely*, *un* is a prefix, *like* is the root word, and *ly* is a suffix.

*See also Skills 1.2d and 2.6*

**SKILL 2.7b   Identifies types of figurative language**

Figurative language is often called by a more familiar term: figures of speech. Poets and writers use figures of speech to sharpen the effect and meaning of their work and to help readers see things in ways they have never seen them before. Marianne Moore observed that a fir tree has "an emerald turkey-foot at the top." Her poem makes us aware of something we probably had never noticed before. The sudden recognition of the likeness yields pleasure in the reading.

Figurative language allows for the statement of truths that more literal language cannot convey. Skillfully used, a figure of speech will help the reader to see more clearly and to focus upon particulars. Figures of speech add many dimensions of richness to the reading and understanding of a poem; they also provide many opportunities for analysis. The approach to analyzing a poem on the basis of its figures of speech is to ask pertinent questions:

- What do they do for the poem?
- Do they underscore meaning?
- Do they intensify understanding?
- Do they increase the intensity of our response?

## Types of Figurative Language

Most of us are aware of a number of types of figures of speech; in fact, if all of them were listed, it would be a very long list! For the purpose of analyzing poetry or literature, the following list is fairly comprehensive.

**Simile:** A direct comparison of two things, often using the term like or as to foster the comparison. A common example is, "My love is like a red, red rose."

**Metaphor:** An indirect comparison of two things. Metaphor is the use of a word or phrase denoting one kind of object or action in place of another. Poets use metaphors extensively, but they are also essential to understanding everyday speech. For example, chairs are said to have "legs" and "arms," even though they are typically unique to humans and other animals.

**Parallelism:** The arrangement of ideas into phrases, sentences, and paragraphs that balance one element with another of equal importance and similar wording. An example from Francis Bacon's *Of Studies* is, "Reading maketh a full man, conference a ready man, and writing an exact man."

**Personification:** The attribution of human characteristics to an inanimate object, an abstract quality, or an animal. For example, John Bunyan wrote characters named Death, Knowledge, Giant Despair, Sloth, and Piety in *Pilgrim's Progress*. The metaphor of the "arm" of a chair is also a form of personification.

**Euphemism:** The substitution of an agreeable or inoffensive term for one that might offend or suggest something unpleasant. Many euphemisms are used to refer to death, including "passed away," "crossed over," or even simply "passed."

**Hyperbole:** A deliberate exaggeration for effect. This passage from Shakespeare's *The Merchant of Venice* is an example:

> Why, if two gods should play some heavenly match
> And on the wager lay two earthly women,
> And Portia one, there must be something else
> Pawned with the other, for the poor rude world
> Hath not her fellow.

**Climax:** A number of phrases or sentences arranged in ascending order of rhetorical forcefulness. This passage from Melville's *Moby Dick* is an example:

> All that most maddens and torments; all that stirs up the lees of things; all truth with malice in it; all that cracks the sinews and cakes the brain; all the subtle demonisms of life and thought; all evil, to crazy Ahab, were visibly personified and made practically assailable in Moby Dick.

**Bathos:** A ludicrous attempt to portray pathos—that is, to evoke pity, sympathy, or sorrow. It may result from inappropriately dignifying the commonplace, using elevated language to describe something trivial, or greatly exaggerating pathos.

**Oxymoron:** A contradiction in terms deliberately employed for effect. It is usually seen in a qualifying adjective whose meaning is contrary to that of the noun it modifies, such as "wise folly." For example, a fairly common oxymoron is "jumbo shrimp."

Irony: The expression of something other than, and particularly the opposite of, the literal meaning, such as words of praise when blame is intended. In poetry, irony is often used as a sophisticated or resigned awareness of contrast between what is and what ought to be; it expresses a controlled pathos without sentimentality. It is a form of indirectness that avoids overt praise or censure. An early example is the Greek comic character Eiron, a clever underdog who, by his wit, repeatedly triumphs over the boastful character Alazon.

Alliteration: The repetition of consonant sounds in two or more neighboring words or syllables. In its simplest form, alliteration reinforces one or two consonant sounds. For example, notice the repetition in Shakespeare's Sonnet 12:

> When I do count the clock that tells the time.

Some poets have used more complex patterns of alliteration by creating similar consonant sounds both at the beginning of words and at the beginning of stressed syllables within words. For example, hear the sounds in Shelley's "Stanzas Written in Dejection Near Naples":

> The City's voice itself is soft like Solitude's

Onomatopoeia: The naming of a thing or action by a vocal imitation of the sound associated with it, such as *buzz* or *hiss*. It is marked by the use of words whose sound suggests the sense. One good example is from "The Brook" by Tennyson:

> I chatter over stony ways,
> In little sharps and trebles,
> I bubble into eddying bays,
> I babble on the pebbles.

Malapropism: A verbal blunder in which one word is replaced by another that is similar in sound but different in meaning. The term itself comes from Sheridan's Mrs. Malaprop in *The Rivals* (1775). Thinking of the geography of contiguous countries, she spoke of the "geometry" of "contagious countries."

## SKILL 2.7c Interprets figurative language

*See Skill 2.7b*

SKILL
2.7d **Analyzes the relationship between word choice and tone in a text**

## Style

> **STYLE:** is the artful adaptation of language to meet various purposes

**STYLE** is the artful adaptation of language to meet various purposes. Authors can modify their word choice, sentence structure, and organization in order to convey certain ideas. For example, an author may write on a topic (such as the environment) in many different styles. In an academic style, the author uses long, complex sentences, advanced vocabulary, and structured paragraphing. However, in an informal explanation in a popular magazine, the author may use a conversational tone with simple words and simple sentence structures.

## Tone

> **TONE:** the attitude an author takes toward his or her subject

**TONE** is the attitude an author takes toward his or her subject. That tone is exemplified in the language of the text. For example, consider the topic of the environment. One author may dismiss the idea of global warming; the tone may be one of derision against environmentalists. A reader might notice this through the style (such as word choice), the details the author decides to present, and the order in which the details are presented. Another author may be angry about global warming and therefore use harsh words and other tones that indicate anger. Finally, yet another author may not care about the issue of the environment one way or the other. Let's say this author is a comedian who likes to poke fun at political activists. His or her tone may be humorous; therefore, he or she will adjust the language used accordingly. In this example, all types of tones are about the same subject—they simply reveal, through language, different opinions and attitudes about the subject.

Finally, yet another author may not care about the issue of the environment one way or the other. Let's say this author is a comedian who likes to poke fun at political activists. His or her tone may be humorous; therefore, he or she will adjust the language used accordingly. In this example, all types of tones are about the same subject—they simply reveal, through language, different opinions and attitudes about the subject.

## SKILL 2.8 Understands the characteristics of conversational, academic, and domain-specific language

Conversational language is often used as the foundation for language development. Development begins as early as infanthood and is reinforced through hearing common words on a frequent basis. Sight words support this development.

High-frequency words are the words most often used in the English language. Depending on the word list used, there are from one hundred to three hundred high-frequency words. It has been estimated that one hundred words make up 50 percent of all words used in reading. Some lists, such as the Dolch and Fry lists, use the most frequently encountered words in early childhood reading texts.

**SIGHT WORDS** are words that the reader learns to read spontaneously, either because of frequency or lack of conformity to orthographic rules; for example, words like the, what, and there, because they don't conform to rules, and words like boy, girl, and book, because they appear frequently in reading texts.

The National Reading Panel has released the following conclusions about vocabulary instruction:

- There is a need for direct instruction of vocabulary items required for a specific text.

- Repeated exposure to vocabulary items is important. Students should be given items that will be likely to appear in many contexts.

- Learning in rich contexts is valuable for vocabulary learning. Vocabulary words should be those that the learner will find useful in many contexts. When vocabulary items are derived from content learning materials, the learner will be better equipped to deal with specific reading matter in content areas.

- There are many methods for directly and explicitly teaching words. The panel identified twenty-one methods that have been found effective in research projects. Many emphasize the underlying concept of a word and its connections to other words using graphics such as semantic mapping and diagrams.

- The keyword method uses words and illustrations that highlight salient features of meaning. The visualization or drawing of a picture either by the student or the teacher was found to be effective. Many words cannot be learned in this way, so effective classrooms provide multiple ways for students to learn and interact with words. The panel also found that computer-assisted activities can have a positive role in the development of vocabulary.

Academic language is acquired starting around age 7, where curricula is used deliberately to shape and develop vocabulary development. Domain-specific vocabulary is often tied to the sciences, where meaning is tied to context. *See Skill 2.8a* for examples of low frequency words, which are commonly domain-specific.

*See also Skill 1.2c*

---

### SKILL 2.8a — Differentiates among the three tiers of vocabulary

The three tiers of vocabulary include basic, high frequency, and low frequency words.

**Tier 4:** **Basic**—common words, often learned through conversation.

*Examples: dog, cat, house, girl, boy, mom, dad*

**Tier 5:** **High Frequency**—academic vocabulary, learned through curricula. These can have multiple meanings.

*Examples: salmon, swimming, push, pull*

**Tier 6:** **Low Frequency**—specialized words, often domain-specific, learned through curricula. Comprehension is often dependent on context.

*Examples: biometric, pharmaceutical, photosynthesis, oceanic*

---

### SKILL 2.8b — Identifies relevant features of language such as word choice, order, and punctuation

*See Skill 2.6*

# Speaking and listening

| SKILL 2.9 | Knows the characteristics of effective collaboration to promote comprehension |
|---|---|

Sharing information in a collaborative environment enhances and reinforces knowledge. Students often find that peer-to-peer interactions clarify their questions quickly and effectively, while offering a different perspective. Because students have the ability to communicate with classmates that have extremely diverse sets of skills and academic backgrounds, the learning experience is enriched through these interactions.

Aside from learning from peers, contributing to collaboration also serves as a boost of confidence. When peers agree with a perspective, they reaffirm what the student was thinking and could open their eyes to the benefits of sharing. Disagreeing is also a huge learning opportunity, ultimately teaching students to debate and support their points with evidence. Students must use active listening skills *(See Skill 2.9b)* to interpret what their instructors and peers are conveying in order to form their own opinion.

| SKILL 2.9a | Identitifies techniques to communicate for a variety of purposes with diverse partners |
|---|---|

Communicating with peers could be an interaction as simple as turning around and asking, "Hey, what did you think about the open ended question on page two?" Time to discuss in partners or small groups can also be established deliberately by an instructor. This is useful when brainstorming on a topic and debriefing on a whole-class discussion or in-class activity.

Group conversations can create extremely positive outcomes, whether set up at random or deliberately. Students can be matched up by skill or interest level, or the instructor could use strategies to randomize the selections. When group conversations happen often, its critical to keep the selections varied so that students are able to learn from the diversity in the class. Also, by following these strategies, students do not expect to be able to pick their partner or group, which often leads to diverse conversations.

Strategies for randomly assigning groups:

- Letters: Everyone whose name begins with "J," stand on this side. After a few groups are formed, select groups of 3–5.

- Birth month: Everyone born in the month of January go to that side of the room. After a few groups are formed, select groups of 3–5.

- Line up alphabetically, group by 4–5

- Count around the room using 1–5.

- Partner up with someone that you've never worked with before.

You can also promote conversations by assigning a simple worksheet or exit slip that asks students to identify the points that their partner(s) have made. For example:

1. When my partner said _____, I agreed with their perspective.

2. When my partner said _____, I had a different point of view. I thought _____.

> SKILL 2.9b  **Identifies the characteristics of active listening**

Listening is a very specific skill for very specific circumstances. There are two aspects of listening that warrant attention: comprehension and purpose. **Comprehension** is simply understanding what someone says, the purpose behind the message, and the context in which it is said. **Purpose** comes in to play when considering that while someone may completely understand a message, they must also know what to do with it. Are they expected to just nod and smile? Go out and take action?

While listening comprehension is a significant skill in itself—one that deserves a lot of focus in the classroom (in the same way that reading comprehension does), we will focus on purpose here. Often, when we understand the purpose of listening in various contexts, comprehension is much easier. Furthermore, when we know the purpose of listening, we can better adjust our comprehension strategies.

*When we are more "active" in our listening, we have greater success in interpreting speech.*

## The Purpose of Listening

When complex or new information is provided to us orally, we must analyze and interpret that information. What is the author's most important point? How do the figures of speech affect meaning? How can we arrive at conclusions? Often, making sense of this information can be difficult for oral presentations—first, because we have no way to go back and review material already stated; second, because oral language is so much less predictable than written language. However, when we focus on extracting the meaning, message, and speaker's purpose, rather than just "listening" and waiting for things to make sense for us—in other words, when we are more "active" in our listening—we have greater success in interpreting speech.

## Listening to literature read aloud

Listening is often done for the purpose of enjoyment. We like to listen to stories, we enjoy poetry, and we like radio dramas and theater. Listening to literature can also be a great pleasure. The problem today is that students have not learned how to extract great pleasure from simply listening. Perhaps that is because we have not done a good enough job of showing students how listening to literature, for example, can be more interesting than television or video games.

In the classrooms of exceptional teachers, we often find that students are captivated by the reading aloud of good literature. It is refreshing and enjoyable to just sit and soak in the language, story, and poetry of literature being read aloud. Therefore, we must teach students *how* to listen and enjoy such work. We do this by making it fun and providing many possibilities and alternatives to capture the wide array of interests in each classroom.

> In the classrooms of exceptional teachers, we often find that students are captivated by the reading aloud of good literature.

## Listening in conversations and discussions

Let us consider listening in large and small group conversations. The difference here is that conversation requires more than just listening: It involves feedback and active involvement. This can be particularly challenging, as in our culture, we are trained to move conversations along, to discourage silence in a conversation, and to always get the last word in. This poses significant problems for the art of listening.

> The difference here is that conversation requires more than just listening: It involves feedback and active involvement.

In a discussion, for example, when we are preparing our next response—rather than listening to what others are saying—we do a large disservice to the entire discussion. Students need to learn how listening carefully to others in discussions actually promotes better responses on the part of subsequent speakers. One way teachers can encourage this in both large and small group discussions is to expect students to respond directly to the previous student's comments before moving ahead with their new comments. This will encourage them to frame their new comments in light of the comments that came just before them.

## Making Sense of Oral Language

Oral speech can also be much less structured than written language. Yet, aside from rereading, many of the skills and strategies that help us in reading comprehension can help us in listening comprehension. For example, as soon as we start listening to something new, we should tap into our prior knowledge in order to attach new information to what we already know. This will not only help us to understand the new information more quickly, but it will also assist us in remembering the material.

## Transitions between ideas

We can also look for transitions between ideas. Sometimes this is simple, such as when voice tone or body language changes; as listeners, we have access to the animation that comes along with live speech. Human beings have to try very hard to be completely nonexpressive in their speech. Listeners should pay attention to how the speaker changes character and voice in order to signal a transition of ideas.

## Nonverbal cues

Listeners can also better comprehend the underlying intent of the author when they notice nonverbal cues. In oral speech, unlike written text, elements like irony are not indicated by the actual words, but rather by the speaker's tone and nonverbal cues. Simply looking to see the expression on the face of a speaker can often do more to communicate irony than trying to extract irony from actual words.

## Note taking

One good way to follow oral speech is to take notes and outline major points. Because oral speech can be more circular than written text, it can be helpful to keep track of an author's message. Students can learn this strategy in many ways in the classroom: They can take notes during the teacher's presentations as well as other students' presentations and speeches.

Other classroom methods can also be used to help students learn good listening skills. For example, teachers can have students practice following complex directions. They can also have students orally retell stories—or retell (in writing or in oral speech) oral presentations of stories or other materials. These activities give students direct practice in the very important skills of listening. They provide students with outlets in which they can slowly improve their abilities to comprehend oral language and take decisive action based on oral speech.

## Analyzing the speech of others

Analyzing the speech of others is an excellent technique for helping students improve their own public speaking abilities. In most circumstances, students cannot view themselves as they give speeches and presentations; however, when they get the opportunity to critique, question, and analyze others' speeches, they begin to learn what works and what doesn't work in effective public speaking.

However, an important word of warning: *Do not* have students critique each others' public speaking skills. It could be very damaging to a student to have his or her peers point out what did not work in a speech. Instead, video is a great tool teachers can use. Any appropriate source of public speaking can be used in the classroom for students to analyze and critique.

*Analyzing the speech of others is an excellent technique for helping students improve their own public speaking abilities.*

| SKILL 2.10 | Knows the characteristics of engaging oral presentations |
|---|---|

Starting with a proper introduction and appropriate clothing to match the environment in which the presentation is being given, there are a variety of factors that should be taught to students to set them up for giving a successful, engaging oral presentation. Students should learn to understand who their audience is before preparing for the presentation so they are aware of the background knowledge they may have on the topic. They should also keep in mind the length of time they will be able to present and the number of people that will be watching while preparing their speech.

Eye contact, asking questions, and accompanying oral presentations with visuals are all excellent strategies for engaging an audience. These can all be included on flashcards while practicing for the presentation. Students should also pay attention to their nonverbal skills *(See Skill 2.9b)* while practicing in order to ensure they use an appropriate amount of hand gestures. Although it seems uncomfortable at the time, students will gain a great deal of knowledge from filming themselves and watching their presentation. While peer to peer feedback may be inappropriate, self-reflection and an individual conference with an instructor could give students specific areas to focus on improving for their next presentation.

*Eye contact, asking questions, and accompanying oral presentations with visuals are all excellent strategies for engaging an audience.*

SKILL
2.10a **Identifies elements of engaging oral presentations** *(e.g., volume, articulation, awareness of audience)*

There are many ways to connect with the audience by bringing them into the conversation. As mentioned in 2.9, watching a recording of a presentation will point to many areas of improvement. Students may realize that the volume of their voice was much too low to hear, they may overuse hand gestures, they could sway back and forth, and they could focus solely on their flashcards instead of making eye contact with audience.

> *Volume level is essential while giving an oral presentation, as students are not typically given microphones or any aids in amplifying their voice.*

Volume level is essential while giving an oral presentation, as students are not typically given microphones or any aids in amplifying their voice. Articulation is critical for the audience to have the ability to comprehend the meaning behind the presentation. Students may stutter or repeat words while giving a speech, and it's important to teach them to keep their confidence high and to move on quickly if a mistake is made.

By researching the audience beforehand, or even by asking a few simple questions at the start of the presentation, a student can capture their awareness on the topic they'll be covering in their presentation. To keep the audience engaged, students should be taught to ask meaningful questions and reflect critically on the subjects discussed.

# DOMAIN II
# MATHEMATICS (5003)

# PERSONALIZED STUDY PLAN

| PAGE | COMPETENCY AND SKILL | KNOWN MATERIAL/ SKIP IT | BRIEFLY REVIEW eSTICKYNOTES | MAKE eFLASHCARDS | TAKE ADDITIONAL SAMPLE TESTS |
|------|---------------------|:---:|:---:|:---:|:---:|
| 85 | **003: Numbers and operations** | ☐ | ☐ | ☐ | ☐ |
| | **Understands place value system** | ☐ | ☐ | ☐ | ☐ |
| | 3.1: Writes numbers using base-10 numerals, number names, and expanded form | ☐ | ☐ | ☐ | ☐ |
| | 3.2: Composes and decomposes multi-digit numbers | ☐ | ☐ | ☐ | ☐ |
| | 3.3: Given a digit, identifies the place the digit is in and its value in that place | ☐ | ☐ | ☐ | ☐ |
| | 3.4: Recognizes that a digit in one place represents ten times what it represents in the place to its right and one-tenth what it represents in the place to its left, and extends this recognition to several places to the right or left | ☐ | ☐ | ☐ | ☐ |
| | 3.5: Uses whole number exponents to denote powers of 10 | ☐ | ☐ | ☐ | ☐ |
| | 3.6: Rounds multi-digit numbers to any place value | ☐ | ☐ | ☐ | ☐ |
| | **Understands operations and properties of rational numbers** | ☐ | ☐ | ☐ | ☐ |
| | 3.7: Solves multistep mathematical and real-world problems using addition, subtraction, multiplication, and division of rational numbers | ☐ | ☐ | ☐ | ☐ |
| | 3.7a: Identifies different problem situations for the operations *(e.g., adding to, taking from, putting together, taking apart, and comparing for subtraction)* | ☐ | ☐ | ☐ | ☐ |
| | 3.7b: Uses the relationship between addition and subtraction and the relationship between multiplication and division to solve problems *(e.g., inverse operations)* | ☐ | ☐ | ☐ | ☐ |
| | 3.7c: Interprets remainders in division problems | ☐ | ☐ | ☐ | ☐ |
| | 3.8: Understands various strategies and algorithms used to perform operations on rational numbers | ☐ | ☐ | ☐ | ☐ |
| | 3.9: Recognizes concepts of rational numbers and their operations | ☐ | ☐ | ☐ | ☐ |
| | 3.9a: Identifies examples where multiplication does not result in a product greater than both factors and division does not result in a quotient smaller than the dividend | ☐ | ☐ | ☐ | ☐ |
| | 3.9b: Composes and decomposes fractions, including the use of unit fractions | ☐ | ☐ | ☐ | ☐ |
| | 3.9c: Recognizes that the value of a unit fraction decreases as the value of the denominator increases | ☐ | ☐ | ☐ | ☐ |
| | 3.9d: Recognizes that the same whole must be used when comparing fractions | ☐ | ☐ | ☐ | ☐ |
| | 3.10: Solves problems using the order of operations, including problems involving whole number exponents | ☐ | ☐ | ☐ | ☐ |
| | 3.11: Identifies properties of operations *(e.g., commutative, associative, distributive)* and uses them to solve problems | ☐ | ☐ | ☐ | ☐ |
| | 3.12: Represents rational numbers and their operations in different ways | ☐ | ☐ | ☐ | ☐ |
| | 3.12a: Uses, interprets, and explains concrete models or drawings of the addition, subtraction, multiplication, and division of rational numbers | ☐ | ☐ | ☐ | ☐ |
| | 3.12b: Represents rational numbers and sums and differences of rational numbers on a number line | ☐ | ☐ | ☐ | ☐ |

# PERSONALIZED STUDY PLAN

| PAGE | COMPETENCY AND SKILL | KNOWN MATERIAL/ SKIP IT | BRIEFLY REVIEW eSTICKYNOTES | MAKE eFLASHCARDS | TAKE ADDITIONAL SAMPLE TESTS |
|------|----------------------|:---:|:---:|:---:|:---:|
| | 3.12c: Illustrates and explains multiplication and division problems using equations, rectangular arrays, and area models | ☐ | ☐ | ☐ | ☐ |
| | 3.13: Compares, classifies, and orders rational numbers | ☐ | ☐ | ☐ | ☐ |
| | 3.14: Converts between fractions, decimals, and percents | ☐ | ☐ | ☐ | ☐ |
| | **Understands proportional relationships and percents** | ☐ | ☐ | ☐ | ☐ |
| | 3.15: Applies the concepts of ratios and unit rates to describe relationships between two quantities | ☐ | ☐ | ☐ | ☐ |
| | 3.16: Understands percent as a rate per 100 | ☐ | ☐ | ☐ | ☐ |
| | 3.17: Solves unit rate problems | ☐ | ☐ | ☐ | ☐ |
| | 3.18: Uses proportional relationships to solve ratio and percent problems | ☐ | ☐ | ☐ | ☐ |
| | **Knows how to use basic concepts of number theory** | ☐ | ☐ | ☐ | ☐ |
| | 3.19: Identifies and uses prime and composite numbers | ☐ | ☐ | ☐ | ☐ |
| | 3.20: Finds factors and multiples of numbers | ☐ | ☐ | ☐ | ☐ |
| | **Knows a variety of strategies to determine the reasonableness of results** | ☐ | ☐ | ☐ | ☐ |
| | 3.21: Recognizes the reasonableness of results within the concept of a given problem | ☐ | ☐ | ☐ | ☐ |
| | 3.22: Uses mental math, estimation, and rounding strategies to solve problems and determine reasonableness of results | ☐ | ☐ | ☐ | ☐ |
| 115 | **004: Algebraic thinking** | ☐ | ☐ | ☐ | ☐ |
| | **Knows how to evaluate and manipulate algebraic expressions, equations, and formulas** | ☐ | ☐ | ☐ | ☐ |
| | 4.1: Differentiates between algebraic expressions and equations | ☐ | ☐ | ☐ | ☐ |
| | 4.2: Adds and subtracts linear algebraic expressions | ☐ | ☐ | ☐ | ☐ |
| | 4.3: Uses the distributive property to generate equivalent linear algebraic expressions | ☐ | ☐ | ☐ | ☐ |
| | 4.4: Evaluates simple algebraic expressions (i.e., one variable, binomial) for given values of variables | ☐ | ☐ | ☐ | ☐ |
| | 4.5: Uses mathematical terms to identify parts of expressions and describe expressions | ☐ | ☐ | ☐ | ☐ |
| | 4.6: Translates between verbal statements and algebraic expressions or equations | ☐ | ☐ | ☐ | ☐ |
| | 4.7: Uses formulas to determine unknown quantities | ☐ | ☐ | ☐ | ☐ |
| | 4.8: Differentiates between dependent and independent variables in formulas | ☐ | ☐ | ☐ | ☐ |
| | **Understands the meanings of solutions to linear equations and inequalities** | ☐ | ☐ | ☐ | ☐ |
| | 4.9: Solves multistep one-variable linear equations and inequalities | ☐ | ☐ | ☐ | ☐ |
| | 4.10: Interprets the solutions of multistep one-variable linear equations and inequalities (e.g., graphs the solution on a number line, states constraints on a situation) | ☐ | ☐ | ☐ | ☐ |

# PERSONALIZED STUDY PLAN

| PAGE | COMPETENCY AND SKILL | KNOWN MATERIAL/ SKIP IT | BRIEFLY REVIEW eSTICKYNOTES | MAKE eFLASHCARDS | TAKE ADDITIONAL SAMPLE TESTS |
|------|----------------------|:---:|:---:|:---:|:---:|
| | 4.11: Uses linear relationships represented by equations, tables and graphs to solve problems | ☐ | ☐ | ☐ | ☐ |
| | **Knows how to recognize and represent patterns** *(e.g., number, shape)* | ☐ | ☐ | ☐ | ☐ |
| | 4.12: Identifies, extends, describes, or generates number and shape patterns | ☐ | ☐ | ☐ | ☐ |
| | 4.13: Makes conjectures, predictions, or generalizations based on patterns | ☐ | ☐ | ☐ | ☐ |
| | 4.14: Identifies relationships between the corresponding terms of two numerical patterns *(e.g., find a rule for a function table)* | ☐ | ☐ | ☐ | ☐ |
| 130 | **005: Geometry and measurement, data, statistics, and probability** | ☐ | ☐ | ☐ | ☐ |
| | **Understands how to classify one-, two-, and three-dimensional figures** | ☐ | ☐ | ☐ | ☐ |
| | 5.1: Uses definitions to identify lines, rays, line segments, parallel lines, and perpendicular lines | ☐ | ☐ | ☐ | ☐ |
| | 5.2: Classifies angles based on their measure | ☐ | ☐ | ☐ | ☐ |
| | 5.3: Composes and decomposes two- and three-dimensional shapes | ☐ | ☐ | ☐ | ☐ |
| | 5.4: Uses attributes to classify or draw polygons and solids | ☐ | ☐ | ☐ | ☐ |
| | **Knows how to solve problems involving perimeter, area, surface area, and volume** | ☐ | ☐ | ☐ | ☐ |
| | 5.5: Represents three-dimensional figures with nets | ☐ | ☐ | ☐ | ☐ |
| | 5.6: Uses nets that are made of rectangles and triangles to determine the surface area of three dimensional figures | ☐ | ☐ | ☐ | ☐ |
| | 5.7: Finds the area and perimeter of polygons, including those with fractional side lengths | ☐ | ☐ | ☐ | ☐ |
| | 5.8: Finds the volume and surface area of right rectangular prisms, including those with fractional edge lengths | ☐ | ☐ | ☐ | ☐ |
| | 5.9: Determines how changes to dimensions change area and volume | ☐ | ☐ | ☐ | ☐ |
| | **Knows the components of the coordinate plane and how to graph ordered pairs on the plane** | ☐ | ☐ | ☐ | ☐ |
| | 5.10: Identifies the *x*-axis, the *y*-axis, the origin, and the four quadrants in the coordinate plane | ☐ | ☐ | ☐ | ☐ |
| | 5.11: Solves problems by plotting points and drawing polygons in the coordinate plane | ☐ | ☐ | ☐ | ☐ |
| | **Knows how to solve problems involving measurement** | ☐ | ☐ | ☐ | ☐ |
| | 5.12: Solves problems involving elapsed time, money, volume, and mass | ☐ | ☐ | ☐ | ☐ |
| | 5.13: Measures and compares lengths of objects using standard tools | ☐ | ☐ | ☐ | ☐ |
| | 5.14: Knows relative sizes of United States customary units and metric units | ☐ | ☐ | ☐ | ☐ |
| | 5.15: Converts units within both the United States customary system and the metric system | ☐ | ☐ | ☐ | ☐ |

# PERSONALIZED STUDY PLAN

| PAGE | COMPETENCY AND SKILL | KNOWN MATERIAL/ SKIP IT | BRIEFLY REVIEW eSTICKYNOTES | MAKE eFLASHCARDS | TAKE ADDITIONAL SAMPLE TESTS |
|---|---|:---:|:---:|:---:|:---:|
| | **Is familiar with basic statistical concepts** | ☐ | ☐ | ☐ | ☐ |
| 5.16: | Identifies statistical questions | ☐ | ☐ | ☐ | ☐ |
| 5.17: | Solves problems involving measures of center (mean, median, mode) and range | ☐ | ☐ | ☐ | ☐ |
| 5.18: | Recognizes which measure of center best describes a set of data | ☐ | ☐ | ☐ | ☐ |
| 5.19: | Determines how change in data affect measures of center or range | ☐ | ☐ | ☐ | ☐ |
| 5.20: | Describes a set of data (e.g., overall patterns, outliers) | ☐ | ☐ | ☐ | ☐ |
| | **Knows how to represent and interpret data presented in various forms** | ☐ | ☐ | ☐ | ☐ |
| 5.21: | Interprets various displays of data (e.g., box plots, histograms, scatterplots) | ☐ | ☐ | ☐ | ☐ |
| 5.22: | Identifies, constructs, and completes graphs that correctly represent given data (e.g., circle graphs, bar graphs, line graphs, histograms, scatterplots, double bar graphs, double line graphs, box plots, and line plots/dot plots) | ☐ | ☐ | ☐ | ☐ |
| 5.23: | Chooses appropriate graphs to display data | ☐ | ☐ | ☐ | ☐ |
| | **Is familiar with how to interpret the probability of events** | ☐ | ☐ | ☐ | ☐ |
| 5.24: | Interprets probabilities relative to likelihood of occurrence | ☐ | ☐ | ☐ | ☐ |

# COMPETENCY 003
## NUMBERS AND OPERATIONS

## Understands place value system

Place value is the basis of our entire number system. A **PLACE VALUE SYSTEM** is one in which the position of a digit in a number determines its value. In the standard system, called **base ten**, each place represents ten times the value of the place to its right. You can think of this as making groups of ten of the smaller unit and combining them to make a new unit.

> **PLACE VALUE SYSTEM:** one in which the position of a digit in a number determines its value

---

**SKILL 3.1** Writes numbers using base-10 numerals, number names, and expanded form

*See also Skills 3.2 and 3.5*

### Base Ten

Ten ones make up one of the next larger unit—tens. Ten of those units make up one of the next larger unit—hundreds. This pattern continues for greater values (ten hundreds = one thousand, ten thousands = one ten thousand, etc.), and lesser, decimal values (ten tenths =1, ten hundredths = one tenth, etc.).

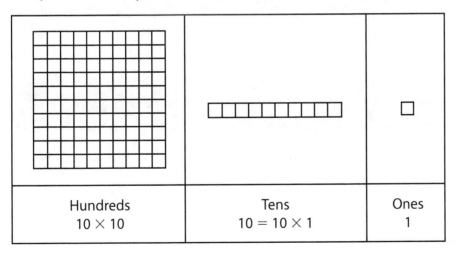

| Hundreds<br>10 × 10 | Tens<br>10 = 10 × 1 | Ones<br>1 |
|---|---|---|

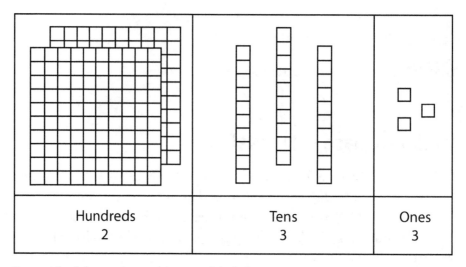

| Hundreds 2 | Tens 3 | Ones 3 |
|---|---|---|

In standard form, the number modeled above is 233.

## Teaching place value

A **PLACE-VALUE CHART** is a way to make sure digits are in the correct places. The value of each digit depends on its position or place. A great way to see the place-value relationships in a number is to model the number with actual objects (place-value blocks, bundles of craft sticks, etc.), write the digits in the chart, and then write the number in the usual, or standard form.

Place value is vitally important to all later mathematics. Without it, keeping track of greater numbers rapidly becomes impossible. (Can you imagine trying to write 999 with only ones?) A thorough mastery of place value is essential to learning the operations with greater numbers. It is the foundation for regrouping ("borrowing" and "carrying") in addition, subtraction, multiplication, and division.

### SKILL 3.2 Composes and decomposes multi-digit numbers

*Any number written in the standard form of base ten can be decomposed into parts separating the powers of ten.*

Any number written in the standard form of base ten can be decomposed into parts separating the powers of ten.

Consider the number 792. We can assign a place value to each digit.

Reading from left to right, the first digit (7) represents the hundreds place. The hundreds place tells us how many sets of one hundred the number contains. Thus, there are 7 sets of one hundred in the number 792.

The second digit (9) represents the tens place. The tens place tells us how many sets of ten the number contains. Thus, there are 9 sets of ten in the number 792.

The last digit (2) represents the ones place. The ones place tells us how many ones the number contains. Thus, there are 2 sets of one in the number 792.

Therefore, there are 7 sets of one hundred, plus 9 sets of ten, plus 2 ones in the number 792. Thus the standard form number 792 can be decomposed and written in expanded form as

$$792 = 700 + 90 + 2.$$

More complex numbers have additional place values to both the left and right of the decimal point. Consider the number 374.8.

Reading from left to right, the first digit (3) is in the hundreds place and tells us the number contains 3 sets of one hundred. The second digit (7) is in the tens place and tells us the number contains 7 sets of ten. The third digit (4) is in the ones place and tells us the number contains 4 ones. Finally, the number after the decimal (8) is in the tenths place and tells us the number contains 8 tenths.

Thus the standard form number 374.8 can be decomposed and written in expanded form as

$$374.8 = 300 + 70 + 4 + 0.8$$

*See also Skill 3.5*

> *More complex numbers have additional place values to both the left and right of the decimal point.*

---

**SKILL 3.3** **Given a digit, identifies the place the digit is in and its value in that place**

*See Skills 3.2 and 3.5*

---

**SKILL 3.4** **Recognizes that a digit in one place represents ten times what it represents in the place to its right and one-tenth what is represents in the place to its left, and extends this recognition to several places to the right or left**

*See Skill 3.5*

## SKILL 3.5 Uses whole number exponents to denote powers of 10

*Each digit to the left of the decimal point increases progressively in powers of ten. Each digit to the right of the decimal point decreases progressively in powers of ten.*

Each digit to the left of the decimal point increases progressively in powers of ten. Each digit to the right of the decimal point decreases progressively in powers of ten.

*Example: The number 12,345.6789 occupies the following powers-of-ten positions:*

| $10^4$ | $10^3$ | $10^2$ | $10^1$ | $10^0$ | 0 | $10^{-1}$ | $10^{-2}$ | $10^{-3}$ | $10^{-4}$ |
|---|---|---|---|---|---|---|---|---|---|
| 1 | 2 | 3 | 4 | 5 | . | 6 | 7 | 8 | 9 |

Names of powers-of-ten positions:

$10^0$ = ones (Note that any non-zero base raised to the power zero is 1.)

$10^1$ = tens            (number 1 and one zero, or 10)

$10^2$ = hundreds      (number 1 and two zeros, or 100)

$10^3$ = thousands     (number 1 and three zeros, or 1000)

$10^4$ = ten-thousands   (number 1 and four zeros, or 10,000)

$10^{-1} = \frac{1}{10^1} = \frac{1}{10}$ = tenths       (1st digit after decimal point, or 0.1)

$10^{-2} = \frac{1}{10^2} = \frac{1}{100}$ = hundredth   (2nd digit after decimal point, or 0.01)

$10^{-3} = \frac{1}{10^3} = \frac{1}{1000}$ = thousandth   (3rd digit after decimal point, or 0.001)

$10^{-4} = \frac{1}{10^4} = \frac{1}{10,000}$ = ten-thousandth   (4th digit after decimal point, or 0.0001)

*Example: Write 73,169.00537 in expanded form.*

We start by listing all the powers-of-ten positions.

| $10^5$ | $10^4$ | $10^3$ | $10^2$ | $10^1$ | $10^0$ | . | $10^{-1}$ | $10^{-2}$ | $10^{-3}$ | $10^{-4}$ | $10^{-5}$ |
|---|---|---|---|---|---|---|---|---|---|---|---|

Multiply each digit by its power of ten. Add the results.

Thus $73,169.00537 = (7 \times 10^4) + (3 \times 10^3) + (1 \times 10^2) + (6 \times 10^1) +$
$(9 \times 10^0) + (0 \times 10^{-1}) + (0 \times 10^{-2}) + (5 \times 10^{-3}) +$
$(3 \times 10^{-4}) + (7 \times 10^{-5})$

*Example: Determine the place value associated with the underlined digit in* 3.16<u>9</u>5.

| $10^0$ | . | $10^{-1}$ | $10^{-2}$ | $10^{-3}$ | $10^{-4}$ |
|---|---|---|---|---|---|
| 3 | . | 1 | 6 | 9 | 5 |

The place value for the digit 9 is the thousandth $\left(10^{-3} \text{ or } \frac{1}{1000}\right)$.

*Example: Write 21 × 10³ in standard form.*

$$21 \times 10^3 = 21 \times 1000$$
$$= 21{,}000$$

*Example: Write 739 × 10⁻⁴ in standard form.*

$$739 \times 10^{-4} = 739 \times \frac{1}{10{,}000}$$
$$= \frac{739}{10{,}000}$$
$$= 0.0739$$

**SKILL 3.6**   **Rounds multi-digit numbers to any place value**

When rounding to a given place value, it is necessary to look at the number in the next smaller place. If this number is 5 or more, the number in the place we are rounding to is increased by 1, and all numbers to the right are changed to zero. If the number is less than 5, the number in the place we are rounding to stays the same, and all numbers to the right are changed to zero.

*When rounding to a given place value, it is necessary to look at the number in the next smaller place.*

*Example: Round the measurement 1 foot 7 inches to the nearest foot.*

Convert the measurement to a decimal number. Then apply the rules for rounding.

$$1 \text{ foot } 7 \text{ inches} = 1\tfrac{7}{12} \text{ feet} = 1.58333 \text{ feet}$$

Since the digit in the tenth place is 5, the number is rounded up to 2 feet.

*Example: Round the number 73.2332 to the nearest hundredth.*

The digit in the thousandth place is 3 which is less than 5. Therefore the digit in the hundredth place is left unchanged and the rounded number is 73.23.

## Understands operations and properties of rational numbers

The rational numbers include integers, fractions and mixed numbers, and terminating and repeating decimals. Just as for integers, the basic operations for fractions, mixed numbers and decimals include addition, subtraction, multiplication and division. However the procedures for carrying out these operations and the conceptual understanding of these operations can be different for numbers that are not integers.

---

### SKILL Solves multistep mathematical and real-world problems using
### 3.7 addition, subtraction, multiplication, and division of rational numbers

The most common use of the operations addition, subtraction, multiplication, and division is to solve real-world problems as in some of the examples below.

*Example: At the end of her shift, a cashier had $96 in the cash register. At the beginning of her shift, she had $15. How much money did the cashier collect during her shift?*

The total collected is the difference between the ending amount and the starting amount.

$$\begin{array}{r} 96 \\ -\ 15 \\ \hline 81 \end{array}$$    The total collected was $81.

*Example: A student buys 4 boxes of crayons. Each box contains 16 crayons. How many crayons does the student have?*

The total number of crayons is $16 \times 4$.

$$\begin{array}{r} 16 \\ \times\ 4 \\ \hline 64 \end{array}$$    Total number of crayons equals 64.

*When adding and subtracting decimals, we align the numbers by place value as we do with whole numbers.*

When adding and subtracting decimals, we align the numbers by place value as we do with whole numbers. After adding or subtracting each column, we bring the decimal down, directly below the decimals in the numbers being added or subtracted.

*Example: Find the sum of 152.3 and 36.342.*

$$\begin{array}{r} 152.300 \\ +\ \ 36.342 \\ \hline 188.642 \end{array}$$

Note that we placed two zeros after the final place value in 152.3 to clarify the column addition.

*Example: Find the difference of 152.3 and 36.342.*

$$
\begin{array}{r}
2\,9\,10 \\
152.\cancel{300} \\
-\ 36.342 \\
\hline
58
\end{array}
\qquad\longrightarrow\qquad
\begin{array}{r}
(4)11(12) \\
1\cancel{52.300} \\
-\ 36.342 \\
\hline
115.958
\end{array}
$$

Note how we borrowed to subtract from the zeros in the hundredths and thousandths places of 152.300.

When multiplying decimal numbers, we multiply exactly as with whole numbers. The number of decimal places in the product is equal to the total number of decimal places contained in the two numbers being multiplied. For example, when multiplying 1.5 and 2.35, we place the decimal in the product 3 places from the left (3.525).

*Example: Find the product of 3.52 and 4.1.*

$$
\begin{array}{r}
3.52 \\
\times\ 4.1 \\
\hline
352 \\
+\ 14{,}080 \\
\hline
14.432
\end{array}
$$

Note that there are 3 total decimal places in the two numbers.

We place the decimal in the product 3 places from the left. Thus, the final product is 14.432.

When dividing decimal numbers, we first remove the decimal in the divisor by moving the decimal in the dividend the same number of spaces to the right. For example, when dividing 1.45 into 5.3, we convert the numbers to 145 and 530 and then perform normal whole number division.

*Example: Find the quotient of 5.3 divided by 1.45.*

First, convert to 145 and 530.

Divide.

$$
\begin{array}{r}
3 \\
145\overline{)530} \\
-\ 435 \\
\hline
95
\end{array}
\qquad\longrightarrow\qquad
\begin{array}{r}
3.65 \\
145\overline{)530.00} \\
-\ 435 \\
\hline
950 \\
-\ 870 \\
\hline
80
\end{array}
$$

Note that we insert the decimal to continue the division.

Because one of the numbers being divided contained one decimal place, we round the quotient to one decimal place. Thus, the final quotient is 3.7.

> ### SKILL 3.7a Identifies different problem situations for the operations (e.g., adding to, taking from, putting together, taking apart, and comparing for subtraction)

**Addition** can be indicated by the expressions: sum, greater than, and, more than, increased by, added to, entire, total.

**Subtraction** can be expressed by: difference, fewer than, minus, less than, decreased by.

**Multiplication** is shown by: product, times, multiplied by, twice.

**Division** is used for: quotient, divided by, ratio.

Multiplication and division problems often include the term "each" or give rates such as "per hour."

Note that all problems may not include these key words. Also, the use of the key words does not automatically indicate the given operation. Key words should only be used as a general guideline. It is still necessary to read and understand the whole problem.

*See example problems in Skill 3.7, 3.7b, 3.7c and throughout the guide.*

> ### SKILL 3.7b Uses the relationship between addition and subtraction and the relationship between multiplication and division to solve problems (e.g., inverse operations)

$a + b = c$ implies that $a = c - b$. Similarly, $a \times b = c$ implies that $a = \frac{c}{b}$. Given the sum, difference, product or quotient of two numbers one of which is unknown, the inverse operation can be used to find the unknown number.

*Example: At the end of a day of shopping, a shopper had $24 remaining in his wallet. He spent $45 on various goods. How much money did the shopper have at the beginning of the day?*

The total amount of money the shopper started with is the sum of the amount spent and the amount remaining at the end of the day.

$$\begin{array}{r} \$\ 24 \\ +\ \ 45 \\ \hline \$\ 69 \end{array}$$

The original total was $69.

*Example: At his job, John gets paid $20 for every hour he works. If John made $940 in a week, how many hours did he work?*

This is a division problem. To determine the number of hours John worked, we divide the total amount made ($940) by the hourly rate of pay ($20). Thus, the number of hours worked equals 940 divided by 20.

$$
\begin{array}{r}
47 \\
20\overline{)940} \\
-80 \\
\hline
140 \\
-140 \\
\hline
0
\end{array}
$$

$\rightarrow$ 20 divides into 940 a total of 47 times with no remainder.

John worked 47 hours.

---

**SKILL 3.7c** | **Interprets remainders in division problems**

If the divisor does not divide evenly into the dividend, we express the leftover amount either as a remainder or as a fraction with the divisor as the denominator. For example, 9 divided by 2 equals 4 with a remainder of 1, or 4 ?.

A remainder usually indicates a fractional answer. However, there may be problem situations where a fractional answer is not appropriate as in the example given below. In the case the answer must be rounded up or down to fit the situation.

*If the divisor does not divide evenly into the dividend, we express the leftover amount either as a remainder or as a fraction with the divisor as the denominator.*

*Example: Each box of apples contains 24 apples How many boxes must a grocer purchase to supply a group of 252 people with one apple each?*

The grocer needs 252 apples. Because he must buy apples in groups of 24, we divide 252 by 24 to determine how many boxes he needs to buy.

$$
\begin{array}{r}
10 \\
24\overline{)252} \\
-24 \\
\hline
12 \\
-0 \\
\hline
12
\end{array}
$$

$\rightarrow$ The quotient is 10 with a remainder of 12.

Thus, the grocer needs 10 boxes plus 12 more apples. Therefore, the minimum number of boxes the grocer can purchase is 11.

**Understands various strategies and algorithms used to perform operations on rational numbers**

*Algorithms are methods or strategies for solving problems.*

Algorithms are methods or strategies for solving problems. There are several different algorithms for solving addition, subtraction, multiplication, and division problems involving integers, rational numbers, and real numbers. In general, algorithms make use of number properties to simplify mathematical operations.

## Addition

Three common algorithms for addition of integers are the partial sums method, the column addition method, and the fast method.

The partial sums method is a two-stage process. First, we sum the columns from left to right. To complete the operation, we add the column values.

$$
\begin{array}{r}
125 \\
+\ \ 89 \\
+\ 376 \\
\hline
400 \\
+\ 170 \\
+\ \ 20 \\
\hline
590
\end{array}
$$

Step 1—column addition

Step 2—final sum

The column addition method is also a two-stage process. First, we add the digits in each column. To complete the operation, we perform the place carries from right to left.

$$
\begin{array}{r}
1\ |\ 2|\ 5 \\
+\ \ |\ 8|\ 9 \\
+\ 3\ |\ 7|\ 6 \\
\hline
4\ |17|20 \\
4\ |19|\ 0 \\
5\ |\ 9|\ 0\ =\ 590
\end{array}
$$

Stage 1 – column addition

← First carry

← Second carry = final answer

The fast method of addition is the traditional method of right-to-left addition. We sum the columns from right to left, performing carries mentally or writing them down.

$$
\begin{array}{r}
12 \\
125 \\
+\ \ 89 \\
+\ 376 \\
\hline
590
\end{array}
$$

← Carries

All of the integer addition algorithms rely on the commutative and associative properties of addition, allowing regrouping and reordering of numbers.

## Subtraction

Three common algorithms of integer subtraction are left-to-right subtraction, partial differences, and the same change rule.

In left-to-right subtraction, we decompose the second number into smaller values and perform the individual subtractions. For example, to solve $335 - 78$, we break 78 down into $70 + 8$.

$$\begin{array}{r} 335 \\ -\ 70 \\ \hline 265 \\ -\ \ \ 8 \\ \hline 257 \end{array}$$

The partial differences method is a two-stage process. First, we operate on each column individually, being careful to record the sign of each result. Then, we sum the results to yield the final answer.

$$\begin{array}{r} 335 \\ -\ 78 \\ \hline +300 \\ -\ 40 \\ -\ \ \ 3 \\ \hline 257 \end{array}$$

The same change rule takes advantage of the fact that subtraction is easier if the smaller number ends in zero. Thus, we change each number by the same amount to produce a smaller number ending in zero.

$$\begin{array}{rcl} 335 & \rightarrow & 337 \\ -\ 78 & \rightarrow & -\ 80 \\ & & \hline \phantom{-\ }257 \end{array}$$

Like the addition algorithms, the subtraction algorithms rely on the commutative and associative properties of addition (because subtraction is addition of a negative number).

## Multiplication

Two common multiplication algorithms are the partial products method and the short method.

In the partial products method, we decompose each term into base-ten form, and multiply each pair of terms.

$$
\begin{array}{r}
84 \\
\times\,26 \\
\hline
\end{array}
$$

$$
\begin{array}{rcl}
80 \times 20 & \rightarrow & 1600 \\
80 \times 6 & \rightarrow & 480 \\
20 \times 4 & \rightarrow & 80 \\
6 \times 4 & \rightarrow & 24 \\
\hline
& & 2184
\end{array}
$$

The short method is a traditional multiplication algorithm. In the short method, we decompose only the second term.

$$
\begin{array}{r}
84 \\
\times\,26 \\
\hline
\end{array}
$$

$$
\begin{array}{rcl}
84 \times 20 & \rightarrow & 1680 \\
84 \times 6 & \rightarrow & 504 \\
\hline
& & 2184
\end{array}
$$

The multiplication algorithms rely on the associative and commutative properties of multiplication and the distribution of multiplication over addition.

> *The multiplication algorithms rely on the associative and commutative properties of multiplication and the distribution of multiplication over addition.*

## Division

A common division algorithm is the partial quotients method. In this method, we make note of two simple products and estimate our way toward a final answer. For example, to find the quotient of 1440 divided by 18, we first make note that $5 \times 18 = 90$ and $2 \times 18 = 36$.

$$
\begin{array}{r r}
18\overline{)1440} & | \\
-\;\;900 & |\;50 \\
\hline
540 & | \\
-\;\;360 & |\;20 \\
\hline
180 & | \\
-\;\;90 & |\;5 \\
\hline
90 & | \\
-\;\;90 & |\;5 \\
\hline
0 & \;\;80
\end{array}
$$

Final quotient = 80, with no remainder

Operations involving rational numbers represented as fractions require unique algorithms. For example, when adding or subtracting fractions, we use the distributive property of multiplication over division to find common denominators.

When completing operations involving real numbers in decimal form, we use algorithms similar to those used with integers. We use the associative, commutative, and distributive properties of numbers to generate algorithms.

| SKILL 3.9 | Recognizes concepts of rational numbers and their operations |

**Number concepts** are commonly drawn from whole numbers, the familiar counting numbers. There is an expectation that when two numbers are multiplied together the result will be greater than both. For example, the product of 3 and 4 is 12, a number greater than both 3 and 4. Similarly, when dealing with whole numbers, division always produces a quotient that is smaller than the number divided. This is not always the case when dealing with fractions and decimals. The sequence 1, 2, 3, 4, ... is increasing while the sequence $\frac{1}{1}, \frac{1}{2}, \frac{1}{3}, \frac{1}{4}$ is decreasing. $\frac{2}{3}$ is not the same as $\frac{2}{5}$ even though both represent two parts out of a whole. These counterintuitive concepts can often be confusing for beginning learners.

| SKILL 3.9a | Identifies examples where multiplication does not result in a product greater than both factors and division does not result in a quotient smaller than the dividend |

The word **"multiply"** is used in ordinary language to denote an increase. Children are often taught to thinking of division as the breaking up of a whole that is then shared. A cake that is cut into five pieces will always produce pieces that are smaller than the whole cake. For rational numbers, in general, however, this instinctive understanding of multiplication and division is misplaced.

Multiplication of a number by a fraction less than one results in a product that is less than the original number. For instance, $2 \times 3$ represents 3 of 2 which is $2 + 2 + 2 = 6$, a number greater than 2. However $\frac{1}{2} \times 2$ represents $\frac{1}{2}$ of 2 which is 1, a number less than 2.

In the following example, the product $3\frac{1}{3}$ is less than the factor $7\frac{1}{3}$.

*Example:* $7\frac{1}{3} \times \frac{5}{11} = \frac{22}{3} \times \frac{5}{11}$  *Reduce like terms (22 and 11).*
$$= \frac{2}{3} \times \frac{5}{1}$$
$$= \frac{10}{3} = 3\frac{1}{3}$$

Likewise, division by a fraction less than one results in a quotient greater than the dividend as shown below.

*Example: 0.3 ÷ 0.2 = 1.5*

### SKILL 3.9b  Composes and decomposes fractions, including the use of unit fractions

Fractions can be broken up into smaller parts. For instance, five parts of a whole is equivalent to one part of the same whole added up five times:

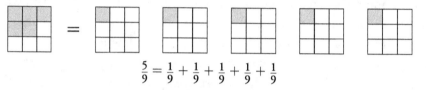

$$\frac{5}{9} = \frac{1}{9} + \frac{1}{9} + \frac{1}{9} + \frac{1}{9} + \frac{1}{9}$$

The same fraction can be decomposed in more than one way:

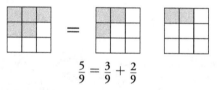

$$\frac{5}{9} = \frac{3}{9} + \frac{2}{9}$$

Note that in the above examples, all the fractions have the same denominator.

It is possible to put together or compose two or more fractions as long as they are expressed in forms that have the same denominator as shown in the example below.

$$\frac{1}{5} + \frac{2}{3} = \frac{3}{15} + \frac{10}{15} = \frac{13}{15}$$

### SKILL 3.9c  Recognizes that the value of a unit fraction decreases as the value of the denominator increases

*The value of a unit fraction decreases as the value of the denominator increases.*

One slice of a pizza that has been cut into six pieces is not the same size as one slice of the same pizza cut into eight pieces. The value of a unit fraction decreases as the value of the denominator increases. This may seem obvious but it may not appear so to a student who has just been introduced to fractions. Multiple pictorial and hands-on demonstrations may be needed for a student to grasp the concept fully.

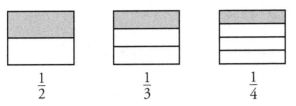

Note that this assertion is valid only when the whole is the same. One-fourth of a large square could be larger than one-half of a smaller square:

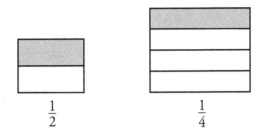

**Recognizes that the same whole must be used when comparing fractions**

*See Skill 3.9c*

**Solves problems using the order of operations, including problems involving whole number exponents**

The order of operations must be followed when evaluating algebraic expressions.

The mnemonic **PEMDAS** (Please Excuse My Dear Aunt Sally) can help you to remember the order of the following steps.

*The order of operations must be followed when evaluating algebraic expressions.*

1. Simplify inside grouping characters such as parentheses (P for Please), brackets, radicals, fraction bars, and so on.

2. Multiply out expressions with exponents (E for Excuse).

3. Do multiplication (M for My) or division (D for Dear) from left to right.

4. Do addition (A for Aunt) or subtraction (S for Sally) from left to right.

*Example: Simplify $3^3 - 5(4 + 2)$*

$$3^3 - 5(4 + 2) = 3^3 - 5(6) \quad \text{(parentheses)}$$
$$= 27 - 5(6) \quad \text{(exponent)}$$
$$= 27 - 30 \quad \text{(multiplication)}$$
$$= \text{-}3 \quad \text{(subtraction)}$$

*Example: Simplify $2 - 4 \times 2^3 - 2(4 - 2 \times 3)$*

$$2 - 4 \times 2^3 - 2(4 - 2 \times 3)$$
$$= 2 - 4 \times 2^3 - 2(4 - 6) \quad \text{(parentheses—multiplication)}$$
$$= 2 - 4 \times 2^3 - 2(\text{-}2) \quad \text{(parentheses—subtraction)}$$
$$= 2 - 4 \times 8 - 2(\text{-}2) \quad \text{(exponent)}$$
$$= 2 - 32 - 2(\text{-}2) \quad \text{(leftmost multiplication)}$$
$$= 2 - 32 - (\text{-}4) \quad \text{(next multiplication)}$$
$$= \text{-}30 - (\text{-}4) \quad \text{(leftmost subtraction)}$$
$$= \text{-}26 \quad \text{(next subtraction)}$$

## SKILL 3.11 Identifies properties of operations *(e.g., commutative, associative, distributive)* and uses them to solve problems

> **PROPERTIES:** rules that apply for addition, subtraction, multiplication, or division of real numbers

**PROPERTIES** are rules that apply for addition, subtraction, multiplication, or division of real numbers. These properties are:

| Commutative | You can change the order of the terms or factors as follows. |
|---|---|
| | **For addition:** $\quad a + b = b + a$ |
| | **For multiplication:** $\quad ab = ba$ |
| | Since subtraction is the inverse operation of addition and division is the inverse operation of multiplication, no separate laws are needed for subtraction and division. |
| | *Example: $5 + \text{-}8 = \text{-}8 + 5 = \text{-}3$* |
| | *Example: $\text{-}2 \times 6 = 6 \times (\text{-}2) = \text{-}12$* |

*Table continued on next page*

| Associative | You can regroup the terms as you like.<br><br>**For addition:** $\qquad a + (b + c) = (a + b) + c$<br><br>**For multiplication:** $\qquad a(bc) = (ab)c$<br><br>This rule does not apply for division and subtraction.<br><br>*Example:* $(-2 + 7) + 5 = -2 + (7 + 5)$<br>$\qquad\qquad 5 + 5 = -2 + 12 = 10$<br><br>*Example:* $(3 \times (-7)) \times 5 = 3 \times (-7 \times 5)$<br>$\qquad\qquad -21 \times 5 = 3 \times -35 = -105$ |
|---|---|
| Identity | An identity is a number that when added to a term gives the original term (additive identity) or that when multiplied by a term gives the original term (multiplicative identity).<br><br>**For addition:** $\qquad a + 0 = a$ (zero is additive identity)<br><br>**For multiplication:** $\quad a \times 1 = a$ (one is multiplicative identity)<br><br>*Example:* $17 + 0 = 17$<br><br>*Example:* $-34 \times 1 = -34$<br><br>The product of any number and one is that number. |
| Inverse | An inverse is a number that when added to another number results in 0, or that when multiplied by another number results in 1.<br><br>**For addition:** $\qquad a + (-a) = 0$<br><br>**For multiplication:** $\qquad a \times \left(\frac{1}{a}\right) = 1$<br><br>$(-a)$ is the additive inverse of $a$; $\left(\frac{1}{a}\right)$, also called the reciprocal, is the multiplicative inverse of $a$.<br><br>*Example:* $25 + -25 = 0$<br><br>*Example:* $5 \times \frac{1}{5} = 1$<br><br>The product of any number and its reciprocal is one. |
| Distributive | The distributive property allows us to operate on terms inside parentheses without first performing operations within the parentheses. This is especially helpful when terms within the parentheses cannot be combined.<br><br>$a (b + c) = ab + ac$<br><br>*Example:* $6 \times (-4 + 9) = (6 \times (-4)) + (6 \times 9)$<br>$\qquad\qquad 6 \times 5 = -24 + 54 = 30$<br><br>To multiply a sum by a number, multiply each addend by the number, then add the products. |

SKILL
3.12
**Represents rational numbers and their operations in different ways**

Blocks or other objects modeled on the base-ten system are useful concrete tools for representing rational numbers. Base-ten blocks represent ones, tens, and hundreds. (*See Skill 3.1 for an example.*)

Number lines and diagrams of different types can also be used to represent rational numbers. Pictorial representations of different types of rational numbers are given in the table below:

*A decimal can be converted to a percent by multiplying by 100, or merely moving the decimal point two places to the right. A percent can be converted to a decimal by dividing by 100, or moving the decimal point two places to the left.*

| COMMON EQUIVALENTS | | | | |
|---|---|---|---|---|
| $\frac{1}{2}$ | = | 0.5 | = | 50% |
| $\frac{1}{3}$ | = | 0.33 | = | $33\frac{1}{3}$% |
| $\frac{1}{4}$ | = | 0.25 | = | 25% |
| $\frac{1}{5}$ | = | 0.2 | = | 20% |
| $\frac{1}{6}$ | = | 0.17 | = | $16\frac{2}{3}$% |
| $\frac{1}{8}$ | = | 0.125 | = | $12\frac{1}{2}$% |
| $\frac{1}{10}$ | = | 0.1 | = | 10% |
| $\frac{2}{3}$ | = | 0.67 | = | $66\frac{2}{3}$% |
| $\frac{5}{6}$ | = | 0.83 | = | $83\frac{1}{3}$% |
| $\frac{3}{8}$ | = | 0.375 | = | $37\frac{1}{2}$% |
| $\frac{5}{8}$ | = | 0.625 | = | $62\frac{1}{2}$% |
| $\frac{7}{8}$ | = | 0.875 | = | $87\frac{1}{2}$% |
| 1 | = | 1.0 | = | 100% |

Diagrams and manipulatives can be used not only to represent rational numbers but also their operations. Concrete and visual representations can help demonstrate the logic behind operational algorithms.

Two groups of four equals eight or $2 \times 4 = 8$ shown in picture form.

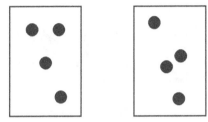

Adding three objects to two or $3 + 2 = 5$ shown in picture form.

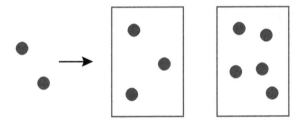

*Example: Use tiles to demonstrate both geometric ideas and number theory. Give each group of students 12 tiles, and instruct each group to build rectangles. Students draw their rectangles on paper.*

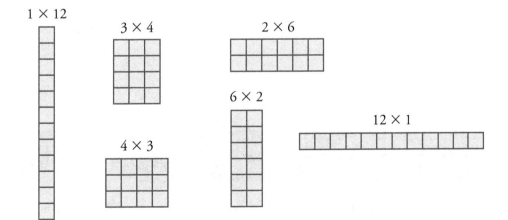

Algorithms for multi-digit numbers can also be modeled using base-ten blocks. Consider the addition of 242 and 193 using the partial sums algorithm. We represent 242 with two "100" blocks, four "10" blocks, and 2 "one" blocks. We represent 193 with one "100" block, nine "10" blocks, and 3 "one" blocks. In the partial sums algorithm, we manipulate each place value separately and total the results. Thus, we group the hundred blocks, ten blocks, and one blocks and derive a total for each place value. We combine the place values to complete the sum.

---

**SKILL 3.12b** **Represents rational numbers and sums and differences of rational numbers on a number line**

Rational numbers can be represented on a number line that shows the distance of the number from 0. Positive numbers are shown on the right hand side of zero while negative numbers are shown on the left hand side.

In the example below, the positive numbers 15, 20, and 25 are represented on a number line:

> *The number line is a particularly helpful tool for teaching negative numbers and for demonstrating addition and subtraction involving negative numbers. These concepts are very difficult for beginning learners to grasp intuitively.*

The number line is a particularly helpful tool for teaching negative numbers and for demonstrating addition and subtraction involving negative numbers. These concepts are very difficult for beginning learners to grasp intuitively.

The addition of 5 to -4 is shown below on the number line:

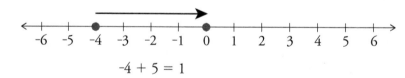

$$-4 + 5 = 1$$

---

**SKILL 3.12c** **Illustrates and explains multiplication and division problems using equations, rectangular arrays, and area models**

An example of a visual representation of an operational algorithm is the modeling of a two-term multiplication as the area of a rectangle. For example, consider the product of 24 and 39. We can represent the product in geometric form. Note that the four sections of the rectangle equate to the four products of the partial products method.

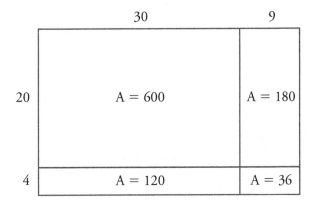

Thus, the final product is the sum of the areas, or $600 + 180 + 120 + 36 = 936$.

*See also Skill 3.12a*

<table>
<tr><td>SKILL<br/>3.13</td><td>**Compares, classifies, and orders rational numbers**</td></tr>
</table>

Fractions, decimals, and percents can be used interchangeably within problems.

If we compare numbers in various forms, we see, for example, that:

The integer $4 = \frac{8}{2}$ (fraction) = 4.0 (decimal) = 400% (percent).

In order to compare and order numbers it is necessary to convert them to the same form as demonstrated in the following example.

*Example: J.C. Nickels has Hunch jeans $\frac{1}{4}$ off the usual price of $36.00. Shears and Roadkill have the same jeans 30% off their regular price of $40. Find the cheaper price.*

$\frac{1}{4} = 0.25$ so $0.25(36) = \$9.00$ off $\$36 - 9 = \$27$ sale price
$30\% = 0.30$ so $0.30(40) = \$12$ off $\$40 - 12 = \$28$ sale price

The price at J.C. Nickels is $1 lower.

*See also Skill 3.14*

**Converts between fractions, decimals, and percents**

A decimal can be converted to a percent by multiplying by 100, or by merely moving the decimal point two places to the right. A decimal can be converted to a fraction by multiplying by the power of 10 needed to get rid of the decimal point and then dividing by the same factor.

*Example: Convert 0.056 to a fraction.*
Multiply 0.056 by $\frac{1000}{1000}$ to get rid of the decimal point:

$$0.056 \times \frac{1000}{1000} = \frac{56}{1000} = \frac{7}{125}$$

A percent can be converted to a decimal by dividing by 100, or moving the decimal point two places to the left.

> *A decimal can be converted to a percent by multiplying by 100, or merely moving the decimal point two places to the right. A percent can be converted to a decimal by dividing by 100, or moving the decimal point two places to the left.*

*Examples:*

| | |
|---|---|
| 0.375 = 37.5% | 84% = 0.84 |
| 0.7 = 70% | 3% = 0.03 |
| 0.04 = 4% | 60% = 0.6 |
| 3.15 = 315% | 110% = 1.1 |
| | $\frac{1}{2}$% = 0.5% = 0.005 |

A percent can be converted to a fraction by placing the percent over 100 and reducing to simplest terms.

*Example: Convert 6.25% to a fraction.*

$$6.25\% = \frac{6.25}{100} = \frac{625}{10,000} = \frac{25}{400} = \frac{1}{16}$$

## Understands proportional relationships and percents

Ratios, unit rates, percents and proportions are used to represent and compare the relative values of two numbers or two ratios. The choice of representation depends on the problem situation.

## SKILL 3.15 Applies the concepts of ratios and unit rates to describe relationships between two quantities

A **RATIO** is a comparison of two numbers. If a class had 11 boys and 14 girls, the ratio of boys to girls could be written one of three ways:

$$11:14 \quad \text{or} \quad 11 \text{ to } 14 \quad \text{or} \quad \frac{11}{14}$$

> **RATIO:** a comparison of two numbers

The ratio of girls to boys is:

$$14:11 \quad \text{or} \quad 14 \text{ to } 11 \quad \text{or} \quad \frac{14}{11}$$

Ratios can be reduced when possible. A ratio of 12 cats to 18 dogs would reduce to 2:3, 2 to 3, or $\frac{2}{3}$.

**Note:** Read ratio questions carefully. Given a group of 6 adults and 5 children, the ratio of children to the entire group would be 5:11.

**PROPORTIONS** are comparisons of ratios. A proportion is an equation that shows two ratios are equal. For example,

$$\frac{1}{3} = \frac{2}{6} \text{ or } 1:3 = 2:6$$

> **PROPORTIONS:** comparisons of ratios

is a proportion that shows the ratios $\frac{1}{3}$ and $\frac{2}{6}$ are equal. In converting from one to the other, both the numerator and the denominator change by the same factor. In the preceding example, both portions of the ratio increase by a factor of 2.

A **UNIT RATE** is a ratio where the second term is one. For instance, the speed of a car travelling 300 miles in 5 hours can be expressed by the ratio 300:5. When this is reduced so that the second term is one, the ratio becomes 60: 1. This indicates that the car travels 60 miles in 1 hour and the speed of the car is 60 miles/hour which is a unit rate. Other examples of unit rate include prices such as \$4/pound or wages such as \$15/hour.

> **UNIT RATE:** a ratio where the second term is one

*See Skills 3.17 and 3.18 for problems involving ratios and unit rates.*

## SKILL 3.16 Understands percent as a rate per 100

A **PERCENT** is a ratio where the second term is 100. If a class has 11 boys and 14 girls, the ratio of the number of boys to the total number of students is 11:25 or $\frac{11}{25}$. This can be converted to a rate per 100 by multiplying both the numerator and denominator by the factor $\frac{100}{25} = 4$. Thus $\frac{11}{25} = \frac{44}{100}$ and 44% of the children in the class are boys.

> **PERCENT:** a ratio where the second term is 100

*See Skill 3.18 for problems involving percentages.*

## SKILL 3.17 Solves unit rate problems

The unit cost for purchasing an item is its price divided by the number of pounds (or ounces, etc.) in the item. The item with the lowest unit cost has the lowest price.

*Example: Find the item with the best unit cost.*

> $1.79 for 10 ounces
> $1.89 for 12 ounces
> $5.49 for 32 ounces

$\frac{1.79}{10}$ .179 per ounce    $\frac{1.89}{12}$ .1575 per ounce    $\frac{5.49}{32}$ .172 per ounce

$1.89 for 12 ounces is the best price.

A second way to find the better buy is to make a proportion, for example, with the price over the number of ounces. Cross-multiply the proportion, writing the products above the numerator that is used. The better price will have the smaller product.

*Example: Find the better buy: $8.19 for forty pounds or $4.89 for twenty-two pounds. Find the unit costs.*

$$\frac{40}{8.19} = \frac{1}{x}$$
$$40x = 8.19$$
$$x = .20475$$

$$\frac{22}{4.89} = \frac{1}{x}$$
$$22x = 4.89$$
$$x = .222\overline{27}$$

Since $.20475 < .222\overline{27}$, $8.19 is the lower price and a better buy.

To find the amount of sales tax on an item, change the percentage of sales tax into an equivalent decimal number. Then multiply the decimal number by the price of the object to find the sales tax. The total cost of the item will be the price of the item plus the sales tax.

## Ratios, Proportions, Percentages

**Proportions** can be used to solve word problems whenever relationships are compared. Some situations include scale drawings and maps, similar polygons, speed, time and distance, cost, and comparison shopping.

*Example: Which is the better buy, six items for $1.29 or eight items for $1.69?*
Find the unit costs.

$6x = 1.29$                        $8x = 1.69$

    $x = 0.215$                    $x = 0.21125$

Thus, eight items for $1.69 is the better buy.

*Example: A car travels 125 miles in two and a half hours. How far will it go in six hours?*
Write a proportion comparing the distance and time.
Let $x$ represent distance in miles. Then,

| | |
|---|---|
| $\frac{125}{2.5} = \frac{x}{6}$ | Set up the proportion. |
| $2.5x = 6 \times 125$ | Cross-multiply. |
| $2.5x = 750$ | Simplify. |
| $2.5x = \frac{750}{2.5}$ | Divide both sides of the equation by 2.5. |
| $x = 300$ miles | Simplify. |

*Example: The scale on a map is one inch = 6 miles. What is the actual distance between two cities if they are 2 inches apart on the map?*
Write a proportion comparing the scale to the actual distance.

$\frac{1}{6} = \frac{2}{x}$; Cross-multiplying, x = 12.

Thus, the actual distance between the cities is twelve miles.

Word problems involving percentages can be solved by writing the problem as an equation, then solving the equation. Keep in mind that *of* means multiplication and *is* means equals.

> *Word problems involving percentages can be solved by writing the problem as an equation, then solving the equation.*

*Example: The ski club has eighty-five members; 80% of the members are able to attend the meeting. How many members attended the meeting?*

| | |
|---|---|
| Restate the problem: | What is 80% of 85? |
| Write an equation: | $n = 0.8 \times 85$ |
| Solve: | $n = 68$ |

Sixty-eight members attended the meeting.

*Example: There are sixty-four dogs in the kennel. Forty-eight are collies. What percentage are collies?*

| | |
|---|---|
| Restate the problem: | 48 is what percentage of 64? |
| Write an equation: | $48 = n \times 64$ |
| Solve: | $48 \div 64 = n$ |
| | $n = .75$ |

Seventy-five percent of the dogs are collies.

*Example: The auditorium was filled to 90% capacity. There were 558 seats occupied. What is the capacity of the auditorium?*

| | |
|---|---|
| Restate the problem: | 90% of what number is 558? |
| Write an equation: | $0.9n = 558$ |
| Solve: | $n = \frac{558}{.9}$ |
| | $n = 620$ |

The capacity of the auditorium is 620 people.

*Example: Shoes cost $42.00. Sales tax is 6%. What is the total cost of the shoes?*

| | |
|---|---|
| Restate the problem: | What is 6% of 42? |
| Write an equation: | $n = 0.06 \times 42$ |
| Solve: | $n = 2.52$ |
| Add the sales tax: | $42.00 + $2.52 = $44.52 |

The total cost of the shoes, including sales tax, is $44.52.

## Knows how to use basic concepts of number theory

Underlying many of the more involved fields of mathematics is an understanding of basic algebra and number theory. One of the fundamental ideas of number theory, explored in the next two sections, is the classification of numbers as "prime" or "composite."

**Identifies and uses prime and composite numbers**

PRIME NUMBERS are numbers whose only factors are 1 and the number itself.

COMPOSITE NUMBERS are whole numbers that have more than two different factors. For example, the number 9 is composite because it has factors of 1, 9, and 3. The number 70 is also composite because, in addition to the factors of 1 and 70, the numbers 2, 5, 7, 10, 14, and 35 are also factors.

Any composite number can be factored into its prime factors. When factoring a number into its prime factors, all the factors must be numbers that cannot be factored again (without using 1). To perform a prime factorization, first choose any two factors of the given number. Check each factor to see if it can be factored again. Continue factoring until all remaining factors are prime. This is the list of prime factors. Regardless of the way in which the original number was factored, the final list of prime factors will always be the same.

> PRIME NUMBERS: numbers whose only factors are 1 and the number itself

> COMPOSITE NUMBERS: whole numbers that have more than two different factors

*Example: Factor 30 into prime factors.*
First, factor 30 into any two factors.

| | |
|---|---|
| $5 \cdot 6$ | Now factor the 6. |
| $5 \cdot 2 \cdot 3$ | These are all prime factors. |

Suppose we begin with two different factors of 30:

| | |
|---|---|
| $3 \cdot 10$ | Now factor the 10. |
| $3 \cdot 2 \cdot 5$ | These are the same prime factors, even |

though the two original factors were different.

*Example: Factor 240 into prime factors.*
Factor 240 into any two factors.

| | |
|---|---|
| $24 \cdot 10$ | Now factor both 24 and 10. |
| $4 \cdot 6 \cdot 2 \cdot 5$ | Now factor both 4 and 6. |
| $2 \cdot 2 \cdot 2 \cdot 3 \cdot 2 \cdot 5$ | These are all prime factors. |

This result can also be written as $2^4 \cdot 3 \cdot 5$.

## SKILL 3.20   Finds factors and multiples of numbers

**GCF (GREATEST COMMON FACTOR):** the largest number that is a factor of all the numbers given in a problem

**GCF** is the abbreviation for the greatest common factor. The GCF is the largest number that is a factor of all the numbers given in a problem. The GCF can be no larger than the smallest number given in the problem. If no other common factor is found, then the GCF is the number 1. To find the GCF, list all possible factors of the smallest number given in the problem (include the number itself). Starting with the largest factor of the smallest number (which is the number itself), determine if it is also a factor of all the other given numbers. If so, that factor is the GCF. If that factor doesn't divide evenly into all the other numbers in the problem, try the same method on the next-smallest factor. Continue until a common factor is found. That is the GCF. *Note:* There can be other common factors besides the GCF.

### Example: Find the GCF of 12, 20, and 36.
The smallest number in the problem is 12. The factors of 12 are 1, 2, 3, 4, 6, and 12. 12 is the largest factor, but it does not divide evenly into 20. Neither does 6, but 4 will divide into both 20 and 36 evenly.

Therefore, 4 is the GCF.

### Example: Find the GCF of 14 and 15.
The factors of 14 are 1, 2, 7, and 14. 14 is the largest factor, but it does not divide evenly into 15. Neither does 7 or 2. Therefore, the only factor common to both 14 and 15 is the number 1, which is the GCF.

**LCM (LEAST COMMON MULTIPLE):** the smallest number that all of the given numbers will divide into

**LCM** is the abbreviation for least common multiple. The least common multiple of a group of numbers is the smallest number that all of the given numbers will divide into. The least common multiple will always be either the largest of the given numbers or a multiple of the largest number.

### Example: Find the LCM of 20, 30, and 40.
The largest number given is 40, but 30 will not divide evenly into 40. The next multiple of 40 is 80 ($2 \times 40$), but 30 will not divide evenly into 80 either. The next multiple of 40 is 120. 120 is divisible by both 20 and 30, so 120 is the LCM.

### Example: Find the LCM of 96, 16, and 24.
The largest number is 96. 96 is divisible by both 16 and 24, so 96 is the LCM.

# Knows a variety of strategies to determine the reasonableness of results

Children are typically taught the steps they need to follow to find the answer to a problem. As long as they don't make any mistakes, the steps lead them to the correct answer. Unfortunately, children do make mistakes and, when they do, it is important for them to be able to identify the mistakes. They can only do that if they have a general sense of what kind of answer they are expecting to get. This is particularly important when calculators are used. Students need to be able to verify that the answer they are getting by punching in numbers is in the correct range and makes sense in the given context.

## SKILL 3.21 Recognizes the reasonableness of results within the concept of a given problem

The following are some simple questions that one can ask to gauge the reasonableness of the result of a math problem:

1. Is the answer positive or negative? If the length of a swimming pool turns out to be negative 17 m, it is obviously wrong. However, a student focused on following the procedure blindly may overlook this indication of error.

2. Is the number a whole number or fraction? Some problems must have answers that are whole numbers. This will require the answer to be rounded up or down to the nearest whole number. (*See Skill 3.7c for an example problem.*)

3. Is the answer the right order of magnitude? A student must have a sense of the size of the answer expected. He must be able to tell that the distance from John's house to his school cannot be 5000 miles.

4. Is the answer expected *more* or *less* than a given number? It is astonishing how many errors of computation can be avoided using this method. For instance, when converting 20 Km to meters, asking whether the expected answer is greater than or less than 20 will help decide whether one should multiply or divide by 1,000 (a common point of confusion in conversion problems).

*See also Skill 3.22*

> ### SKILL Uses mental math, estimation, and rounding strategies to solve
> ### 3.22 problems and determine reasonableness of results

Mental calculations may be used to estimate and check the reasonableness of answers. The highest place value in a number can be used to make a mental estimate of its "order of magnitude". For instance, if the highest place value of a number is $10^6$, one can say that the number is in the millions. This will place the estimate within a factor of 10 of the exact answer. Although this is a very rough estimate, it can be useful in many situations.

Estimation and approximation may be used to check the reasonableness of answers.

*Example: Find the sum of 4387 + 7226 + 5893.*

$4300 + 7200 + 5800 = 17300$      Estimation.

$4387 + 7226 + 5893 = 17506$      Actual sum.

By comparing the estimate to the actual sum, students can determine that their answer is reasonable.

*Example: Estimate the answer.*   $\frac{58 \times 810}{1989}$

58 becomes 60, 810 becomes 800 and 1989 becomes 2000.

$$\frac{60 \times 800}{2000} = 24$$

An estimate may sometimes be all that is needed to solve a problem.

*Example: Janet goes into a store to purchase a CD on sale for $13.95. While shopping, she sees two pairs of shoes, prices $19.95 and $14.50. She only has $50. Can she purchase everything?*

Solve by rounding:

     $19.95 \rightarrow \$20.00$

     $14.50 \rightarrow \$15.00$

     $13.95 \rightarrow \underline{\$14.00}$

             $49.00$      Yes, she can purchase the CD and the shoes.

Note: In this problem it is important to round up and not round down. If Janet underestimates the total cost of the items she may find herself short of cash that the checkout counter.

# COMPETENCY 004
## ALGEBRAIC THINKING

## Knows how to evaluate and manipulate algebraic expressions, equations, and formulas

**Symbolic representation** is the basic language of mathematics. Converting data to symbols allows for easy manipulation and problem solving. Students should have the ability to recognize what the symbolic notation represents and convert information into symbolic form.

Many algebraic procedures are similar to and rely upon number operations and algorithms. For example, addition of rational expressions is similar to fraction addition. The basic algorithm of addition for both fractions and rational expressions is the common denominator method. Both number operations and operations with algebraic expressions are based on the same principles: the commutative, associative and distributive properties.

---

**SKILL 4.1** Differentiates between algebraic expressions and equations

An **EQUATION** expresses a complete idea and is equivalent to an English sentence. An **EXPRESSION**, on the other hand, encompasses only part of an idea similar to a phrase in the English language. Equations are formed using equal signs to set one expression equal to another.

Some examples of algebraic expressions are given below.

**Examples:**

| | |
|---|---|
| 7 added to a number | $n + 7$ |
| a number decreased by 8 | $n - 8$ |
| 12 times a number divided by 7 | $12n \div 7$ |
| 28 less than a number | $n - 28$ |
| the ratio of a number to 55 | $n/55$ |
| 4 times the sum of a number and 21 | $4(n + 21)$ |

The following are examples of equations that make use of some of the above expressions:

> **EQUATION:** expresses a complete idea and is equivalent to an English sentence

> **EXPRESSION:** encompasses only part of an idea similar to a phrase in the English language

**Examples:** 7 added to a number is 28 less than the number $\quad n + 7 = n - 28$

The ratio of a number to 55 is the number decreased by 8 $\quad \frac{n}{55} = n - 8$

12 times a number divided by 7 is equal to 5 $\qquad 12n \div 7 = 5$

---

**SKILL 4.2** **Adds and subtracts linear algebraic expressions**

In order to add or subtract linear algebraic expressions, follow these steps:

1. Remove the parentheses, and identify like terms (terms involving the same variable or no variable.)

2. Group the like terms together.

3. Add the like terms.

**Example:** $(2x + 3) + (3x - 2)$

$= 2x + 3 + 3x - 2$ $\qquad$ (remove parentheses)

$= 2x + 3x + 3 - 2$ $\qquad$ (group like terms)

$= 5x + 1$ $\qquad$ (add like terms)

**Example:** $(5x + 2 + x) - (3x - 2)$

$= 5x + 2 + x - 3x + 2$ $\qquad$ (remove parentheses)

$= 5x + x - 3x + 2 + 2$ $\qquad$ (group like terms)

$= 3x + 4$

**Example:** $(2x + 3 + y) + (3x - 2) - (2 + 6y)$

$= 2x + 3 + y + 3x - 2 - 2 - 6y$ $\qquad$ (remove parentheses)

$= 2x + 3x + y - 6y + 3 - 2 - 2$ $\qquad$ (group like terms)

$= 5x - 5y - 1$ $\qquad$ (add like terms)

## SKILL 4.3 Uses the distributive property to generate equivalent linear algebraic expressions

According to the distributive property, for all real numbers $a$, $b$, and $c$, $a(b + c) = ab + ac$.

This property can be used to reduce an expression involving parentheses to an equivalent linear expression.

*Example: Simplify 3(4x + 2).*
Using the distributive property,
$$3(4x + 2) = 3(4x) + 3(2) = 12x + 6$$

*Example: Simplify 6x(3 − 5) + 2(4 − 3x).*
Using the distributive property,
$$6x(3 - 5) + 2(4 - 3x) = 6x(3) - 6x(5) + 2(4) - 2(3x)$$
$$= 18x - 30x + 8 - 6x$$
$$= 18x - 30x - 6x + 8$$
$$= -18x + 8$$

## SKILL 4.4 Evaluates simple algebraic expressions *(i.e., one variable, binomial)* for given values of variables

**VARIABLES** in algebraic expressions stand for unknown numbers. To evaluate the value of an algebraic expression for a particular value of the variable, simply substitute the given value for the variable and carry out the indicated operation.

**VARIABLES** in algebraic expressions stand for unknown numbers

*Example: Evaluate x + 5 for x = 3.*
$$x + 5 = 3 + 5 = 8$$

*Example: Evaluate 5x − 9 for x = 2.*
$$5x - 9 = 5(2) - 9$$
$$= 10 - 9$$
$$= 1$$

*Example: Evaluate 5(x − 7) for x = 1.*
$$5(x - 7) = 5(1 - 7)$$
$$= 5(-6)$$
$$= -30$$

## SKILL 4.5 Uses mathematical terms to identify parts of expressions and describe expressions

Mathematical terms such as variable, constant, factor, term, and coefficient are used to describe parts of expressions and equations.

*Example: Describe the parts of the expression 7x + 20y + 3*

**Variables** are symbols that represent unknown quantities. In this expression the variables are "$x$" and "$y$."

**Constants** are fixed numbers. Here "3" is a constant. So are "7" and "20."

Parts of the expression separated by + or − are known as **terms**. This expression has three terms "$7x$," "$20y$," and "3."

**Factors** are parts that are multiplied together. For instance, the term "$7x$" has the factors "7" and "$x$."

**Coefficients** are constant factors that multiply a variable. In this expression, "7" is the coefficient of "$x$" and "20" is the coefficient of "$y$."

## SKILL 4.6 Translates between verbal statements and algebraic expressions or equations

*Example: Write the following statement as an algebraic equation: "The height of the rocket is the product of the velocity and the amount of time in flight, plus the starting height."*

First, define the variables involved in the problem. Express the height of the rocket, $h$, in terms of the velocity; $v$, the time in flight, $t$; and the initial height, $s$. If ambiguity arises, such as if the statement is spoken instead of written (the lack of a comma might lead to the question as to whether the second term in the product is $t$ or $(t + s)$), choose the interpretation that makes the most sense according to the situation.

Next, write the equation using the defined variables:

$$h = vt + s$$

This equation, along with the definitions of each parameter, constitutes the solution to this problem.

*Example: Write an equation based on the following statement: "I want to know the price of a single banana if bananas are sold by the dozen for x dollars."*

In this case, what is needed is the given price, $x$, divided by 12, since this gives the price per banana, $b$. This is written in algebraic form as follows:

$$b = \frac{x}{12}$$

The preceding examples are simple, but they are representative of the types of processes needed to convert verbal or written statements into algebraic expressions. Mastery of this skill is important for solving word problems.

*Also, see Skill 4.1.*

| SKILL 4.7 | Uses formulas to determine unknown quantities |
|---|---|

An algebraic formula is an equation that describes a relationship among variables. While it is not often necessary to derive the formula, one must know how to rewrite a given formula in terms of a desired variable.

*Example: Given that the relationship of voltage, V, applied across a material with electrical resistance, R, when a current, I, is flowing through the material is represented by the formula V = IR, find the resistance of the material when a current of 10 milliamps is flowing, when the applied voltage is 2 volts.*

$V = IR$      Solve for $R$.

$IR = V; R = \frac{V}{I}$      Divide both sides by $I$.

When $V = 2$ volts; $I = 10 \times 10^{-3}$ amps;

$R = \frac{2}{10^1 \times 10^{-3}}$

$R = \frac{2}{10^{-2}}$      Substituting $R = \frac{V}{I}$, we get,

$R = 2 \times 10^2$

$R = 200$ ohms

The resistance is 200 ohms.

*Example: Given the formula I = PRT, where I is the simple interest paid or realized when an amount P, the principal, is deposited at simple interest rate R (in decimal form) and T is the time expressed in years, find the principal that must be deposited to yield an interest payment of $586 over a period of 2 years at an interest rate of 23.5%.*

$I = PRT$ Solve for $P$: $P = \frac{I}{RT}$ (divide both sides by $RT$).

$$I = 586; R = 23.5\% = 0.235; T = 2$$

$$\frac{586}{0.235 \times 2} = \frac{586}{0.47} \qquad \text{(Substitute)}$$

$$= \$1246.80$$

Check: $I = PRT$; $1246.8 \times 0.235 \times 2 = 586$

---

## SKILL 4.8 Differentiates between dependent and independent variables in formulas

*Loosely speaking, an equation describes a relationship between the independent variable x and the dependent variable y.*

Loosely speaking, an equation describes a relationship between the independent variable $x$ and the dependent variable $y$. Thus, y is written as $f(x)$, or a "function of $x$." This represents a relationship between a set of all input numbers (values of independent variable $x$) and a set of all outputs (values of dependent variable $y$). Since the value of $x$ is used to calculate the value of $y$, $y$ is dependent on $x$.

Another way to describe a function is as a process in which one or more numbers are input into an imaginary machine that produces another number as the output. If 5 (the value of $x$) is input into a machine with a process of $y = x + 1$, the output will be 6 (the value of $y$). The input is the independent variable and the output is the dependent variable.

Many real-life relationships can be described mathematically. The function $y = x + 1$ can be used to describe the idea that people age one year on each birthday. To describe the relationship in which a person's monthly medical costs are 6 times the person's age, we could write $y = 6x$. In this situation, the person's age is the independent variable and the monthly medical cost is the dependent variable.

## Understands the meanings of solutions to linear equations and inequalities

A variable in an algebraic expression can take on any value. However, when the variable is part of an equation or inequality, the relationship between the expressions on both sides constrains the values that the variable can take on. For instance, the "$x$" in the expression $x + 5$ can take on any value. However, the inequality $x + 5 > 0$ restricts possible values of $x$ to values greater than -5. The solutions of equations or inequalities are the admissible values of the unknown variable that make the equation or inequality true. Thus $x > -5$ is the solution to the inequality $x + 5 > 0$.

**Solves multistep one variable linear equations and inequalities**

To solve an equation or inequality, follow these steps:

**Task 1:** If there are parentheses, use the distributive property to eliminate them.

**Task 2:** If there are fractions, determine their LCD (least common denominator). Multiply every term of the equation by the LCD. This will cancel out all of the fractions while solving the equation or inequality.

**Task 3:** If there are decimals, find the largest decimal. Multiply each term by a power of 10 (10, 100, 1000, etc.) with the same number of zeros as the length of the decimal. This will eliminate all decimals while solving the equation or inequality.

**Task 4:** Combine like terms on each side of the equation or inequality.

**Task 5:** If there are variables on both sides of the equation, add or subtract one of those variable terms to move it to the other side. Combine like terms.

**Task 6:** If there are constants on both sides, add or subtract one of those constants to move it to the other side. Combine like terms.

**Task 7:** If there is a coefficient in front of the variable, divide both sides by this number. This is the answer to an equation. However, remember:

**Dividing or multiplying an inequality by a negative number will reverse the direction of the inequality sign.**

**Task 8:** The solution of a linear equation solves to one single number. The solution of an inequality is always stated including the inequality sign.

*Example: Solve:* $3(2x + 5) - 4x = 5(x + 9)$

| | |
|---|---|
| $6x + 15 - 4x = 5x + 45$ | ref. step 1 |
| $2x + 15 = 5x + 45$ | ref. step 4 |
| $-3x + 15 = 45$ | ref. step 5 |
| $-3x = 30$ | ref. step 6 |

$$x = -10 \qquad \text{ref. step 7}$$

*Example: Solve:* $\frac{1}{2}(5x + 34) = \frac{1}{4}(3x - 5)$

$$\frac{5}{2}x + 17 = \frac{3}{4}x - \frac{5}{4} \qquad \text{ref. step 1}$$

LCD of $\frac{5}{2}$, $\frac{3}{4}$, and $\frac{5}{4}$ is 4.

Multiply by the LCD of 4.

$$4\left(\frac{5}{2}x + 17\right) = \left(\frac{3}{4}x - \frac{5}{4}\right)4 \qquad \text{ref. step 2}$$

$$10x + 68 = 3x - 5$$

$$7x + 68 = -5 \qquad \text{ref. step 5}$$

$$7x + -73 \qquad \text{ref. step 6}$$

$$x = -\frac{73}{7} \text{ or } -10\frac{3}{7} \qquad \text{ref. step 7}$$

Check:

$$\frac{1}{2}\left[5\frac{-13}{7} + 34\right] = \frac{1}{4}\left[3\left(\frac{-13}{7}\right) - \frac{5}{4}\right]$$

$$\frac{1}{2}\left[\frac{-13(5)}{7} + 34\right] = \frac{1}{4}\left[3\left(\frac{-13}{7}\right) - \frac{5}{4}\right]$$

$$\frac{-13(5)}{7} + 17 = \frac{3(-13)}{28} - \frac{5}{4}$$

$$\frac{-13(5) + 17(14)}{14} = \frac{3(-13)}{28} - \frac{5}{4}$$

$$\emptyset -13(5) + 14(14)]2 = \frac{3(-13) - 35}{28}$$

$$\frac{-130 + 476}{28} = \frac{-219 - 35}{28}$$

$$\frac{-254}{28} = \frac{-254}{28}$$

*Example: Solve:* $6x + 21 < 8x + 31.$

$$-2x + 21 < 31 \qquad \text{ref. step 5}$$

$$-2x < 10 \qquad \text{ref. step 6}$$

$$x > -5 \qquad \text{ref. step 7}$$

Note that the inequality sign has changed.

---

### SKILL 4.10 Interprets the solutions of multistep one-variable linear equations and inequalities *(e.g., graphs the solution on a number line, states constraints on a situation)*

When graphing a first-degree equation, solve for the variable. The graph of this solution will be a single point on the number line. There will be no arrows.

When graphing a linear inequality, the dot will be hollow if the inequality sign is $<$ or $>$. If the inequality sign is either $\leq$ or $\geq$, the dot on the graph will be solid. The arrow goes to the right for $\geq$ or $>$. The arrow goes to the left for $\leq$ or $<$.

*Example: Solve $5(x + 2) + 2x = 3(x - 2)$.*

$$5(x + 2) + 2x = 3(x - 2)$$
$$5x + 10 + 2x = 3x - 6$$
$$7x + 10 = 3x - 6$$
$$4x = -16$$
$$x = -4$$

*Example: Solve $2(3x - 7) > 10x - 2$.*

$$2(3x - 7) > 10x - 2$$
$$6x - 14 > 10x - 2$$
$$-4x > 12$$
$$x < -3 \quad \text{Note the change in inequality when dividing by negative numbers.}$$

| SKILL 4.11 | Uses linear relationships represented by equations, tables and graphs to solve problems |
|---|---|

A relationship between two quantities can be represented using a table, a graph, or a written rule. In the following example, the rule $y = 9x$ describes the relationship between the total amount earned, $y$, and the number of pairs of $9 sunglasses sold, $x$.

A table using these data would appear as:

| number of sunglasses sold | 1 | 5 | 10 | 15 |
|---|---|---|---|---|
| total dollars earned | 9 | 45 | 90 | 135 |

Each (*x, y*) relationship between a pair of values is called the **coordinate pair** that can be plotted on a graph. The coordinate pairs (1, 9), (5, 45), (10, 90), and (15, 135) are plotted on the graph below.

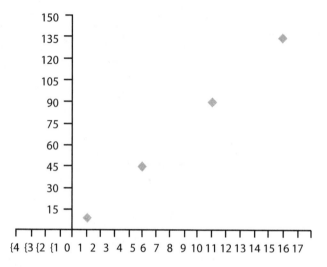

| LINEAR RELATIONSHIP: a relationship in which a fixed change in one quantity results in a fixed change in the other quantity |
| :--- |

The graph above shows a linear relationship. A **LINEAR RELATIONSHIP** between two quantities is a one in which a fixed change in one quantity results in a fixed change in the other quantity. In the example given above, when *x* changes by 5, *y* changes by 9. On a graph, a straight line depicts a linear relationship.

The general form of a linear function is $f(x) = ax + b$ where *a* and *b* are constants. In order to determine the linear function that best models a set of data, we need to figure out *a* and *b*.

*Example: Johnny delivers flyers for ABC Hardware after school. He is paid a weekly salary of $25 plus a 1% commission on any sales resulting from the flyers. The table of data looks like this:*

| Sales, *s* ($) | Earnings, *E(s)* ($) |
| :---: | :---: |
| 100 | 26 |
| 200 | 27 |
| 300 | 28 |
| 400 | 29 |
| 500 | 30 |

The linear function is given by $E(s) = (0.01)s + 25$, where *E(s)* represents total earnings, 0.01 substitutes for *a*, *s* represents sales, and 25 substitutes for *b*.

The following examples use linear relationships to model real life situations.

*Example: The YMCA wants to sell raffle tickets to raise at least $32,000. If it must pay $7,250 in expenses and prizes out of the money collected from the tickets, how many tickets worth $25 each must the YMCA sell?*

Since they want to raise *at least* $32,000, that means they would be happy to get 32,000 *or more*. This requires an inequality.

Let $x$ = number of tickets sold

Then $25x$ = total money collected for $x$ tickets

Total money minus expenses is greater than $32,000:

$$25x - 7,250 \geq 32,000$$
$$25x \geq 39,250$$
$$x \geq 1,570$$

If the YMCA sells *1,570 tickets or more,* they will raise *at least* $32,000.

*Example: The Simpsons went out for dinner. All four of them ordered the aardvark steak dinner. Bert paid for the four meals and included a tip of $12.00 for a total of $84.60. How much was an aardvark steak dinner?*

Let $x$ = the price of one aardvark dinner

So $4x$ = the price of four aardvark dinners

$$4x + 12 = 84.60$$
$$4x = 72.60$$
$$x = \$18.15 \text{ for each dinner}$$

# Knows how to recognize and represent patterns

Mathematics is essentially the study of patterns. Different areas of mathematics study different kinds of patterns and represent then using numbers, symbols and diagrams. The study of patterns is what connects mathematics with other areas of learning such as music and the sciences. Patterns observed in these areas are expressed in the language of math. Humans understand things by identifying patterns. Most importantly, patterns allow us to make predictions and draw conclusions about unknown situations.

SKILL 4.12 **Identifies, extends, describes, or generates number and shape patterns**

Consider the series 1, 1, 2, 3, 5, 8, ....

Inspecting the terms in the series, one finds that every term in the series is a sum of the previous two terms.

Thus, the next term = 5 + 8 = 13.

This particular sequence is a well-known series named the Fibonacci sequence.

Other patterns can be created using algebraic variables. Patterns may also be pictorial. In each case, one can predict subsequent terms or find a missing term by first discovering the rule that governs the pattern.

*Example: Find the next term in the sequence $ax^2y$, $ax^4y^2$, $ax^6y^3$, ....*
Inspecting the pattern we see that this is a geometric sequence with common ratio $x^2y$.

Thus, the next term = $ax^6y^3 \times x^2y = ax^8y^4$.

*Example: Find the next term in the pattern:*

Inspecting the pattern one observes that it has alternating squares and circles that include a number of hearts that increases by two for each subsequent term.

Hence, the next term in the pattern will be as follows:

Sometimes a diagram makes it easier to see the next number in a series. Take the following:

1   3   6   10   15

Organizing the diagram gives:

| | 1st term | 2nd term | 3rd term | 4th term | 5th term | 6th term | $n$th term |
|---|---|---|---|---|---|---|---|
| | | | | | * | | |
| | | | | * | ** | | |
| | | | * | ** | *** | | |
| | | * | ** | *** | **** | | |
| | * | ** | *** | **** | ***** | | |
| Total | 1 | 3 | 6 | 10 | 15 | | |
| # Added: | 1 | 2 | 3 | 4 | 5 | | |

The 6th term will be $1 + 2 + 3 + 4 + 5 + 6 = 21$

The 10th term will be $1 + 2 + 3 + 4 + 5 + 6 + 7 + 8 + 9 + 10 = 55$

The $n$th terms will be $1 + 2 + 3 + 4 + \ldots + n$

**SKILL 4.13** **Makes conjectures, predictions, or generalizations based on patterns**

The following table represents the number of problems Mr. Rodgers is assigning his math students for homework each day, starting with the first day of class.

| Day | 1 | 2 | 3 | 4 | 5 | 6 | 7 | 8 | 9 | 10 | 11 |
|---|---|---|---|---|---|---|---|---|---|---|---|
| Number of Problems | 1 | 1 | 2 | 3 | 5 | 8 | 13 | | | | |

*If Mr. Rodgers continues this pattern, how many problems will he assign on the 11th day?*

If we look for a pattern, it appears that the number of problems assigned each day is equal to the sum of the problems assigned for the previous two days. We test this as follows:

Day 2 = 1 + 0 = 1
Day 3 = 1 + 1 = 2

Day 4 = 2 + 1 = 3
Day 5 = 3 + 2 = 5
Day 6 = 5 + 3 = 8
Day 7 = 8 + 5 = 13

Therefore, Day 8 would correlate to 21 problems; Day 9, 34 problems; Day 10, 55 problems; and Day 11, 89 problems.

A sequence is a pattern of numbers arranged in a particular order. When a list of numbers is arranged in a sequence, the pattern may be expressed in terms of variables. Suppose we have the sequence 8, 12, 16.… If we assign the variable $a$ to the initial term 8 and the variable $d$ to the difference between the first two terms, we can formulate a pattern of $a, a + d, a + 2d, ..., a + (n - 1)d$. With this formula, we can determine any number in the sequence. For example, let's say we want to know what the 400th term would be. Using the formula, we get

$a + (n - 1)d$
$= 8 + (400 - 1)4$
$= 8 + 399(4)$
$= 8 + 1696$
$= 1704$

We have determined that the 400th term would be 1704. This kind of sequence, with a common difference $d$, is known as an arithmetic sequence.

A **RECURRENCE RELATION** is an equation that defines a sequence recursively; in other words, each term of the sequence is defined as a function of the preceding terms.

*Example: You deposit $5,000 in your savings account. Your bank pays 5% interest compounded annually. How much will your account be worth at the end of 10 years?*

Let $V$ represent the amount of money in the account and $V_n$ represent the amount of money after $n$ years. The amount in the account after $n$ years equals the amount in the account after $n - 1$ years plus the interest for the $n$th year. This can be expressed as the recurrence relation $V_0$ where your initial deposit is represented by $V_0 = 5,000$.

$V_0 = V_0$
$V_1 = 1.05V_0$
$V_2 = 1.05V_1 = (1.05)^2V_0$
$V_3 = 1.05V_2 = (1.05)^3V_0$
…
$V_n = (1.05)V_{n-1} = (1.05)^nV_0$

Inserting the values into the equation, you get $V_{10} = (1.05)^{10}(5,000) = 8,144.$

> SKILL **Identifies relationships between the corresponding terms of two**
> 4.14 **numerical patterns** *(e.g., find a rule for a function table)*

*Example: Kepler discovered a relationship between the average distance of a planet from the sun and the time it takes the planet to orbit the sun.*

The following table shows the data for the six planets closest to the sun:

|  | Mercury | Venus | Earth | Mars | Jupiter | Saturn |
|---|---|---|---|---|---|---|
| **Average distance, $x$** | 0.387 | 0.723 | 1 | 1.523 | 5.203 | 9.541 |
| $x^3$ | 0.058 | 0.378 | 1 | 3.533 | 140.852 | 868.524 |
| **Time, $y$** | 0.241 | 0.615 | 1 | 1.881 | 11.861 | 29.457 |
| $y^2$ | 0.058 | 0.378 | 1 | 3.538 | 140.683 | 867.715 |

Looking at the data in the table, we see that $x^3 \approx y^2$. We can conjecture the following function for Kepler's relationship: $y = \sqrt{x^3}$.

*See also Skill 4.11*

# COMPETENCY 005
## GEOMETRY AND MEASUREMENT, DATA, STATISTICS, AND PROBABILITY

## Understands how to classify one-, two-, and three-dimensional figures

Two and three dimensional figures in geometry are classified according to the characteristics of the lines and angles forming them. These characteristics include the number of lines or angles, angle and line size and whether the lines are parallel or perpendicular to each other.

> **SKILL 5.1** Uses definitions to identify lines, rays, line segments, parallel lines, and perpendicular lines

Point, line, and plane are the basic undefined components used to represent geometric figures. Although they are undefined, their properties and characteristics give a clear understanding of what they are.

A **point** indicates place or position. A point has no length, width, or thickness.

&bull;     point *A*
*A*

A **line** is considered a set of points. Lines may be straight or curved, but the term line commonly denotes a straight line. Lines extend indefinitely in both directions.

 line *AB*

*A*      *B*

A **plane** is a set of points composing a flat surface. A plane also has no boundaries.

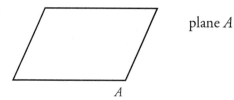 plane *A*

*A*

A **line segment** has two endpoints.

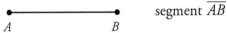

segment $\overline{AB}$

A **ray** has exactly one endpoint. It extends indefinitely in one direction.

ray $\overrightarrow{AB}$

An infinite number of lines can be drawn through any point.

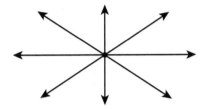

Exactly one line can be drawn through two points.

Two lines intersect at exactly one point. Two lines are **perpendicular** if their intersection forms right angles.

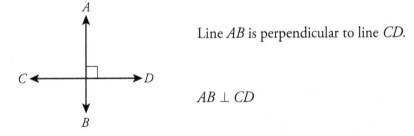

Line *AB* is perpendicular to line *CD*.

$AB \perp CD$

Two lines in the same plane that do not intersect are **parallel**. Parallel lines are everywhere equidistant.

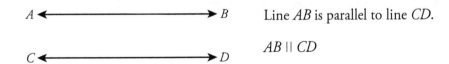

Line *AB* is parallel to line *CD*.

$AB \parallel CD$

## SKILL 5.2 Classifies angles based on their measure

An **angle** is formed by the intersection of two rays.

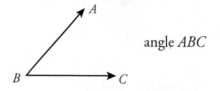

angle *ABC*

Angles are measured in degrees. $1° = \frac{1}{360}$ of a circle.

A **right angle** measures 90°.

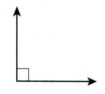

An **acute angle** measures more than 0° and less than 90°.

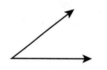

An **obtuse angle** measures more than 90° and less than 180°.

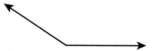

A **straight angle** measures 180°.

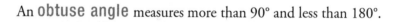

A **reflexive angle** measures more than 180° and less than 360°.

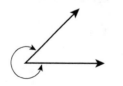

---

**SKILL 5.3** **Composes and decomposes two- and three-dimensional shapes**

*See Skills 5.5, 5.7, and 5.8*

---

**SKILL 5.4** **Uses attributes to classify or draw polygons and solids**

**Polygons**, which are simple, closed **two-dimensional figures** composed of line segments, are named according to the number of sides they have.

A **quadrilateral** is a polygon with four sides.

The sum of the measures of the angles of a quadrilateral is 360°.

A **trapezoid** is a quadrilateral with exactly one pair of parallel sides.

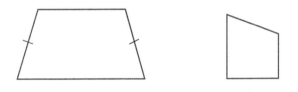

In an **isosceles trapezoid**, the non-parallel sides are congruent.

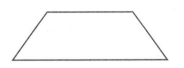

A **parallelogram** is a quadrilateral with two pairs of parallel sides.

In a parallelogram:

- The diagonals bisect each other.

- Each diagonal divides the parallelogram into two congruent triangles.

- Both pairs of opposite sides are congruent.

- Both pairs of opposite angles are congruent.

- Two adjacent angles are supplementary.

A **rectangle** is a parallelogram that contains a right angle.

A **rhombus** is a parallelogram with all sides of equal length.

A **square** is a rectangle with all sides of equal length.

*Example: True or false?*

| | |
|---|---|
| All squares are rhombuses. | True |
| All parallelograms are rectangles. | False. *Some* parallelograms are rectangles. |
| All rectangles are parallelograms. | True |
| Some rhombuses are squares. | True |
| Some rectangles are trapezoids. | False. Trapezoids have only one pair of parallel sides. |
| All quadrilaterals are parallelograms. | False. *Some* quadrilaterals are parallelograms. |
| Some squares are rectangles. | False. *All* squares are rectangles. |
| Some parallelograms are rhombuses. | True |

A **triangle** is a polygon with three sides.

Triangles can be classified by their types of angles or the lengths of their sides.

An **acute triangle** has *exactly three acute* angles.

A **right triangle** has *one right* angle.

An **obtuse triangle** has *one obtuse* angle.

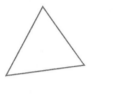  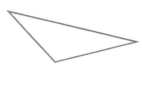

acute                  right                  obtuse

All *three* sides of an **equilateral triangle** are the same length.

*Two* sides of an **isosceles triangle** are the same length.

*None* of the sides of a **scalene triangle** are the same length.

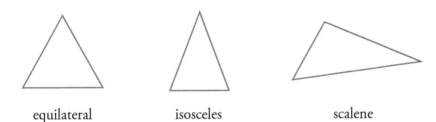

equilateral           isosceles           scalene

*Example: Can a triangle have two right angles?*
No. A right angle measures 90°. Therefore, the sum of two right angles would be 180°, and there could not be third angle (since the sum of the angles of a triangle is 180°).

*Example: Can a triangle have two obtuse angles?*
No. Since an obtuse angle measures more than 90°, the sum of two obtuse angles would be greater than 180°.

A **cylinder** has two congruent circular bases that are parallel.

A **sphere** is a space figure having all its points the same distance from the center.

A **cone** is a space figure having a circular base and a single vertex.

A **pyramid** is a space figure with a square base and 4 triangle-shaped sides.

A **tetrahedron** is a 4-sided space triangle. Each face is a triangle.

A **prism** is a space figure with two congruent, parallel bases that are polygons.

# Knows how to solve problems involving perimeter, area, surface area, and volume

The study of geometry began in ancient times with the practical need to measure land or materials for construction. These needs still exist along with many others in all areas of science and engineering. Calculation of perimeter, area and volume is one of the basic uses of geometry.

## SKILL 5.5 Represents three-dimensional figures with nets

A **NET** is a two-dimensional figure that can be cut out and folded up to make a three-dimensional solid. Below are models of some regular solids with their corresponding face polygons and nets. Nets clearly show the shape and number of faces of a solid.

> **NET:** a two-dimensional figure that can be cut out and folded up to make a three-dimensional solid

| | | | |
|---|---|---|---|
| Cube |  | 6 squares |  |
| Tetrahedron |  | 4 equilateral triangles |  |
| Octahedron |  | 8 equilateral triangles |  |
| Icosahedron |  | 20 equilateral triangles | 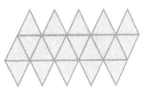 |

Dodecahedron  12 regular
pentagons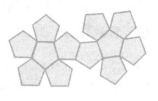

There can be more than one possible net for a particular three-dimensional figure. For instance, here are two more nets for a tetrahedron.

---

**SKILL 5.6** **Uses nets that are made of rectangles and triangles to determine the surface area of three dimensional figures**

---

A net effectively transforms the surface of a three-dimensional figure into a two-dimensional figure. This makes it easy to calculate the surface area.

*Example: A triangular prism has bases that are equilateral triangles of side 1 cm. If the height of the prism is 5 cm, what is the surface area of the prism?*

The net of a triangular prism consists of three rectangles and two triangles.

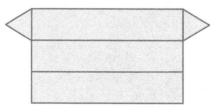

The area of each rectangle $= 1 \text{ cm} \times 5 \text{ cm} = 5 \text{ cm}^2$

The area of each triangle $= \dfrac{\sqrt{3}}{4}(1)^2 = 0.433 \text{ cm}^2$

The total surface area of the prism $= 5 \times 3 + 0.433 \times 2$
$$= 15 + 0.866 = 15.87 \text{ cm}^2$$

*See also Skill 5.8*

The **perimeter** of any polygon is the sum of the lengths of the sides. The **area** of a polygon is the number of square units covered by the figure. In the area formulae below, *b* refers to the base and *h* to the height or altitude of a figure. For a trapezoid, *a* and *b* are the two parallel bases.

> **PERIMETER:** the sum of the lengths of the sides of any polygon

> **AREA:** the number of square units covered by a polygon

| Figure | Area Formula | Perimeter Formula |
|---|---|---|
| Rectangle | $LW$ | $2(L + W)$ |
| Triangle | $\frac{1}{2}bh$ | $a + b + c$ |
| Parallelogram | $bh$ | sum of lengths of sides |
| Trapezoid | $\frac{1}{2}h(a + b)$ | sum of lengths of sides |

*Example: What is the cost of carpeting a rectangular office that measures 12 feet by 15 feet if the carpet costs $12.50 per square yard?*

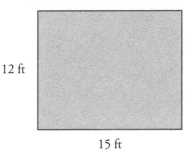

12 ft

15 ft

You first need to determine the area of the office. The area of a rectangle is $A = length \times width$.

Substitute the given values in the equation $A = lw$.

$$A = (12 \text{ ft})(15 \text{ ft})$$
$$A = 180 \text{ ft}^2$$

Now determine the cost of carpeting 180 ft² at $12.50 per square yard.

First, you need to convert 180 ft² into square yards.

$$1 \text{ yd} = 3 \text{ ft}$$
$$(1 \text{ yd})(1 \text{ yd}) = (3 \text{ ft})(3 \text{ ft})$$
$$1 \text{ yd}^2 = 9 \text{ ft}^2$$

Hence, $\frac{180 \text{ ft}^2}{1} \times \frac{1 \text{ yd}^2}{9 \text{ ft}^2} = \frac{20}{1} = 20 \text{ yd}^2$

The carpet costs \$12.50 per square yard; thus the cost of carpeting the office described is \$12.50 × 20 = \$250.00.

*Example: Find the area of a parallelogram with base 6.5 cm and altitude 3.7 cm.*

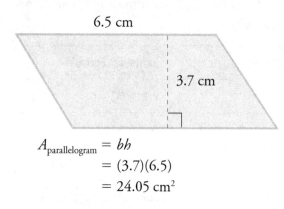

$$A_{\text{parallelogram}} = bh$$
$$= (3.7)(6.5)$$
$$= 24.05 \text{ cm}^2$$

*Example: A farmer has a piece of land shaped as shown below. He wishes to fence this land at an estimated cost of \$25 per linear foot. What is the total cost of fencing this property to the nearest foot?*

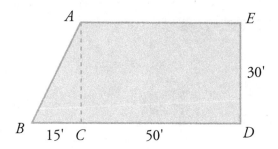

From the right triangle *ABC*, *AC* = 30 and *BC* = 15.

Since $(AB) = (AC)^2 + (BC)^2$, $(AB) = (30)^2 + (15)^2$. So, *AB* is feet, or about 33.5 feet. To the nearest foot, *AB* = 34 feet. The perimeter of the piece of land is
= 34 + 15 + 50 + 30 + 50 = 179 feet

The cost of fencing is \$25 × 179 = \$4,475.00.

### SKILL 5.8 Finds the volume and surface area of right rectangular prisms, including those with fractional edge lengths

For figures such as prisms, the volume and surface areas must be derived by breaking the figure into portions for which these values can be calculated easily. For instance, consider the following figure.

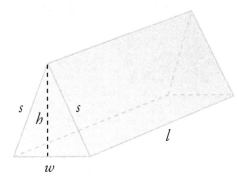

The volume of this figure can be found by calculating the area of the triangular cross section and then multiplying by $l$.

$$V = \tfrac{1}{2}hwl$$

The lateral surface area can be found by adding the areas of each side.

$$S = 2sl + lw$$

Similar reasoning applies to other figures composed of sides that are defined by triangles, quadrilaterals and other planar or linear elements.

*Example: What is the volume of a shoe box with a length of 35 cm, a width of 20 cm, and a height of 15 cm?*

Volume of a rectangular solid
$$= \text{length} \times \text{width} \times \text{height}$$
$$= 35 \times 20 \times 15$$
$$= 10{,}500 \text{ cm}^3$$

*See also Skill 5.6*

### SKILL 5.9  Determines how changes to dimensions change area and volume

Two figures that have the same shape are similar. Corresponding parts of similar polygons are proportional.

*Example: Given the rectangles below, compare their areas and perimeters.*

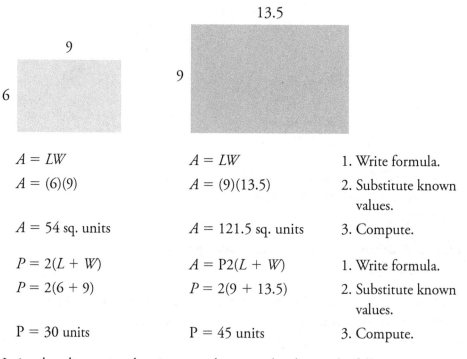

| | | |
|---|---|---|
| $A = LW$ | $A = LW$ | 1. Write formula. |
| $A = (6)(9)$ | $A = (9)(13.5)$ | 2. Substitute known values. |
| $A = 54$ sq. units | $A = 121.5$ sq. units | 3. Compute. |
| $P = 2(L + W)$ | $A = P2(L + W)$ | 1. Write formula. |
| $P = 2(6 + 9)$ | $P = 2(9 + 13.5)$ | 2. Substitute known values. |
| $P = 30$ units | $P = 45$ units | 3. Compute. |

Notice that the areas and perimeters relate to each other in the following manner:

Ratio of sides: $\frac{9}{13.5} = \frac{2}{3}$

Ratio of perimeters: $\frac{30}{45} = \frac{2}{3}$

Ratio of areas: $\frac{54}{121.5} = 0.4444 = \frac{4}{9} = \left(\frac{2}{3}\right)^2$

In general, when the dimensions of two polygons are in the proportion $a{:}b$,

The ratio of perimeters $= a{:}b$

The ratio of areas $= a^2{:}b^2$

Similar solids also share the same shape but are not necessarily the same size. The ratio of any two corresponding measurements of similar solids is the scale factor. For example, the scale factor for two square pyramids, one with a side measuring 2 inches and the other with a side measuring 4 inches, is 2:4.

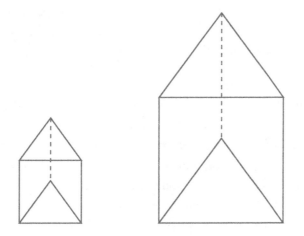

The base perimeters, the surface areas, and the volumes of similar solids are directly related to the scale factor. If the scale factor of two similar solids is $a:b$, then:

The ratio of base perimeters $= a:b$

The ratio of areas $= a^2:b^2$

The ratio of volumes $= a^3:b^3$

Thus, for the above example,

The ratio of base perimeters is 2:4.

The ratio of areas is $2^2:4^2 = 4:16$.

The ratio of volumes is $2^3:4^3 = 8:64$.

*Example: What happens to the volume of a square pyramid when the lengths of the sides of the base are doubled?*

Scale factor $= a:b = 1:2$

Ratio of volume $= 1^3:2^3 = 1:8$

(The volume is increased by a factor of 8.)

## Knows the components of the coordinate plane and how to graph ordered pairs on the plane

We can represent any two-dimensional geometric figure in the Cartesian or rectangular coordinate system. The Cartesian or rectangular coordinate system is formed by two perpendicular axes (coordinate axes): the $x$-axis and the $y$-axis. If we know the dimensions of a two-dimensional, or planar, figure, we can use this coordinate system to visualize the shape of the figure and use algebraic methods to solve geometry problems.

### SKILL 5.10 Identifies the *x*-axis, the *y*-axis, the origin, and the four quadrants in the coordinate plane

**COORDINATE PLANE:** a plane with a point selected as an origin, some length selected as a unit of distance, and two perpendicular lines that intersect at the origin, with positive and negative direction selected on each line

A **COORDINATE PLANE** is a plane with a point selected as an origin, some length selected as a unit of distance, and two perpendicular lines that intersect at the origin, with positive and negative direction selected on each line. Traditionally, the lines are called *x* (drawn from left to right, with positive direction to the right of the origin) and *y* (drawn from bottom to top, with positive direction upward of the origin). The coordinates of a point are determined by the distance of the point from these lines, and the signs of the coordinates are assigned by determining whether the point is in the positive or negative direction from the origin. The standard coordinate plane consists of a plane divided into four quadrants by the intersection of two axes, the *x*-axis (horizontal axis) and the *y*-axis (vertical axis).

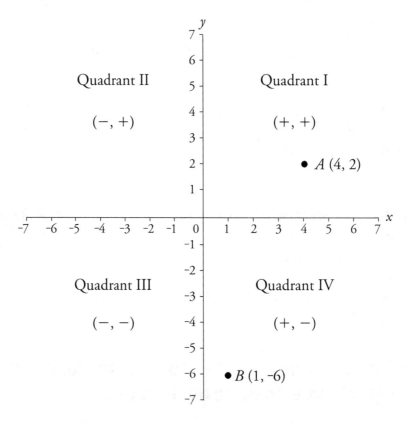

The coordinates (*x*, *y*) of a point refer to the unique ordered pair of numbers that identifies the point on the coordinate plane. The first number in the ordered pair identifies the position of the point with regard to the *x*-axis, and the second number identifies the point's position with regard to the *y*-axis.

In the coordinate plane shown above, point *A* is given by the ordered pair (4, 2), and point *B* is given by the ordered pair (1, -6).

**SKILL Solves problems by plotting points and drawing polygons in the**
**5.11 coordinate plane**

We can represent any two-dimensional geometric figure in the Cartesian or rectangular coordinate system. The Cartesian or rectangular coordinate system is formed by two perpendicular axes (coordinate axes): the *X*-axis and the *Y*-axis. If we know the dimensions of a two-dimensional, or planar, figure, we can use this coordinate system to visualize the shape of the figure.

*Example: Represent an isosceles triangle with two sides of length 4 on the coordinate plane.*

Draw the two sides along the *x*- and *y*- axes and connect the points (vertices).

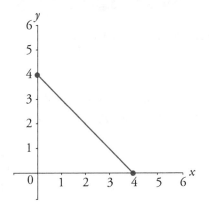

The distance between points $(x_1, y_1)$ and $(x_2, y_2)$ on the coordinate plane is given by the distance formula

$$D = \sqrt{(x_2 - x_1)^2 + (y_2 - y_1)^2}$$

*Example: Find the perimeter of a figure with vertices at (4, 5), (-4, 6) and (-5, -8).*
The figure being described is a triangle. Therefore, the distance for all three sides must be found. Carefully, identify all three sides before beginning.

Side 1 = (4, 5) to (-4, 6)
Side 2 = (-4, 6) to (-5, -8)
Side 3 = (-5, -8) to (4, 5)

$$D_1 = \sqrt{(-4 - 4)^2 + (6 - 5)^2} = \sqrt{65}$$

$$D_2 = \sqrt{((-5 - (-4))^2 + (-8 - 6)^2} = \sqrt{197}$$

$$D_3 = \sqrt{((4 - (-5))^2 + (5 - (-8))^2} = \sqrt{250} \text{ or } 5\sqrt{10}$$

$$\text{Perimeter} = \sqrt{65} + \sqrt{197} + 5\sqrt{10}$$

# Knows how to solve problems involving measurement

Solving measurement problems requires familiarity with units. Commonly used units belong to two different systems, the metric system and the United States customary system. Within each system there are many different units for different quantities such as mass and length. Each type of quantity also has several units within the same system. It is important, therefore, that students know how to convert between units within the same system and between systems.

> **SKILL 5.12** Solves problems involving elapsed time, money, volume, and mass

The most common measurement problems in everyday life involve time, money, volume and mass.

*Example: The winner of a race spent 1 hr 58 min 12 sec on the first half of the race and 2 hr 9 min 57 sec on the second half of the race. How much time did the entire race take?*

$$
\begin{array}{lll}
 & 1 \text{ hr} & 58 \text{ min} & 12 \text{ sec} \\
+ & 2 \text{ hr} & 9 \text{ min} & 57 \text{ sec} \\
\hline
 & 3 \text{ hr} & 67 \text{ min} & 69 \text{ sec} \\
+ & 0 \text{ hr} & 1 \text{ min} & -60 \text{ sec} \\
\hline
 & 3 \text{ hr} & 68 \text{ min} & 9 \text{ sec}
\end{array}
$$

Add these numbers.

Change 60 seconds to 1 minute.

$$
\begin{array}{lll}
 & 3 \text{ hr} & 68 \text{ min} & 9 \text{ sec} \\
+ & 1 \text{ hr} & -60 \text{ min} & 0 \text{ sec} \\
\hline
 & 4 \text{ hr} & 8 \text{ min} & 9 \text{ sec}
\end{array}
$$

Change 60 minutes to 1 hour.

The entire race took 4 hr 8 min 9 sec.

*Example: Kathy has a bag of potatoes that weighs 5 lb 10 oz. She uses one third of the bag to make mashed potatoes. How much does the bag weigh now?*

1 lb = 16 oz

5(16 oz) + 10 oz

= 80 oz + 10 oz = 90 oz (original weight)

$90 - \left(\frac{1}{3}\right)90$ oz

= 90 oz − 30 oz

= 60 oz

60 ÷ 16 = 3.75 lb

The bag weighs 60 oz, or 3.75 lb.

*See also Skills 3.7b and 5.15*

## SKILL 5.13  Measures and compares lengths of objects using standard tools

Any measurement obtained with a measuring device is approximate. Variations in measurement are defined in terms of precision and accuracy. The precision of a measuring device is the smallest fractional or decimal division on the instrument. The smaller the unit or fraction of a unit on the measuring device, the more precisely it can measure. Accuracy is a measure of how close the result of measurement comes to the "true" value. In the game of darts, the true value is the bull's eye. If three darts are tossed and each lands on the bull's eye, the dart thrower is both precise (all land near the same spot) and accurate (the darts all land on the "true" value).

The tool chosen for measurement will depend on the purpose of measurement and the degree of precision needed. For example, to measure the length of a room for carpeting, it may be sufficient to measure the length to the nearest centimeter. The length of a memory card inserted into a tablet, on the other hand, may need to be accurate to the tenth of a millimeter. For more precise measurements it is necessary to use tools with smaller fractional or decimal divisions.

The number of decimal points used to express a measurement indicates its precision. If the length of a pencil is given as 6.0 cm, the measurement precision is 0.1 cm. If, instead, the measurement is written as 6.00 cm, it indicates that the degree of precision is higher at 0.01 cm.

When the lengths of two objects are compared, it is important that both the lengths are measured to the same precision. For example, saying that a book of length 10.14 inches is longer than another book of length 10.1 inches is incorrect since the length of the second book has been measured to a lower precision. However, it would be correct to say that a book of length 10.14 inches is longer than a book of length 10.10 inches.

> ### SKILL 5.14 Knows relative sizes of United States customary units and metric units
>
> *See Skill 5.15*

> ### SKILL 5.15 Converts units within both the United States customary system and the metric system

There are many methods for converting measurements among various units within a system or between systems. One method is multiplication of the given measurement by a conversion factor. This conversion factor is the following ratio, which is always equal to unity.

$$\frac{\text{new units}}{\text{old units}} \quad \text{OR} \quad \frac{\text{what you want}}{\text{what you have}}$$

The fundamental feature of unit analysis or dimensional analysis is that conversion factors can be multiplied together and units can be cancelled in the same way as numerators and denominators of numerical fractions. The following examples help clarify this point.

*Example: Convert 3 miles to yards.*

Multiply the initial measurement by the conversion factor, cancel the mile units, and solve:

$$\frac{3 \text{ miles}}{1} \times \frac{1{,}760 \text{ yards}}{1 \text{ mile}} = 5{,}280 \text{ yards}$$

*Example: It takes Cynthia 45 minutes to get ready each morning. How many hours does she spend getting ready each week?*

Multiply the initial measurement by the conversion factors from minutes to hours and from days to weeks, then cancel the minute and day units and solve:

$$\frac{45 \text{ min}}{1 \text{ day}} \times \frac{1 \text{ hour}}{60 \text{ min}} \times \frac{7 \text{ days}}{1 \text{ week}} = 5.25 \frac{\text{hours}}{\text{week}}$$

Conversion factors for different types of units are listed below:

| MEASUREMENTS OF LENGTH (ENGLISH SYSTEM) | | |
|---:|:---:|:---|
| 12 inches (in) | = | 1 foot (ft) |
| 3 feet (ft) | = | 1 yard (yd) |
| 1760 yards (yd) | = | 1 mile (mi) |

| MEASUREMENTS OF LENGTH (METRIC SYSTEM) | | |
|---|---|---|
| Kilometer (km) | = | 1000 meters (m) |
| Hectometer (hm) | = | 100 meters (m) |
| Decameter (dam) | = | 10 meters (m) |
| Meter (m) | = | 1 meter (m) |
| Decimeter (dm) | = | 1/10 meter (m) |
| Centimeter (cm) | = | 1/100 meter (m) |
| Millimeter (mm) | = | 1/1000 meter (m) |

| CONVERSION OF LENGTH FROM ENGLISH TO METRIC | | |
|---|---|---|
| 1 inch | = | 2.54 centimeters |
| 1 foot | ≈ | 30.48 centimeters |
| 1 yard | ≈ | 0.91 meters |
| 1 mile | ≈ | 1.61 kilometers |

| MEASUREMENTS OF WEIGHT (METRIC SYSTEM) | | |
|---|---|---|
| kilogram (kg) | = | 1000 grams (g) |
| gram (g) | = | 1 gram (g) |
| milligram (mg) | = | 1/1000 gram (g) |

| CONVERSION OF WEIGHT FROM METRIC TO ENGLISH | | |
|---|---|---|
| 28.35 grams (g) | = | 1 ounce (oz) |
| 16 ounces (oz) | = | 1 pound (lb) |
| 2000 pounds (lb) | = | 1 ton (t) (short ton) |
| 1.1 ton (t) | = | 1 metric ton (t) |

| CONVERSION OF WEIGHT FROM ENGLISH TO METRIC | | |
|---|:---:|---|
| 1 ounce | ≈ | 28.35 grams |
| 1 pound | ≈ | 0.454 kilogram |
| 1.1 ton | = | 1 metric ton |

| MEASUREMENT OF VOLUME (ENGLISH SYSTEM) | | |
|---|:---:|---|
| 8 fluid ounces (oz) | = | 1 cup (c) |
| 2 cups (c) | = | 1 pint (pt) |
| 2 pints (pt) | = | 1 quart (qt) |
| 4 quarts (qt) | = | 1 gallon (gal) |

| MEASUREMENT OF VOLUME (METRIC SYSTEM) | | |
|---|:---:|---|
| Kiloliter (kl) | = | 1000 liters (l) |
| Liter (l) | = | 1 liter (l) |
| Milliliter (ml) | = | 1/1000 liter (ml) |

| CONVERSION OF VOLUME FROM ENGLISH TO METRIC | | |
|---|:---:|---|
| 1 teaspoon (tsp) | ≈ | 5 milliliters |
| 1 fluid ounce | ≈ | 29.57 milliliters |
| 1 cup | ≈ | 0.24 liters |
| 1 pint | ≈ | 0.47 liters |
| 1 quart | ≈ | 0.95 liters |
| 1 gallon | ≈ | 3.8 liters |

*Note: ( ' ) represents feet and ( " ) represents inches.*

*Example: Convert 8,750 meters to kilometers.*

$$\frac{8{,}750 \text{ meters}}{1} \times \frac{1 \text{ kilometer}}{1{,}000 \text{ meters}} = 8.75 \text{ km}$$

*Example: A car skidded 170 yards on an icy road before coming to a stop. How long is the skid distance in kilometers?*

Since 1 yard $\approx$ 0.9 meters, multiply 170 yards by $\frac{0.9 \text{ meters}}{1 \text{ yard}}$.

Since 1000 meters $=$ 1 kilometer, multiply 153 meters by $\frac{1 \text{ kilometer}}{1000 \text{ meters}}$.

$$153 \text{ m} \times \frac{1 \text{ km}}{1000 \text{ m}} = 0.153 \text{ km}$$

*Example: If the temperature is 90°F, what is it expressed in Celsius units?*

To convert between Celsius (C) and Fahrenheit (F), use the following formula.

$$\frac{°C}{5} = \frac{°F - 32}{9}$$

If F $=$ 90°, then C $= 5\frac{(90 - 32)}{9} = \frac{5 \times 58}{9} = 32.2°$.

*Example: A map shows a scale of 1 inch $=$ 2 miles. Convert this scale to a numerical ratio so that any unit system (such as metric) can be used to measure distances.*

The scale is a ratio—1 inch : 2 miles. If either value is converted so that the two values have the same units, then this scale can be converted to a purely numerical ratio. To avoid fractions, convert miles to inches.

$$2 \text{ mi} = 2 \text{ mi} \times \frac{5{,}280 \text{ ft}}{1 \text{ mi}} \times \frac{12 \text{ in}}{1 \text{ ft}} = 126{,}720 \text{ in}$$

The ratio is then 1:126,720.

# Is familiar with basic statistical concepts

Statistics are cited almost invariably, in one form or another, in studies and publications that seek to prove a point about people, animals, food, drugs, or any number of other subjects. Using summary statistics and graphs appropriately to support conclusions and predictions is a crucial skill to this end.

## SKILL 5.16 Identifies statistical questions

Statistics identifies the patterns in a set of data and uses certain measures to describe characteristics of the data set and draw conclusions about the information it contains.

**MEDIAN:** the middle of a data set

**MODE:** the value that appears the most often in a data set

**RANGE:** the difference between the highest and lowest values in a data set

**VARIANCE:** the average squared distance from each value of a data set to the mean

Center and spread are the two main concepts that describe the characteristics of a data set. Measures of central tendency define the center of a data set, and measures of dispersion define the amount of spread.

The most common measures of central tendency are mean, median and mode. MEAN is the average value of a data set, MEDIAN is the middle value of a data set, and MODE is the value that appears the most often in a data set.

The most common measures of spread are range, variance, and standard deviation. RANGE is the difference between the highest and lowest values in a data set. The VARIANCE is the average squared distance from each value of a data set to the mean. The standard deviation is the square root of the variance. A data set clustered around the center has a small variance and small standard deviation, while a disperse data set with many gaps has a large variance and large standard deviation.

> **SKILL 5.17** Solves problems involving measures of center (mean, median, mode) and range

The arithmetic mean (or average) of a set of numbers is the sum of the numbers divided by the number of items being averaged.

*Example: Find the mean and range of the following data values. Round to the nearest tenth.*

$$24.6 \quad 57.3 \quad 44.1 \quad 39.8 \quad 64.5$$

Mean = 230.3 ÷ 5 = 46.06, which is rounded to 46.1.

The range is the difference between the highest and lowest data values.

Range = 64.5 − 24.6 = 39.9

The median of a set of data is the middle number when the data values are arranged in order. If there is an even number of data values, the median is the mean of the two middle values.

*Example: Find the median of the data values.*

$$12 \quad 14 \quad 27 \quad 3 \quad 13 \quad 7 \quad 17 \quad 12 \quad 22 \quad 6 \quad 16$$

Rearrange the terms from smallest to largest.

$$3 \quad 6 \quad 7 \quad 12 \quad 12 \quad 13 \quad 14 \quad 16 \quad 17 \quad 22 \quad 27$$

Since there are 11 numbers, the middle number is the sixth number, or 13.

The **mode** of a set of numbers is the number that occurs with the greatest frequency. A set can have no mode if each term appears exactly one time. Similarly, a set can have more than one mode.

*Example: Find the mode of the data set.*

26   15   37   26   35   26   15

The number 26 appears three times; therefore, the mode is 26.

*Example: Find the mean, median, and mode of the test scores listed below:*

| 85 | 77 | 65 |
|----|----|----|
| 92 | 90 | 54 |
| 88 | 85 | 70 |
| 75 | 80 | 69 |
| 85 | 88 | 60 |
| 72 | 74 | 95 |

Mean: sum of all scores ÷ number of scores = 78

Median: Put the numbers in order from smallest to largest. Pick the middle number.

54 60 65 69 70 72 74 75 77 80 85 85 85 88 88 90 92 95

Both values are in the middle.

Therefore, median is average of two numbers in the middle, or 78.5. The mode, or most frequent number is 85.

---

SKILL 5.18 **Recognizes which measure of center best describes a set of data**

Different situations require different information. The mean is the most descriptive value for tightly-clustered data with few outliers. Outlier data, which are values in a data set that are unusually high or low, can greatly distort the mean of a data set. Median, on the other hand, may better describe widely dispersed data and data sets with outliers because outliers and dispersion have little effect on the median value.

If we examine the circumstances under which an ice cream store owner may use statistics collected in the store, we find different uses for different information. Over a 7-day period, the store owner collected data on the ice cream flavors sold. He found the mean number of scoops sold was 174 per day. The most frequently sold flavor was vanilla. This information was useful in determining how much ice cream to order in all and in what amounts for each flavor. In the case of the ice cream store, the median and range had little business value for the owner.

Retail store owners may be most concerned with the most common dress size so they may order more of that size than any other.

Consider the set of test scores from a math class: 0, 16, 19, 65, 65, 65, 68, 69, 70, 72, 73, 73, 75, 78, 80, 85, 88, and 92. The mean is 64.06 and the median is 71. Since there are only three scores less than the mean out of the eighteen scores, the median (71) would be a more descriptive score.

## SKILL 5.19 Determines how change in data affect measures of center or range

Changes to a data set may or may not affect measures of center and range.

Measures of center will increase or decrease if the data values, on the average, increase or decrease. If a data set is modified by adding both high and low values, though, the measures of central tendency may remain unchanged. For example, the data sets (1,2,3,4,5) and (0,1,2,3,4,5,6) both have the same mean and median values. The data set (2,3,4,5,6), on the other hand, has higher mean and median values than the data set (1,2,3,4,5).

The changes to the data sets in the two examples given above have the opposite effect on the range. Adding higher and lower values increases the range. Thus, the data set (1,2,3,4,5) has a range of 4 whereas the data set (0,1,2,3,4,5,6) has a range of 6. Increasing every value in the data set by 1 leaves the range unchanged. Thus the data set (2,3,4,5,6) has the same range as the data set (1,2,3,4,5).

## SKILL 5.20 Describes a set of data (e.g., overall patterns, outliers)

*See Skills 5.16, 5.17, 5.18, 5.21, and 5.22*

# Knows how to represent and interpret data presented in various forms

A visual is a compact way to present information contained in a large data set. It is also easier to grasp the essential characteristics of a data set when it is presented as a graph or diagram of some sort.

| SKILL 5.21 | **Interprets various displays of data** *(e.g., box plots, histograms, scatterplots)* |

An **INFERENCE** is a statement that is derived from reasoning. When reading a graph, inferences help us to interpret the data that is being presented. Using these interpretations, we can form conclusions and make predictions based on the data.

> **INFERENCE:** a statement that is derived from reasoning

A **trend line** on a line graph, for instance, shows the correlation between two sets of data. A trend may show positive correlation (both sets of data values increase together), negative correlation (one set of data values increases as the other decreases), or no correlation.

*Example: Katherine and Tom were both doing poorly in math class. Their teacher had a conference with each of them in November. The following graph shows their math test scores during the school year.*

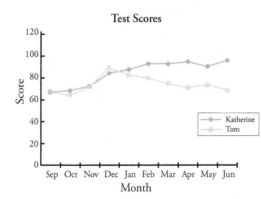

This graph shows that there is a positive trend in Katherine's test scores and a negative trend in Tom's test scores.

We can infer that Katherine's test scores rose steadily after November. Tom's test scores spiked in December but then began to fall again, showing a negative trend after December.

We can conclude that Katherine took her teacher's meeting seriously and began to study in order to do better on the exams. It seems as though Tom tried harder for a bit, but his test scores eventually slipped back down to the level at which he began.

*See also Skill 5.22*

> **SKILL Identifies, constructs, and completes graphs that correctly represent 5.22 given data** *(e.g., circle graphs, bar graphs, line graphs, histograms, scatterplots, double bar graphs, double line graphs, box plots, and line plots/dot plots)*

There are many graphical ways in which to represent data, such as line plots, line graphs, scatter plots, stem and leaf plots, histograms, bar graphs, pie charts, and pictographs.

A **line plot** organizes data in numerical order along a number line. An x is placed above the number line for each occurrence of the corresponding number. Line plots allow viewers to see at a glance a range of data and where typical and atypical data falls. These plots are generally used to summarize relatively small sets of data.

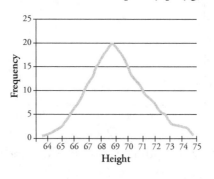

A **line graph** compares two variables, and each variable is plotted along an axis. A line graph highlights trends by drawing connecting lines between data points. This representation is particularly appropriate for data that varies continuously. Line graphs are sometimes referred to as frequency polygons.

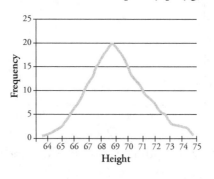

**Bar graphs** are similar to histograms. However, bar graphs are often used to convey information about categorical data where the horizontal scale represents a non-numeric attributes such as cities or years. Another difference is that the bars in bar graphs rarely touch. Bar graphs are also useful in comparing data about two or more similar groups of items.

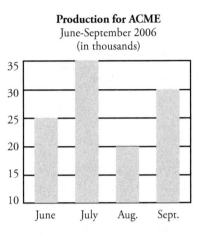

**Production for ACME**
June-September 2006
(in thousands)

A **pie chart**, also known as a **circle graph**, is used to represent relative amounts of a whole.

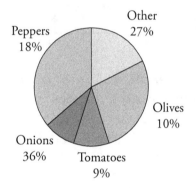

**Scatter plots** compare two characteristics of the same group of things or people and usually consist of a large body of data. They show how much one variable is affected by another. The relationship between the two variables is their **correlation**. The closer the data points come to making a straight line when plotted, the closer the correlation.

**Stem and leaf plots** are visually similar to line plots. The **stems** are the digits in the greatest place value of the data values, and the **leaves** are the digits in the next greatest place values. Stem and leaf plots are best suited for small sets of data and are especially useful for comparing two sets of data. The following is an example using test scores:

| 4 | 9 |
| 5 | 4 9 |
| 6 | 1 2 3 4 6 7 8 8 |
| 7 | 0 3 4 6 6 6 7 7 7 7 8 8 8 8 |
| 8 | 3 5 5 7 8 |
| 9 | 0 0 3 4 5 |
| 10 | 0 0 |

A **box-and-whisker plot** displays five statistics: a minimum and maximum score (neither of which should be considered outliers) and three quartiles. The box is composed of the first quartile, the median (or second quartile) and the third quartile, as shown in the example below. The (non-outlier) minimum and maximum values are shown at the end of the "whiskers" attached to the box.

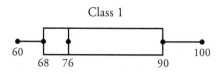

Class 1

The above box-and-whisker example summarizes the scores on a mathematics test for the students in Class I. It indicates that the lowest score is 60 and the highest score is 100. Twenty-five percent of the class scored 68 or lower (the first quartile), 50% scored 76 or lower (the second quartile), and 25% scored 90 or higher (the third quartile).

Box-and-whisker plots help relate the measures of central tendency to data outliers, clusters, and gaps. Consider the hypothetical box-and-whisker plot given below, with one outlier value on each end of the distribution.

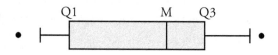

Note that the beginning of the box is the value of the first quartile of the data set, and the end of the box is the value of the third quartile. We represent the median as a vertical line in the box. The "whiskers" extend to the last point that is not an outlier. The points beyond the figure represent outlier values.

**Histograms** are used to summarize information from large sets of data that can be naturally grouped into intervals. The vertical axis indicates **frequency** (the number of times any particular data value occurs), and the horizontal axis indicates data values or ranges of data values. The number of data values in any interval is the **frequency of the interval**.

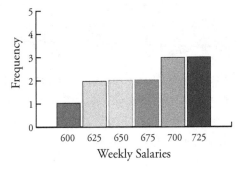

A **pictograph** uses small figures or icons to represent data. Pictographs are used to summarize relative amounts, trends, and data sets, and they are useful in comparing quantities.

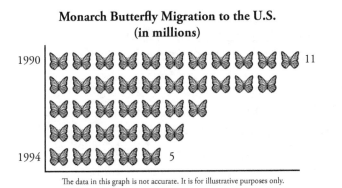

**Monarch Butterfly Migration to the U.S.**
**(in millions)**

The data in this graph is not accurate. It is for illustrative purposes only.

---

**SKILL 5.23**  **Chooses appropriate graphs to display data**

*See Skill 5.22*

## Is familiar with how to interpret the probability of events

Probability assigns a number to the likelihood of an event occurring. An event with no chance of occurring has probability zero whereas an event that will definitely occur has a probability of 1. All other events can be assigned a probability in the intermediate range.

### SKILL 5.24  Interprets probabilities relative to likelihood of occurrence

In the study of probability, the **sample space** is a list of all possible outcomes of an experiment. For example, the sample space of tossing two coins is the set {HH, HT, TT, TH}, the sample space of rolling a six-sided die is the set {1, 2, 3, 4, 5, 6}, and the sample space of measuring the height of students in a class is the set of all real numbers {R}. **Probability** measures the chance of an event occurring. The probability of an event that *must* occur, or a *certain event,* is **1**. The probability of an impossible event (there is no "favorable outcome") is **0**.

$$P(\text{event}) = \frac{\text{number of favorable outcomes}}{\text{number of possible outcomes}}$$

*Example: A fair die is rolled.*
  *a) Find the probability of rolling an even number*
  *b) Find the probability of rolling a number less than 3.*

a)  The sample space is

  $S = \{1, 2, 3, 4, 5, 6\}$

  and the event "roll an even number" is

  $E = \{2, 4, 6\}$

  Hence, the probability of rolling an even number is
  $P(E) = \frac{n(E)}{n(S)} = \frac{3}{6} = \frac{1}{2}$

b)  The event of rolling a number less than 3 is represented by

  $A = \{1, 2\}$

  Hence, the probability of rolling a number less than 3 is
  $P(A) = \frac{n(A)}{n(S)} = \frac{2}{6} = \frac{1}{3}$

*Example: The results of a survey of 47 students are summarized in the table below.*

|  | Black Hair | Blonde Hair | Red Hair | Total |
|---|---|---|---|---|
| Male | 10 | 8 | 6 | 24 |
| Female | 6 | 12 | 5 | 23 |
| Total | 16 | 20 | 11 | 47 |

Use the table to answer the following questions.

a) If one student is selected at random, find the probability of selecting a male student.

$$\frac{\text{Number of male students}}{\text{Number of students}} = \frac{24}{47}$$

b) If one student is selected at random, find the probability of selecting a female with red hair.

$$\frac{\text{Number of red hair females}}{\text{Number of students}} = \frac{5}{47}$$

c) If one student is selected at random, find the probability of selecting a student who does not have red hair.

$$\frac{\text{Red hair students}}{\text{Number of students}} = \frac{11}{47}$$

Probability of selecting a student without red hair $= 1 - \frac{11}{47} = \frac{36}{47}$

# DOMAIN III

## SOCIAL STUDIES (5004)

# PERSONALIZED STUDY PLAN

| PAGE | COMPETENCY AND SKILL | KNOWN MATERIAL/ SKIP IT | BRIEFLY REVIEW eSTICKYNOTES | MAKE eFLASHCARDS | TAKE ADDITIONAL SAMPLE TESTS |
|---|---|---|---|---|---|
| 165 | **006: United States history, government, and citizenship** | ☐ | ☐ | ☐ | ☐ |
| | 6.1: Knows European exploration and colonization in United States history and growth and expansion of the United States | ☐ | ☐ | ☐ | ☐ |
| | 6.2: Knows about the American Revolution and the founding of the nation in United States history | ☐ | ☐ | ☐ | ☐ |
| | 6.3: Knows the major events and developments in United States history from founding to present (e.g., westward expansion, industrialization, Great Depression) | ☐ | ☐ | ☐ | ☐ |
| | 6.4: Knows about twentieth-century developments and transformations in the United States (e.g., assembly line, space age) | ☐ | ☐ | ☐ | ☐ |
| | 6.5: Understands connections between causes and effects of events | ☐ | ☐ | ☐ | ☐ |
| | 6.6: Understands the nature, purpose, and forms (e.g., federal, state, local) of government | ☐ | ☐ | ☐ | ☐ |
| | 6.7: Knows key documents and speeches in the history of the United States (e.g., United States Constitution, Declaration of Independence, Gettysburg Address) | ☐ | ☐ | ☐ | ☐ |
| | 6.8: Knows the rights and responsibilities of citizenship in a democracy | ☐ | ☐ | ☐ | ☐ |
| 201 | **007: Geography, anthropology, and sociology** | ☐ | ☐ | ☐ | ☐ |
| | 7.1: Knows world and regional geography (e.g., spatial terms, places, and regions) | ☐ | ☐ | ☐ | ☐ |
| | 7.2: Understands the interaction of physical and human systems (e.g., how humans change the environment, how the environment changes humans, importance of natural and human resources) | ☐ | ☐ | ☐ | ☐ |
| | 7.3: Knows the uses of geography (e.g., apply geography to interpret past, to interpret present, to plan for future) | ☐ | ☐ | ☐ | ☐ |
| | 7.4: Knows how people of different cultural backgrounds interact with their environment, family, neighborhoods, and communities | ☐ | ☐ | ☐ | ☐ |
| 213 | **008: World history and economics** | ☐ | ☐ | ☐ | ☐ |
| | 8.1: Knows the major contributions of classical civilizations (e.g., Egypt, Greece, Rome) | ☐ | ☐ | ☐ | ☐ |
| | 8.2: Understands twentieth-century developments and transformations in world history | ☐ | ☐ | ☐ | ☐ |
| | 8.3: Understands the role of cross-cultural comparisons in world history instruction | ☐ | ☐ | ☐ | ☐ |
| | 8.4: Knows key terms and basic concepts of economics (e.g., supply and demand, scarcity and choice, money and resources) | ☐ | ☐ | ☐ | ☐ |
| | 8.5: Understands how economics affects population, resources, and technology | ☐ | ☐ | ☐ | ☐ |
| | 8.6: Understands the government's role in economics and impact of economics on government | ☐ | ☐ | ☐ | ☐ |

# COMPETENCY 006
## UNITED STATES HISTORY, GOVERNMENT, AND CITIZENSHIP

> **SKILL 6.1** **Knows European exploration and colonization in United States history and growth and expansion of the United States**

Colonists from England, France, Holland, Sweden, and Spain all settled in North America on lands once frequented by Native Americans. Spanish colonies were mainly in the south, French colonies were mainly in the extreme north and in the middle of the continent, and the rest of the European colonies were in the northeast and along the Atlantic coast. These colonists got along with their new neighbors with varying degrees of success.

The French colonists seemed the most willing to work with the Native Americans. Even though their pursuit of animals to fill the growing demand for the fur trade was overpowering, they managed to find a way to maintain a relative peace with their new neighbors; the French and Native Americans even fought on the same side of the war against England. The Dutch and Swedish colonists were interested mostly in surviving in their new homes. However, they didn't last long in their struggles against England.

The English and Spanish colonists had the worst relations with the Native Americans, mainly because the Europeans made a habit of taking land, signing and then breaking treaties, massacring, and otherwise abusing their new neighbors. The Native Americans were only too happy to share their agriculture and jewelry-making secrets with the Europeans; what they got in return was grief and deceit. The term Manifest Destiny meant nothing to the Native Americans, who believed that they lived on land loaned to them by the gods above.

The colonies were generally divided into three regions: New England, Middle Atlantic, and Southern. The culture of each region was distinct and affected attitudes, ideas about politics, religion, and economic activities. The geography of each region also contributed to the colonies' unique characteristics.

## The New England Colonies

The **NEW ENGLAND COLONIES** consisted of Massachusetts, Rhode Island, Connecticut, and New Hampshire. Life in these colonies was centered on the

> **NEW ENGLAND COLONIES:** consisted of Massachusetts, Rhode Island, Connecticut, and New Hampshire

towns. Each family farmed its own plot of land, but a short summer growing season and limited amount of good soil gave rise to other economic activities such as manufacturing, fishing, shipbuilding, and trade. The vast majority of the settlers had similar origins, most having arrived from England and Scotland. Towns were carefully planned and laid out in similar fashion. The form of government was the town meeting where all adult males met to make the laws. The legislative body, the General Court, consisted of an upper and a lower house.

## The Middle Atlantic Colonies

> **MIDDLE OR MIDDLE ATLANTIC COLONIES:** included New York, New Jersey, Pennsylvania, Delaware, and Maryland

The MIDDLE or MIDDLE ATLANTIC COLONIES included New York, New Jersey, Pennsylvania, Delaware, and Maryland. New York and New Jersey were at one time the Dutch colony of New Netherland, and Delaware was at one time New Sweden. These five colonies, from their beginnings, were considered "melting pots," with settlers from many different nations and backgrounds. The main economic activity was farming; the settlers were scattered over the countryside cultivating rather large farms. The Native Americans were not as much of a threat as they were in New England so the colonists did not have to settle in small farming villages. The soil was very fertile, the land was gently rolling, and a milder climate provided a longer growing season. These farms produced a large surplus of food, not only for the colonists themselves but also for sale. This colonial region became known as the "breadbasket" of the New World, and the New York and Philadelphia seaports were constantly filled with ships being loaded with meat, flour, and other foodstuffs for the West Indies and England.

Other economic activities in these colonies included shipbuilding, iron mining, and the production of paper, glass, and textiles in factories. The legislative body in Pennsylvania was unicameral (consisting of one house). In the other four colonies, the legislative body had two houses. Units of local government were found in counties and towns.

## The Southern Colonies

> **SOUTHERN COLONIES:** Virginia, North and South Carolina, and Georgia

> *Virginia was the first permanent successful English colony and Georgia was the last.*

The SOUTHERN COLONIES were Virginia, North and South Carolina, and Georgia. Virginia was the first permanent successful English colony and Georgia was the last. The year 1619 was a very important year in the history of Virginia as well as the United States, with the occurrence of three significant events:

- Sixty women were sent to Virginia to marry and establish families

- Twenty Africans, the first of thousands, arrived

- The Virginia colonists were granted the right to self-government

The granting of the right to self-government was the most important event. The colonists immediately elected their own representatives to the House of Burgesses—their own legislative body.

The major economic activity in this region was farming. Here too the soil was very fertile, and the climate was mild, with an even longer growing season than farther north. The large plantations, eventually requiring large numbers of slaves, were found in the coastal or tidewater areas. Although the wealthy slave-owning planters set the pattern of life in this region, most of the people lived inland, away from coastal areas. They were small farmers and few, if any, owned slaves.

The settlers in these four colonies came from diverse backgrounds and cultures. Virginia was colonized mostly by people from England, while Georgia was started as a haven for debtors from English prisons. Pioneers from Virginia settled in North Carolina, while South Carolina welcomed people from England and Scotland, French Protestants, Germans, and emigrants from islands in the West Indies.

Products from farms and plantations included rice, tobacco, indigo, cotton, some corn, and wheat. Other economic activities in the southern colonies included lumber and naval stores (tar, pitch, rosin, and turpentine) from the pine forests and fur trade on the frontier. Cities such as Savannah and Charleston were important seaports and trading centers.

## SKILL 6.2 Knows about the American Revolution and the founding of the nation in United States history

### Causes of the War of Independence

With the end of the French and Indian War (the Seven Years' War), England decided to reassert control over the colonies in America. The government particularly needed the revenue from the control of trade to pay for the recent war and to defend the new territory obtained as a result of the war.

English leaders decided to impose a tax that would pay for the military defense of the American lands. The colonists rejected this idea for two reasons: 1) They were undergoing an economic recession, and 2) They believed it unjust to be taxed unless they had representation in Parliament.

England passed a series of laws that provoked fierce opposition:

- The Proclamation Act prohibited English settlement beyond the Appalachian Mountains to appease the Native Americans

- The Sugar Act imposed a tax on foreign molasses, sugar, and other goods imported into the colonies

- The Currency Act prohibited colonial governments from issuing paper money

Opposition arose in Massachusetts. Leaders denounced "taxation without representation" and a boycott was organized against imported English goods. The movement rapidly spread to other colonies.

## The Stamp Act

The Stamp Act placed a tax on newspapers, legal documents, licenses, almanacs, and playing cards. This was the first instance of an "internal" tax on the colonies. In response, the colonists formed secret groups called the "Sons of Liberty" and staged riots against the agents who collected the taxes and marked items with a special stamp.

In October of 1765, representatives of nine colonies met in the Stamp Act Congress. They drafted resolutions stating their reasons for opposing the act and sent them to England. Merchants throughout the colonies applied pressure with a large boycott of imported English goods. The Stamp Act was repealed three months later.

## The Townshend Acts

England then had a dual concern: to generate revenue and to regain control of the colonists. They passed the Townshend Acts in 1767. These acts placed taxes on lead, glass, paint, paper, and tea.

This led to another very successful boycott of English goods. England responded by limiting the tax to tea. This ended the boycotts of everything except tea.

The situation between colonists and British troops was becoming increasingly strained. Despite a skirmish in New York and the Boston Massacre in 1770, tensions abated over the next few years.

## The Boston Tea Party

The Tea Act of 1773 gave the British East India Company a monopoly on sales of tea. The colonists responded with the Boston Tea Party. England responded with the Coercive Acts (called the Intolerable Acts by the colonists) in 1774. This closed the port of Boston, changed the charter of the Massachusetts colony, and suppressed town meetings.

## Continental Congress

Eleven colonies sent delegates to the First Continental Congress in 1774. The group issued the Declaration of Rights and Grievances, which vowed allegiance to the king but protested the right of Parliament to tax the colonies. The boycotts resumed at the same time.

Massachusetts mobilized its colonial militia in anticipation of difficulties with England. The British troops attempted to seize their weapons and ammunition. The result was two clashes with minutemen at Lexington and Concord. The Second Continental Congress met a month later. Many of the delegates recommended a declaration of independence from Britain. The group established an army and commissioned George Washington as its commander.

British forces attacked patriot strongholds at Breed's Hill and Bunker Hill. Although the colonists withdrew, the the British lost nearly half of their army. The next month King George III declared the American colonies to be in a state of rebellion. The war quickly began in earnest. On July 3, 1776, British General Howe arrived in New York harbor with 10,000 troops to prepare for an attack on the city. The following day, the Second Continental Congress accepted the final draft of the Declaration of Independence by unanimous vote.

## Colonial Army versus British Army

Although the colonial army was quite small compared to the British army, and lacked formal military training, the colonists had learned a new method of warfare from the Native Americans. To be sure, many battles were fought in the traditional style of two lines of soldiers facing off and firing weapons, but the advantage the patriots had was the understanding of guerilla warfare—fighting from behind trees and other defenses.

## Founding of the Nation

When the war began, the colonies began to establish state governments. To a significant extent, the government that was defined for the new nation was intentionally weak. The colonies/states feared centralized government; however, the lack of continuity between the individual governments was confusing and economically damaging.

SKILL
6.3 **Knows the major events and developments in United States history from founding to present** *(e.g., westward expansion, industrialization, Great Depression)*

The Constitutional Convention of 1787 devised an entirely new form of government and outlined it in the Constitution of the United States. The Constitution was ratified quickly and took effect in 1789. Concerns that had been raised in or by the states regarding civil liberties and states' rights led to the immediate adoption of twelve amendments to the Constitution; the first ten are known as the Bill of Rights.

## The American Political System

It is important to realize that political parties are never mentioned in the U.S. Constitution. In fact, George Washington himself warned against the creation of "factions" in American politics that cause "jealousies and false alarms" as well as the damage they could cause to the body politic. Thomas Jefferson echoed this warning, yet he would come to lead a party himself.

*It is important to realize that political parties are never mentioned in the U.S. Constitution.*

Americans had good reason to fear the emergence of political parties. They had witnessed how parties worked in Great Britain. Parties, called "factions" in Britain, were made up of a few people who schemed to win favors from the government, and who were more interested in their own personal profits and advantages than in the public good. Thus, the new American leaders were interested in keeping factions from forming. It was, ironically, disagreements between two of Washington's chief advisors, **Thomas Jefferson** and **Alexander Hamilton**, which spurred the formation of the first political parties in the newly formed United States of America.

## Formation of the two-party system

The two parties that developed in the early 1790s were led by Jefferson as the secretary of state and Hamilton as the secretary of the treasury. Jefferson and Hamilton were different in many ways, including their views on what should be the proper form of government of the United States. This difference helped to shape the parties that formed around them.

Hamilton wanted the federal government to be stronger than the state governments. Jefferson believed that the state governments should be stronger. Hamilton supported the creation of the first bank of the United States; Jefferson opposed it because he felt that it gave too much power to wealthy investors who would help to run it. Jefferson interpreted the Constitution strictly; he argued that nowhere did the Constitution give the federal government the power to create a national bank.

Hamilton interpreted the Constitution much more loosely. He pointed out that the Constitution gave Congress the power to make all laws "necessary and proper" to carry out its duties. He reasoned that since Congress had the right to collect taxes, then Congress had the right to create the bank.

Hamilton also wanted the government to encourage economic growth. He favored the growth of trade, manufacturing, and the rise of cities as necessary parts of economic growth. He favored business leaders and mistrusted the common people. Jefferson believed that the common people, especially farmers, were the backbone of the nation. He thought that the rise of big cities and manufacturing would corrupt American life.

Before long, leaders in other states began to organize support for either Jefferson or Hamilton. Jefferson's supporters called themselves **Democratic-Republicans** (often this was shortened to just Republicans, though in actuality this was the forerunner of today's Democratic Party). Hamilton and his supporters were known as **Federalists**, because they favored a strong federal government. The Federalists had the support of the merchants and shipowners in the Northeast and some planters in the South. Small farmers, craftspeople, and some of the wealthier landowners supported Jefferson and the Democratic-Republicans.

By the time Washington retired from office in 1796, the new political parties would come to play an important role in choosing his successor. Each party would put up its own candidates for office. The election of 1796 was the first one in which political parties played a role. By the beginning of the 1800s, the Federalist Party, torn by internal divisions, began suffering a decline. This was exacerbated in 1800 when Thomas Jefferson was elected president. After the leader of the Federalist Party, Alexander Hamilton, was killed in 1804 in a duel with Aaron Burr, the Federalist Party began to collapse. By 1816, after losing a string of important elections (Jefferson was reelected in 1804, and James Madison, a Democratic-Republican was elected in 1808), the Federalist Party ceased to be an effective political force, and soon passed off the national stage.

By the late 1820s, new political parties had grown up. The Democratic-Republican Party, or simply the Republican Party, had been the major party for many years, but differences within the party about the direction the country was headed caused a split after 1824. Those who favored strong national growth took the name **Whigs** after a similar party in Great Britain and united around then-President John Quincy Adams. Many businesspeople in the Northeast as well as some wealthy planters in the South supported it.

Those who favored slower growth and were more worker- and small farmer-oriented went on to form the new **Democratic Party**, with Andrew Jackson acting as its first leader (he also became its first president). This was the forerunner of today's party of the same name.

In the mid-1850s, the slavery issue was beginning to heat up; in 1854, those opposed to slavery, the Whigs, along with some Northern Democrats, united to form the Republican Party. Before the Civil War, the Democratic Party was more heavily represented in the South and was thus primarily pro-slavery.

*By the time of the Civil War, the present configuration of the major political parties had been formed.*

Therefore, by the time of the Civil War, the present configuration of the major political parties had been formed. Though there would sometimes be drastic changes in ideology and platforms over the years, no other political parties would manage to gain enough strength to seriously challenge the "Big Two" parties.

In fact, they have shown themselves adaptable to changing times. In many instances, they have managed to shut out other parties by simply adapting their platforms, such as in the 1930s during the Great Depression and in the years immediately preceding. The Democratic Party adapted much of the Socialist Party platform and, under Franklin Roosevelt, put much of it into effect, thus managing to eliminate the Socialist Party as a serious threat.

Since the Civil War, no other political party has managed to gain enough support to either elect a substantial number of members of Congress or to elect a president. Some have come closer than others, but barring unforeseen circumstances, the absolute monopoly on national political debate seems secure in the hands of the Republican and Democratic parties.

## Westward Movement

In the United States, territorial expansion occurred in the expansion westward under the banner of **Manifest Destiny**. In addition, the United States was involved in the War with Mexico, the Spanish-American War, and the support of the Latin American colonies of Spain in their revolt for independence. In Latin America, the Spanish colonies were successful in their fight for independence and self-government.

After the United States purchased the Louisiana Territory, Jefferson appointed Captains Meriwether Lewis and William Clark to explore it, to find out exactly what had been bought. The expedition, called the Corps of Discovery, eventually included a slave named York, a dog, forty young men, a female Shoshone Indian named Sacagawea, and her infant son. They went all the way to the Pacific Ocean, returning two years later with maps, journals, and artifacts. This led the way for future explorers to discover more about the territory; it also resulted in the westward movement and the later belief in the doctrine of Manifest Destiny.

Initially, the United States and Britain shared the Oregon country. By the 1840s, with the increase in the free and slave populations and the demand of the settlers for control and government by the United States, the conflict had to be resolved. In a treaty signed in 1846 by both nations, a peaceful resolution occurred, with Britain giving up its claims south of the 49th parallel.

In the American Southwest, the results were exactly the opposite. Spain had claimed this area since the 1540s, had spread northward from Mexico City, and, in the 1700s, had established missions, forts, villages, towns, and very large ranches. After the purchase of the Louisiana Territory in 1803, Americans began moving into Spanish territory. A few hundred American families in what is now Texas were allowed to live there but had to agree to become loyal subjects of Spain.

In 1821, Mexico successfully revolted against Spanish rule, won independence, and chose to be more tolerant of American settlers and traders. The Mexican government encouraged and allowed extensive trade and settlement, especially in Texas. Many of the new settlers were southerners who brought their slaves with them. Slavery was outlawed in Mexico and technically illegal in Texas, although the Mexican government often looked the other way.

Friction increased between land-hungry Americans swarming into western lands and the Mexican government that controlled these lands. The clash was not only political but also cultural and economic. The Spanish influence permeated all parts of southwestern life: law, language, architecture, and customs. By this time, the doctrine of Manifest Destiny was in the hearts and on the lips of those seeking new areas of settlement and a new life. Americans were demanding U.S. control of not only the Mexican Territory but also of Oregon. Although peaceful negotiations with Great Britain secured Oregon, it took two years of war to gain control of the southwestern United States.

To make tensions worse, the Mexican government owed debts to U.S. citizens whose property had been damaged or destroyed during its struggle for independence from Spain. By the time war broke out in 1845, Mexico had not paid its war debts. The government was weak, corrupt, irresponsible, torn by revolutions, and in poor financial condition. Mexico was also bitter over American expansion into Texas and the 1836 revolution, which resulted in Texas's independence. In the 1844 presidential election, the Democrats pushed for the annexation of Texas and Oregon and after winning, they started the procedure to admit Texas to the Union.

When statehood was granted, diplomatic relations between the United States and Mexico were ended. President Polk wanted U.S. control of the entire Southwest, from Texas to the Pacific Ocean. He sent a diplomatic mission with an offer to purchase New Mexico and upper California, but the Mexican government refused to even receive the diplomats. Consequently, in 1846, each nation claimed aggression on the part of the other and war was declared. The treaty signed in 1848 and a subsequent treaty in 1853 completed the southwestern boundary of the United States, reaching to the Pacific Ocean, as President Polk wished.

The impact of the entire westward movement resulted in the completion of the borders of the present-day contiguous United States. Overall, the major contributing factors included the bloody War with Mexico; the ever-growing controversy over slave versus free states, which affected the balance of power in the U.S. Congress, especially the Senate; and the Civil War.

## Civil War

The Civil War began through a series of events that spanned decades. Tensions between the southern states and the northern states were increasing; in 1833, Congress lowered tariffs, this time to a level acceptable to South Carolina, which had been growing increasingly dissatisfied with the federal government. Although President Jackson believed in states' rights, he also firmly believed in and was determined to preserve the Union. Through Jackson's efforts, a constitutional crisis had been averted, but sectional divisions were getting deeper and more pronounced. The abolition movement was also growing rapidly, becoming an important issue in the North. The slavery issue was at the root of every problem, crisis, event, decision, and struggle from then on.

The next crisis involved the issue concerning Texas. By 1836, Texas was an independent republic with its own constitution. During its fight for independence, Americans were sympathetic to and supportive of the Texans, and some individuals recruited volunteers who crossed into Texas to help the struggle. Problems arose when the state petitioned Congress for statehood. Texas wanted to allow slavery, but Northerners in Congress opposed admission to the Union because it would disrupt the balance between free and slave states and give Southerners in Congress increased influence.

A few years later, Congress took up consideration of new territories between Missouri and present-day Idaho. Again, heated debate over permitting slavery in these areas flared up. Those opposed to slavery used the **Missouri Compromise** to prove their point showing that the land being considered for territories was part of the area the Compromise had designated as banned for slavery.

On May 25, 1854, Congress passed the infamous **Kansas-Nebraska Act,** which nullified the provision creating the territories of Kansas and Nebraska. This allowed the people of these two territories to decide for themselves whether or not to permit slavery there. Feelings were so deep and divided that any further attempts to compromise met with little success. Political and social turmoil swirled everywhere. Kansas was called "Bleeding Kansas" because of the extreme violence and bloodshed throughout the territory due to the two governments that existed there: one pro-slavery and the other anti-slavery.

## Dred Scott decision

In 1857, the Supreme Court handed down a decision guaranteed to cause explosions throughout the country. Dred Scott was a slave whose owner had taken him from slave state Missouri, then to free state Illinois, into Minnesota Territory (free under the provisions of the Missouri Compromise), and finally back to slave state Missouri. Abolitionists pursued the issue by presenting a court case, stating that since Scott had lived in a free state and free territory, he was in actuality a free man.

Two lower courts ruled before the Supreme Court became involved: one ruling in favor and one against. The Supreme Court decided that residing in a free state and free territory did not make Scott a free man because Scott (like all other slaves) was not a U.S. citizen or a state citizen of Missouri. Therefore, he did not have the right to sue in state or federal courts. The Court went a step further and ruled that the old Missouri Compromise was now unconstitutional because Congress did not have the power to prohibit slavery in the Territories.

## Lincoln-Douglas debates

In 1858, Abraham Lincoln and Stephen A. Douglas were running for the office of U.S. Senator from Illinois; they participated in a series of debates that directly affected the outcome of the 1860 presidential election. Douglas, a Democrat, was up for reelection and knew that if he won that race, he had a good chance of becoming president in 1860. Lincoln, a Republican, was not an abolitionist but he believed that slavery was morally wrong. He firmly believed in and supported the Republican Party principle that slavery must not be allowed to extend any further. The final straw came with the election of Lincoln to the presidency the next year. Due to a split in the Democratic Party, there were four candidates from four political parties. With Lincoln receiving a minority of the popular vote and a majority of electoral votes, the southern states, one by one, voted to secede from the Union, as they had promised they would if Lincoln and the Republicans were victorious. The die was cast.

## North versus South

Both sides quickly prepared for war. The North had more in its favor: a larger population; superiority in finances and transportation facilities; and manufacturing, agricultural, and natural resources. The North possessed most of the nation's gold, had about 92 percent of all industries, and had almost all the known supplies of copper, coal, iron, and various other minerals. Most of the nation's railroads were in the North and Midwest; men and supplies could be moved wherever needed and food could be transported from the farms of the Midwest to workers in the East as well as to soldiers on the battlefields. Trade with nations overseas could go on as usual due to control of the navy and the merchant fleet.

The Northern states numbered twenty-four and included Western (California and Oregon) and border (Maryland, Delaware, Kentucky, Missouri, and West Virginia) states. The Southern states numbered eleven and included South Carolina, Georgia, Florida, Alabama, Mississippi, Louisiana, Texas, Virginia, North Carolina, Tennessee, and Arkansas, making up the Confederacy.

Although outnumbered in population, the South was completely confident of victory. They knew that all they had to do was fight a defensive war and protect their own territory. The North had to invade and defeat an area almost the size of Western Europe. Another advantage of the South was that a number of its best officers had graduated from the U.S. Military Academy at West Point and had long years of army experience. Many had exercised varying degrees of command in the Indian Wars and the War with Mexico. Men from the South were conditioned to living outdoors and were more familiar with horses and firearms than men from northeastern cities. Since cotton was such an important crop, Southerners felt that British and French textile mills were so dependent on raw cotton that they would be forced to help the Confederacy in the war.

The South was winning the war until the **Battle of Gettysburg**, July 1–3, 1863. Until Gettysburg, Lincoln's commanders, McDowell and McClellan, were less than desirable; Burnside and Hooker, not what was needed. Lee, on the other hand, had many able officers; he depended heavily on Jackson and Stuart. Jackson died at Chancellorsville and was replaced by Longstreet. Lee decided to invade the North and depended on J. E. B. Stuart and his cavalry to keep him informed of the location of Union troops and their strengths.

The day after Gettysburg, on July 4, Vicksburg, Mississippi surrendered to Union General Ulysses Grant, thus severing the western Confederacy from the eastern part. In September 1863, the Confederacy won its last important victory at Chickamauga. In November, the Union victory at Chattanooga made it possible for Union troops to go into Alabama and Georgia, splitting the eastern Confederacy in two. Lincoln gave Grant command of all Northern armies in March of 1864. Grant led his armies into battles in Virginia while General Philip Sheridan and his cavalry did as much damage as possible. In a skirmish at a place called Yellow Tavern, Virginia, Sheridan's and Stuart's forces met, with Stuart being fatally wounded.

*The Civil War took more American lives than any other American war in history.*

The Civil War took more American lives than any other American war in history, the South losing one-third of its soldiers in battle compared to about one-sixth for the North. More than half of the total deaths were caused by disease and the horrendous conditions of field hospitals. Destruction was pervasive in towns, farms, trade, and industry. After the war, the South had no voice in the political, social, and cultural affairs of the nation, lessening to a great degree the influence of the more traditional Southern ideals. The Northern Yankee Protestant ideals of hard work, education, and economic freedom became the standard of the United States and helped influence the development of the nation into a modern, industrial power.

## Effects of the Civil War

The effects of the Civil War were tremendous. It changed the methods of waging war and has been called the first modern war. It introduced weapons and tactics which, when improved later, were used extensively in wars of the late 1800s and 1900s. Civil War soldiers were the first to fight in trenches, the first to fight under a unified command, and the first to wage a defense called "major cordon defense" (a strategy of advancing on all fronts). They were also the first to use repeating and breech-loading weapons. Observation balloons were first used during the war along with submarines, ironclad ships, and mines. Telegraphy and railroads were also first put to use during this time.

By executive proclamation and constitutional amendment, slavery was officially ended, although there remained deep prejudice and racism (still apparent today). The Union was preserved and the states were finally truly united. Sectionalism, especially in the area of politics, remained strong for another hundred years but not to the degree and with the violence that existed before 1861.

It has been noted that the Civil War may have been American democracy's greatest failure, as calm reason, which is basic to democracy, fell victim to human passion. Yet democracy did survive. The victory of the North established that no state has the right to end or leave the Union. Because of this unity, the United States became a major global power. It is important to remember that Lincoln never proposed to punish the South. He was most concerned with restoring the South to the Union in a program that was flexible and practical rather than rigid and unbending. In fact, he never really felt that the states had succeeded in leaving the Union, but rather that they had left the "family circle" for a short time.

The conclusion of the Civil War opened the floodgates for westward migration and the settlement of new land. The availability of cheap land and the expectation of great opportunities prompted thousands to travel across the Mississippi River and settle the Great Plains and California. The primary activities of the new western economy were farming, mining, and ranching. Both migration and the economy were facilitated by the expansion of the railroad and the completion of the transcontinental railroad in 1869.

*The conclusion of the Civil War opened the floodgates for westward migration and the settlement of new land.*

Migration and settlement were not easy. As the settlers moved west, they encountered Native American tribes who believed they had a natural right to the lands upon which their ancestors had lived for generations. Resentment of the encroachment of new settlers was particularly strong among the tribes that had been ordered to relocate to "Indian Country" prior to 1860. Conflict was intense and frequent until 1867, when the government established two large tracts of land called "reservations" in Oklahoma and the Dakotas, to which all tribes would be confined.

With the war over, troops were sent west to enforce the relocation and reservation containment policies. There were frequent wars, particularly as white settlers attempted to move onto Native American lands and the tribes resisted their confinement.

Continuing conflict led to the passage of the Dawes Act of 1887. This was a recognition that confinement in reservations was not working. The law was intended to break up the Native American communities and bring about assimilation into white culture by deeding portions of the reservation lands to individual Native Americans who were expected to farm their land. The policy continued until 1934.

Armed resistance essentially came to an end by 1890. The surrender of Geronimo and the massacre at Wounded Knee led to a change of strategy by the Indians. Thereafter, the resistance strategy was to preserve their culture and traditions.

## Industrialization

There was a marked degree of industrialization before and during the Civil War, but at war's end, there was not much industry in the United States. After the war, dramatic changes took place: machines replaced hand labor; extensive nationwide railroad service facilitated the wider distribution of goods; new products were made available in large quantities; and large amounts of money from bankers and investors were available for the expansion of business operations.

American life was significantly affected by this phenomenal industrial growth. Cities became the centers of this new business activity, resulting in mass population movements and tremendous growth. This new boom in business resulted in huge fortunes for some Americans and extreme poverty for many others. The discontent this caused resulted in a number of new reform movements from which came measures controlling the power and size of big business and helping the poor.

The use of machines in industry enabled workers to produce a large quantity of goods much faster than they could by hand. With the increase in business, hundreds of workers were hired and assigned to perform specific jobs in the production process. This was a method of organization called the "division of labor"; because of its ability to increase the rate of production, businesses lowered prices for their products, making the products affordable for more people. As a result, sales and businesses were increasingly successful and profitable.

A great variety of new products and inventions became available, including the typewriter, the telephone, barbed wire, the electric light, the phonograph, and the gasoline-powered automobile. From this list, the one that had the greatest effect on America's economy was the automobile.

The increase in business and industry was greatly affected by the many rich **natural resources** that were found throughout the nation. The industrial machines were powered by an abundant water supply. The construction industry as well as products made from wood depended heavily on lumber from the forests. Coal and iron ore in abundance were needed for the steel industry, which profited and increased from the use of steel in such things as skyscrapers, automobiles, bridges, railroad tracks, and machines. Other minerals such as silver, copper, and petroleum played a large role in industrial growth (especially petroleum, from which gasoline was refined as fuel for the increasingly popular automobile).

The developments in communication, such as the telephone and telegraph, increased the efficiency and prosperity of big business. Steam-power generation, sophisticated manufacturing equipment, the ability to move about the country quickly by railroad, and the invention of the steam-powered tractor resulted in a phenomenal growth in industrial output. The new steel and oil industries provided a significant impetus to industrial growth and added thousands of new jobs. The inventive spirit of the time was a major force propelling the industrial revolution forward. This spirit led to an improvement in products, the development of new production processes and equipment, and even to the creation of entirely new industries. During the last forty years of the nineteenth century, inventors registered almost seven hundred thousand new patents.

*During the last forty years of the nineteenth century, inventors registered almost seven hundred thousand new patents.*

One result of industrialization was the growth of the **Labor Movement**. There were numerous boycotts and strikes that often became violent when the police or the militias were called in. Labor and farmer organizations were created and became a political force. Industrialization also brought an influx of immigrants from Asia (particularly from China and Japan) and from Europe (particularly European Jews, the Irish, and Russians). High rates of immigration led to the creation of cultural communities within various cities, such as "little Russia" or "little Italy."

Industrialization also led to the overwhelming growth of cities as workers moved closer to their places of work. The economy was booming, but it was based on basic needs and luxury goods, for which there was to be only limited demand, especially during times of economic recession or depression.

## The Great Depression and Its Aftermath

In September 1929, stock prices began to slip somewhat, yet people remained optimistic. On Monday, October 21, prices began to fall quickly. The volume traded was so high that the tickers were unable to keep up. Investors were frightened, and they started selling very quickly. This caused further collapse. For the next two days prices stabilized somewhat. On **Black Thursday**, October 24, 1929, prices plummeted again. By this time investors had lost confidence. On Friday and Saturday an attempt to stop the crash was made by some leading bankers. But on Monday the 28th, prices began to fall again, declining by 13% in one day. The next day, **Black Tuesday, October 29**, saw 16.4 million shares traded. Stock prices fell so far that at many times no one was willing to buy at any price.

Unemployment quickly reached 25 percent nationwide. People thrown out of their homes created makeshift domiciles of cardboard, scraps of wood, and tents. With unmasked reference to President Hoover, who was quite obviously overwhelmed by the situation and incompetent to deal with it, these communities were called **Hoovervilles**. Families stood in bread lines, rural workers left the dust bowl of the plains to search for work in California, and banks failed. More than one hundred thousand businesses failed between 1929 and 1932. The despair that swept the nation left an indelible scar on all who endured the Depression.

When the stock market crashed, businesses collapsed. Without demand for products, other businesses and industries collapsed. This set in motion a domino effect, bringing down the businesses and industries that provided raw materials or components to these industries. Hundreds of thousands became jobless. Then the jobless often became homeless. Desperation prevailed. Little had been done to assess the toll hunger, inadequate nutrition, or starvation took on the health of those who were children during this time. While food was cheap, relatively speaking, there was little money to buy it.

Everyone who lived through the Great Depression was permanently affected in some way. Many never trusted banks again. Many people of this generation later hoarded cash so they would not risk losing everything again. Some permanently rejected the use of credit.

In the immediate aftermath of the stock market crash, many urged President Herbert Hoover to provide government relief. Hoover responded by urging the nation to be patient. By the time he signed relief bills in 1932, it was too late.

Hoover's bid for reelection in 1932 failed. The new president, Franklin D. Roosevelt, won the White House on his promise to the American people of a "new deal." Upon assuming office, Roosevelt and his advisers immediately launched a massive program of innovation and experimentation to try to bring the Depression to an end and get the nation back on track. Congress gave the president unprecedented power to act to save the nation. During the next eight years, the most extensive and broad-based legislation in the nation's history was enacted. The legislation was intended to accomplish three goals: relief, recovery, and reform.

## The New Deal

The first step in the New Deal was to relieve suffering. This was accomplished through a number of job-creation projects. The second step, the recovery aspect, was to stimulate the economy. The third step was to create social and economic change through innovative legislation.

The National Recovery Administration attempted to accomplish a number of goals:

- Restore employment

- Increase general purchasing power

- Provide character-building activity for unemployed youth

- Encourage decentralization of industry and thus divert population from crowded cities to rural or semirural communities

- Develop river resources in the interest of navigation and inexpensive power and light

- Complete flood control on a permanent basis

- Enlarge the national program of forest protection and develop forest resources

- Control farm production and improve farm prices

- Assist home builders and homeowners

- Restore public faith in banking and trust operations

- Recapture the value of physical assets, whether in real property, securities, or other investments

These objectives and their accomplishment implied a restoration of public confidence and courage.

Among the "alphabet organizations" set up to work out the details of the recovery plan, the most prominent were:

- **Agricultural Adjustment Administration (AAA):** Designed to readjust agricultural production and prices, thereby boosting farm income

- **Civilian Conservation Corps (CCC):** Designed to give wholesome, useful activity in the forestry service to unemployed young men
- **Civil Works Administration (CWA) and the Public Works Administration (PWA):** Designed to give employment in the construction and repair of public buildings, parks, and highways
- **Works Progress Administration (WPA):** Designed to move individuals from relief rolls to work projects or private employment

The **Tennessee Valley Authority (TVA)** was of a more permanent nature, designed to improve the navigability of the Tennessee River and increase productivity of the timber and farm lands in its valley. This program built sixteen dams that provided water control and hydroelectric generation.

The **Public Works Administration** employed Americans on over thirty-four thousand public works projects at a cost of more than $4 billion. Among these projects was the construction of a highway that linked the Florida Keys and Miami, the Boulder Dam (now the Hoover Dam), and numerous highway projects.

To provide economic stability and prevent another crash, Congress passed the **Glass-Steagall Act**, which separated banking and investing. The Securities and Exchange Commission was created to regulate dangerous speculative practices on Wall Street. The Wagner Act guaranteed a number of rights to workers and unions in an effort to improve worker-employer relations.

The **Social Security Act of 1935** established pensions for the aged and infirm as well as a system of unemployment insurance.

Much of the recovery program was designed to respond to an emergency, but certain permanent national policies emerged. The intention of the public was to employ their government in supervising and, to an extent, regulating business operations—from corporate activities to labor problems. This included protecting bank depositors and the credit system of the country, employing gold resources and currency adjustments to aid permanent restoration of normal living, and, if possible, establishing a line of subsistence below which no useful citizen would be permitted to sink.

Many of the steps taken by the Roosevelt administration have had far-reaching effects. They alleviated the economic disaster of the Great Depression, enacted controls that would mitigate the risk of another stock market crash, and provided greater security for workers. The nation's economy, however, did not fully recover until the United States entered World War II.

## U.S. Policy after World War II

In the aftermath of the Second World War, with the Soviet Union having emerged as the second strongest power in the world, the United States embarked on a policy known as containment of the Communist menace. This involved what came to be known as the Marshall Plan and the Truman Doctrine. The **MARSHALL PLAN** involved the economic aid that was sent to Europe in the aftermath of the Second World War aimed at preventing the spread of communism. To that end, the U.S. has devoted a larger and larger share of its foreign policy, diplomacy, and both economic and military might to combating it.

The **TRUMAN DOCTRINE** offered military aid to those countries that were in danger of communist upheaval. This led to the era known as the cold war, in which the United States took the lead along with the Western European nations against the Soviet Union and the Eastern Bloc countries. It was also at this time that the United States finally gave up on George Washington's advice against "European entanglements" and joined the **NORTH ATLANTIC TREATY ORGANIZATION (NATO).** This was formed in 1949 and comprised the United States and several Western European nations for the purposes of opposing communist aggression.

The United Nations was also formed at this time (1945) to replace the defunct League of Nations for the purposes of ensuring world peace. Even with American involvement, the UN would prove largely ineffective in maintaining world peace.

In the 1950s, the United States embarked on what was called the Eisenhower Doctrine, after then-President Eisenhower. This aimed at trying to maintain peace in a troubled area of the world, the Middle East. However, unlike the Truman Doctrine in Europe, it would have little success.

The United States also became involved in a number of world conflicts in the ensuing years. Each had at the core the struggle against communist expansion. Among these were the Korean Conflict (1950–1953), the Vietnam War (1965–1975), and various continuing entanglements in Central and South America and the Middle East. By the early 1970s under the leadership of then-Secretary of State Henry Kissinger, the United States and its allies embarked on the policy that came to be known as détente. This was aimed at the easing of tensions between the United States and its allies and the Soviet Union and its allies.

By the 1980s, the United States embarked on what some saw as a renewal of the cold war. This owed to the fact that the United States was becoming more involved in trying to prevent communist insurgency in Central America. A massive expansion of its armed forces and the development of space-based weapons systems were undertaken at this time. As this occurred, the Soviet Union, with a failing economic system and a foolhardy adventure in Afghanistan, found itself

> **MARSHALL PLAN:** aimed at preventing the spread of communism, involved the economic aid that was sent to Europe in the aftermath of the Second World War

> **TRUMAN DOCTRINE:** offered military aid to countries in danger of communist upheaval

> **NORTH ATLANTIC TREATY ORGANIZATION (NATO):** formed in 1949 for the purposes of opposing communist aggression

unable to compete. By 1989, events had come to a head. This ended with the breakdown of the Communist Bloc, the virtual end of the monolithic Soviet Union, and the collapse of the communist system by the early 1990s.

> **SKILL 6.4** **Knows about twentieth-century developments and transformations in the United States** (e.g., assembly line, space age)

## Social and Economic Changes

The United States underwent significant social and economic changes during the twentieth century, and it became a dominant world power internationally. Economically, the United States saw great prosperity as well as severe depression emerging as primary economic forces.

*A huge wave of immigration at the turn of the century provided industry with a large labor pool and established millions of immigrants and their families in the working class.*

The industrialization that had started following the end of the Civil War in the mid-nineteenth century continued into the early decades of the twentieth century. A huge wave of immigration at the turn of the century provided industry with a large labor pool and established millions of immigrants and their families in the working class.

**POPULISM:** philosophy concerned with the common-sense needs of average people

**POPULISM** is a philosophy concerned with the common-sense needs of average people. Populism often finds expression as a reaction against perceived oppression of the average people by the wealthy elite in society. The prevalent claim of populist movements is that they will put the people first. Populist movements claim to represent the majority of the people and call them to stand up to institutions or practices that seem detrimental to their well-being.

Populism flourished in the late nineteenth and early twentieth centuries in the United States. Several political parties were formed out of this philosophy, including the Greenback Party, the Populist Party, the Farmer-Labor Party, the Single Tax movement of Henry George, the Share Our Wealth movement of Huey Long, the Progressive Party, and the Union Party.

The tremendous changes caused by the Industrial Revolution led to a demand for reform that would control the power wielded by big corporations. The gap between the industrial moguls and the working people was growing; this disparity resulted in a public outcry for reform at the same time there was an outcry for governmental reform that would end the political corruption and elitism of the day.

The reforms initiated by leaders and the spirit of Progressivism were far-reaching. Politically, many states enacted initiatives and referendums for progressive movements. The adoption of the recall occurred in many states, and several states enacted legislation that would undermine the power of political machines. On a national level, the two most significant political changes were:

- The ratification of the Seventeenth Amendment, which required that all U.S. Senators be chosen by popular election

- The ratification of the Nineteenth Amendment, which granted women the right to vote

Major economic reforms of the period included the aggressive enforcement of the **Sherman Antitrust Act** and the passage of the **Elkins Act** and the **Hepburn Act**, which gave the Interstate Commerce Commission greater power to regulate the railroads. The **Pure Food and Drug Act** prohibited the use of harmful chemicals in food; the **Meat Inspection Act** regulated the meat industry to protect the public against tainted meat; over two-thirds of the states passed laws prohibiting child labor; workmen's compensation was mandated; and the Department of Commerce and Labor was created.

Responding to concern over the environmental effects of the timber, ranching, and mining industries, Roosevelt set aside 238 million acres of federal lands to be protected from development. Wildlife preserves were established, the national park system was expanded, and the National Conservation Commission was created. The **Newlands Reclamation Act** also provided federal funding for the construction of irrigation projects and dams in semi-arid areas of the country.

The Wilson Administration carried out additional reforms. The **Federal Reserve Act** created a national banking system, providing a more stable money supply. The **Sherman Act** and the **Clayton Antitrust Act** defined unfair competition, made corporate officers liable for the illegal actions of employees, and exempted labor unions from antitrust lawsuits. The Federal Trade Commission was established to enforce these measures. Finally, the Sixteenth Amendment was ratified, establishing an income tax. This measure was designed to relieve the poor of a disproportionate burden in funding the federal government and to make the wealthy pay a greater share of the nation's tax burden.

Before 1800, most manufacturing took place in small shops or in homes. However, starting in the early 1800s, factories with modern machines were built, making it easier to produce goods faster. The eastern part of the country became a major industrial area, although some industry also developed in the west. At about the same time, improvements began to be made in building roads, railroads, canals, and steamboats.

The increased ease of travel facilitated westward movement and boosted the economy with faster and cheaper shipment of goods and products, covering larger and larger areas. Some of the innovations arising from these changes included the Erie Canal, which connects the interior and Great Lakes with the Hudson River and the coastal port of New York. Many other natural waterways were connected by canals during this time.

Robert Fulton's Clermont, the first commercially successful steamboat, led the pack as the fastest way to ship goods, making it the most important means to do so. Later, steam-powered railroads became the biggest rival of the steamboat as a means of shipping, eventually becoming the most important transportation method opening the west.

*With expansion into the interior of the country, the United States became the leading agricultural nation in the world.*

With expansion into the interior of the country, the United States became the leading agricultural nation in the world. The hardy pioneer farmers produced a vast surplus, and emphasis went to producing products with a high sale value. Implements such as the cotton gin and the reaper aided in higher production. Travel and shipping were greatly assisted in areas not yet reached by railroad; they were also facilitated by improved and new roads, such as the National Road in the east and the Oregon and Santa Fe trails in the west.

As travel and communication became faster, people became more exposed to works of literature, art, newspapers, drama, live entertainment, and political rallies. More information was desired about previously unknown areas of the country, especially the West, and the discovery of gold and other mineral wealth resulted in a literal surge of settlers.

Public schools were established in many states, and more and more children were able to get an education. With higher literacy and more participation in literature and the arts, the young nation was developing its own unique culture, and becoming less and less influenced by and dependent on European culture.

At the same time, more industries and factories required more labor. Women, children, and, at times, entire families worked dangerously long hours until the 1830s. By that time, factories were getting even larger and employers began hiring immigrants who were coming to America in huge numbers. Before then, efforts were made to organize a labor movement to improve working conditions and increase wages. These efforts never really caught on until after the Civil War.

## World War I and World War II

The prosperity of industrial and economic changes was interrupted by America's entry into the First World War in 1917. While reluctant to enter the hostilities, the United States played a decisive role in ending the war and in the creation of the League of Nations that followed, establishing its central position in international relations that would increase in importance through the century.

The World War I effort required a massive production of weapons, ammunition, radios, and other equipment of war. During wartime, work hours were shortened, wages were increased, and working conditions improved. When the war ended, and business and industrial owners attempted to return to prewar conditions, the workers revolted. These conditions contributed to the establishment of new labor laws.

The United States resumed its prosperous industrial growth in the years after World War I, but even as industrial profits and stock market investments skyrocketed, farm prices and wages fell, creating an unbalanced situation that caused an economic collapse in 1929, when the stock market crashed. The United States plummeted into economic depression with high unemployment. This period is known as the Great Depression.

President Franklin Roosevelt proposed that the federal government assist in rebuilding the economy, something his predecessor, President Hoover, thought the government should not do. Roosevelt's New Deal policies were adopted to wide success, and marked an important shift in the role that the U.S. government plays in economic matters and social welfare.

The nation's recovery was underway when, in late 1941, it entered the Second World War to fight against Japan and Germany and their allied Axis powers. Fifty-nine nations became embroiled in World War II, which began September 1, 1939 and ended September 2, 1945. These dates include both the European and Pacific theaters of war. The horribly tragic results of this second global conflagration were more deaths and more destruction than those of any other armed conflict. Millions of people were uprooted and displaced. The end of the war brought renewed power struggles, especially in Europe and China; many Eastern European nations as well as China came under the control and domination of the communists, supported and backed by the Soviet Union.

With the development of atomic bombs and their deployment against two Japanese cities, the world found itself in the nuclear age. The peace settlement established by the United Nations after the war still operates today.

The years between World War I and World War II produced significant advancements in aircraft technology, and the pace of aircraft development and production dramatically increased during World War II. Major developments included flight-based weapon delivery systems, the long-range bomber, the first jet fighter, the first cruise missile, and the first ballistic missile. Although they were invented, cruise and ballistic missiles were not widely used during the war. Glider planes were heavily used in World War II because they were silent upon approach. Another significant development was the broad use of paratrooper units. Hospital planes also came into use to extract the seriously wounded from the front and to transport them to hospitals for treatment.

Weapons and technology in other areas also improved rapidly during this time. These advances were critical in determining the outcome of the war. Radar, electronic computers, nuclear weapons, and new tank designs were used for the first time. More new inventions were registered for patents than ever before; most of these new ideas were aimed either to kill or to prevent people from being killed.

The war began with essentially the same weaponry that had been used in World War I. However, as the war progressed, so did technology. The aircraft carrier joined the battleship; the Higgins boat, the primary landing craft, was invented; light tanks were developed to meet the needs of a changing battlefield; and other armored vehicles were developed. Submarines were also perfected during this period.

Numerous other weapons were also developed or invented to meet the needs of battle during World War II: the bazooka, the rocket-propelled grenade, anti-tank weapons, assault rifles, the tank destroyer, mine-clearing Flail tanks, Flame tanks, submersible tanks, cruise missiles, rocket artillery and air-launched rockets, guided weapons, torpedoes, self-guiding weapons, and napalm. The atomic bomb was also developed and used for the first time during World War II.

> The 1950s saw the emergence of a large consumer culture in the United States.

The war industry fueled another period of economic prosperity that lasted through the postwar years. The 1950s saw the emergence of a large consumer culture in the United States, which has not only bolstered the American economy ever since, but has been an important development for other countries that produce goods for the U.S. market.

The United States first established itself as an important world military leader at the turn of the twentieth century during the Spanish American War; it cemented this position during the two world rars. Following World War II, with Europe struggling to recover from the fighting, the United States and the Soviet Union emerged as the two dominant world powers. This remained the situation for three decades while the two super powers engaged in a cold war between the ideals of communism and capitalism. In the 1980s, the Soviet Union underwent a series of reforms that resulted in the collapse of the country and the end of the cold war, leaving the United States as the true world power. Thus, the United States changed from a reluctant participant in international affairs into a central leader.

## Technological Developments Post-World War II

Major technological developments in the post–World War–II era include:

- Discovery of penicillin (1945)

- Detonation of the first atomic bombs (1945)

- Xerography process invented (1946)

- Exploration of the South Pole

- Studies of X-ray radiation

- U.S. airplane first flies at supersonic speed (1947)

- Invention of the transistor (1947)

- Long-playing record invented (1948)

- Studies begin in the science of chemo-genetics (1948)

- Mount Palomar reflecting telescope created (1948)

- Idlewild Airport (now known as JFK International Airport) opens in New York City

- Cortisone discovered (1949)

- USSR tests first atomic bomb (1949)

- U.S. guided missile launched and travels 250 miles (1949)

- Plutonium separated (1950)

- Tranquilizer meprobamate comes into wide use (1950)

- Antihistamines become popular in treating colds and allergies (1950)

- Electric power produced from atomic energy (1951)

- First heart-lung machine devised (1951)

- First solo flight over the North Pole (1951)

- Yellow fever vaccine developed (1951)

- Isotopes used in medicine and industry (1952)

- Contraceptive pill produced (1952)

- First hydrogen bomb exploded (1952)

- Nobel Prize in medicine awarded for discovery of streptomycin (1952)

- Cave Cougnac discovered with prehistoric paintings (1953)

- USSR explodes hydrogen bomb (1953)

- Hillary and Tenzing reach the summit of Mount Everest (1953)

- Lung cancer connected to cigarette smoking (1953)

- First U.S. submarine converted to nuclear power (1954)

- Polio vaccine invented (1954)

- Discovery of Vitamin B12 (1955)

- Discovery of the molecular structure of insulin (1955)

- First artificial manufacture of diamonds (1955)

- Beginning of development of "visual telephone" (1956)

- Beginning of transatlantic cable telephone service (1956)

- USSR launches first Earth satellites (Sputnik I and II ) (1957)

- Mackinac Straits Bridge in Michigan opens as the longest suspension bridge (1957)

- Stereo recordings introduced (1958)

- NASA created (1958)

- USSR launches rocket with two monkeys aboard (1959)

- Nobel Prize in Medicine for synthesis of RNA and DNA (1959)

---

**SKILL 6.5**    **Understands connections between causes and effects of events**

*See Skills 6.1, 6.2, 6.3, and 6.4*

---

**SKILL 6.6**    **Understands the nature, purpose, and forms** *(e.g., federal, state, local)* **of government**

## The Nature and Purpose of Government

Historically, the functions of government (or people's concepts of government and its purpose and function) have varied considerably. In the theory of political science, the function of government is to secure the common welfare of the members of the given society over which it exercises control. In different historical eras, governments have attempted to achieve the common welfare in accordance with the traditions and ideologies of the given society.

Among primitive peoples, systems of control were rudimentary at best. They arose directly from the ideas of right and wrong that had been established in the group and that were common in that particular society. Control was exercised most

*The function of government is to secure the common welfare of the members of the given society over which it exercises control.*

often by means of group pressure, typically in the form of taboos and superstitions—and in many cases by ostracism, or banishment from the group. Thus, in most cases, because of the extreme tribal nature of society in those early times, this led to very unpleasant circumstances for the individual so treated. Without the protection of the group, a lone individual did not survive long.

Among civilized peoples, governments began to assume more institutional forms. They rested on a well-defined legal system. They imposed penalties on violators of the social order. They used force, which was supported and sanctioned by their people. The government was charged with establishing the social order and was supposed to do so in order to discharge its functions.

Eventually, the ideas of government, such as who should govern and how, came to be considered by various thinkers and philosophers. The most influential of these were the ancient Greek philosophers Plato and Aristotle.

Aristotle's conception of government was based on a simple idea. The function of government was to provide for the general welfare of its people. A good government, and one that should be supported, was one that did so in the best way possible, with the least pressure on the people. Bad governments were those that subordinated the general welfare to that of the individuals who ruled. At no time should any function of any government be that of personal interest of any one individual, no matter who that individual is. This does not mean that Aristotle had no sympathy for the individual or individual happiness (accusations that have sometimes been made against Plato). Rather, Aristotle believed that a society is greater than the sum of its parts, or that "the good of the many outweighs the good of the few and also of the one."

Yet, a good government, and one that carries out its functions well, will always weigh the relative merits of what is good for a given individual in society and what is good for the society as a whole. This basic concept has continued to our own time and has found its fullest expression in the idea of representative democracy and political and personal freedom. In addition, the most ideal government is one that maintains social order while allowing the greatest possible autonomy for individuals.

| FORMS OF GOVERNMENT | |
| --- | --- |
| Anarchism | A political movement believing in the elimination of all government and its replacement by a cooperative community of individuals. Anarchism has sometimes involved political violence, such as assassinations of important political or governmental figures. The historical banner of this movement is a black flag. |

*Table continued on next page*

| Communism | A belief as well as a political system characterized by a classless, stateless social organization. Communism calls for the common ownership of national goods. This ideology is the same as Marxism. The historical banner of the movement is a red flag and variation of stars, hammer, and sickle, representing the various types of workers. |
|---|---|
| Dictatorship | Also called an oligarchy, rule by an individual or small group of individuals; a dictatorship centralizes all political control in itself and enforces its will with a strong police force. |
| Fascism | A belief as well as a political system opposed ideologically to Communism, though similar in basic structure, with a one-party state and centralized political control. Unlike Communism, fascism tolerates private ownership of the means of production, although it maintains tight overall control. Central to its belief is the idolization of the leader, a "cult of personality," and most often an expansionist ideology. Examples have been German Nazism and Italian Fascism. |
| Monarchy | The rule of a nation by a monarch (a nonelected, usually hereditary leader), most often a king or queen. This form of government may or may not be accompanied by some measure of democratically open institutions and elections at various levels. A modern example is Great Britain, which is called a constitutional monarchy. |
| Parliamentary System | A system of government with a legislature, usually involving a multiplicity of political parties and often coalition politics. There is division between the head of state and head of government. The head of government is usually known as a prime minister, who is also usually the head of the largest party. The head of government and cabinet usually both sit and vote in the parliament. The head of state is most often an elected president (though in the case of a constitutional monarchy, like Great Britain, the sovereign may take the place of a president as head of state). A government may fall when a majority in parliament votes "no confidence" in the government. |
| Presidential System | A system of government with a legislature, involving few or many political parties, with no division between head of state and head of government: The president serves in both capacities. The president is elected either by direct or indirect election. A president and cabinet usually do not sit or vote in the legislature, and the president may or may not be the head of the largest political party. A president can thus rule even without a majority in the legislature. He or she can only be removed from office for major infractions of the law. |
| Socialism | A political belief and system in which the state takes a guiding role in the national economy and provides extensive social services to its population. The state may or may not own outright the means of production, but even where it does not, it exercises tight control. It usually promotes democracy (Democratic-Socialism), though the heavy state involvement produces excessive bureaucracy and usually inefficiency. Taken to an extreme, it may lead to Communism as government control increases and democratic practice decreases. Ideologically, the two movements are very similar in belief and practice, as Socialists also preach the superiority of their system to all others and that it will become the eventual natural order. For that reason it is also considered a variant of Marxism. Socialism has also used a red flag as a symbol. |

## U.S. Government System

The various governments of the United States and of Native American tribes have many similarities and a few notable differences. They are more similar than not; all in all, they reflect the tendency of their people to prefer a representative government that has checks and balances and that looks out for the people as a whole.

The United States government has three distinct branches: the executive, the legislative, and the judicial. Each has its own function and its own "check" on the other two.

*The United States government has three distinct branches: the executive, the legislative, and the judicial.*

### Legislative branch

The legislative branch consists primarily of the House of Representatives and the Senate. Each house has a set number of members, the House with 435 apportioned according to national population trends and the Senate with one hundred (two from each state). House members serve two-year terms; senators serve six-year terms. Each house can initiate a bill, but that bill must be passed by a majority of both houses in order to become a law. The House is primarily responsible for initiating spending bills; the Senate is responsible for ratifying treaties that the president might sign with other countries.

### Executive branch

The executive branch has the president and vice-president as its two main figures. The president is the commander-in-chief of the armed forces and the person who can approve or veto all bills from Congress. (Vetoed bills can become law anyway if two-thirds of each house of Congress votes to pass them over the president's objections.) The president is elected to a four-year term by the electoral college, which usually mirrors the popular will of the people. The president can serve a total of two terms. The executive branch also has several departments consisting of advisors to the president. These departments include State, Defense, Education, Treasury, and Commerce, among others. Members of these departments are appointed by the president and approved by Congress.

### Judicial branch

The judicial branch consists of a series of courts and related entities, with the top body being the Supreme Court. The Court decides whether laws of the land are constitutional; any law invalidated by the Supreme Court is no longer in effect. The Court also regulates the enforcement and constitutionality of the amendments to the Constitution. The Supreme Court is the highest court in the land.

Cases make their way to it from federal appeals courts, which hear appeals of decisions made by federal district courts. These lower two levels of courts are found in regions around the country. Supreme Court justices are appointed by the president and confirmed by the Senate. They serve for life. Lower-court judges are elected in popular votes in their states.

## State and local government

State governments are mirror images of the federal government, with a few important exceptions:

- Governors are not technically commanders-in-chief of armed forces

- State supreme court decisions can be appealed to federal courts

- Terms of state representatives and senators vary

- Judges, even of the state supreme courts, are elected by popular vote

- Governors and legislators have term limits that vary by state

Local governments vary widely across the country, although none of them has a judicial branch per se. Some local governments consist of a city council, of which the mayor is a member who has limited powers; in other cities, the mayor is the head of the government and the city council members are the chief lawmakers. Local governments also have fewer strict requirements for people running for office than do the state and federal governments.

The form of government of the various Native American tribes varies as well. Most tribes have governments along the lines of the U.S. federal or state governments. An example is the Cherokee Nation, which has a fifteen-member tribal council as the head of the legislative branch; a principal chief and deputy chief who head the executive branch and carry out the laws passed by the tribal council; and a judicial branch made up of the judicial appeals tribunal and the Cherokee Nation district court. Members of the tribunal are appointed by the principal chief. Members of the other two branches are elected by popular vote of the Cherokee Nation.

SKILL **Knows key documents and speeches in the history of the United**
6.7 **States** *(e.g., United States Constitution, Declaration of Independence, Gettysburg Address)*

# Declaration of Independence

The **DECLARATION OF INDEPENDENCE** was written in 1776 by Thomas Jefferson. It was a call to the colonies to unite against the king, detailing the grievances of the colonies and articulating the philosophical framework upon which the United States is founded.

The Declaration of Independence is an outgrowth of both ancient Greek ideas of democracy and individual rights and the ideas of the European Enlightenment and the Renaissance, especially the ideology of the political thinker John Locke. Thomas Jefferson (1743–1826), the principle author of the Declaration, borrowed much from Locke's theories and writings.

John Locke was one of the most influential political writers of the seventeenth century, who put great emphasis on human rights and put forth the belief that when governments violate those rights people should rebel. In 1690, he wrote the book *Two Treatises of Government*, which had tremendous influence on political thought in the American colonies and helped shape the U.S. Constitution and Declaration of Independence.

The Declaration of Independence was the founding document of the United States of America. The Articles of Confederation were the first attempt of the newly independent states to reach a new understanding among themselves. The Declaration was intended to demonstrate the reasons that the colonies were seeking separation from Great Britain. Conceived by and written for the most part by Thomas Jefferson, it is not only important for what it says, but also for how it says it. The Declaration is in many respects a poetic document. Instead of a simple recitation of the colonists' grievances, it set out clearly the reasons the colonists were seeking their freedom from Great Britain. They had tried all means to resolve the dispute peacefully. It was the right of a people, when all other methods of addressing their grievances have been tried and have failed, to separate themselves from that power that was keeping them from fully expressing their rights to "life, liberty, and the pursuit of happiness."

**DECLARATION OF INDEPENDENCE:** written in 1776 by Thomas Jefferson, it was a call to the colonies to unite against the king, articulating the philosophical framework upon which the United States is founded

*The Declaration of Independence is an outgrowth of both ancient Greek ideas of democracy and individual rights and the ideas of the European Enlightenment and the Renaissance, especially the ideology of the political thinker John Locke.*

*For more information about this important document, go to:*

*http://www.archives.gov/ exhibits/charters/declaration. html*

U.S. CONSTITUTION:
the written document that
describes and defines the
system and structure of the
U.S. government

# U.S. Constitution

The **U.S. CONSTITUTION** is the written document that describes and defines the system and structure of the U.S. government. Ratification of the Constitution by the required number of states (nine of the original thirteen), was completed on June 21, 1788, and thus the Constitution officially became the law of the land.

In 1786, an effort to regulate interstate commerce ended in what is known as the **Annapolis Convention**. Because only five states were represented, this convention was not able to accomplish definitive results. The debates, however, made it clear that foreign and interstate commerce could not be regulated by a government with as little authority as the government established by the Confederation. Congress was therefore asked to call a convention to provide a constitution that would address the emerging needs of the new nation.

The convention met under the presidency of George Washington, with fifty-five of the sixty-five appointed members present. A constitution was written in four months. The Constitution of the United States is the fundamental law of the republic. It is a precise, formal, written document of the extraordinary, or supreme, type of constitution. The founders of the Union established it as the highest governmental authority. There is no national power superior to it. The foundations were so broadly laid as to provide for the expansion of national life and to make it an instrument that would last for all time.

To maintain the stability of the Constitution, its framers created a difficult process for making any changes to it. No amendment can become valid until it is ratified by three-fourths of all of the states.

The British system of government was part of the basis of the final document. However, significant changes were necessary to meet the needs of a partnership of states that were tied together as a single federation yet sovereign in their own local affairs. This constitution established a system of government that was unique and advanced far beyond other systems of its day.

There were, to be sure, differences of opinion. The compromises that resolved these conflicts are reflected in the final document. The first point of disagreement and compromise was related to the presidency. Some wanted a strong, centralized, individual authority. Others feared autocracy or the growth of monarchy. The compromise was to give the president broad powers but to limit the amount of time, through term of office, that any individual could exercise that power. The power to make appointments and to conclude treaties was controlled by the requirement of the consent of the Senate.

The second conflict was between large and small states. The large states wanted power proportionate to their voting strength; the small states opposed this plan.

The compromise was that all states should have equal voting power in the Senate, but to have membership in the House of Representatives be determined in proportion to population.

The third conflict was about slavery. The compromise was:

- Fugitive slaves should be returned by states to which they might flee for refuge

- No law would be passed for twenty years prohibiting the importation of slaves

The fourth major area of conflict was how the president would be chosen. One side argued for election by direct vote of the people. The other side thought that the president should be chosen by Congress. One group feared the ignorance of the people; the other feared the power of a small group of people. The compromise was the electoral college.

The Constitution binds the states in a governmental unity in everything that affects the welfare of all. At the same time, it recognizes the rights of the people of each state to independence of action in matters that relate only to them. Since the federal Constitution is the law of the land, all other laws must conform to it.

The debates conducted during the Continental Congress represent the issues and the arguments that led to the compromises in the final document. The debates also reflect the concerns of the founding fathers that the rights of the people be protected from abrogation by the government itself as well as the determination that no branch of government should have enough power to override the others. There is, therefore, a system of checks and balances.

## Federalist Papers

The **FEDERALIST PAPERS** were written to win popular support for the new proposed Constitution. In these publications, the debates of the Congress and the concerns of the founding fathers were made available to the people of the nation. In addition to providing an explanation of the underlying philosophies and concerns of the Constitution and the compromises that were made, the Federalist Papers conducted what has frequently been called the most effective marketing and public relations campaign in human history.

## Constitutional Amendments

An **AMENDMENT** is a change or addition to the U.S. Constitution. To date, only twenty-seven amendments to the Constitution have passed. An amendment may be used to cancel out a previous one (e.g., the Eighteenth Amendment of 1919, known as Prohibition, was canceled by the Twenty-First Amendment in 1933). Amending the Constitution is an extremely difficult thing to do.

**FEDERALIST PAPERS:** the debates of the Congress and the concerns of the founding fathers were made available to the people of the nation in order to win popular support for the new proposed Constitution

*The Federalist Papers conducted what has frequently been called the most effective marketing and public relations campaign in human history.*

**AMENDMENT:** a change or addition to the U.S. Constitution

An amendment must start in Congress. One or more lawmakers propose it, and then each house votes on it in turn. The amendment must have the support of two-thirds of each house separately in order to progress on its path into law. (It should be noted here that this two-thirds need be only two-thirds of a quorum, which is just a simple majority. Thus, it is theoretically possible for an amendment to be passed and to become legal even though it has been approved by less than half of one or both houses.)

The final and most difficult step for an amendment is the ratification of the state legislatures. A total of three-fourths of those must approve the amendment. Approvals there need be only a simple majority, but the number of states that must approve the amendment is thirty-eight. Hundreds of amendments have been proposed through the years.

A key element in some of those failures has been the time limit that Congress has the option to put on amendment proposals. A famous example of an amendment that got close but didn't reach the threshold before the deadline expired was the Equal Rights Amendment, which was proposed in 1972 but couldn't muster enough support for passage, even though its deadline was extended from seven to ten years.

**THE BILL OF RIGHTS:** the first ten amendments of the Constitution, approved at the same time, shortly after the Constitution was ratified

The first ten amendments are called **THE BILL OF RIGHTS**; they were approved at the same time, shortly after the Constitution was ratified. The Eleventh and Twelfth amendments were ratified around the turn of the nineteenth century and, respectively, voided foreign suits against states and revised the method of presidential election. The Thirteenth, Fourteenth, and Fifteenth amendments were passed in succession after the end of the Civil War. Slavery was outlawed by the Thirteenth Amendment. The Fourteenth and Fifteenth amendments provided for equal protection and for voting rights, respectively, without consideration of skin color.

The first amendment of the twentieth century was the Sixteenth Amendment, which provided for a federal income tax. Providing for direct election to the Senate was the Seventeenth Amendment. (Before this, senators were appointed by state leaders, not elected by the public at large.)

*The long battle for voting rights for women ended in success with the passage of the Nineteenth Amendment.*

The Eighteenth Amendment prohibited the use or sale of alcohol across the country. The long battle for voting rights for women ended in success with the passage of the Nineteenth Amendment. The date for the beginning of terms for the president and the Congress was changed from March to January by the Twentieth Amendment. With the Twenty-first Amendment came the only instance in which an amendment was repealed. In this case, it was the Eighteenth Amendment and its prohibition of alcohol consumption or sale.

The Twenty-second Amendment limited the number of terms that a president could serve to two. Presidents since George Washington had followed Washington's practice of not running for a third term; this changed when Franklin D. Roosevelt ran for reelection a second time, in 1940. He was reelected that time and a third time, too, four years later. He didn't live out his fourth term, but he did convince Congress and most of the state legislature that some sort of term limit should be in place.

The little-known Twenty-third Amendment provided for representation of Washington, D.C., in the electoral college. The Twenty-fourth Amendment prohibited poll taxes, which people had had to pay in order to vote.

Presidential succession is the focus of the Twenty-fifth Amendment, which provides a blueprint of what to do if the president is incapacitated or killed. The Twenty-sixth Amendment lowered the legal voting age for Americans from twenty-one to eighteen. The final amendment, the Twenty-seventh, prohibits members of Congress from substantially raising their own salaries. This amendment was one of twelve originally proposed in the late eighteenth century. Ten of those twelve became the Bill of Rights, and one has yet to become law.

A host of potential amendments have made news headlines in recent years. A total of six amendments have been proposed by Congress and passed muster in both houses but have not been ratified by enough state legislatures. The aforementioned Equal Rights Amendment is one. Another one, which would grant the District of Columbia full voting rights equivalent to states' rights, has not passed; like the Equal Rights Amendment, its deadline has expired. A handful of others remain on the books without expiration dates, including an amendment to regulate child labor.

*For detailed information and images of the Constitution and the Bill of Rights, go to:*

*http://www.archives.gov/exhibits/charters/constitution.html*

## Gettysburg Address

The **GETTYSBURG ADDRESS** was given by President Abraham Lincoln when he visited Gettysburg several months after the Battle of Gettysburg in 1863 at the dedication of the national cemetery in Gettysburg. In this short speech, Lincoln gave voice to a spirit that inspired many by referring to this time as a "new birth of freedom." His eloquence is remembered by many and often quoted.

**GETTYSBURG ADDRESS:** given by President Abraham Lincoln in 1863 at the dedication of the national cemetery in Gettysburg

**Knows the rights and responsibilities of citizenship in a democracy**

## Bill of Rights

The first ten amendments to the U.S. Constitution address civil liberties and civil rights. They were written mostly by James Madison. Here they are in brief:

1. Freedom of religion

2. Right to bear arms

3. Security from the quartering of troops in homes

4. Right against unreasonable search and seizure

5. Right against self-incrimination

6. Right to trial by jury, right to legal council

7. Right to jury trial for civil actions

8. No cruel or unusual punishment allowed

9. These rights shall not deny other rights the people enjoy

10. Powers not mentioned in the Constitution shall be retained by the states or the people

It is presumed that all citizens of the United States will recognize their responsibilities to the country and that the surest way of protecting their rights is by exercising those rights, which also entail a responsibility. Some examples include the *right* to vote and the *responsibility* to be well-informed on various issues, the *right* to a trial by jury and the *responsibility* to ensure the proper working of the justice system by performing jury duty (rather than avoiding it). In the end, it is only by the mutual recognition of the fact that an individual has both rights and responsibilities in society that enables the society to function in order to protect those very rights.

# COMPETENCY 007
## GEOGRAPHY, ANTHROPOLOGY, AND SOCIOLOGY

> **SKILL 7.1** **Knows world and regional geography** (e.g., spatial terms, places, and regions)

**SPATIAL ORGANIZATION** is a description of how things are grouped in a given space. In geographical terms, this can describe people, places, and environments anywhere and everywhere on Earth.

The most basic form of spatial organization for people is where they live. The vast majority of people live near other people in villages, towns, cities, and settlements. People live near others in order to take advantage of the goods and services that naturally arise from cooperation. The villages, towns, cities, and settlements they live in are, to varying degrees, near bodies of water. Water is a staple of survival for every person on the planet; it is also a good source of energy for factories and industries, as well as a form of transportation for people and goods.

Another way to describe where people live is by the **geography** and **topography** around them. The vast majority of people on the planet live in areas that are very hospitable. Yes, people live in the Himalayas and in the Sahara, but the populations of those areas are very small when compared to those of the plains of China, India, Europe, and the United States. People naturally want to live where they do not have to work really hard just to survive, and world population patterns reflect this.

We can examine the spatial organization of the places where people live. For example, in a city, where are the factories and heavy industrial buildings? Are they near airports or train stations? Are they on the edge of town, near major roads? What about housing developments? Are they near these industries, or are they far away? Where are the other industrial buildings? Where are the schools and hospitals and parks? What about the police and fire stations? How close are people's homes to these various things?

Towns, and especially cities, are routinely organized into neighborhoods so that each house or home is near most things that its residents might need on a regular basis. This means that large cities have multiple schools, hospitals, grocery stores, fire stations, and so on.

> **SPATIAL ORGANIZATION:** a description of how things are grouped in a given space; in geographical terms, this can describe people, places, and environments anywhere and everywhere on Earth

## Settlement Patterns

The distances between cities, towns, villages, or settlements are also related to settlement patterns. In certain parts of the United States and in many European countries, population settlement patterns achieve megalopolis standards, with no clear boundaries from one town to the next. Other, more sparsely populated areas have towns that are few and far between with relatively few people in them. Some exceptions to this exist, of course, like oases in the deserts; for the most part, however, population centers tend to be relatively near one another or at least near smaller towns.

Most populated places in the world also tend to be close to agricultural lands. Food makes the world go round. Although some cities are more agriculturally inclined than others, it is rare to find a city that grows absolutely no crops. The kind of food grown is almost entirely dependent on the kind of available land and the climate of the area. Rice doesn't grow well in the desert, for instance, nor do bananas grow well in snowy lands. Certain crops are easier to transport than others, and the ones that aren't are usually grown near ports or other centers of exporting.

**RELATIVE LOCATION:** refers to the surrounding geography (e.g., on the banks of the Mississippi River)

**ABSOLUTE LOCATION:** refers to a specific point, such as latitude 41° north, longitude 90° west, or 123 Main Street

## Five Themes of Geography

The five themes of geography are:

1. Location: This includes relative and absolute location. A **RELATIVE LOCATION** refers to the surrounding geography (e.g., on the banks of the Mississippi River). **ABSOLUTE LOCATION** refers to a specific point, such as latitude 41° north, longitude 90° west, or 123 Main Street.

2. Place: This is something that has both human and physical characteristics. Physical characteristics include features such as mountains, rivers, and deserts. Human characteristics are the features created by human interaction with the environment (such as canals and roads).

3. Human-environmental interaction: The theme of human-environmental interaction has three main concepts: humans adapt to the environment (wearing warm clothing in a cold climate); humans modify the environment (planting trees to block a prevailing wind); and humans depend on the environment (for food, water, and raw materials).

4. **Movement:** The theme of movement covers how humans interact with one another through trade, communications, emigration, and other forms of contact.

5. **Regions:** A region is an area that has some kind of unifying characteristic, such as a common language or a common government. There are three main types of regions: FORMAL REGIONS are areas defined by actual political boundaries, such as a city, county, or state. FUNCTIONAL REGIONS are defined by a common function, such as the area covered by a telephone service. VERNACULAR REGIONS are less formally defined areas that are formed by people's perception (e.g., "the Middle East" or "the South").

## Landforms

A LANDFORM comprises a geomorphological unit. Landforms are categorized by characteristics such as elevation, slope, orientation, stratification, rock exposure, and soil type. By name, they include such features as berms, mounds, hills, cliffs, and valleys. Oceans and continents exemplify highest-order landforms; however, landform elements can be further broken down. The generic landform elements are pits, peaks, channels, ridges, passes, pools, and planes; these can often be extracted from a digital elevation model using automated or semiautomated techniques.

Elementary landforms (segments, facets, and relief units) are the smallest homogeneous divisions of the land surface at a given scale or resolution. A plateau or a hill can be observed at various scales, ranging from a few hundred meters to hundreds of kilometers. Hence, the spatial distribution of landforms is often fuzzy and scale-dependent, as is the case for soils and geological strata.

A number of factors, ranging from plate tectonics to erosion and deposition, can generate and affect landforms. Biological factors can also influence landforms—for example, consider the role of plants in the development of dune systems and salt marshes, and the work of corals and algae in the formation of coral reefs.

The Earth's surface is made up of 70 percent water and 30 percent land. Physical features of the land surface include mountains, hills, plateaus, valleys, and plains. Other minor landforms include deserts, deltas, canyons, mesas, basins, foothills, marshes, and swamps. Earth's water features include oceans, seas, lakes, rivers, and canals.

**FORMAL REGIONS:** areas defined by actual political boundaries, such as a city, county, or state

**FUNCTIONAL REGIONS:** are defined by a common function, such as the area covered by a telephone service

**VERNACULAR REGIONS:** are less formally defined areas that are formed by people's perception (e.g., "the Middle East" or "the South")

**LANDFORM:** comprises a geomorphological unit, categorized by characteristics such as elevation, slope, orientation, stratification, rock exposure, and soil type

*The Earth's surface is made up of 70 percent water and 30 percent land.*

| EARTH'S PHYSICAL FEATURES | |
|---|---|
| Mountains | Landforms with rather steep slopes at least 2,000 feet or more above sea level. Mountains are found in groups called mountain chains or mountain ranges. At least one range can be found on six of the Earth's seven continents. North America has the Appalachian and Rocky Mountains; South America, the Andes; Asia, the Himalayas; Australia, the Great Dividing Range; Europe, the Alps; and Africa, the Atlas, Ahaggar, and Drakensburg Mountains. Mountains are commonly formed by volcanic activity, or when land is thrust upward where two tectonic plates collide. |
| Hills | Elevated landforms rising to an elevation of about five hundred to two thousand feet. Hills are found everywhere on Earth—including Antarctica, where they are covered by ice. |
| Plateaus | Elevated landforms that are usually level on top. Some plateaus are dry because they are surrounded by mountains that keep out any moisture. The plateau extending north from the Himalayas is extremely dry, while those in Antarctica and Greenland are covered with ice and snow. Plateaus can be formed by underground volcanic activity, erosion, or colliding tectonic plates. |
| Plains | Areas of flat or slightly rolling land, usually lower than the landforms next to them. Sometimes called *lowlands* (and often located along *seacoasts*), plains support the majority of the world's people. Many have been formed by large rivers, which provided extremely fertile soil for successful cultivation of crops and numerous large settlements of people. In North America, the vast plains areas extend from the Gulf of Mexico north to the Arctic Ocean and between the Appalachian and Rocky Mountains. In Europe, rich plains extend east from Great Britain into central Europe on into the Siberian region of Russia. Plains in river valleys are found in China (the Yangtze River valley), India (the Ganges River valley), and Southeast Asia (the Mekong River valley). |
| Valleys | Land areas that are found between hills and mountains. Some have gentle slopes containing trees and plants; others have very steep walls and are referred to as canyons. One famous example is Arizona's Grand Canyon of the Colorado River, which was formed by erosion. |
| Deserts | Large dry areas of land receiving ten inches or less of rainfall each year. Among the better known deserts are Africa's large Sahara desert, the Arabian desert on the Arabian Peninsula, and the desert outback covering roughly one-third of Australia. Deserts are found mainly in the tropical latitudes and are formed when surrounding features such as mountain ranges extract most of the moisture from the prevailing winds. |
| Deltas | Areas of lowlands formed by soil and sediment deposited at the mouths of rivers. The soil is generally very fertile; most fertile river deltas are important crop-growing areas. One well-known example is the delta of Egypt's Nile River, known for its production of cotton. |
| Mesas | The flat tops of hills or mountains, usually with steep sides. Mesas are similar to plateaus, but smaller. |
| Basins | Low areas drained by rivers or low spots in mountains. |
| Foothills | A low series of hills found between a plain and a mountain range. |

*Table continued on next page*

| Marshes and Swamps | Wet lowlands providing growth of such plants as rushes and reeds. |
|---|---|
| Oceans | The largest bodies of water on the planet. Five major oceans are usually recognized: the Pacific, Atlantic, Indian, Arctic, and Southern oceans; the last two listed are sometimes consolidated into the first three. The *Atlantic Ocean* is one-half the size of the Pacific and separates North and South America from Africa and Europe; the *Pacific Ocean* covers almost one-third of the entire surface of the Earth and separates North and South America from Asia and Australia; the *Indian Ocean* touches Africa, Asia, and Australia; the ice-filled *Arctic Ocean* extends from North America and Europe to the North Pole; and the *Southern Ocean* is made up of the southern portions of the Pacific, Atlantic, and Indian Oceans,which touch the shores of Antarctica. |
| Seas | Bodies of water smaller than oceans and surrounded by land. Some examples include the Mediterranean Sea found between Europe, Asia, and Africa and the Caribbean Sea, which touches the West Indies, South America, and Central America. |
| Lakes | Bodies of water surrounded by land. The Great Lakes in North America are a good example. |
| Rivers | Considered a nation's lifeblood, usually beginning as very small streams, formed by melting snow and rainfall. Rivers flow from higher to lower land, emptying into a larger body of water—usually a sea or an ocean. Examples of important rivers include the Nile, Niger, and Zaire rivers of Africa; the Rhine, Danube, and Thames rivers of Europe; the Yangtze, Ganges, Mekong, Hwang He, and Irrawaddy rivers of Asia; the Murray-Darling in Australia; and the Orinoco in South America. River systems are made up of large rivers as well as the numerous smaller rivers or tributaries flowing into them. Examples include the vast Amazon River system in South America and the Mississippi River system in the United States. |
| Canals | Man-made water passages constructed to connect two larger bodies of water. Famous examples include the *Panama Canal* across Panama's isthmus, which connects the Atlantic and Pacific oceans, and the *Suez Canal* in the Middle East between Africa and the Arabian Peninsula, connecting the Red and Mediterranean seas. |

# Weather and Climate

WEATHER is the condition of the air that affects the day-to-day atmospheric conditions. It includes factors such as temperature, air pressure, wind, and moisture or precipitation (which includes rain, snow, hail, or sleet).

CLIMATE is the term used to describe the average weather or daily weather conditions for a specific region over a long period of time. Studying the climate of an area includes information gathered on the area's monthly and yearly temperatures as well as its monthly and yearly amounts of precipitation. Another characteristic of an area's climate is the length of its growing season.

**WEATHER:** the condition of the air that affects the day-to-day atmospheric conditions

**CLIMATE:** the term used to describe the average weather or daily weather conditions for a specific region over a long period of time

## Humid continental climate

Studying the climate of an area includes information gathered on the area's monthly and yearly temperatures as well as its monthly and yearly amounts of precipitation.

In northern and central United States, northern China, south central and southeastern Canada, and the western and southeastern parts of the former Soviet Union, there is a "climate of four seasons." This is also known as the humid continental climate, which includes spring, summer, fall, and winter. Cold winters, hot summers, and enough rainfall to grow a variety of crops are the major characteristics of this climate. In areas where the humid continental climate is found, there are some of the world's best farmlands as well as important activities such as trading and mining. Differences in temperatures throughout the year are typically determined by how far inland a place is, away from the coast.

### Steppe or prairie climate

The steppe or prairie climate is located in the interiors of the large continents like Asia and North America. These dry flatlands are far from ocean breezes and are called prairies (or the Great Plains in Canada and the United States and steppes in Asia). Although the summers are hot and the winters are cold, the big difference is rainfall. In the steppe climate, rainfall is light and uncertain at ten to twenty inches per year. Where rain is more plentiful, grass grows; in areas of less rainfall, the steppes or prairies gradually become deserts. Examples of this are the Gobi desert of Asia, deserts in central and western Australia and the southwestern United States, and the smaller deserts found in Pakistan, Argentina, and Africa south of the equator.

### Tundra and taiga

The two major climates found in the high latitudes are tundra and taiga. The word *tundra*, meaning marshy plain, is Russian; it aptly describes the climatic conditions in the northern areas of Russia, Europe, and Canada. Winters are extremely cold and very long. Most of the year the ground is frozen, but it becomes rather mushy during the very short summer months. Surprisingly, less snow falls in the area of the tundra than in the eastern part of the United States. However, due to the harshness of the extreme cold, very few people live there and almost no crops can be raised. Despite the small human population, many plants and animals are found there.

The taiga is the northern forest region located south of the tundra. The world's largest forestlands are found here, along with vast mineral wealth and fur-bearing animals. The climate is so extreme that very few people live here, as they are not able to raise crops due to the extremely short growing season. The winter temperatures are colder and the summer temperatures hotter than those in the tundra because the taiga climate region is farther from the waters of the Arctic Ocean. The taiga is found in the northern parts of Russia, Sweden, Norway, Finland, Canada, and Alaska, with most of their lands covered with marshes and swamps.

## Subtropical climate

The humid subtropical climate is found north and south of the tropics. It is characterized by its high levels of moisture. The areas with this type of climate include the southeastern coasts of Japan, mainland China, Australia, Africa, South America, and the United States. One interesting feature of these locations is that warm ocean currents are found there. The winds that blow across these currents bring in warm moist air all year round. Long, warm summers; short, mild winters; and a long growing season allow for different crops to be grown several times a year. These conditions contribute to the productivity of this climate, which supports more people than any of the other climates.

## Marine climate

The marine climate is found in Western Europe, the British Isles, the Pacific Northwest of the United States, the western coast of Canada, southern Chile, southern New Zealand, and southeastern Australia. A common characteristic of these lands is that they are either near water or surrounded by it. The ocean winds are wet and warm, bringing a mild rainy climate to these areas. In the summer, the daily temperatures average at or below 70° F. During the winter, because of the warming effect of the ocean waters, the temperatures rarely fall below freezing.

In certain areas of the Earth, there is a type of climate unique to areas with high mountains. This type of climate is called a **vertical climate** because the temperatures, crops, vegetation, and human activities change as one ascends through the different levels of elevation. At the foot of the mountain, a hot and rainy climate is found, with the cultivation of many lowland crops. As one climbs higher, the air becomes cooler, the climate changes sharply, and economic activities change to things such as grazing sheep and growing corn. At the top of many mountains, snow is found year round.

---

**SKILL 7.2** **Understands the interaction of physical and human systems** *(e.g., how humans change the environment, how the environment changes humans, importance of natural and human resources)*

# Culture and Geography

Social scientists use the term **CULTURE** to describe the way of life of a group of people. This term includes not only art, music, and literature but also beliefs, customs, languages, traditions, and inventions—in short, any way of life, whether complex or simple. Although the term **GEOGRAPHY** is defined as the study of the Earth's features, it also includes the study of living things as it pertains to their

> **CULTURE:** the way of life of a group of people, including not only art, music, and literature, but also beliefs, customs, languages, traditions, and inventions

location, the relationships of these locations with each other, how they came to be there, and what impact these have on the world.

**PHYSICAL GEOGRAPHY** is concerned with the locations of such features as climate, water, and land as well as how these relate to and affect each other. It includes how they affect human activities and what forces shaped and changed them.

All three of these features of the Earth (climate, water, and land) affect the lives of all humans, ultimately having a direct influence on what is made and produced, where this production occurs, how it occurs, and what makes it possible. The combination of the different climatic conditions and types of landforms and other surface features work together all around the Earth to give the many varied cultures their unique characteristics and distinctions.

**CULTURAL GEOGRAPHY** studies the location, characteristics, and influence of the physical environment on different cultures around the Earth. Also included in these studies are comparisons and influences of the many varied cultures.

**Physical locations** of the Earth's surface features include the four major hemispheres and the parts of the Earth's continents in them. **Political locations** are the political divisions, if any, within each continent. Both physical and political locations are precisely determined in two ways:

1. Surveying is done to determine boundary lines and distance from other features.

2. Exact locations are precisely determined by imaginary lines of latitude (**parallels**) and longitude (**meridians**).

The intersection of these lines at right angles forms a grid, making it possible to pinpoint an exact location of any place using any two grid coordinates.

## The Earth's Hemispheres

The **Eastern Hemisphere** is located between the North and South poles, between the prime meridian (0° longitude) east to the international date line (180º longitude). It consists of most of Europe, all of Australia, most of Africa, and all of Asia (except for a tiny piece of the easternmost part of Russia that extends east of 180° longitude).

The **Western Hemisphere** is located between the North and South poles, between the prime meridian (0° longitude) west to the international date line (180° longitude). It consists of all of North and South America, a tiny part of the easternmost part of Russia that extends east of 180° longitude, and a part of Europe that extends west of the prime meridian.

**GEOGRAPHY:** the study of the Earth's features, including the study of living things as it pertains to their location, the relationships of these locations with each other, how they came to be there, and what impact these have on the world

**PHYSICAL GEOGRAPHY:** concerned with the locations of such features as climate, water, and land as well as how these relate to and affect each other

**CULTURAL GEOGRAPHY:** studies the location, characteristics, and influence of the physical environment on different cultures around the Earth

The **Northern Hemisphere**, located between the North Pole and the equator, contains all of the continents of Europe and North America and parts of South America, Africa, and most of Asia.

The **Southern Hemisphere**, located between the South Pole and the equator, contains all of Australia, a small part of Asia, about one-third of Africa, most of South America, and all of Antarctica.

## The Seven Continents

Of the seven continents, **Australia** is the only one that contains just one country. It is also the only island continent. Its political divisions consist of six states and one territory: Western Australia, South Australia, Tasmania, Victoria, New South Wales, Queensland, and Northern Territory.

**Africa** is made up of fifty-four separate countries, including Egypt, Nigeria, South Africa, Zaire, Kenya, Algeria, Morocco, and the large island of Madagascar.

**Asia** consists of forty-nine separate countries, including China, Japan, India, Turkey, Israel, Iraq, Iran, Indonesia, Jordan, Vietnam, Thailand, and the Philippines.

Some of **Europe**'s forty-three separate nations include France, Russia, Malta, Denmark, Hungary, Greece, and Bosnia.

**North America** consists of Canada, the United States of America, the island nations of the West Indies, and the "land bridge" of Middle America, including Cuba, Jamaica, Mexico, Panama, and other nations.

Thirteen separate nations together occupy the continent of **South America**; among them are the nations of Brazil, Paraguay, Ecuador, and Suriname.

The continent of **Antarctica** has no political boundaries or divisions but has a number of science and research stations managed by nations such as Russia, Japan, France, Australia, and India.

---

SKILL **Knows the uses of geography** (e.g., apply geography to interpret past, to
7.3 interpret present, to plan for future)

*Studying the geographic features of the Earth is essential to understanding the history of the physical environment and the history of humanity.*

Studying the geographic features of the Earth is essential to understanding the history of the physical environment and the history of humanity. Only when a comprehensive worldview is obtained through extensive geographical research can we have a complete understanding of the Earth, its lands, and its peoples throughout time. In this way, geography is useful as a historical and evaluative tool.

At the same time, geography is also useful for looking toward the future. To understand the world we live in today and the world we will inhabit in the future, we have to be aware of the geographic concepts that drive world events. These include, but are not limited to, environmental concerns.

Geography is often studied within the context of anthropology and sociology, areas of social studies that encompass human development as it relates to place and society.

**ANTHROPOLOGY: the scientific study of human culture and humanity: the relationship between humans and their cultures**

**ANTHROPOLOGY** is the scientific study of human culture and humanity: the relationship between humans and their cultures. Anthropologists study different groups, patterns of behavior, how they relate to one another, and their similarities and differences. Their research is twofold: it is cross-cultural and comparative. The major method of study is referred to as "participant observation." In this method, the anthropologist studies and learns about the culture's members by living among them and participating with them in their daily lives. Other methods may be used, but this is the most common. For example, in the 1920s, Margaret Mead lived among the Samoans, observing their ways of life. Her study resulted in the book *Coming of Age in Samoa*. The Leakey family, consisting of Louis, his wife Mary, and their son Richard, were anthropologists who did much fieldwork to further the study of human origins.

Many aspects of anthropology and the study of human cultures intersect with the study of geography. Because the Earth's physical features contribute to the actions and livelihoods of all cultures around the globe, the two fields of study are inexorably linked. Therefore, it is not uncommon to find discussions of geography interspersed in cultural studies.

In general, geographical studies are divided into several categories:

- **Regional:** The elements and characteristics of a place or region
- **Topical:** An Earth feature or one human activity occurring throughout the entire world
- **Physical:** Earth's physical features; what creates and changes them; their relationships to each other; and their relationships to human activities
- **Human:** Human activity patterns and how they relate to the environment including political, cultural, historical, urban, and social geographical fields of study

Special research methods used by geographers include mapping, interviewing, field studies, mathematics, statistics, and scientific instruments.

**Knows how people of different cultural backgrounds interact with their environment, family, neighborhoods, and communities**

## Natural Resources

NATURAL RESOURCES are naturally occurring substances that are considered valuable in their natural form. A commodity is generally considered a natural resource when the primary activities associated with it are extraction and purification, as opposed to creation. Thus, mining, petroleum extraction, fishing, and forestry are generally considered natural resource industries while agriculture is not.

Natural resources are often classified into renewable and nonrenewable resources. RENEWABLE RESOURCES are generally living resources (fish, coffee, and forests, for example), which can restock (renew) themselves if they are not over-harvested. Renewable resources can restock themselves and be used indefinitely if they are sustained. Once renewable resources are consumed at a rate that exceeds their natural rate of replacement, the standing stock will diminish and eventually run out.

The rate of sustainable use of a renewable resource is determined by the replacement rate and amount of standing stock of that particular resource. Nonliving renewable natural resources include soil, water, wind, tides, and solar radiation. NONRENEWABLE RESOURCES are natural resources that cannot be remade or regenerated in the same proportion in which they are used. Examples of nonrenewable resources are fossil fuels such as coal, petroleum, and natural gas.

In recent years, the renewal of natural capital and attempts to move to sustainable development have been a major focus of development agencies. This is of particular concern in rainforest regions, which hold most of the Earth's natural biodiversity—irreplaceable genetic natural capital. Conservation of natural resources is the major focus of Natural Capitalism, environmentalism, the ecology movement, and Green parties. Some view this depletion as a major source of social unrest and conflicts in developing nations.

## Environmental Policy

ENVIRONMENTAL POLICY is concerned with the sustainability of the Earth. The concern of environmental policy is the preservation of a region, habitat, or ecosystem. Because humans, both individually and within communities, rely upon the environment to sustain human life, social and environmental policies must be mutually supportable.

If modern societies have no understanding of the limitations of natural resources or how their actions affect the environment, and they act without regard for the sustainability of the Earth, it will become impossible for the Earth to sustain

**NATURAL RESOURCES:** naturally occurring substances considered valuable in their natural form

*The rate of sustainable use of a renewable resource is determined by the replacement rate and amount of standing stock of that particular resource.*

**RENEWABLE RESOURCES:** living resources, which can restock themselves if they are not over-harvested

**NONRENEWABLE RESOURCES:** natural resources that cannot be regenerated in the same proportion in which they are used

**ENVIRONMENTAL POLICY:** concerned with the sustainability of the Earth and the preservation of a region, a habitat, or an ecosystem

human existence. For centuries, social, economic, and political policies have ignored the impact of human existence and human civilization upon the environment. Human civilization has disrupted the ecological balance, contributed to the extinction of animal and plant species, and destroyed ecosystems through uncontrolled harvesting.

In an age of global warming and unprecedented demand on natural resources, social and environmental policies must become increasingly interdependent if the planet is to continue to support life and human civilization.

# COMPETENCY 008
## WORLD HISTORY AND ECONOMICS

> ### SKILL 8.1 Knows the major contributions of classical civilizations (e.g., Egypt, Greece, Rome)

### Mesopotamia

The ancient civilization of the Sumerians invented the wheel; developed irrigation through the use of canals, dikes, and devices for raising water; devised the system of cuneiform writing; learned to divide time; and built large boats for trade. The Babylonians devised the famous Code of Hammurabi, a code of laws.

### Egypt

Egypt made numerous significant contributions, including construction of the great pyramids, development of hieroglyphic writing, preservation of bodies after death, creation of paper from papyrus, developments in arithmetic and geometry, invention of the method of counting in groups of 1-10 (the decimal system), completion of a solar calendar, and formation of the foundation for science and astronomy.

The earliest historical record of the Kush civilization is in Egyptian sources, which describe a region upstream from the first cataract of the Nile as "wretched." This civilization was characterized by a settled way of life in fortified mud-brick villages. The people subsisted on hunting and fishing, herding cattle, and gathering grain. Skeletal remains suggest that they were a blend of Negroid and Mediterranean peoples. This civilization appears to be the second oldest in Africa (after Egypt).

During the period of Egypt's Old Kingdom (ca. 2700–2180 BCE), this civilization was essentially a diffused version of Egyptian culture and religion. When Egypt came under the domination of the Hyksos, Kush reached its greatest power and cultural energy (1700–1500 BCE). When the Hyksos were eventually expelled from Egypt, the New Kingdom brought Kush back under Egyptian colonial control.

## China

China is considered by some historians to be the oldest uninterrupted civilization in the world; it was in existence at about the same time as the ancient civilizations found in Egypt, Mesopotamia, and the Indus Valley. The Chinese studied nature and weather; stressed the importance of education, family, and a strong central government; followed the religions of Buddhism, Confucianism, and Taoism; and invented such things as gunpowder, paper, printing, and the magnetic compass. China began building the Great Wall, practiced crop rotation and terrace farming, increased the importance of the silk industry, and developed caravan routes across Central Asia for extensive trade. The Chinese also increased proficiency in rice cultivation and developed a written language based on drawings or pictographs.

## Persia

The ancient Persians developed an alphabet; contributed the religions and philosophies of Zoroastrianism, Mithraism, and gnosticism; and allowed conquered peoples to retain their own customs, laws, and religions.

## Greece

The classical civilization of Greece reached the highest levels of human achievement based on the foundations already laid by such ancient groups as the Egyptians, Phoenicians, Minoans, and Mycenaeans.

Among the more important contributions of Greece was the Greek alphabet derived from the Phoenician letters, which formed the basis for the Roman alphabet and our present-day alphabet. Extensive trading and colonization resulted in the spread of Greek civilization. The love of sports, with emphasis on a physically sound body, led to the tradition of the Olympic Games. Greece was responsible for the rise of independent, strong city-states. Other important areas that the Greeks are credited with influencing include drama, epic and lyric poetry, fables, myths centered on their many gods and goddesses, science, astronomy, medicine, mathematics, philosophy, art, architecture, and the recording of historical events.

The conquests of Alexander the Great spread Greek ideas to the lands he conquered and brought many ideas from Asia to the Greek world. The desire to learn as much about the world as possible was a major objective of his conquests.

Ancient Greece is often called the cradle of western civilization because of the enormous influence it had, not only on the time in which it flourished, but on western culture ever since.

Early Greek institutions have survived for thousands of years and have influenced the entire world. The Athenian form of democracy, with all citizens having an equal vote in their own government, is a philosophy upon which all modern democracies are based. In the United States, the Greek tradition of democracy was honored in the choice of Greek architectural styles for the nation's government buildings. The modern Olympic Games are a revival of an ancient Greek tradition, and many of the events are re-creations of original contests.

The works of the Greek epic poet Homer, author of the *Iliad* and the *Odyssey*, are considered the earliest in western literature, and are still read and taught today. The tradition of the theater was born in Greece, with the plays of Aristophanes and others. In philosophy, Aristotle developed an approach to learning that emphasized observation and thought, and Socrates and Plato contemplated the nature of being and the origins and ideals of government and political relations. Greek mythology has been the source of inspiration for literature into the present day.

In the field of mathematics, Pythagoras and Euclid laid the foundations of geometry and Archimedes calculated the value of *pi*. Herodotus and Thucydides were the first to apply research and interpretation to written history.

In the arts, Greek sensibilities were held as perfect forms which others might strive for. In sculpture, the Greeks achieved an idealistic aesthetic that had not been perfected before that time.

The Greek civilization served as an inspiration to the Roman Republic, which followed in its tradition of democracy and was directly influenced by its achievements in art and science. Later, during the Renaissance, European scholars and artists would rediscover ancient Greece's love for dedicated inquiry and artistic expression, leading to a surge in scientific discoveries and advancements in the arts.

## Rome

The ancient civilization of Rome owed much to the Greeks. Romans admired Greek architecture and arts, and built upon these traditions to create a distinct tradition of their own that would influence the western world for centuries.

The ancient civilization of Rome lasted approximately a thousand years (including the periods of the Roman Republic and the Roman Empire), although its influence on Europe and its history was felt for a much longer period. There was a sharp contrast between the curious, imaginative, inquisitive Greeks and the

The ancient civilization of Rome lasted approximately a thousand years.

practical, simple, down-to-earth Romans, who spread and preserved the ideas of ancient Greece and other cultural groups. The accomplishments of the Romans are numerous, but their greatest contributions included language, engineering, building, law, government, roads, trade, and the Pax Romana. The Pax Romana was the long period of peace allowing free travel and trade, spreading people, cultures, goods, and ideas all over a vast area of the known world.

In government, the Romans took the Athenian concept of democracy and built it into a complex system of a representative government that included executive, legislative, and judicial functions. In the arts, Romans created a realistic approach to portraiture, in contrast to the more idealized form of the Greeks. In architecture, Rome borrowed directly from the Greek tradition, but also developed the dome and the arch, allowing for larger and more dramatic forms. The Romans continued the Greek tradition of learning, often employing Greeks to educate their children.

The Roman Republic flourished in the centuries leading up to the advent of the Christian era. An organized bureaucracy and active political population provided elite Roman citizens with the means to ascend to positions of considerable authority. During the first century BCE, Gaius Julius Caesar ambitiously began to gather support among the ruling authorities of the Republic, eventually being named one of the two consuls who were elected annually. Caesar was ultimately named dictator for life, and was the transitional leader between the Roman Republic and what would become the Roman Empire.

Like the Republic, the Roman Empire also looked to the east, to Greece, for inspiration. The Macedonian conqueror Alexander, who had unified Greece and introduced the culture throughout the eastern world, provided many Roman emperors with a role model.

The Roman Empire extended through much of Europe, and Roman culture extended with it. Everywhere the Romans went, they built roads, established cities, and left their mark on the local population. The Roman language, Latin, spread as well and was transformed into the Romance languages of French and Spanish. The Roman alphabet, which was based on the Greek transformation of Phoenician letters, was adopted throughout the empire and is still used today.

The empire itself has served as a model for modern government, especially in federal systems such as that found in the United States. The eventual decline and fall of the empire has been a subject that has occupied historians for centuries.

## SKILL 8.2 Understands twentieth-century developments and transformations in world history

During the twentieth century, the world witnessed unprecedented strides in communications, a major expansion of international trade, and significant international diplomatic and military activity, including two world wars.

The rise of **nationalism** in Europe at the end of the nineteenth century led to a series of alliances and agreements among European nations. These agreements eventually led to the First World War, as nations called on their military allies to provide assistance and defense.

A new model of international relations was proposed following the devastation of World War I, one based on the mission to preserve peace. The **League of Nations** was formed to promote this peace, but it ultimately failed, having no way to enforce its resolutions. When Germany, led by Adolph Hitler, rebelled against the restrictions placed on it following World War I and began a campaign of military expansion through Europe, the Second World War ensued. Great Britain, the United States, and other allied nations combined forces to defeat Germany and the Axis powers.

Taking a lesson from the failure of the League of Nations, the world's nations organized the **United Nations**, an international assembly given the authority to arrange and enforce international resolutions.

World War II left Europe in ruins. As a result, the United States and the Soviet Union emerged as the two major world powers. Although allies in the war, tension arose between the two powers as the United States engaged in a policy of halting the spread of communism sponsored by the Soviets and China. The United States and the Soviet Union never engaged in direct military conflict during this **cold war**, but they were both involved in protracted conflicts in Korea and Vietnam. The threat of nuclear war increased as each power produced more and more weapons in an extended arms race. The threat of the spread of nuclear weapons largely diminished after the fall of the Soviet Union in the early 1990s, which ended the cold war.

In Asia, new economies matured and the formerly tightly-controlled Chinese market became more open to foreign investment, increasing China's influence as a major economic power. In Europe, the **European Union** made a bold move to a common currency, the euro, in a successful effort to consolidate the region's economic strength. In South America, countries such as Brazil and Venezuela

> *During the twentieth century, the world witnessed unprecedented strides in communications, a major expansion of international trade, and significant international diplomatic and military activity, including two world wars.*

showed growth despite political unrest, as Argentina suffered a near complete collapse of its economy. As the technology sector expanded, so did the economy of India, where high-tech companies found a highly educated workforce.

Conflict between the Muslim world and the United States increased during the last decade of the twentieth century, culminating in a terrorist attack on New York City and Washington, D.C., in 2001. These attacks, sponsored by the radical group Al Qaeda, prompted a military invasion by the United States of Afghanistan, where the group is based. Shortly afterwards, the United States, England, and several smaller countries addressed further instability in the region by ousting Iraqi dictator Saddam Hussein in a military campaign. In the eastern Mediterranean, tension between Israelis and Palestinians continued to build, regularly erupting into violence.

## SKILL 8.3 Understands the role of cross-cultural comparisons in world history instruction

Maintaining an awareness of the variations among cultures is crucial to understanding world history. Each country or group has its own perspective on key events. Some cultures developed in isolation, while others developed in direct relation to others. Understanding these differences and similarities allows for a fuller understanding of historical events.

CULTURAL IDENTITY: the identification of individuals or groups as they are influenced by their belonging to a particular group or culture

CULTURAL IDENTITY is the identification of individuals or groups as they are influenced by their belonging to a particular group or culture. This refers to the sense of who one is, what values are important, and what racial or ethnic characteristics are important in one's self-understanding and manner of interacting with the world and with others. In a nation such as the United States, with a well-deserved reputation as a "melting pot," the attachment to cultural identities can become a divisive factor in communities and societies. Cosmopolitanism, its alternative, tends to blur those cultural differences in the creation of a shared new culture.

*In order for a society to function as a cohesive and unifying force, there must be some degree of enculturation of all groups.*

Throughout history, groups have defined themselves and/or assimilated into the larger population to varying degrees. In order for a society to function as a cohesive and unifying force, there must be some degree of enculturation of all groups. The alternative is a competing, and often conflicting, collection of subgroups that are not able to cohere into a society. The failure to assimilate often results in culture wars as values and lifestyles come into conflict.

Cross-cultural exchanges, however, can enrich every involved group of persons with the discovery of shared values and needs, as well as an appreciation for the unique cultural characteristics of each. Historically, as the main civilizations grew and came into contact with each other, cultural exchanges took place at an increasing rate. Nevertheless, distinct religions, governments, and technological differences existed among the major civilizations during the first millennium CE. Such patterns of exchange and difference are woven throughout history and continue into the twenty-first century.

## SKILL 8.4 Knows key terms and basic concepts of economics (e.g., supply and demand, scarcity and choice, money and resources)

A **MARKET** is defined as the mechanism that brings buyers and sellers in contact with each other so that they can buy and sell. Buyers and sellers do not have to meet face to face; for example, when the consumer buys a good from a catalog or through the Internet, the buyer never comes face to face with the seller, yet both buyer and seller are part of a bona fide market.

> **MARKET:** the mechanism that brings buyers and sellers in contact with each other so that they can buy and sell

Markets exist in both the input and output sides of the economy. The **INPUT MARKET** is the market in which factors of production, or resources, are bought and sold. Factors of production, or inputs, fall into four broad categories:

- Land
- Labor
- Capital
- Entrepreneurship

> **INPUT MARKET:** the market in which factors of production, or resources, are bought and sold

Each of these four inputs is used in the production of every good and service. **OUTPUT MARKETS** refer to the market in which goods and services are sold. When the consumer goes to the local shoe store to buy a pair of shoes, the shoes are the output, and the consumer is taking part in the output market. However, the shoe store is a participant in both the input and output market. The sales clerk and workers are hiring out their resource of labor in return for a wage rate. Therefore they are participating in the input market.

> **OUTPUT MARKETS:** the market in which goods and services are sold

In a **market-oriented economy**, all of these markets function on the basis of supply and demand. The **EQUILIBRIUM PRICE** is determined as the overlap of the buying decisions of buyers with the selling decision of sellers. This is true whether the market is an input market, with a market rate of wage, or an output market,

> **EQUILIBRIUM PRICE:** the overlap of the buying decisions of buyers with the selling decision of sellers

with a market price of the output. A market-oriented economy results in the most efficient allocation of resources.

The best place to see **supply and demand** and markets in action is at a stock exchange or a commodity futures exchange. Buyers and sellers come face to face in the trading pit and accomplish trades by open outcry. Sellers who want to sell stocks or futures contracts call out the prices at which they will sell. Buyers who want to buy stocks or futures contracts call out the prices at which they will buy. When the two sides agree on price, a trade is made. This process goes on throughout trading hours. It is easiest to see how markets and supply and demand function in this kind of setting because it is open and obvious.

The same kinds of forces are at work at your local shopping mall or grocery store, even though the price appears as a given to you, the consumer. The price you see was arrived at through the operation of supply and demand. In this way, the equilibrium price is the price that clears the markets. The phrase "clears the market" means that there are no shortages or surpluses. If the price is too high, consumers won't buy the product and the store will have a surplus of the good. The stores then have to lower prices to eliminate the surplus merchandise. If the price is too low, consumers will buy so much that there will be a shortage. The shortage is then alleviated as the price goes up, rationing the good to those who are willing and able to pay the higher price for it.

In cases where government imposes legally mandated prices, the result can either be a shortage—with a price imposed that is above the market price—or a surplus, with a price imposed below the market price. The existence of price supports in agriculture is the reason for the surplus in agricultural products.

## SKILL 8.5 Understands how economics affects population, resources, and technology

The scarcity of resources is the basis for the existence of economics. Economics is defined as a study of how scarce resources are allocated to satisfy unlimited wants. In this sense, **resources** refer to these four factors of production:

- **Labor:** Anyone who sells his or her ability to produce goods and services.

- **Capital:** Anything that is manufactured to be used in the production process.

- **Land:** The land itself and everything occurring naturally on it (such as oil, minerals, and lumber).

- **Entrepreneurship:** The ability of an individual to combine the three inputs with his or her own talents to produce a viable good or service. The entrepreneur takes the risk and experiences the losses or profits.

The fact that the supply of these resources is finite means that society cannot have as much of everything that it wants. There is a constraint on production and consumption as well as on the kinds of goods and services that can be produced and consumed.

Scarcity means that choices have to be made. If society decides to produce more of one good, this means that fewer resources are available for the production of other goods. For example, assume that a society can produce two goods: good $x$ and good $y$. The society uses resources in the production of each good. If producing one unit of good $x$ requires the same amount of resources used to produce three units of good $y$, then producing one more unit of good $x$ results in a decrease in three units of good $y$. In effect, one unit of good $x$ "costs" three units of good $y$. This cost is referred to as **opportunity cost**.

Opportunity cost is essentially the value of the sacrificed alternative: the value of what had to be given up in order to have the output of good $x$. Opportunity cost does not just refer to production. Your opportunity cost of studying with this guide is the value of what you are not doing because you are studying, whether it is watching TV, spending time with family, or working. Every choice has an opportunity cost.

If wants were limited and/or if resources were unlimited, the concepts of choice and opportunity cost would not exist, and neither would the field of economics. There would be enough resources to satisfy the wants of consumers, businesses, and governments. The allocation of resources wouldn't be a problem. Society could have more of both good $x$ and good $y$ without having to give up anything. There would be no opportunity cost. However, this isn't the situation that societies are faced with.

Because resources are scarce, society doesn't want to waste them. Society wants to obtain the most satisfaction it can from the consumption of the goods and services produced with its scarce resources. The members of society don't want their scarce resources wasted through inefficiency. This means that producers must choose an efficient production process, which is the lowest-cost means of production. High costs mean wasted resources.

Consumers also don't want society's resources to be wasted by producing goods that they don't want. Producers reduce this kind of inefficiency by determining which goods their consumers want. They do this by watching how consumers spend their money, essentially "voting" with their dollar spending. A desirable good, one that consumers want, earns profits. A good that incurs losses is a good that society doesn't want its resources wasted on. This signals the producer that society, as a whole, wants its resources used in another way.

> SKILL 8.6  **Understands the government's role in economics and impact of economics on government**

## The Role of Government

*Government is required to provide the framework for the functioning of the economy.*

Even in a capitalist economy, there is a role for government. Government is required to provide the framework for the functioning of the economy. This requires a legal system, a monetary system, and a "watchdog" authority to protect consumers from bad or dangerous products and practices. Society needs a government to correct for the misallocation of resources when the market doesn't function properly, as in the case of externalities, like pollution. Another function of the government is to correct for the unequal distribution of income that results from a market-oriented system. Government functions to provide public goods, like national defense, and to correct for macro-instability like inflation and unemployment through the use of monetary and fiscal policies. Although there are countless more ways in which the government acts on the economy, these are the more important ways.

In the same way, economics has an impact on government. First, the government has to respond to economic situations. Inflation and unemployment call on the government to implement various economic policies. The business cycle and the policies implemented to counter the business cycle affect the level of tax revenues that the government receives. This affects the budget and the amount of dollars that government has to spend on various programs.

A government that has lower tax revenues due to economic conditions has to postpone certain discretionary spending programs until the economy improves. Unlike individuals, government can spend more tax dollars than it receives and operate in a debt condition financed by selling bonds. These are dollars that have to be repaid at some future date. Different economic conditions and situations call on the government to respond with different policies; the government has to figure out what to do and how much to do in each situation.

## Types of Economic Systems

Economic systems refer to the arrangements a society has devised to answer what are known as the "three questions":

1. What goods to produce

2. How to produce the goods

3. For whom the goods are being produced (or how the allocation of the output is determined)

Different economic systems answer these questions in different ways.

A **MARKET ECONOMY** answers these questions in terms of demand and supply and the use of markets. Consumers vote for the products they want with their dollar spending. Goods acquiring enough dollar votes are profitable, signaling to the producers that society wants its scarce resources used in this way. This is how the *what* question is answered. The producer then hires inputs in accordance with the goods consumers want, looking for the most efficient or lowest-cost method of production. The lower a firm's costs for any given level of revenue, the higher the firm's profits. This is the way the *how* question is answered in a market economy. The for *whom* question is answered in the marketplace by the determination of the equilibrium price. Price serves to ration the goods to those who can and will transact at the market price or better. Those who can't or won't are excluded from the market. The United States has a market economy.

The opposite of the market economy is called the **CENTRALLY PLANNED ECONOMY**. This used to be called Communism, even though the term is not correct in a strict Marxian sense. In a planned economy, the means of production are publicly owned, with little, if any private ownership. Instead of the "three questions" being solved by markets, there is a planning authority that makes the decisions. The planning authority decides what will be produced and how. Since most planned economies direct resources into the production of capital and military goods, there is little remaining for consumer goods; the result is often chronic shortages. Price functions as an accounting measure and does not reflect scarcity. The former Soviet Union and most of the Eastern Bloc countries were planned economies of this sort.

In between the two extremes is **MARKET SOCIALISM**. This is a mixed economic system that uses both markets and planning. Planning is usually used to direct resources at the upper levels of the economy, with markets used to determine the prices of consumer goods and wages. This kind of economic system answers the "three questions" with planning and markets. The former Yugoslavia was a market socialist economy.

**MARKET ECONOMY:** an economy that operates by voluntary exchange in a free market and is not planned or controlled by a central authority

*The United States has a market economy.*

**CENTRALLY PLANNED ECONOMY:** the opposite of the market economy, the means of production are publicly owned, with little, if any private ownership

**MARKET SOCIALISM:** a mixed economic system that uses both markets and planning

You can put each nation of the world on a continuum in terms of these characteristics and rank them from most capitalistic to most planned. The United States would probably rank as the most capitalistic and North Korea would probably rank as the most planned, but this doesn't mean that the United States doesn't engage in planning or that economies like mainland China don't use markets.

# DOMAIN IV

## SCIENCE (5005)

# PERSONALIZED STUDY PLAN

| PAGE | COMPETENCY AND SKILL | KNOWN MATERIAL/ SKIP IT | BRIEFLY REVIEW eSTICKYNOTES | MAKE eFLASHCARDS | TAKE ADDITIONAL SAMPLE TESTS |
|------|----------------------|:---:|:---:|:---:|:---:|
| 229 | **009: Earth science** | ☐ | ☐ | ☐ | ☐ |
| | 9.1: Understands the structure of the Earth system *(e.g., structure and properties of the solid Earth, the hydrosphere, the atmosphere)* | ☐ | ☐ | ☐ | ☐ |
| | 9.2: Understands processes of the Earth system *(e.g., earth processes of the solid Earth, the hydrosphere, the atmosphere)* | ☐ | ☐ | ☐ | ☐ |
| | 9.3: Understands Earth history *(e.g., origin of Earth, paleontology, the rock record)* | ☐ | ☐ | ☐ | ☐ |
| | 9.4: Understands Earth and the universe *(e.g., stars and galaxies, the solar system and planets; Earth, Sun, and Moon relationships)* | ☐ | ☐ | ☐ | ☐ |
| | 9.5: Understands Earth patterns, cycles, and change | ☐ | ☐ | ☐ | ☐ |
| | 9.6: Understands science as a human endeavor, process, and career | ☐ | ☐ | ☐ | ☐ |
| | 9.7: Understands science as inquiry *(e.g., questioning, gathering data, drawing reasonable conclusions)* | ☐ | ☐ | ☐ | ☐ |
| | 9.8: Understands how to use resource and research material in science | ☐ | ☐ | ☐ | ☐ |
| | 9.9: Understands the unifying processes of science *(e.g., systems, order, and organization)* | ☐ | ☐ | ☐ | ☐ |
| 249 | **010: Life science** | ☐ | ☐ | ☐ | ☐ |
| | 10.1: Understands the structure and function of living systems *(e.g., living characteristics and cells, tissues and organs, life processes)* | ☐ | ☐ | ☐ | ☐ |
| | 10.2: Understands reproduction and heredity *(e.g., growth and development, patterns of inheritance of traits, molecular basis of heredity)* | ☐ | ☐ | ☐ | ☐ |
| | 10.3: Understands change over time in living things *(e.g., life cycles, mutations, adaptation and natural selection)* | ☐ | ☐ | ☐ | ☐ |
| | 10.4: Understands regulation and behavior *(e.g., life cycles, responses to external stimuli, controlling the internal environment)* | ☐ | ☐ | ☐ | ☐ |
| | 10.5: Understands unity and diversity of life, adaptation, and classification | ☐ | ☐ | ☐ | ☐ |
| | 10.6: Understands the interdependence of organisms *(e.g., ecosystems, populations, communities)* | ☐ | ☐ | ☐ | ☐ |
| | 10.7: Knows about personal health *(e.g., nutrition, communicable diseases, substance abuse)* | ☐ | ☐ | ☐ | ☐ |
| | 10.8: Understands science as a human endeavor, process, and career | ☐ | ☐ | ☐ | ☐ |
| | 10.9: Understands science as inquiry *(e.g., questioning, gathering data, drawing reasonable conclusions)* | ☐ | ☐ | ☐ | ☐ |
| | 10.10: Understands how to use resource and research material in science | ☐ | ☐ | ☐ | ☐ |
| | 10.11: Understands the unifying processes of science *(e.g., systems, order, organization)* | ☐ | ☐ | ☐ | ☐ |

# PERSONALIZED STUDY PLAN

| PAGE | COMPETENCY AND SKILL | KNOWN MATERIAL/ SKIP IT | BRIEFLY REVIEW eSTICKYNOTES | MAKE eFLASHCARDS | TAKE ADDITIONAL SAMPLE TESTS |
|------|---------------------|:---:|:---:|:---:|:---:|
| 280 | **011: Physical science** | ☐ | ☐ | ☐ | ☐ |
| | 11.1: Understands the physical and chemical properties and structure of matter *(e.g., changes of states, mixtures and solutions, atoms and elements)* | ☐ | ☐ | ☐ | ☐ |
| | 11.2: Understands forces and motions *(e.g., types of motion, laws of motion, forces and equilibrium)* | ☐ | ☐ | ☐ | ☐ |
| | 11.3: Understands energy *(e.g., forms of energy, transfer and conservation of energy, simple machines)* | ☐ | ☐ | ☐ | ☐ |
| | 11.4: Understands interactions of energy and matter *(e.g., electricity, magnetism, sound)* | ☐ | ☐ | ☐ | ☐ |
| | 11.5: Understands science as a human endeavor, process, and career | ☐ | ☐ | ☐ | ☐ |
| | 11.6: Understands science as inquiry *(e.g., questioning, gathering data, drawing reasonable conclusions)* | ☐ | ☐ | ☐ | ☐ |
| | 11.7: Understands how to use resource and research material in science | ☐ | ☐ | ☐ | ☐ |
| | 11.8: Understands the unifying processes of science *(e.g., systems, order, and organization)* | ☐ | ☐ | ☐ | ☐ |

# COMPETENCY 009
## EARTH SCIENCE

> **SKILL** **Understands the structure of the Earth system** (e.g., structure and
> **9.1** properties of the solid Earth, the hydrosphere, the atmosphere)

## Earth's Plates

Data obtained from many sources led scientists to develop the theory of **PLATE TECTONICS**. This theory is the most current model that explains not only the movement of the continents but also the changes in the Earth's crust caused by internal forces.

**PLATES** are rigid blocks of the Earth's crust and upper mantle. These rigid solid blocks make up the lithosphere. The Earth's lithosphere is broken into nine large sections and several small ones. These moving slabs are called plates. The major plates are named after the continents they are "transporting." The plates float on and move with a layer of hot, plastic-like rock in the upper mantle. Geologists believe that the heat currents circulating within the mantle cause this plastic zone of rock to slowly flow, carrying along the overlying crustal plates.

Movement of these crustal plates creates areas where the plates diverge as well as areas where the plates converge. A major area of **divergence** is located in the Mid-Atlantic. Currents of hot mantle rock rise and separate at this point of divergence, creating new oceanic crust at the rate of two to ten centimeters per year. **Convergence** is when the oceanic crust collides with either another oceanic plate or a continental plate. The oceanic crust sinks, forming an enormous trench and generating volcanic activity. Convergence also includes continent-to-continent plate collisions. When two plates slide past one another, a transform fault is created.

These movements produce many major features of the Earth's surface, such as mountain ranges, volcanoes, and earthquake zones. Most of these features are located at plate boundaries, where the plates interact by spreading apart, pressing together, or sliding past each other. These movements are very slow, averaging only a few centimeters a year.

Boundaries form between spreading plates where the crust is forced apart in a process called **rifting**. Rifting generally occurs at mid-ocean ridges. Rifting can also take place within a continent, splitting the continent into smaller landmasses that drift away from each other, thereby forming an ocean basin between them.

> **PLATE TECTONICS:** theory that explains not only the movement of the continents but also the changes in the Earth's crust caused by internal forces

> **PLATES:** rigid blocks of the Earth's crust and upper mantle

The Red Sea is a product of rifting. As the seafloor spreading takes place, new material is added to the inner edges of the separating plates. In this way the plates grow larger, and the ocean basin widens. This is the process that broke up the supercontinent Pangaea and created the Atlantic Ocean.

Boundaries between plates that are colliding are zones of intense crustal activity. When a plate of ocean crust collides with a plate of continental crust, the more dense oceanic plate slides under the lighter continental plate and plunges into the mantle. This process is called subduction, and the site where it takes place is called a subduction zone. A subduction zone is usually seen on the sea floor as a deep depression called a trench.

The crustal movement identified by plates sliding sideways past each other produces a plate boundary characterized by major faults that are capable of unleashing powerful earthquakes. The San Andreas fault forms such a boundary between the Pacific plate and the North American plate.

## Atmosphere

Dry air has three basic components: dry gas, water vapor, and solid particles (dust from soil, etc.).

The most abundant dry gases in the atmosphere are:

$(N_2)$ Nitrogen 78.09 %          $(Ar)$ Argon 0.93 %

$(O_2)$ Oxygen 20.95 %          $(CO_2)$ Carbon Dioxide 0.03 %

The atmosphere is divided into four main layers based on temperature:

- **Troposphere:** This layer is the closest to the Earth's surface. All weather phenomena occur here because it is the layer with the most water vapor and dust. Air temperature decreases with increasing altitude. The average thickness of the troposphere is seven miles (eleven kilometers).

- **Stratosphere:** This layer contains very little water. Clouds within this layer are extremely rare. The ozone layer is located in the upper portions of the stratosphere. Air temperature is fairly constant but does increase somewhat with height due to the absorption of solar energy and ultraviolet rays from the ozone layer.

- **Mesosphere:** Air temperature again decreases with height in this layer. This is the coldest layer, with temperatures in the range of -1000C at the top.

- **Thermosphere:** This layer extends upward into space. Oxygen molecules in this layer absorb energy from the Sun, causing temperatures to increase with height. The lower part of the thermosphere is called the ionosphere. Here, charged particles (ions) and free electrons can be found. When gases in the ionosphere are excited by solar radiation, the gases give off light and glow in the sky. These glowing lights are called the aurora borealis in the Northern Hemisphere and aurora australis in the Southern Hemisphere. The upper portion of the thermosphere is called the exosphere. Gas molecules are very far apart in this layer. Layers of exosphere are also known as the Van Allen belts and are held together by the Earth's magnetic field.

> **SKILL 9.2** **Understands processes of the Earth system** (e.g., earth processes of the solid Earth, the hydrosphere, the atmosphere)

## Mountains

OROGENY is the term given to natural mountain building. A mountain is terrain that has been raised high above the surrounding landscape by volcanic action, or some form of tectonic plate collisions. The plate collisions could either be intercontinental collisions or ocean floor collisions with a continental crust (subduction).

The physical composition of mountains includes igneous, metamorphic, and sedimentary rocks; some may have rock layers that are tilted or distorted by plate collision forces.

There are many different types of mountains. The physical attributes of a mountain range depend upon the angle at which plate movement thrusts layers of rock to the surface. Many mountains (the Adirondacks, the Southern Rockies) were formed along high-angle faults.

Folded mountains (the Alps, the Himalayas) are produced by the folding of rock layers during their formation. The Himalayas are the highest mountains in the world; they contain Mount Everest, which rises almost nine kilometers above sea level. The Himalayas were formed when India collided with Asia. The movement that created this collision is still in process at the rate of a few centimeters per year.

Fault-block mountains (in Utah, Arizona, and New Mexico) are created when plate movement produces tension forces instead of compression forces. The area under tension produces normal faults, and rock along these faults is displaced upward.

Dome mountains are formed as magma tries to push up through the crust but fails to break the surface. Dome mountains resemble a huge blister on the Earth's surface.

OROGENY: natural mountain building

*The physical composition of mountains includes igneous, metamorphic, and sedimentary rocks*

Upwarped mountains (the Black Hills of South Dakota) are created in association with a broad arching of the crust. They can also be formed by rock thrust upward along high angle faults.

## The Formation of Mountains

Mountains are produced by different types of processes. Most major mountain ranges are formed by the processes of folding and faulting.

In folding, mountains are produced by the folding of rock layers. Crustal movements may press horizontal layers of sedimentary rock together from the sides, squeezing them into wavelike folds. Up-folded sections of rock are called anticlines; down-folded sections of rock are called synclines. The Appalachian Mountains are an example of folded mountains, with long ridges and valleys in a series of anticlines, and synclines formed by folded rock layers.

*The Appalachian Mountains are an example of folded mountains.*

Faults are fractures in the Earth's crust that have been created by either tension or compression forces transmitted through the crust. These forces are produced by the movement of separate blocks of crust. Faultings are categorized on the basis of the relative movement between the blocks on both sides of the fault plane. The movement can be horizontal, vertical, or oblique.

A dip-slip fault occurs when the movement of the plates is vertical and opposite. The displacement is in the direction of the inclination, or dip, of the fault. Dip-slip faults are classified as normal faults when the rock above the fault plane moves down relative to the rock below.

Reverse faults are created when the rock above the fault plane moves up relative to the rock below. Reverse faults with a very low angle to the horizontal are also referred to as thrust faults.

Faults in which the dominant displacement is horizontal movement along the trend or strike (length) of the fault are called strike-slip faults. When a large strike-slip fault is associated with plate boundaries it is called a transform fault. The San Andreas fault in California is a well-known transform fault.

Faults that have both vertical and horizontal movement are called oblique-slip faults.

## Volcanoes

VOLCANISM: the movement of magma through the crust and its emergence as lava onto the Earth's surface

VOLCANISM is the term given to the movement of magma through the crust and its emergence as lava onto the Earth's surface. Volcanic mountains are built up by successive deposits of volcanic materials.

An **ACTIVE VOLCANO** is one that is currently erupting or building to an eruption. A **DORMANT VOLCANO** is one that is between eruptions but still shows signs of internal activity that might lead to an eruption in the future. An **EXTINCT VOLCANO** is said to be no longer capable of erupting. Most of the world's active volcanoes are found along the rim of the Pacific Ocean, which is also a major earthquake zone. This curving belt of active faults and volcanoes is often called the Ring of Fire. The world's best known volcanic mountains include Mount Etna in Italy and Mount Kilimanjaro in Africa. The Hawaiian Islands are actually the tops of a chain of volcanic mountains that rise from the ocean floor.

There are three types of volcanic mountains:

- **Shield volcanoes** are associated with quiet eruptions. Lava emerges from the vent or opening in the crater and flows freely out over the Earth's surface until it cools and hardens into a layer of igneous rock. A repeated lava flow builds this type of volcano into the largest volcanic mountain. Mauna Loa in Hawaii is the largest shield volcano on Earth.

- **Cinder-cone volcanoes** are associated with explosive eruptions as lava is hurled high into the air in a spray of droplets of various sizes. These droplets cool and harden into cinders and particles of ash before falling to the ground. The ash and cinder pile up around the vent to form a steep, cone-shaped hill called the cinder cone. Cinder-cone volcanoes are relatively small but may form quite rapidly.

- **Composite volcanoes** are those built by both lava flows and layers of ash and cinders. Mount Fuji in Japan, Mount St. Helens in the United States (Washington), and Mount Vesuvius in Italy are all famous composite volcanoes.

When lava cools, igneous rock is formed. This formation can occur either above or below ground.

**INTRUSIVE ROCK** includes any igneous rock that was formed below the Earth's surface. Batholiths are the largest structures of intrusive rock and are composed of near-granite materials; they are the core of the Sierra Nevada Mountains. **EXTRUSIVE ROCK** includes any igneous rock that was formed at the Earth's surface.

**DIKES** are old lava tubes formed when magma entered a vertical fracture and hardened. Sometimes magma squeezes between two rock layers and hardens into a thin horizontal sheet called a sill. A laccolith is formed in much the same way as a sill, but the magma that creates a laccolith is very thick and does not flow easily. It pools and forces the overlying strata creating an obvious surface dome.

**ACTIVE VOLCANO:** one that is currently erupting or building to an eruption

**DORMANT VOLCANO:** one that is between eruptions but still shows signs of internal activity that might lead to an eruption in the future

**EXTINCT VOLCANO:** no longer capable of erupting

**INTRUSIVE ROCK:** any igneous rock that was formed below the Earth's surface

**EXTRUSIVE ROCK:** any igneous rock that was formed at the Earth's surface

**DIKES:** old lava tubes formed when magma entered a vertical fracture and hardened

CALDERA: normally formed by the collapse of the top of a volcano

A **CALDERA** is normally formed by the collapse of the top of a volcano. This collapse can be caused by a massive explosion that destroys the cone and empties most, if not all, of the magma chamber below the volcano. The cone collapses into the empty magma chamber, forming a caldera.

An inactive volcano may have magma solidified in its pipe. This structure, called a volcanic neck, is resistant to erosion and today may be the only visible evidence of the past presence of an active volcano.

## Rocks

There are three major subdivisions of rocks:

- **Sedimentary rocks** are created through a process known as lithification. It occurs when fluid sediments are transformed into solid rocks. One common process affecting sediments is compaction, when the weights of overlying materials compress and compact the deeper sediments. The compaction process leads to cementation. Cementation is when sediments are converted to sedimentary rock.

- **Igneous rocks** can be classified according to their texture, their composition, and the way they formed. They are made from molten rock. Molten rock is called **magma**. As magma cools, the elements and compounds begin to form crystals. The more slowly the magma cools, the larger the crystals grow. Rocks with large crystals are said to have a coarse-grained texture. Granite is an example of a coarse-grained igneous rock. Rocks that cool rapidly before any crystals can form have a glassy texture like obsidian, also commonly known as volcanic glass.

- **Metamorphic rocks** are formed by high temperatures and great pressures. The process by which the rocks undergo these changes is called **metamorphism**. The outcome of metamorphic changes includes deformation by extreme heat and pressure, compaction, destruction of the original characteristics of the parent rock, bending and folding while in a plastic stage, and the emergence of completely new and different minerals due to chemical reactions with heated water and dissolved minerals.

  Metamorphic rocks are classified into two groups: foliated (leaflike) rocks and unfoliated rocks. Foliated rocks consist of compressed, parallel bands of minerals, which give the rocks a striped appearance. Examples of such rocks include slate, schist, and gneiss. Unfoliated rocks are not banded; examples of unfoliated rocks include quartzite, marble, and anthracite.

MINERALS are natural, nonliving solids with a definite chemical composition and a crystalline structure. ORES are minerals or rock deposits that can be mined for a profit. ROCKS are Earth materials made of one or more minerals. A ROCK FACIES is a rock group that differs from comparable rocks (as in composition, age, or fossil content).

## Glaciation

About twelve thousand years ago, a vast sheet of ice covered a large part of the northern United States. This huge, frozen mass moved southward from the northern regions of Canada as several large bodies of slow-moving ice. These bodies of ice, called GLACIERS, are large masses of ice that move or flow over the land in response to gravity. Glaciers form among high mountains and in other cold regions. A time period in which glaciers advance over a large portion of a continent is called an ICE AGE.

Evidence of glacial coverage remains as abrasive grooves, large boulders from northern environments dropped in southerly locations, glacial troughs created by the rounding out of steep valleys through glacial scouring, and the remains of glacial sources called cirques that were created by frost wedging the rock at the bottom of the glacier. Remains of plants and animals typically found in warm climates that have been discovered in the moraines and outwash plains help support the theory of periods of warmth during the past ice ages.

The major ice age began about two to three million years ago. This age saw the advancement and retreat of glacial ice over millions of years. Theories relating to the origin of glacial activity include plate tectonics, through which it can be demonstrated that some continental masses, now in temperate climates, were at one time blanketed by ice and snow. Another theory involves changes in the Earth's orbit around the Sun, changes in the angle of the Earth's axis, and the wobbling of the Earth's axis. Support for the validity of this theory has come from deep-ocean research that indicates a correlation between climatic-sensitive microorganisms and the changes in the Earth's orbital status.

There are two main types of glaciers: valley glaciers and continental glaciers. Erosion by valley glaciers is characteristic of U-shaped erosion. Valley glaciers produce sharp-peaked mountains such as the Matterhorn in Switzerland. Erosion by continental glaciers is characteristic of the movement of glaciers over mountains, leaving smoothed, rounded mountains and ridges in their paths.

MINERALS: natural, non-living solids with a definite chemical composition and a crystalline structure

ORES: minerals or rock deposits that can be mined for a profit

ROCKS: Earth materials made of one or more minerals

ROCK FACIES: a rock group that differs from comparable rocks (as in composition, age, or fossil content)

GLACIERS: large masses of ice that move or flow over the land in response to gravity

ICE AGE: a time period in which glaciers advance over a large portion of a continent

## Fossilization

A **FOSSIL** is the remains or trace of an ancient organism that has been preserved naturally in the Earth's crust. Sedimentary rocks usually are rich sources of fossil remains. Those fossils found in layers of sediment were embedded in the slowly forming sedimentary rock strata. The oldest fossils known are the traces of 3.5 billion-year-old bacteria found in sedimentary rocks. Few fossils are found in metamorphic rock, and virtually none are found in igneous rocks. The magma is so hot that any organism trapped in the magma is destroyed.

Although the fairly well preserved remains of a woolly mammoth embedded in ice were found in Russia in May 2007, the best-preserved animal remains are typically discovered in natural tar pits. When an animal accidentally falls into the tar, it becomes trapped, sinking to the bottom. Preserved bones of the saber-toothed cat have been found in tar pits.

Prehistoric insects have been found trapped in ancient amber or fossil resin that was excreted by some extinct species of pine trees. Fossil molds are the hollow spaces in a rock previously occupied by bones or shells. A fossil cast is a fossil mold that fills with sediments or minerals and later hardens, forming a cast.

Fossil tracks are the imprints in hardened mud left behind by birds or animals.

## Types of Weathering

**EROSION** is the inclusion and transportation of surface materials by another moveable material—usually water, winds, or ice. The most important cause of erosion is running water. Streams, rivers, and tides are constantly at work removing weathered fragments of bedrock and carrying them away from their original location.

A stream erodes bedrock by the grinding action of the sand, pebbles, and other rock fragments. This grinding against each other is called **abrasion**. Streams also erode rocks by dissolving or absorbing their minerals. Limestone and marble are readily dissolved by streams.

**DEPOSITION**, also known as sedimentation, is the term for the process by which material from one area is slowly deposited into another area. This is usually due to the movement of wind, water, or ice containing particles of matter. When the rate of movement slows down, particles filter out and remain behind, causing a buildup of matter. Note that this is a result of matter being eroded and removed from another site.

**FOSSIL:** the remains or trace of an ancient organism that has been preserved naturally in the Earth's crust

Sedimentary rocks usually are rich sources of fossil remains.

**EROSION:** the inclusion and transportation of surface materials by another moveable material—usually water, winds, or ice

The most important cause of erosion is running water.

**DEPOSITION:** also known as sedimentation, the process by which material from one area is slowly deposited into another area

The breaking down of rocks at or near the Earth's surface is known as **WEATHER-ING**. Weathering breaks down these rocks into smaller and smaller pieces. There are two types of weathering: physical weathering and chemical weathering.

**Physical weathering** is the process by which rocks are broken down into smaller fragments without undergoing any change in chemical composition. Physical weathering is mainly caused by the freezing of water, the expansion of rock, and the activities of plants and animals.

One example of physical weathering occurs through frost wedging, which is the cycle of daytime thawing and refreezing at night. This cycle causes large rock masses, especially the rocks exposed on mountaintops, to be broken into smaller pieces. Another example is the peeling away of the outer layers from a rock, which is called **exfoliation**. Rounded mountaintops are called exfoliation domes; they have been formed in this way.

**Chemical weathering** is the breaking down of rocks through changes in their chemical composition. Water, oxygen, and carbon dioxide are the main agents of chemical weathering. When water and carbon dioxide combine chemically, they produce a weak acid that breaks down rocks. An example of this is the change of feldspar in granite to clay.

> **WEATHERING:** the breaking down of rocks at or near the Earth's surface

## SKILL 9.3 Understands Earth history (e.g., origin of Earth, paleontology, the rock record)

Earth's history extends over more than four billion years and is reckoned in terms of a scale. Paleontologists who study the history of the Earth have divided this huge period of time into four large time units called **eons**. Eons are divided into smaller units of time called **eras**. An era refers to a time interval in which particular plants and animals were dominant or present in great abundance. The end of an era is most often characterized by:

• A general uplifting of the crust

• The extinction of the dominant plants or animals

• The appearance of new life forms

Each era is divided into several smaller divisions of time called periods. Some periods are divided into smaller time units called epochs. The table below outlines these eras and periods by their major characteristics.

| ERA | PERIOD | TIME | CHARACTERISTICS |
|---|---|---|---|
| Cenozoic | Quaternary | 1.6 million years ago to the present | The ice age occurred, and human beings evolved. |
| | Tertiary | 65-1.64 million years ago | Mammals and birds evolved to replace the great reptiles and dinosaurs that had just become extinct. Forests gave way to grasslands, and the climate become cooler. |
| Mesozoic | Cretaceous | 135-65 million years ago | Reptiles and dinosaurs roamed the Earth. Most of the modern continents had split away from the large landmass, Pangaea, and many were flooded by shallow chalk seas. |
| | Jurassic | 350-135 million years ago | Reptiles were beginning to evolve. Pangaea started to break up. Deserts gave way to forests and swamps. |
| | Triassic | | |
| Paleozoic | Permian | 355-250 million years ago | Continents came together to form one big landmass, Pangaea. Forests (that formed today's coal) grew on deltas around the new mountains, and deserts formed. |
| | Carboniferous | | |
| | Devonian | 410-355 million years ago | Continents started moving toward each other. The first land animals, such as insects and amphibians, existed. Many fish swam in the seas. |
| | Silurian | 510-410 million years ago | Sea life flourished, and the first fish evolved. The earliest land plants began to grow around shorelines and estuaries. |
| | Ordovician | | |
| | Cambrian | 570-510 million years ago | No life on land, but many kinds of sea animals existed. |
| Precambrian | Proterozoic | Beginning of the Earth to 570 million years ago (seven-eighths of the Earth's history) | Some sort of life existed. |
| | Archaean | | No life. |

## Using Geologic Evidence to Understand the Past

The process of determining the age of rocks by cataloging their composition has been outmoded since the middle 1800s. Today, a sequential history can be determined by the fossil content (principle of fossil succession) of a rock system as well as its superposition within a range of systems. This classification process was termed stratigraphy and permitted the construction of a geologic column in which rock systems are arranged in their correct chronological order.

UNIFORMITARIANISM is a fundamental concept in modern geology. It simply states that the physical, chemical, and biological laws that operated in the geologic past operate in the same way today. The forces and processes that we observe presently shaping our planet have been at work for a very long time. This idea is commonly stated as, "The present is the key to the past." CATASTROPHISM is the concept that the Earth was shaped by catastrophic events of a short-term nature.

Estimates of the Earth's age have been made possible with the discovery of radioactivity and the invention of instruments that can measure the amount of radioactivity in rocks. The use of radioactivity to make accurate determinations of Earth's age is called ABSOLUTE DATING. This process depends upon comparing the amount of radioactive material in a rock with the amount that has decayed in another element. Studying the radiation given off by atoms of radioactive elements is the most accurate method of measuring the Earth's age.

Radioactive atoms are unstable and are continuously breaking down or undergoing decay. The radioactive element that decays is called the parent element. The new element that results from the radioactive decay of the parent element is called the daughter element. The time required for one half of a given amount of a radioactive element to decay is called the half-life of that element or compound. Geologists also commonly use carbon dating to calculate the age of a fossil substance.

> **UNIFORMITARIANISM:** states that the physical, chemical, and biological laws that operated in the geologic past operate in the same way today

> **CATASTROPHISM:** the concept that the Earth was shaped by catastrophic events of a short-term nature

> **ABSOLUTE DATING:** the use of radioactivity to make accurate determinations of Earth's age

*Studying the radiation given off by atoms of radioactive elements is the most accurate method of measuring the Earth's age.*

---

**SKILL 9.4** **Understands Earth and the universe** *(e.g., stars and galaxies, the solar system and planets; Earth, Sun, and Moon relationships)*

Earth is the third planet away from the Sun in our solar system. Earth's numerous types of motion and states of orientation greatly affect global conditions, such as seasons, tides, and lunar phases. The Earth orbits the Sun within a period of 365 days. During this orbit, the average distance between the Earth and the Sun is 93 million miles.

The shape of the Earth's orbit around the Sun deviates from the shape of a circle only slightly. This deviation, known as the Earth's eccentricity, has a very small effect on the Earth's climate. The Earth is closest to the Sun at perihelion, occurring around January 2 of each year, and farthest from the Sun at aphelion, occurring around July 2. Because the Earth is closest to the Sun in January, the northern winter is slightly warmer than the southern winter.

## Planets

There are eight established planets in our solar system: Mercury, Venus, Earth, Mars, Jupiter, Saturn, Uranus, and Neptune. For many years Pluto was an established planet in our solar system, but as of 2006, it was reclassified as a dwarf planet.

The planets are divided into two groups based on distance from the Sun. The inner planets include Mercury, Venus, Earth, and Mars. The outer planets include Jupiter, Saturn, Uranus, and Neptune.

| PLANETS IN THE SOLAR SYSTEM | |
|---|---|
| Mercury | The closest planet to the Sun. Its surface has craters and rocks. The atmosphere is composed of hydrogen, helium, and sodium. Mercury was named after the Roman messenger god. |
| Venus | Has a slow rotation when compared to Earth. Venus and Uranus rotate in opposite directions from the other planets. This opposite rotation is called retrograde rotation. The surface of Venus is not visible due to the extensive cloud cover. The atmosphere is composed mostly of carbon dioxide, while sulfuric acid droplets in the dense cloud cover give Venus a yellow appearance. Venus has a greater greenhouse effect than that observed on Earth, and the dense clouds combined with carbon dioxide trap heat. Venus was named after the Roman goddess of love. |
| Earth | Considered a water planet, with 70 percent of its surface covered by water. Gravity holds the masses of water in place. The different temperatures observed on Earth allow for the different states of water (solid, liquid, gas) to exist. The atmosphere is composed mainly of oxygen and nitrogen. Earth is the only planet known to support life. |
| Mars | Surface contains numerous craters, active and extinct volcanoes, ridges, and valleys with extremely deep fractures. Iron oxide found in the dusty soil makes the surface seem rust-colored and the skies seem pink in color. The atmosphere is composed of carbon dioxide, nitrogen, argon, oxygen, and water vapor. Mars has polar regions with ice caps composed of water as well as two satellites (moons). Mars was named after the Roman war god. |
| Jupiter | The largest planet in the solar system. Jupiter has sixteen moons. The atmosphere is composed of hydrogen, helium, methane, and ammonia. There are white-colored bands of clouds indicating rising gas and dark-colored bands of clouds indicating descending gases. The gas movement is caused by heat resulting from the energy of Jupiter's core. Jupiter has a strong magnetic field and a great red spot that is thought to be a hurricane-like cloud. |

*Table continued on next page*

| PLANETS IN THE SOLAR SYSTEM | |
|---|---|
| Saturn | The second largest planet in the solar system. Saturn has rings of ice, rock, and dust particles circling it. Its atmosphere is composed of hydrogen, helium, methane, and ammonia. It has more than twenty satellites. Saturn was named after the Roman god of agriculture. |
| Uranus | The third largest planet in the solar system and has retrograde revolution. Uranus is a gaseous planet. It has ten dark rings and fifteen satellites. Its atmosphere is composed of hydrogen, helium, and methane. Uranus was named after the Greek god of the heavens. |
| Neptune | Another gaseous planet with an atmosphere consisting of hydrogen, helium, and methane. Neptune has three rings and two satellites. It was named after the Roman sea god because its atmosphere is the same color as the seas. |
| Pluto | Once considered the smallest planet in the solar system, its status was changed to that of a dwarf planet in 2006. Pluto's atmosphere probably contains methane, ammonia, and frozen water. Pluto has one satellite. It revolves around the Sun every 250 years. Pluto was named after the Roman god of the underworld. |

## The Sun and Stars

### The Sun

The Sun is considered the nearest star to Earth that produces solar energy. By the process of nuclear fusion, hydrogen gas is converted to helium gas. Energy flows out of the core to the surface; radiation then escapes into space.

Parts of the Sun include:

- **The core:** The inner portion of the Sun where fusion takes place.

- **The photosphere:** Considered the surface of the Sun, it also produces sunspots (cool, dark areas that can be seen on the Sun's surface).

- **The chromosphere:** Hydrogen gas causes this portion to be red. Also found here are solar flares (sudden brightness of the chromosphere) and solar prominences (gases that shoot outward from the chromosphere).

- **The corona:** The transparent area of the Sun visible only during a total eclipse.

Solar radiation is energy traveling from the Sun that radiates into space. Solar flares produce excited protons and electrons that shoot outward from the chromosphere at great speeds reaching Earth. These particles disturb radio reception and also affect the magnetic field on Earth.

## Stars

A star is a ball of hot, glowing gas that is hot enough and dense enough to trigger nuclear reactions, which fuel the star. In comparing the mass, light production, and size of the Sun to other stars, astronomers find that the Sun is a perfectly ordinary star. It behaves exactly the way they would expect a star of its size to behave. The main difference between the Sun and other stars is that the Sun is much closer to Earth.

Most stars have masses similar to that of the Sun. The majority of stars' masses are between 0.3 to 3.0 times the mass of the Sun. Theoretical calculations indicate that in order to trigger nuclear reactions and to create its own energy—that is, to become a star—a body must have a mass greater than 7 percent of the mass of the Sun. Astronomical bodies that are less massive than this become planets or objects called brown dwarfs. The largest accurately determined stellar mass is of a star called V382 Cygni; it is twenty-seven times the mass of the Sun.

The range of brightness among stars is much larger than the range of mass. Astronomers measure the brightness of a star by measuring its magnitude and luminosity. Magnitude allows astronomers to rank how bright different stars appear to humans. Because of the way our eyes detect light, a lamp ten times more luminous than another lamp will appear less than ten times brighter to human eyes. This discrepancy affects the magnitude scale, as does the tradition of giving brighter stars lower magnitudes. The lower a star's magnitude, the brighter it is. Stars with negative magnitudes are the brightest of all.

Magnitude is given in terms of absolute and apparent values. Absolute magnitude is a measurement of how bright a star would appear if viewed from a set distance away. Astronomers also measure a star's brightness in terms of its luminosity. A star's absolute luminosity, or intrinsic brightness, is the total amount of energy radiated by the star per second. Luminosity is often expressed in units of watts.

**MAGNITUDE STARS:**
twenty-one of the brightest stars that can be seen from Earth

MAGNITUDE STARS are twenty-one of the brightest stars that can be seen from Earth. These are the first stars noticed at night. In the Northern Hemisphere, there are fifteen commonly observed first-magnitude stars.

**CONSTELLATIONS:**
groups, or patterns, of stars

Astronomers use groups, or patterns, of stars called CONSTELLATIONS as reference points to locate other stars in the sky. Familiar constellations include Ursa Major (also known as Great Bear or Big Bear) and Ursa Minor (known as Little Bear). Within Ursa Major, the smaller constellation the Big Dipper is found. Within Ursa Minor, the smaller constellation the Little Dipper is found. Different constellations appear as the Earth continues its revolution around the Sun with the seasonal changes.

Vast collections of stars are defined as GALAXIES. Galaxies are classified as irregular, elliptical, and spiral. An irregular galaxy has no real structured appearance; most are in their early stages of life. An elliptical galaxy consists of smooth ellipses, containing little dust and gas but composed of millions or trillions of stars. Spiral galaxies are disk shaped and have extending arms that rotate around their dense centers. Earth's galaxy is the Milky Way. It is a spiral galaxy.

A PULSAR is defined as a variable radio source that emits signals in very short, regular bursts; it is believed to be a rotating neutron star. A QUASAR is defined as an object that photographs like a star but has an extremely large redshift and a variable energy output; it is believed to be the active core of a very distant galaxy.

BLACK HOLES are defined as objects that have collapsed to such a degree that light cannot escape from the surface; light is trapped by the intense gravitational field.

The forces of gravity acting on particles of gas and dust in a cloud in an area of space produce stars. This cloud is called a nebula. Particles in this cloud attract each other; as the star grows, its temperature increases. With the increased temperature, the star begins to glow. Fusion occurs in the core of the star, releasing radiant energy at the star's surface.

When hydrogen becomes exhausted in a small, or even an average star, its core will collapse and cause its temperature to rise. The released heat causes nearby gases to heat, contract, carry out fusion, and produce helium. Stars at this stage are nearing the end of their life. These stars are called red giants or super giants. A white dwarf is the dying core of a giant star. A nova is an ordinary star that experiences a sudden increase in brightness and then fades back to its original brightness. A supernova radiates even greater light energy. A neutron star is the result of mass left behind after a supernova. A black hole is a star with condensed matter and gravity so intense that light cannot escape.

## Comets, Asteroids, and Meteors

Astronomers believe that rocky fragments may have been the remains of the birth of the solar system that never formed into a planet. These asteroids are found in the region between Mars and Jupiter.

COMETS are masses of frozen gases, cosmic dust, and small rocky particles. Astronomers think that most comets originate in a dense comet cloud beyond Pluto. A comet consists of a nucleus, a coma, and a tail. A comet's tail always points away from the Sun. The most famous comet, Halley's comet, is named after the person who first discovered it in 240 BCE. It returns to the skies near Earth every seventy-five to seventy-six years.

GALAXIES: vast collections of stars

PULSAR: a variable radio source that emits signals in very short, regular bursts, believed to be a rotating neutron star

QUASAR: an object that photographs like a star but has an extremely large red-shift and a variable energy output, believed to be the active core of a very distant galaxy

BLACK HOLES: objects that have collapsed to such a degree that light cannot escape from the surface

COMETS: masses of frozen gases, cosmic dust, and small rocky particles

Astronomers think that most comets originate in a dense comet cloud beyond Pluto.

**METEOROIDS:** composed of particles of rock and metal of various sizes

**METEOR:** a burning meteoroid falling through the Earth's atmosphere also known as a "shooting star"

**METEORITES:** meteors that strike the Earth's surface

**OORT CLOUD:** a hypothetical spherical cloud surrounding our solar system extending approximately three light years or 30 trillion kilometers from the Sun

**KUIPER BELT:** a vast population of small bodies orbiting the Sun beyond Neptune

**METEOROIDS** are composed of particles of rock and metal of various sizes. When a meteoroid travels through the Earth's atmosphere, friction causes its surface to heat up and it begins to burn. A burning meteoroid falling through the Earth's atmosphere is called a **METEOR** (also known as a "shooting star").

**METEORITES** are meteors that strike the Earth's surface. A physical example of a meteorite's impact on the Earth's surface can be seen in Arizona; the Barringer Crater is a huge meteor crater. There are many other meteor craters throughout the world.

## Oort Cloud and Kuiper Belt

The **OORT CLOUD** is a hypothetical spherical cloud surrounding our solar system. It extends approximately three light years or 30 trillion kilometers from the Sun. The cloud is believed to be made up of materials that were ejected from the inner solar system because of interaction with Uranus and Neptune, but are gravitationally bound to the Sun. It is named the Oort cloud after Jan Oort, who suggested its existence in 1950. Comets from the Oort cloud exhibit a wide range of sizes, inclinations, and eccentricities; they are often referred to as long-period comets because they have a period of greater than 200 years.

The **KUIPER BELT** is the name given to a vast population of small bodies orbiting the Sun beyond Neptune. There are more than 70,000 of these small bodies, some with diameters larger than 100 kilometers extending outwards from the orbit of Neptune to 50AU. They exist mostly within a ring or belt surrounding the Sun. It is believed that the objects in the Kuiper Belt are primitive remnants of the earliest phases of the solar system. It is also believed that the Kuiper Belt is the source of many short-period comets (comets with periods of less than 200 years). It is a reservoir for the comets in the same way that the Oort cloud is a reservoir for long-period comets.

Occasionally, the orbit of a Kuiper Belt object will be disturbed by the interactions of the giant planets in such a way as to cause the object to cross the orbit of Neptune. It will then very likely have a close encounter with Neptune, sending it out of the solar system or into an orbit crossing those of the other giant planets or even into the inner solar system. Prevailing theory states that scattered disk objects began as Kuiper Belt objects, which were scattered through gravitational interactions with the giant planets.

It seems that the Oort cloud objects were formed closer to the Sun than the Kuiper Belt objects. Small objects formed near the giant planets would have been ejected from the solar system by gravitational encounters. Those that didn't escape entirely formed the distant Oort cloud. Small objects formed farther out had no such interactions and remained as the Kuiper Belt objects.

# Origins of the Solar System and Universe

There are two main hypotheses about the origin of the solar system:

- **The tidal hypothesis** proposes that the solar system began with a near collision of the Sun and a large star. Some astronomers believe that as these two stars passed each other, the great gravitational pull of the large star extracted hot gases from the Sun. The mass from the hot gases started to orbit the Sun, which began to cool, then condensing into the nine planets. (Few astronomers support this hypothesis.)

- **The condensation hypothesis** proposes that the solar system began with rotating clouds of dust and gas. Condensation occurred in the center, forming the Sun, and the smaller parts of the cloud formed the nine planets. (This hypothesis is accepted by many astronomers.)

The two main theories to explain the origins of the universe include:

- **The big bang theory,** widely accepted by many astronomers, states that the universe originated from a magnificent explosion spreading mass, matter, and energy into space. Galaxies formed from this material as it cooled during the next half-billion years.

- **The steady state theory,** the least accepted theory, states that the universe is continuously being renewed. Galaxies move outward and new galaxies replace the older galaxies. Astronomers have not found any evidence to prove this theory.

The future of the universe is hypothesized by the **oscillating universe hypothesis,** which states that the universe will oscillate, or expand and contract. Galaxies will move away from one another and will, in time, slow down and stop. Then a gradual moving toward each other will again activate an explosion—another big bang.

| SKILL 9.5 | Understands Earth patterns, cycles, and change |
|---|---|

## Seasons

The rotation axis of the Earth is not perpendicular to the orbital (ecliptic) plane. The axis of the Earth is tilted 23.45 degrees from the perpendicular; the tilt of this axis is known as the obliquity of the ecliptic, and is mainly responsible for the four seasons of the year by influencing the intensity of solar rays received by the Northern and Southern hemispheres.

The four seasons—spring, summer, fall, and winter—are extended periods of characteristic average temperature, rainfall, storm frequency, and vegetation growth or dormancy. The effect of the Earth's tilt on climate is best demonstrated at the solstices, the two days of the year when the Sun is farthest from the Earth's equatorial plane. At the summer solstice (June), the Earth's tilt on its axis causes the Northern Hemisphere to lean toward the Sun, while the Southern Hemisphere leans away. Consequently, the Northern Hemisphere receives more intense rays from the Sun and experiences summer during this time, while the Southern Hemisphere experiences winter. At the winter solstice (December), it is the Southern Hemisphere that leans toward the Sun and thus experiences summer. Spring and fall are produced by varying degrees of the same leaning toward or away from the Sun.

## Tides

SPRING TIDES: occuring during the full and new moon, the especially strong tides that occur when the Earth, Sun, and moon are in line, allowing both the Sun and the moon to exert gravitational force on the Earth, thereby increasing tidal bulge height

The orientation of and gravitational interaction between the Earth and the moon are responsible for the ocean tides that occur on Earth. The term tide refers to the cyclic rise and fall of large bodies of water. Gravitational attraction is defined as the force of attraction between all bodies in the universe. At the location on Earth closest to the moon, the gravitational attraction of the moon draws seawater toward the moon in the form of a tidal bulge. On the opposite side of the Earth, another tidal bulge forms in the direction away from the moon because at this point, the moon's gravitational pull is the weakest.

NEAP TIDES: occuring during quarter moons, especially weak tides during which the gravitational forces of the moon and the Sun are perpendicular to one another

SPRING TIDES are the especially strong tides that occur when the Earth, Sun, and moon are in line, allowing both the Sun and the moon to exert gravitational force on the Earth, thereby increasing tidal bulge height. These tides occur during the full moon and the new moon. NEAP TIDES are especially weak tides occurring when the gravitational forces of the moon and the Sun are perpendicular to one another. These tides occur during quarter moons.

## Phases of the Moon

LUNAR PHASES: the changes in the appearance of the moon from the Earth

The Earth's orientation in relation to the solar system is also responsible for our perception of the phases of the moon. While the Earth orbits the Sun within a period of 365 days, the moon orbits the Earth every twenty-seven days. As the moon circles the Earth, its shape in the night sky appears to change. The changes in the appearance of the moon from the Earth are known as LUNAR PHASES.

These phases vary cyclically according to the relative positions of the moon, the Earth, and the Sun. At all times, half of the moon is facing the Sun; thus, it is illuminated by reflecting the Sun's light. As the moon orbits the Earth and the Earth orbits the Sun, the half of the moon that faces the Sun changes. However, the moon is in synchronous rotation around the Earth, meaning that nearly the same side of the moon faces the Earth at all times. This side is referred to as the near side of the moon. Lunar phases occur as the Earth and moon orbit the Sun and the fractional illumination of the moon's near side changes.

When the Sun and moon are on opposite sides of the Earth, observers on Earth perceive a **full moon**, meaning the moon appears circular because the entire illuminated half of the moon is visible. As the moon orbits the Earth, the moon "wanes" as the amount of the illuminated half of the moon that is visible from Earth decreases. A **gibbous moon** is between a full moon and a half moon, or between a half moon and a full moon. When the Sun and the moon are on the same side of Earth, the illuminated half of the moon is facing away from Earth, and the moon appears invisible. This lunar phase is known as the **new moon**. The time between full moons is approximately 29.53 days.

| PHASES OF THE MOON | |
|---|---|
| New Moon | The moon is invisible or the first signs of a crescent appear |
| Waxing Crescent | The right crescent of the moon is visible |
| First Quarter | The right quarter of the moon is visible |
| Waxing Gibbous | Only the left crescent is not illuminated |
| Full Moon | The entire illuminated half of the moon is visible |
| Waning Gibbous | Only the right crescent of the moon is not illuminated |
| Last Quarter | The left quarter of the moon is illuminated |
| Waning Crescent | Only the left crescent of the moon is illuminated |

Viewing the moon from the Southern Hemisphere causes these phases to occur in the opposite order.

## SKILL 9.6 Understands science as a human endeavor, process, and career

*See Skill 10.8*

**SKILL 9.7** Understands science as inquiry *(e.g., questioning, gathering data, drawing reasonable conclusions)*

*See Skill 10.9*

**SKILL 9.8** Understands how to use resource and research material in science

*See Skill 10.10*

**SKILL 9.9** Understands the unifying processes of science *(e.g., systems, order, and organization)*

*See Skill 10.11*

# COMPETENCY 010
## LIFE SCIENCE

> **SKILL 10.1** **Understands the structure and function of living systems** *(e.g., living characteristics and cells, tissues and organs, life processes)*

The organization of living systems builds by levels from small to increasingly larger and more complex. All living things, from cells to ecosystems, have the same requirements to sustain life.

Life is organized from simple to complex in the following ways: Organelles make up cells. Cells make up tissues, and tissues make up organs. Groups of organs make up organ systems. Organ systems work together to provide life for an organism.

Several characteristics identify living versus nonliving things:

- **Living things are made of cells:** They grow, respond to stimuli and are capable of reproduction

- **Living things must adapt to environmental changes or perish**

- **Living things carry on metabolic processes:** They use and make energy

All organic life has a common element: carbon. Carbon is recycled through the ecosystem through both biotic and abiotic means. It is the link between biological processes and the chemical makeup of life.

## Prokaryotic and Eukaryotic Cells

The cell is the basic unit of all living things. The two types of cells are prokaryotic and eukaryotic.

Prokaryotic cells consist only of bacteria and blue-green algae. Bacteria were most likely the first cells; they date back in the fossil record 3.5 billion years. These cells are grouped together because of the following characteristics:

- They have no defined nucleus or nuclear membrane. The DNA and ribosomes float freely within the cell.

- They have a thick cell wall. This is for protection, to give shape, and to keep the cell from bursting.

> The cell is the basic unit of all living things.

- The cell walls contain amino sugars (glycoproteins). Penicillin works by disrupting the cell wall, which is bad for the bacteria but does not harm the host.

- Some have a capsule made of polysaccharides that make them sticky.

- Some have a pilus, which is a protein strand. This also allows for attachment of the bacteria and may be used for sexual reproduction (conjugation).

- Some have flagella for movement.

**Eukaryotic cells** are found in protists, fungi, plants, and animals. Some features of eukaryotic cells include the following:

- They are usually larger than prokaryotic cells.

- They contain many organelles, which are membrane-bound areas for specific cell functions.

- They contain a cytoskeleton that provides a protein framework for the cell.

- They contain cytoplasm, which supports the organelles and contains the ions and molecules necessary for cell function.

## Parts of eukaryotic cells

1. **Nucleus:** The brain of the cell. The nucleus contains:

    - **Chromosomes:** DNA, RNA, and proteins tightly coiled to conserve space while providing a large surface area.

    - **Chromatin:** The loose structure of chromosomes. Chromosomes are called chromatin when the cell is not dividing.

    - **Nucleoli:** Where ribosomes are made. These are seen as dark spots in the nucleus.

    - **Nuclear membrane:** Contains pores that let RNA out of the nucleus. The nuclear membrane is continuous with the endoplasmic reticulum, which allows the membrane to expand or shrink if needed.

2. **Ribosomes:** The site of protein synthesis. Ribosomes may be free floating in the cytoplasm or attached to the endoplasmic reticulum. There may be up to a half million ribosomes in a cell, depending on how much protein is made by the cell.

3. **Endoplasmic reticulum:** These are folded and provide a large surface area. They are the "roadway" of the cell and allow for transport of materials. The lumen of the endoplasmic reticulum helps to keep materials out of the cytoplasm and headed in the right direction. The endoplasmic reticulum is capable of building new membrane material. There are two types:

– **Smooth endoplasmic reticulum:** Contain no ribosomes on their surface.

– **Rough endoplasmic reticulum:** Contain ribosomes on their surface. This form of endoplasmic reticulum is abundant in cells that make many proteins, as in the pancreas, which produces many digestive enzymes.

4. **Golgi complex or Golgi apparatus:** This structure is stacked to increase surface area. The Golgi complex functions to sort, modify, and package molecules that are made in other parts of the cell. These molecules are either sent out of the cell or to other organelles within the cell.

5. **Lysosomes:** Found mainly in animal cells. These contain digestive enzymes that break down food, substances not needed, viruses, damaged cell components, and eventually the cell itself. It is believed that lysosomes are responsible for the aging process.

6. **Mitochondria:** Large organelles that make ATP to supply energy to the cell. Muscle cells have many mitochondria because they use a great deal of energy. The folds inside the mitochondria are called **cristae**. They provide a large surface where the reactions of cellular respiration occur. Mitochondria have their own DNA and are capable of reproducing themselves if a greater demand is made for additional energy. Mitochondria are found only in animal cells.

7. **Plastids:** Found in photosynthetic organisms only. They are similar to the mitochondria due to their double membrane structure. They also have their own DNA and can reproduce if increased capture of sunlight becomes necessary. There are several types of plastids:

– **Chloroplasts:** Green in color, they function in photosynthesis. They are capable of trapping sunlight.

– **Chromoplasts:** Make and store yellow and orange pigments. They provide color to leaves, flowers, and fruits.

– **Amyloplasts:** Store starch and are used as a food reserve. They are abundant in roots like potatoes.

8. **Cell wall:** Found in plant cells only, composed of cellulose and fibers. It is thick enough for support and protection, yet porous enough to allow water and dissolved substances to enter. Cell walls are cemented to each other.

9. **Vacuoles:** Hold stored food and pigments. Vacuoles are very large in plants. This allows them to fill with water in order to provide turgor pressure. Lack of turgor pressure causes a plant to wilt.

10. **Cytoskeleton:** Composed of protein filaments attached to the plasma membrane and organelles. They provide a framework for the cell and aid in cell movement. They constantly change shape and move about. Three types of fibers make up the cytoskeleton:

– **Microtubules:** Largest of the three, they are made up of cilia and flagella for locomotion. Flagella grow from a basal body. Some examples are sperm cells and tracheal cilia. Centrioles are also composed of microtubules. They form the spindle fibers that pull the cell apart into two cells during cell division. Centrioles are not found in the cells of higher plants.

– **Intermediate filaments:** Smaller than microtubules but larger than microfilaments. They help the cell keep its shape.

– **Microfilaments:** Smallest of the three, they are made of actin and small amounts of myosin (as in muscle cells). They function in cell movement such as cytoplasmic streaming, endocytosis, and ameboid movement. This structure pinches the two cells apart after cell division, forming two cells.

> **SKILL 10.2** **Understands reproduction and heredity** (e.g., growth and development, patterns of inheritance of traits, molecular basis of heredity)

## Reproductive System

Sexual reproduction greatly increases diversity due to the many combinations possible through meiosis and fertilization. **GAMETOGENESIS** is the production of the sperm and egg cells. **Spermatogenesis** begins at puberty in the male. One spermatozoa produces four sperm. The sperm mature in the seminiferous tubules located in the testes. **Oogenesis**, the production of egg cells, is usually complete by the birth of a female. Egg cells are not released until menstruation begins at puberty. Meiosis forms one ovum with all the cytoplasm and three polar bodies, which are reabsorbed by the body. The ovum are stored in the ovaries and released each month from puberty to menopause.

**GAMETOGENESIS:** the production of the sperm and egg cells

## Path of the sperm

Sperm are stored in the seminiferous tubules in the testes where they mature. Mature sperm are found in the epididymis, located on top of the testes. After ejaculation, the sperm travel up the vas deferens where they mix with semen made in the prostate and seminal vesicles; they then travel out the urethra.

## Path of the egg

Eggs are stored in the ovaries. Ovulation releases the egg into the fallopian tubes, which are ciliated to move the egg along. Fertilization normally occurs in the fallopian tube. If pregnancy does not occur, the egg passes through the uterus and is expelled through the vagina during menstruation. Levels of progesterone and estrogen stimulate menstruation. In the event of pregnancy, hormonal levels are affected by the implantation of a fertilized egg, so menstruation does not occur.

## Pregnancy

If fertilization occurs, the zygote implants in about two to three days in the uterus. Implantation promotes secretion of human chorionic gonadotropin (HCG). This is what is detected in pregnancy tests. The HCG keeps the level of progesterone elevated to maintain the uterine lining in order to feed the developing embryo until the umbilical cord forms. Labor is initiated by oxytocin, which causes labor contractions and dilation of the cervix. Prolactin and oxytocin cause the production of milk.

## Cellular Reproduction

The purpose of cell division is to provide growth and repair in body (somatic) cells and to replenish or create sex cells for reproduction. There are two forms of cell division:

- **Mitosis** is the division of somatic cells

- **Meiosis** is the division of sex cells (eggs and sperm)

| MAJOR DIFFERENCES BETWEEN MITOSIS AND MEIOSIS | |
|---|---|
| **Mitosis** | **Meiosis** |
| Division of somatic cell | Division of sex cells |
| Two cells result from each division | Four cells or polar bodies result from each division |
| Chromosome number is identical | Chromosome number is half the number of parent cells |
| Division is for cell growth and repair | Recombinations provide genetic diversity |

Some terms to know:

- **Gamete:** Sex cell or germ cell; eggs and sperm
- **Chromatin:** Loose chromosomes; this state is found when the cell is not dividing
- **Chromosome:** Tightly coiled, visible chromatin; this state is found when the cell is dividing
- **Homologues:** Chromosomes that contain the same information—they are of the same length and contain the same genes
- **Diploid:** Two in number; diploid chromosomes are a pair of chromosomes (somatic cells)
- **Haploid:** One in number; haploid chromosomes are half of a pair (sex cells)

## Mitosis

The cell cycle is the life cycle of the cell. It is divided into two stages: **interphase** and **mitotic division** (when the cell is actively dividing).

Interphase is divided into three steps:

1. **G1 Period (growth):** The cell is growing and metabolizing
2. **S Period (synthesis):** New DNA and enzymes are being made
3. **G2 Period (growth):** New proteins and organelles are being made to prepare for cell division

The mitotic stage consists of the stages of mitosis and the division of the cytoplasm. The stages of mitosis and their events are as follows. Be sure to know the correct order of steps (IPMAT).

1. **Interphase:** Chromatin is loose, chromosomes are replicated, and cell metabolism is occurring. Interphase is technically not a stage of mitosis.
2. **Prophase:** Once the cell enters prophase, it proceeds through the following steps continuously, without stopping. The chromatin condenses to become visible chromosomes. The nucleolus disappears and the nuclear membrane breaks apart. Mitotic spindles form, which will eventually pull the chromosomes apart. They are composed of microtubules. The cytoskeleton breaks down and the spindles are pushed to the poles or opposite ends of the cell by the action of centrioles.

3. **Metaphase:** Kinetechore fibers attach to the chromosomes, which causes the chromosomes to line up in the center of the cell (think middle for metaphase).

4. **Anaphase:** Centromeres split in half and homologous chromosomes separate. The chromosomes are pulled to the poles of the cell, with identical sets at either end.

5. **Telophase:** There are two nuclei with a full set of DNA identical to the parent cell. The nucleoli become visible and the nuclear membrane reassembles. A cell plate is visible in plant cells, whereas a cleavage furrow is formed in animal cells. The cell is pinched into two cells. Cytokinesis, or division, of the cytoplasm and organelles occurs.

## Meiosis

Meiosis consists of the same five stages as mitosis, but is repeated in order to reduce the chromosome number by one half. This way, when the sperm and egg join during fertilization, the haploid number is reached. The steps of meiosis are:

- **Meiosis I:** The major function is to replicate chromosomes; cells remain diploid.

- **Prophase I:** Replicated chromosomes condense and pair with homologues. This forms a tetrad. Crossing over (the exchange of genetic material between homologues to further increase diversity) occurs during Prophase I.

- **Metaphase I:** Homologous sets attach to spindle fibers after lining up in the middle of the cell.

- **Anaphase I:** Sister chromatids remain joined and move to the poles of the cell.

- **Telophase I:** Two new cells are formed and the chromosome number is still diploid.

- **Meiosis II:** The major function is to reduce the chromosome number in half.

- **Prophase II:** Chromosomes condense.

- **Metaphase II:** Spindle fibers form again, sister chromatids line up in center of cell, centromeres divide, and sister chromatids separate.

- **Anaphase II:** Separated chromosomes move to opposite ends of cell.

- **Telophase II:** Four haploid cells form for each original sperm germ cell. One viable egg cell gets all the genetic information and three polar bodies form with no DNA. The nuclear membrane reforms and cytokinesis occurs.

## Mutations

During these very intricate steps, mistakes do happen. Inheritable changes in DNA are called MUTATIONS. Mutations may be errors in replication or a spontaneous rearrangement of one or more segments by factors like radioactivity, drugs, or chemicals. The amount of the change is not as critical as where the change is. Mutations may occur on somatic or sex cells. Usually changes on sex cells are more dangerous since they contain the basis of all information for the developing offspring.

> MUTATIONS: inheritable changes in DNA

Mutations are not always bad. They are the basis of evolution, and if they make a more favorable variation that enhances the organism's survival, then they are beneficial. However, mutations may also lead to abnormalities, birth defects, and even death.

There are several types of mutations. Here are a few examples. First, suppose a normal sequence was as follows:

**Normal**                                             **A B C D E F**

Here are a few types of mutations:

- **Duplication** (one gene is repeated):            A B C C D E F
- **Inversion** (a segment of the sequence is flipped around):  A E D C B F
- **Deletion** (a gene is left out):                 A B C E F
- **Insertion, or translocation** (a segment from another place on the DNA is inserted in the wrong place):  A B C R S D E F
- **Breakage** (a piece is lost):                    A B C (DEF is lost)

Nondisjunction occurs during meiosis when chromosomes fail to separate properly. One sex cell may get both genes and another may get none. Depending on the chromosomes involved, this may or may not be serious. Offspring end up with either an extra chromosome or missing one. An example of nondisjunction is Down syndrome, in which three of chromosome 21 are present.

## Genetics

Gregor Mendel is recognized as the father of genetics. His work in the late 1800s is the basis of our knowledge of genetics. Although unaware of the presence of DNA or genes, Mendel realized there were factors (now known as genes) that were transferred from parents to their offspring. Mendel worked with pea plants; he fertilized the plants himself, keeping track of subsequent generations. His findings led to the Mendelian laws of genetics. Mendel found that two "factors" governed each trait, one from each parent. Traits or characteristics came in several forms, known as alleles. For example, the trait of flower color had white alleles and purple alleles.

Mendel established three laws:

- **Law of dominance:** In a pair of alleles, one trait may cover up the allele of the other trait. Example: Brown eyes are dominant (over blue eyes).

- **Law of segregation:** Only one of the two possible alleles from each parent is passed on to the offspring. (During meiosis, the haploid number ensures that half the sex cells get one allele and half get the other.)

- **Law of independent assortment:** Alleles sort independently of each other. (Many combinations are possible, depending on which sperm ends up with which egg. Compare this to the many combinations of hands possible when dealing a deck of cards.)

**Punnet squares** are used to show the possible ways that genes combine and indicate probability of the occurrence of a certain genotype or phenotype. One parent's genes are put at the top of the box and the other parent's at the side of the box. Genes combine on the square just like numbers that are added in addition tables we learned in elementary school. Below is an example of a **monohybrid cross**, which is a cross using only one trait—in this case, a trait labeled *g*.

### Punnet Square

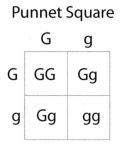

|   | G | g |
|---|---|---|
| **G** | GG | Gg |
| **g** | Gg | gg |

In a **dihybrid cross**, sixteen gene combinations are possible, as each cross has two traits.

Some definitions to know:

- **Dominant:** The stronger of two traits. If a dominant gene is present, it will be expressed. It is shown by a capital letter.

- **Recessive:** The weaker of two traits. In order for the recessive gene to be expressed, there must be two recessive genes present. It is shown by a lower case letter.

- **Homozygous (purebred):** Having two of the same genes present; an organism may be homozygous dominant with two dominant genes or homozygous recessive with two recessive genes.

- **Heterozygous (hybrid):** Having one dominant gene and one recessive gene. Due to the law of dominance, the dominant gene will be expressed.

- **Genotype:** The genes the organism has. Genes are represented with letters. AA, Bb, and tt are examples of genotypes.

- **Phenotype:** How the trait is expressed in an organism. Blue eyes, brown hair, and red flowers are examples of phenotypes.

- **Incomplete dominance:** Neither gene masks the other; a new phenotype is formed. For example, red flowers and white flowers may have equal strength. A heterozygote (Rr) would have pink flowers. If a problem occurs with a third phenotype, incomplete dominance is occurring.

- **Codominance:** Genes may form new phenotypes. The ABO blood grouping is an example of codominance. A and B are of equal strength and O is recessive. Therefore, Type A blood may have the genotypes of AA or AO, Type B blood may have the genotypes of BB or BO, Type AB blood has the genotype A and B, and Type O blood has two recessive O genes.

- **Linkage:** Genes that are found on the same chromosome usually appear together unless crossing over has occurred in meiosis (e.g., blue eyes and blonde hair commonly occur together).

- **Lethal alleles:** These are usually recessive due to the early death of the offspring. If a 2:1 ratio of alleles is found in offspring, a lethal gene combination may be the reason. Some examples of lethal alleles include sickle cell anemia, Tay-Sachs disease, and cystic fibrosis. In most cases, the coding for an important protein is affected.

- **Inborn errors of metabolism:** These occur when the protein affected is an enzyme. Examples include PKU (phenylketonuria) and albinism.

- **Polygenic characters:** Many alleles code for a phenotype. There may be as many as twenty genes that code for skin color. This is why there is such a variety of skin tones. Another example is height. A couple of medium height may have very tall offspring.

- **Sex-linked traits:** The Y chromosome found only in males (XY) carries very little genetic information, whereas the X chromosome found in females (XX) carries very important information. Since men have no second X chromosome to cover up a recessive gene, the recessive trait is expressed more often in men. Women need the recessive gene on both X chromosomes to show the trait. Examples of sex-linked traits include hemophilia and color blindness.

- **Sex-influenced traits:** Traits are influenced by the sex hormones. Male-pattern baldness is an example of a sex-influenced trait. Testosterone influences the expression of the gene. Most men lose their hair due to this trait.

**Understands change over time in living things** *(e.g., life cycles, mutations, adaptation and natural selection)*

Charles Darwin defined the theory of natural selection in the mid-1800s. Through the study of finches on the Galapagos Islands, Darwin theorized that nature selects the traits that are advantageous to the organism. Organisms that do not possess the desirable trait die, and do not pass on their genes. Those more fit to survive get the opportunity to reproduce, thus increasing that gene in the population.

Darwin listed four principles to define natural selection:

1. The individuals in a certain species vary from generation to generation

2. Some of the variations are determined by the genetic makeup of the species

3. More individuals are produced than will survive

4. Some genes allow for better survival of an animal

## Causes of Evolution

Certain factors increase the chances of variability in a population, thus leading to evolution. Factors that increase variability include mutations, sexual reproduction, immigration, and large population. Factors that decrease variation include natural selection, emigration, small population, and random mating.

## Sexual selection

Genes that happen to come together determine the makeup of the gene pool. Animals that use mating behaviors may be successful or unsuccessful. An animal that lacks attractive plumage or has a weak mating call will not attract the female, thereby eventually limiting that gene in the gene pool. Mechanical isolation, where sex organs do not fit the female, has an obvious disadvantage.

**Understands regulation and behavior** *(e.g., life cycles, responses to external stimuli, controlling the internal environment)*

**ANIMAL COMMUNICATION** is defined as any behavior by one animal that affects the behavior of another animal. Animals use body language, sound, and smell to communicate. Perhaps the most common type of animal communication is the presentation or movement of distinctive body parts. Many animal species reveal or conceal body parts to communicate with potential mates, predators, and prey.

**ANIMAL COMMUNICATION:** any behavior by one animal that affects the behavior of another animal

In addition, many species communicate with sound. Examples of vocal communication include the mating "songs" of birds and frogs and warning cries of monkeys. Many animals also release scented chemicals called pheromones and secrete distinctive odors from specialized glands to communicate with other animals. Pheromones are important in reproduction and mating, and glandular secretions of long-lasting smell alert animals to the presence of others.

Ecological and behavioral factors affect the interrelationships among organisms in many ways. Two important ecological factors are environmental conditions and resource availability.

There are four important types of organismal behavior:

1. **Competitive:** In any system, organisms compete with other species for scarce resources. Organisms also compete with members of their own species for mates and territory. Many competitive behaviors involve rituals and dominance hierarchies. Rituals are symbolic activities that often settle disputes without undue harm. For example, dogs bare their teeth, erect their ears, and growl to intimidate competitors. A dominance hierarchy, or "pecking order," organizes groups of animals, simplifying interrelationships, conserving energy, and minimizing the potential for harm in a community.

2. **Instinctive:** Instinctive, or innate, behavior is common to all members of a given species; it is genetically preprogrammed. Environmental differences do not affect instinctive behaviors. For example, baby birds of many types and species beg for food by raising their heads and opening their beaks.

3. **Territorial:** Many animals act aggressively to protect their territory from other animals. Animals protect territories for use in feeding, mating, and the rearing of young.

4. **Mating:** Mating behaviors are very important interspecies interactions. The search for a mate with which to reproduce is an instinctive behavior. Mating interrelationships often involve ritualistic and territorial behaviors that are competitive.

Environmental conditions such as climate influence organismal interrelationships by changing the dynamic of the ecosystem. Changes in climate (such as moisture levels and temperature) can alter the environment, changing the characteristics that are advantageous. For example, an increase in temperature will favor those organisms that can tolerate the temperature change. Thus, those organisms gain a competitive advantage. In addition, the availability of necessary resources influences interrelationships. For example, when necessary resources are scarce, interrelationships are more competitive than when resources are abundant.

Behavior may be innate or learned. INNATE BEHAVIOR is defined as behavior that is inborn or instinctual. An environmental stimulus (such as the length of day or temperature) results in a behavior. Hibernation among some animals is an innate behavior. LEARNED BEHAVIOR is any behavior that is modified due to past experience.

## Basic Life Functions

Members of the five different kingdoms of the classification system of living organisms often differ in their basic life functions. Here we compare and analyze how members of the five kingdoms obtain nutrients, excrete waste, and reproduce.

### Bacteria

Bacteria are prokaryotic, single-celled organisms that lack cell nuclei. The different types of bacteria obtain nutrients in a variety of ways. Most bacteria absorb nutrients from the environment through small channels in their cell walls and membranes (chemotrophs) while some perform photosynthesis (phototrophs). Chemoorganotrophs use organic compounds as energy sources while chemolithotrophs can use inorganic chemicals. Depending on the type of metabolism and energy source, bacteria release a variety of waste products (e.g., alcohols, acids, carbon dioxide) to the environment through diffusion.

All bacteria reproduce through binary fission (asexual reproduction), producing two identical cells. Bacteria reproduce very rapidly, dividing or doubling every twenty minutes in optimal conditions. Asexual reproduction does not allow for genetic variation, but bacteria achieve genetic variety by absorbing DNA from ruptured cells and conjugating or swapping chromosomal or plasmid DNA with other cells.

### Animals

Animals are multicellular, eukaryotic organisms. All animals obtain nutrients by eating food (ingestion). Different types of animals derive nutrients from eating plants, other animals, or both. Animal cells perform digestion that converts food molecules, mainly carbohydrates and fats, into energy. The excretory systems of animals, like animals themselves, vary in complexity. Simple invertebrates eliminate waste through a single tube, while complex vertebrates have a specialized system of organs that process and excrete waste.

> **INNATE BEHAVIOR:** behavior that is inborn or instinctual

> **LEARNED BEHAVIOR:** behavior that is modified due to past experience

Most animals, unlike bacteria, exist in two distinct sexes. Members of the female sex give birth or lay eggs. Some less-developed animals can reproduce asexually. For example, flatworms can divide in two, and some unfertilized insect eggs can develop into viable organisms. Most animals reproduce sexually through various mechanisms. For example, many aquatic animals reproduce by external fertilization of eggs, while mammals reproduce by internal fertilization. More-developed animals possess specialized reproductive systems and cycles that facilitate reproduction and promote genetic variation.

## Plants

Plants, like animals, are multicellular, eukaryotic organisms. Plants obtain nutrients from the soil through their root systems and convert sunlight into energy through photosynthesis. Many plants store waste products in vacuoles or organs (e.g., leaves, bark) that are discarded. Some plants also excrete waste through their roots.

More than half of the plant species reproduce by producing seeds from which new plants grow. Depending on the type of plant, flowers or cones produce seeds. Other plants reproduce by spores, tubers, bulbs, buds, and grafts. The flowers of flowering plants contain their reproductive organs. Pollination is the joining of male and female gametes that is often facilitated by movement of wind or animals.

## Fungi

Fungi are eukaryotic, mostly multicellular organisms. All fungi are heterotrophs, obtaining nutrients from other organisms. More specifically, most fungi obtain nutrients by digesting and absorbing nutrients from dead organisms. Fungi secrete enzymes outside of their bodies to digest organic material and then absorb the nutrients through their cell walls.

Most fungi can reproduce asexually and sexually. Different types of fungi reproduce asexually by mitosis, budding, sporification, or fragmentation. The sexual reproduction of fungi is different from the sexual reproduction of animals. The two mating types of fungi are plus and minus, not male and female. The fusion of hyphae, the specialized reproductive structure in fungi, between plus and minus types, produces and scatters diverse spores.

## Protists

Protists are eukaryotic, single-celled organisms. Most protists are heterotrophic, obtaining nutrients by ingesting small molecules and cells and digesting them in vacuoles. All protists reproduce asexually by either binary or multiple fission. Like bacteria, protists achieve genetic variation by exchange of DNA through conjugation.

## SKILL 10.5 Understands unity and diversity of life, adaptation, and classification

Carolus Linnaeus is called the father of taxonomy. **TAXONOMY** is the science of classification. Linnaeus based his system on morphology, the study of structure. Later, evolutionary relationships (phylogeny) were also used to sort and group species.

> **TAXONOMY:** the science of classification

The modern classification system uses binomial nomenclature. This consists of a two-word name for every species. The genus is the first part of the name and the species is the second part. Notice, in the levels explained below, that Homo sapiens is the scientific name for humans. Starting with the kingdom, the groups get smaller and more alike as one moves down the levels in the classification of humans.

| Kingdom | Animalia |
| --- | --- |
| Phylum | Chordata |
| Subphylum | Vertebrata |
| Class | Mammalia |
| Order | Primate |
| Family | Hominidae |
| Genus | Homo |
| Species | Sapiens |

Species are defined by the ability to successfully reproduce with members of their own kind.

## The Five Kingdoms of Living Organisms

Living organisms are divided into five major kingdoms:

- Monera
- Protista
- Fungi
- Plantae
- Animalia

## Kingdom Monera

This kingdom includes bacteria and blue-green algae; these are prokaryotic, unicellular organisms with no true nucleus.

Bacteria are classified according to their morphology (shape). Bacilli are rod shaped, cocci are round, and spirillia are spiral shaped. The gram stain is a staining procedure used to identify bacteria. Gram-positive bacteria pick up the stain and turn purple. Gram-negative bacteria do not pick up the stain and are pink in color.

### Methods of locomotion

Flagellates have a flagellum; ciliates have cilia; and ameboids move through use of pseudopodia.

### Methods of reproduction

Binary fission is simply dividing in half and is asexual. All new organisms are exact clones of the parent. Sexual modes provide more diversity. Bacteria can reproduce sexually through conjugation, where genetic material is exchanged.

### Methods of obtaining nutrition

Photosynthetic organisms, or producers, convert sunlight to chemical energy, while consumers, or heterotrophs, eat other living things. Saprophytes are consumers that live off dead or decaying material.

## Kingdom Protista

This kingdom includes eukaryotic, unicellular organisms; some are photosynthetic, and some are consumers. Microbiologists use methods of locomotion, reproduction, and how the organism obtains its food to classify protista.

## Kingdom Fungi

Organisms in this kingdom are eukaryotic, multicellular, absorptive consumers, and contain a chitin cell wall.

## Kingdom Plantae

This kingdom contains nonvascular plants and vascular plants.

### Nonvascular plants

Small in size, these plants do not require vascular tissue (xylem and phloem) because individual cells are close to their environment. The nonvascular plants have no true leaves, stems, or roots.

- **Division Bryophyta:** Mosses and liverworts; these plants have a dominant gametophyte generation. They possess rhizoids, which are root-like structures. Moisture in their environment is required for reproduction and absorption.

### Vascular plants

The development of vascular tissue enables these plants to grow in size. Xylem and phloem allow for the transport of water and minerals up to the top of the plant, as well as for the transport of food manufactured in the leaves to the bottom of the plant. All vascular plants have a dominant sporophyte generation.

- **Division Lycophyta:** Club mosses; these plants reproduce with spores and require water for reproduction.

- **Division Sphenophyta:** Horsetails; also reproduce with spores. These plants have small, needle-like leaves and rhizoids. They require moisture for reproduction.

- **Division Pterophyta:** Ferns; they reproduce with spores and flagellated sperm. These plants have a true stem and need moisture for reproduction.

- **Gymnosperms:** The word means "naked seed." These were the first plants to evolve with seeds, which made them less dependent on water for reproduction. Their seeds can travel by wind; pollen from the male is also easily carried by the wind. Gymnosperms have cones that protect the seeds.

- **Division Cycadophyta:** Cycads; these plants look like palms with cones.

- **Divison Ghetophyta:** Desert dwellers.

- **Division Coniferophyta:** Pines; these plants have needles and cones.

- **Divison Ginkgophyta:** The ginkgo is the only member of this division.

### Angiosperms (division Anthophyta)

The largest group in the plant kingdom. Plants in this kingdom are the flowering plants that produce true seeds for reproduction.

## Kingdom Animalia

### Annelida

This phylum includes the segmented worms. The Annelida have specialized tissue. The circulatory system is more advanced in these worms; it is a closed system with blood vessels. The nephridia are their excretory organs. They are hermaphroditic, and each worm fertilizes the other upon mating. They support themselves with a hydrostatic skeleton and have circular and longitudinal muscles for movement.

*Mollusca*

This phylum includes clams, octopi, and soft-bodied animals. These animals have a muscular foot for movement. They breathe through gills, and most are able to make a shell for protection from predators. They have an open circulatory system, with sinuses bathing the body regions.

*Arthropoda*

This phylum includes insects, crustaceans, and spiders; this is the largest group of the animal kingdom. Phylum Arthropoda accounts for about 85 percent of all the animal species. Animals in this phylum possess an exoskeleton made of chitin. They must molt to grow. Insects, for example, go through four stages of development. They begin as an egg, hatch into a larva, form a pupa, then emerge as an adult. Arthropods breathe through gills, trachea, or book lungs. Movement varies, with members being able to swim, fly, and crawl. There is a division of labor among the appendages (legs, antennae, etc.). This is an extremely successful phylum, with members occupying diverse habitats.

*Echinodermata*

This phylum includes sea urchins and starfish; these animals have spiny skin. Their habitat is marine. They have tube feet for locomotion and feeding.

*Chordata*

This phylum includes all animals with a notocord or a backbone. The classes in this phylum include Agnatha (jawless fish), Chondrichthyes (cartilage fish), Osteichthyes (bony fish), Amphibia (frogs and toads; gills that are replaced by lungs during development), Reptilia (snakes, lizards; the first to lay eggs with a protective covering), Aves (birds; warm-blooded with wings consisting of a particular shape and composition designed for flight), and Mammalia (warm-blooded animals with body hair who bear their young alive and possess mammary glands for milk production).

SKILL **Understands the interdependence of organisms** (e.g., ecosystems,
10.6 populations, communities)

**Ecology** is the study of organisms: where they live and their interactions with the environment. A **population** is a group of the same species in a specific area. A **community** is a group of populations residing in the same area. Communities that are ecologically similar in relation to temperature, rainfall, and the species that live there are called **biomes**.

| BIOMES | |
|---|---|
| Marine | Covers 75 percent of the Earth. This biome is organized by the depth of the water. The intertidal zone is located from the tide line to the edge of the water. The littoral zone is from the water's edge to the open sea. It includes coral reef habitats and is the most densely populated area of the marine biome. The open sea zone is divided into the epipelagic zone and the pelagic zone. The epipelagic zone receives more sunlight and has a larger number of species. The ocean floor is called the benthic zone and is populated with bottom feeders. |
| Tropical Rain Forest | Temperature is constant (25°C), and rainfall exceeds 200 cm per year. Located around the area of the equator, the rain forest has abundant, diverse species of plants and animals. |
| Savanna | Temperatures range from 0 to 25°C, depending on the location. Rainfall is from 90 to 150 cm per year. Plants include shrubs and grasses. The savanna is a transitional biome between the rain forest and the desert. |
| Desert | Temperatures range from 10 to 38°C. Rainfall is under 25 cm per year. Plant species include xerophytes and succulents. Lizards, snakes, and small mammals are common animals. |
| Temperate | Deciduous forest temperatures range from -24 to 38°C. Rainfall is from 65 to 150 cm per year. Deciduous trees are common, as are deer, bear, and squirrels. |
| Taiga | Temperatures range from -24 to 22°C. Rainfall is from 35 to 40 cm per year. Taiga is located far north and far south of the equator, close to the poles. Plant life includes conifers and plants that can withstand harsh winters. Animals include weasels, mink, and moose. |
| Tundra | Temperatures range from -28 to 15°C. Rainfall is limited, ranging from 10 to 15 cm per year. The tundra is located even farther north and south than the taiga. Common plants include lichens and mosses. Animals include polar bears and musk ox. |
| Polar or Permafrost | Temperatures range from -40 to 0°C. It rarely gets above freezing. Rainfall is below 10 cm per year. Most water is bound up as ice. Life is limited. |

Succession is defined as an orderly process of replacing a community that has been damaged or has begun where no life previously existed. Primary succession occurs after a community has been totally wiped out by a natural disaster or where life never existed before, as in a flooded area. Secondary succession takes place in communities that were once flourishing but were disturbed by some force, either human or natural, but not totally stripped. A climax community is a community that is established and flourishing.

## Definitions of Feeding Relationships

- Parasitism: When two species occupy a similar place, but the parasite benefits from the relationship while the host is harmed.

- **Commensalism:** When two species occupy a similar place and neither species is harmed or benefits from the relationship.

- **Mutualism (symbiosis):** When two species occupy a similar place and both species benefit from the relationship.

- **Competition:** When two species occupy the same habitat or eat the same food.

- **Predation:** When animals eat other animals. The animals they feed on are called the prey. Population growth depends upon competition for food, water, shelter, and space. The number of predators determines the number of prey, which in turn affects the number of predators.

- **Carrying capacity:** The total amount of life a habitat can support. Once the habitat runs out of food, water, shelter, or space, the carrying capacity decreases and then restabilizes.

## Ecological Problems

Nonrenewable resources are fragile and must be conserved for use in the future. Humankind's impact on the environment and knowledge of conservation will control our future. The following are just some of the ways in which the Earth's ecology is altered by human interaction:

- **Biological magnification:** Chemicals and pesticides accumulate along the food chain. Tertiary consumers have more accumulated toxins than animals at the bottom of the food chain.

- **Simplification of the food web:** Three major crops feed the world—rice, corn, and wheat. Planting these foods in abundance wipes out habitats and pushes animals residing there into other habitats, causing overpopulation or extinction.

- **Fuel sources:** Strip mining and the overuse of oil reserves have depleted these resources. At the current rate of consumption, the only way to guarantee our future fuel sources is conservation or alternate fuel sources.

- **Pollution:** Although technology gives us many advances, pollution is a side effect of production. Waste disposal and the burning of fossil fuels have polluted our land, water, and air. Global warming and acid rain are two results of the burning of hydrocarbons and sulfur.

- **Global warming:** Rainforest depletion and the use of fossil fuels and aerosols have caused an increase in carbon dioxide production. This leads to a decrease in the amount of oxygen, which is directly proportional to the amount of ozone. As the ozone layer depletes, more heat enters our atmosphere and is trapped. This causes an overall warming effect, which may eventually melt polar ice caps and cause a rise in water levels or changes in climate that will affect weather systems worldwide.

- **Endangered species:** Construction of homes to house people has caused the destruction of habitats for other animals, leading to their extinction.

- **Overpopulation:** The human race is still growing at an exponential rate. Carrying capacity has not been met due to our ability to use technology to produce more food and housing. However, space and water cannot be manufactured; eventually, our nonrenewable resources will reach a crisis state. Our overuse affects every living thing on this planet.

SKILL **Knows about personal health** *(e.g., nutrition, communicable diseases,*
10.7 *substance abuse)*

## Overview of Systems in the Human Body

The function of the skeletal system is support. Vertebrates have an endoskeleton, with muscles attached to bones. Skeletal proportions are controlled by area-to-volume relationships. Body size and shape is limited due to the forces of gravity. Surface area is increased to improve efficiency in all organ systems.

The function of the muscular system is movement. There are three types of muscle tissue. Skeletal muscle is voluntary. Skeletal muscles are attached to bones. Smooth muscle is involuntary. It is found in organs and enables functions such as digestion and respiration. Cardiac muscle is a specialized type of smooth muscle.

The neuron is the basic unit of the nervous system. It consists of an axon, which carries impulses away from the cell body; the dendrite, which carries impulses toward the cell body; and the cell body, which contains the nucleus. Synapses are spaces between neurons. Chemicals called neurotransmitters are found close to the synapse. The myelin sheath, composed of Schwann cells, covers the neurons and provides insulation.

The function of the digestive system is to break down food and absorb it into the bloodstream, where it can be delivered to all cells of the body for use in cellular respiration. As animals evolved, digestive systems changed from simple absorption to a system with a separate mouth and anus, capable of allowing the animal to become independent of a host.

The respiratory system functions in the gas exchange of oxygen (needed) and carbon dioxide (waste). It delivers oxygen to the bloodstream and picks up carbon dioxide for release out of the body. Simple animals diffuse gases from and to their environment. Gills allow aquatic animals to exchange gases in a fluid medium by removing dissolved oxygen from the water. Lungs maintain a fluid environment for gas exchange in terrestrial animals.

The function of the **circulatory system** is to carry oxygenated blood and nutrients to all cells of the body and return carbon dioxide waste to be expelled from the lungs. Animals evolved from an open system to a closed system with vessels leading to and from the heart.

## Nutrition and Exercise

The components of nutrition are:

- **Carbohydrates:** The main source of energy (glucose) in the human diet. There are two types: simple and complex. Complex carbohydrates have greater nutritional value because they take longer to digest, contain dietary fiber, and do not excessively elevate blood sugar levels. Common sources of carbohydrates are fruits, vegetables, grains, dairy products, and legumes.

- **Proteins:** Necessary for growth, development, and cellular function. The body breaks down consumed protein into component amino acids for future use. Major sources of protein are meat, poultry, fish, legumes, eggs, dairy products, and grains.

- **Fats:** A concentrated energy source and important component of the human body. The types of fats are saturated, monounsaturated, and polyunsaturated. Polyunsaturated fats are the healthiest because they may lower cholesterol levels, while saturated fats increase cholesterol levels. Common sources of saturated fats include dairy products, meat, coconut oil, and palm oil. Common sources of unsaturated fats include nuts, most vegetable oils, and fish.

- **Vitamins and minerals:** Organic substances that the body requires in small quantities for proper functioning. People acquire vitamins and minerals in their diets and in supplements. Important vitamins include A, B, C, D, E, and K. Important minerals include calcium, phosphorus, magnesium, potassium, sodium, chlorine, and sulfur.

- **Water:** Makes up 55–75 percent of the human body. Essential for most bodily functions. Acquired through foods and liquids.

Nutritional requirements vary from person-to-person. General guidelines for meeting adequate nutritional needs are:

- No more than 30 percent of total caloric intake from fats (preferably 10 percent from saturated fats, 10 percent from monounsaturated fats, and 10 percent from polyunsaturated fats)

- No more than 15 percent of total caloric intake from protein (complete)

- *At least* 55 percent of total caloric intake from carbohydrates (mainly complex carbohydrates)

Exercise and diet help maintain proper body weight by equalizing caloric intake and caloric output.

Regular exercise improves overall health. Benefits of regular exercise include a stronger immune system; stronger muscles, bones, and joints; reduced risk of premature death; reduced risk of heart disease; improved psychological well-being; and weight management. The health risk factors improved by physical activity include cholesterol levels, blood pressure, stress-related disorders, heart disease, weight and obesity disorders, early death, certain types of cancer, musculoskeletal problems, mental health, and susceptibility to infectious diseases.

## SKILL 10.8 Understands science as a human endeavor, process, and career

Science is tentative. By definition, it is about humans searching for information by making educated guesses. It must be replicable. Another scientist must be able to achieve the same results under the same conditions at a later time. The term **empirical** means that a phenomenon must be assessed through tests and observations. Science changes over time. Science is limited by available technology. An example of this would be the relationship of the discovery of the cell and the invention of the microscope. As our technology improves, more hypotheses will become theories and possibly laws.

Science is also limited by the data that can be collected. Data may be interpreted differently on different occasions. The limitations of science cause explanations to be changed as new technologies emerge. New technologies gather previously unavailable data and enable us to build upon current theories with new information.

## The Nature of Science

The nature of science mainly consists of three important things:

1. **The scientific world view:** It is possible to understand this highly organized world and its complexities with the help of the latest technology. Scientific ideas are subject to change. After repeated experiments, a theory is established, but this theory can be changed or supported in the future. Only laws that occur naturally do not change. Scientific knowledge may not be discarded but can be modified (e.g., Albert Einstein didn't discard Newtonian

principles but modified them in his theory of relativity). Also, science can't answer all of our questions. We can't find answers to questions related to our beliefs, moral values, and norms.

2. **Scientific inquiry:** Scientific inquiry starts with a simple question. This simple question leads to information gathering and an educated guess otherwise known as a hypothesis. To prove the hypothesis, an experiment has to be conducted, which yields data and the conclusion. All experiments must be repeated at least twice to get reliable results. Thus, scientific inquiry leads to new knowledge or the verification of established theories. Science requires proof or evidence. Science is dependent on accuracy, not bias or prejudice. In science, there is no place for preconceived ideas or premeditated results. By using their senses and modern technology, scientists will be able to get reliable information. Science is a combination of logic and imagination. A scientist needs to think and imagine and be able to reason.

3. **Scientific enterprise:** Science is a complex activity involving various people and places. A scientist may work alone or in a laboratory, in a classroom, or almost anywhere. Most of the time, it is a group activity requiring the social skills of cooperation, communication of results or findings, consultations, and discussions. Science demands a high degree of communication to governments, funding authorities, and the public.

Science explains, reasons, and predicts. These three actions are interwoven and inseparable. While reasoning is absolutely important for science, there should be no bias or prejudice. Science is not authoritarian because it has been shown that scientific authority can be wrong. No one can determine or make decisions for others on any issue.

Science is a process of checks and balances. It is expected that scientific findings will be challenged, and in many cases retested. Often, one experiment will be the beginning point for another. While bias does exist, the use of controlled experiments and an awareness on the part of the scientist can go far to ensure a sound experiment. Even if the science is well done, it may still be questioned. It is through this continual search that hypotheses develop into theories and sometimes become laws. It is also through this search that new information is discovered.

## Science as a career

Society is not the same as it used to be even twenty-five years ago. Technology has changed our lifestyles, our behavior, our ethical and moral thinking, our economy, and our career opportunities.

Science is an interesting, innovative, and thoroughly enjoyable subject. Science careers are challenging and stimulating, and the possibilities for scientific careers are endless.

Why do people choose careers in science? This is a very important question. The reasons are manifold and may include:

- A passion for science

- A desire to experiment and gain knowledge

- A desire to contribute to society's betterment

- An inquiring mind

- Wanting to work on a team

There are a number of opportunities in science. For the sake of ease and convenience, they are grouped under various categories.

- **Biological sciences:** The study of living organisms and their life cycles, medicinal properties, and the like

  – Botanist

  – Microbiologist

- **Physical science:** The study of matter and energy

  – Analytical chemist

  – Biochemist

  – Chemist

  – Physicist

- **Earth science:** The study of the Earth, its changes over the years, and natural disasters such as earthquakes and hurricanes

  – Geologist

  – Meteorologist

  – Oceanographer

  – Seismologist

  – Volcanologist

- **Space science:** The study of space, the universe, and planets

  – Astrophysicist

  – Space scientist

- **Forensic science:** The solving of crimes using various techniques
  - Forensic pathologist
- **Medical science:** Science with practical applications in the care and cure of diseases
  - Biomedical scientist
  - Clinical scientist
- **Agricultural science:** The use of science to grow and improve upon crops
  - Agriculturist
  - Agricultural service industry worker
  - Agronomist
  - Veterinary science worker

---

**SKILL 10.9** **Understands science as inquiry** *(e.g., questioning, gathering data, drawing reasonable conclusions)*

Science can be defined as a body of knowledge that is systematically derived from study, observations, and experimentation. Its goal is to identify and establish principles and theories that can be applied to solve problems. Pseudoscience, on the other hand, is a belief that is not warranted. There is no scientific methodology or application involved in pseudoscience. Classic examples of pseudoscience include witchcraft, alien encounters, or any topics that are explained by hearsay.

*Scientific inquiry starts with observation.*

Scientific inquiry starts with observation. Observation is an important skill by itself, as it leads to experimentation and communicating the experimental findings to the public. After observation, a question is formed, which starts with *why* or *how*. To answer these questions, experimentation is necessary. Between observation and experimentation there are three more important steps: gathering information (or researching the problem), forming a hypothesis, and designing the experiment.

The design of an experiment is very important since it involves identifying a control, constants, independent variables, and dependent variables. A **control** is something we compare our results with at the end of the experiment. It is like a reference. **Constants** are the factors that are kept the same in an experiment to get reliable results. **Independent variables** are factors we change in an experiment. **Dependent variables** are the changes that arise from the experiment. It is important to bear in mind that there should be more constants than variables to obtain reproducible results in an experiment.

After the experiment is done, it is repeated and results are graphically presented. The results are then analyzed and conclusions drawn. After the conclusion is drawn, the final step is communication. It is the responsibility of scientists to share the knowledge they obtain through their research. In this age, much emphasis is put on the form and the method of communication. The conclusions must be communicated by clearly describing the information using accurate data and visual presentations like graphs (bar/line/pie), tables/charts, diagrams, artwork, and other appropriate media. Modern technology should be used whenever necessary. The method of communication must be suitable to the audience.

Written communication is as important as oral communication. This is essential for submitting research papers to scientific journals, newspapers, and other magazines.

# Planning and Conducting Investigations

## The scientific method

The scientific method is the basic process behind science. It involves several steps, beginning with hypothesis formulation and working through to the conclusion:

1. **Posing a question:** Although many discoveries happen by chance, the standard thought process of a scientist begins with forming a question to research. The more limited the question, the easier it is to set up an experiment to answer it.

2. **Forming a hypothesis:** Once the question is formulated, researchers should take an educated guess about the answer to the problem or question. This "best guess" is the hypothesis.

3. **Doing the test:** To make a test fair, data from an experiment must have a variable or a condition that can be changed, such as temperature or mass. A good test will try to manipulate as few variables as possible to see which variable is responsible for the result. This requires a second example of a control. A control is an extra setup in which all the conditions are the same except for the variable being tested.

4. **Observing and recording the data:** Reporting the data should include the specifics of how measurements were calculated. For example, a graduated cylinder needs to be read with proper procedures. For beginning students, technique must be part of the instructional process so as to give validity to the data.

5. **Drawing a conclusion:** After recording data, compare your data with the data of other groups. A conclusion is the judgment derived from the data results.

## Graphs and lab reports

Graphs utilize numbers to demonstrate patterns. The patterns offer a visual representation, making it easier to draw conclusions.

Normally, knowledge is integrated in the form of a **lab report**. A report has many sections. It should include a specific **title** that tells exactly what is being studied. The **abstract** is a summary of the report written at the beginning of the paper. The **purpose** should always be defined to state the problem. The purpose should include the **hypothesis** (educated guess) of what is expected from the outcome of the experiment. The entire experiment should relate to this problem.

It is important to describe exactly what was done to prove or disprove a hypothesis. A **control** is necessary to prove that the results occurred from the changed conditions and would not have happened normally. Only one variable should be manipulated at a time. **Observations** and **results** of the experiment, including all results from data, should be recorded. Drawings, graphs, and illustrations should be included to support information. Observations are objective, whereas analysis and interpretation are subjective. A **conclusion** should explain why the results of the experiment either proved or disproved the hypothesis.

A **SCIENTIFIC THEORY** is an explanation of a set of related observations based on a proven hypothesis. A **SCIENTIFIC LAW** usually lasts longer than a scientific theory and has more experimental data to support it.

> **SCIENTIFIC THEORY:** an explanation of a set of related observations based on a proven hypothesis

> **SCIENTIFIC LAW:** usually lasts longer than a scientific theory and has more experimental data to support it.

## Gathering and Using Data to Draw Reasonable Conclusions

Whenever scientists begin an experiment or project, they must decide what pieces of data they are going to collect. This data can be qualitative or quantitative. Scientists use a variety of methods to gather and analyze this data. These methods include storing the data in a table or analyzing the data using a graph. Scientists also make notes of their observations (what they see, hear, smell, etc.), throughout the experiment. Scientists are then able to use the data and observations to make inferences and draw conclusions about a question or problem.

Several steps should be followed in the interpretation and evaluation of data:

1. **Apply critical analysis and thinking strategies**, asking questions about the accuracy of the data and the procedures of the experiment and procurement of the data.

2. **Determine the importance of information and its relevance to the essential question.** Any experiment may produce a plethora of data, not all of which is necessary to consider when analyzing the hypothesis. The useful information must then be **separated into component parts.**

3. Make inferences, identify trends, and interpret data.

4. Determine the most appropriate method of communicating these inferences and conclusions to the intended audience.

---

**SKILL Understands how to use resource and research material in science
10.10**

Professional journals provide core information about scientific research. Popular magazines focused on science also provide summaries of research as well as everyday translations of interesting scientific research. Many newspapers report on scientific endeavors; some publish a special section on science news. All of these sources are useful to teachers and students of science. However, much information utilized in the classroom comes from texts specifically designed for particular grade levels.

While a certain amount of information will always be presented in lecture form or using traditional written materials (i.e., textbooks), there are also many alternative resources available for teaching science at the elementary level. Several examples are listed below:

## Hands-on Experiments and Games

Some simple experiments in the life and environmental sciences may be appropriate for elementary-level students. For instance, they might examine samples of pond water under a microscope or assist with the dissection of plants or lower animals. Students can also model environmental scenarios, perhaps pretending to be either predatory or prey animals. Such interactive experiences help students visualize principles explained elsewhere and help them become more involved with the subject matter.

## Software and Simulations

When hands-on experiments are costly, complicated, dangerous, or otherwise not possible, students may benefit from software programs that simulate them. Multimedia software packages can be used to expose students to the sounds of the life forms and the environmental settings they are studying.

*The following Web site lists many publishers of multimedia software packages:*

*http://www.educational-software-directory.net/science/*

## Natural History Museums, Zoos, and Wildlife Preserves

Visits to facilities that aim to spread information about the life and environmental sciences, such as museums and zoos, can be an exciting change from classroom learning. Wildlife preserves and similar facilities often provide educational opportunities and allow students to observe living things in their native environments.

## Professional Scientists and State/National Government Employees

Research scientists and other professionals may be a good resource to teach students more about certain subjects. This is especially true when they can present demonstrations or invite students to their labs or other places of work. In some cases an agency such as the Department of Natural Resources, Environmental Protection Agency, or state Extension Service may also be a resource.

*These Web sites list resources for science teachers:*
- *http://sciencepage.org/teachers.htm*
- *http://www.nbii.gov/portal/server.pt?open=512&objID=236&mode=2&cached=true*
- *http://www.biologycorner.com/*

---

**SKILL 10.11** **Understands the unifying processes of science** *(e.g., systems, order, organization)*

---

The following concepts and processes are generally recognized as common to all scientific disciplines:

1. **Systems, order, and organization:** Because the natural world is so complex, the study of science involves the **organization** of items into smaller groups based on interaction or interdependence. These groups are called **systems**. Examples of organization are the periodic table of elements and the five-kingdom classification scheme for living organisms. Examples of systems are the solar system, the cardiovascular system, Newton's laws of force and motion, and the laws of conservation. **Order** refers to the behavior and measurability of organisms and events in nature. The arrangement of planets in the solar system and the life cycle of bacterial cells are examples of order.

2. **Evidence, models, and explanation:** Scientists use **evidence** and **models** to form **explanations** of natural events. Models are miniaturized representations of a larger event or system. Evidence is anything that furnishes proof.

3. **Constancy, change, and measurement:** **Constancy** and **change** describe the observable properties of natural organisms and events. Scientists use different systems of **measurement** to observe change and constancy. For example, the freezing and melting points of given substances and the speed of sound are the same under constant conditions. Growth, decay, and erosion are all examples of natural changes.

4. **Evolution and equilibrium: Evolution** is the process of change over a long period of time. While biological evolution is the most common example, one can also classify technological advancement, changes in the universe, and changes in the environment as evolution.

5. **Equilibrium** is the state of balance between opposing forces of change. Homeostasis and ecological balance are examples of equilibrium.

6. **Form and function: Form** and **function** are properties of organisms and systems that are closely related. The function of an object usually dictates its form, and the form of an object usually facilitates its function. For example, the form of the heart (e.g., muscle and valves) allows it to perform its function of circulating blood through the body.

## Structure and Function Model

The function of different systems in organisms from bacteria to humans dictates system structure. The basic principle that "form follows function" applies to all organismal systems. We will discuss a few examples to illustrate this principle. Keep in mind that we can relate the structure and function of all organismal systems.

Mitochondria, subcellular organelles present in eukaryotic cells, provide energy for cell functions. Much of the energy-generating activity takes place in the mitochondrial membrane. To maximize this activity, the mitochondrial membrane has many folds to pack a relatively large amount of membrane into a small space.

Bacterial cells maintain a high surface area-to-volume ratio to maximize contact with the environment and to allow for the exchange of nutrients and waste products. Bacterial cells achieve this high ratio by maintaining a small internal volume by cell division.

The cardiovascular system of animals has many specialized structures that help to achieve the function of delivering blood to all parts of the body. The heart has four chambers for the delivery and reception of blood. The blood vessels vary in size to accommodate the necessary volume of blood. For example, vessels near the heart are large to accommodate large amounts of blood, and vessels in the extremities are very small to limit the amount of blood delivered.

The structure of the skeletal systems of different animals varies based on the animal's method of movement. For example, the honeycombed structure of bird bones provides a lightweight skeleton of great strength to accommodate flight. The bones of the human skeletal system are dense, strong, and aligned in such a way as to allow walking on two legs in an upright position.

# COMPETENCY 011
## PHYSICAL SCIENCE

> **SKILL 11.1** Understands the physical and chemical properties and structure of matter (e.g., changes of states, mixtures and solutions, atoms and elements)

## Matter

Everything in our world is made up of **matter**, whether it is a rock, a building, an animal, or a person. Matter is defined by its characteristics: It takes up space and it has mass.

> **MASS:** a measure of the amount of matter in an object

**MASS** is a measure of the amount of matter in an object. Two objects of equal mass will balance each other on a simple balance scale no matter where the scale is located. For instance, two rocks with the same amount of mass that are in balance on Earth will also be in balance on the moon. They will feel heavier on the Earth than on the moon because of the gravitational pull of the Earth. Therefore, although the two rocks have the same mass, they will have different weight.

> **WEIGHT:** the measure of the Earth's pull of gravity on an object

**WEIGHT** is the measure of the Earth's pull of gravity on an object. It can also be defined as the pull of gravity between other bodies. The units of weight measurement commonly used are the pound (English measure) and the kilogram (metric measure).

> **VOLUME:** the amount of cubic space that an object occupies

In addition to mass, matter also has the property of volume. **VOLUME** is the amount of cubic space that an object occupies. Volume and mass together give a more exact description of an object. Two objects may have the same volume, but different mass, or the same mass but different volumes.

> **DENSITY:** the mass of a substance contained per unit of volume

For instance, consider two cubes that are each one cubic centimeter, one made from plastic and one from lead. They have the same volume, but the lead cube has more mass. The measure that we use to describe the cubes takes into consideration both the mass and the volume. **DENSITY** is the mass of a substance contained per unit of volume. If the density of an object is less than the density of a liquid, the object will float in the liquid. If the object is denser than the liquid, then the object will sink.

Density is stated in grams per cubic centimeter ($g/cm^3$), where the gram is the standard unit of mass. To find an object's density, you must measure its mass and its volume. Then divide the mass by the volume ($D = m/V$).

To discover an object's density, first use a balance scale to find its mass. Then calculate its volume. If the object is a regular shape, you can find the volume by multiplying the length, width, and height together. However, if it is an irregular shape, you can find the volume by seeing how much water it displaces. Measure the water in the container before and after the object is submerged. The difference is the volume of the object.

**SPECIFIC GRAVITY** is the ratio of the density of a substance to the density of water. For instance, the specific density of one liter of alcohol is calculated by comparing its mass (0.81 kg) to the mass of one liter of water (1 kg):

$$\frac{\text{mass of 1 L alcohol}}{\text{mass of 1 L water}} = \frac{0.81 \text{ kg}}{1.00 \text{ kg}} = 0.81$$

> **SPECIFIC GRAVITY:** the ratio of the density of a substance to the density of water

## Physical and Chemical Properties of Matter

Physical and chemical properties of matter describe the appearance or behavior of a substance. A physical property can be observed without changing the identity of a substance. For instance, you can describe the color, mass, shape, and volume of a book. Chemical properties describe the ability of a substance to be changed into new substances. Baking powder goes through a chemical change as it changes into carbon dioxide gas during the baking process.

Matter constantly changes. A physical change is a change that does not produce a new substance. The freezing and melting of water is an example of physical change. A chemical change (or chemical reaction) is any change of a substance into one or more other substances. Burning materials turn into smoke; a seltzer tablet fizzes into gas bubbles. The phase of matter (solid, liquid, or gas) is identified by its shape and volume.

A solid has a definite shape and volume. A liquid has a definite volume, but no shape. A gas has no shape or volume because it will spread out to occupy the entire space of whatever container it is in. While plasma is really a type of gas, its properties are so unique that it is considered a unique phase of matter.

Plasma is a gas that has been ionized, meaning that at least one electron has been removed from some of its atoms. Plasma shares some characteristics with gas, specifically, the high kinetic energy of its molecules. Thus, plasma exists as a diffuse "cloud," though it sometimes includes tiny grains (this is called dusty plasma). What most distinguishes plasma from gas is that it is electrically conductive and exhibits a strong response to electromagnetic fields. This property is a consequence of the charged particles that result from the removal of electrons from the molecules in the plasma.

Energy is the ability to cause changes in matter. Applying heat to a frozen liquid changes it from solid back to liquid. Continue heating it and it will boil and give off steam, a gas. Evaporation is the change in phase from liquid to gas. Condensation is the change in phase from gas to liquid.

## Composition of Matter

An ELEMENT is a substance that cannot be broken down into other substances. To date, scientists have identified 109 elements: 89 are found in nature and 20 are synthetic.

> **ELEMENT:** a substance that cannot be broken down into other substances

An ATOM is the smallest particle of an element that retains the properties of that element. All of the atoms of a particular element are the same. The atoms of each element are different from the atoms of other elements. Elements are assigned an identifying symbol of one or two letters. The symbol for oxygen is O; it stands for one atom of oxygen. However, because oxygen atoms in nature are joined together in pairs, the symbol $O_2$ represents oxygen.

> **ATOM:** the smallest particle of an element that retains the properties of that element

This pair of oxygen atoms is a molecule. A MOLECULE is the smallest particle of a substance that can exist independently and still have all of the properties of that substance. A molecule of most elements is made up of one atom. However, oxygen, hydrogen, nitrogen, and chlorine molecules are made of two atoms each.

> **MOLECULE:** the smallest particle of a substance that can exist independently and still have all of the properties of that substance

A COMPOUND is made of two or more elements that have been chemically combined. Atoms join together when elements are chemically combined. The result is that the elements lose their individual identities; the compound that they become has different properties.

> **COMPOUND:** two or more elements that have been chemically combined

We use a formula to show the elements of a chemical compound. A chemical formula is a shorthand way of showing what is in a compound through symbols and subscripts. The letter symbols let us know what elements are involved and the number subscript indicates how many atoms of each element are involved. No subscript is used if there is only one atom involved. For example, carbon dioxide is made up of one atom of carbon (C) and two atoms of oxygen ($O_2$), so the formula would be represented as $CO_2$.

Substances can combine without a chemical change. A mixture is any combination of two or more substances in which the substances keep their own properties. A fruit salad is a mixture (so is an ice cream sundae, although you might not recognize each part if it is stirred together). Colognes and perfumes are other examples. You may not readily recognize the individual elements; however, they can be separated.

Compounds and mixtures are similar in that they are made up of two or more substances. However, they have the opposite characteristics, as shown in the table:

| Compounds | Made up of one kind of particle<br>Formed during a chemical change<br>Broken down only by chemical changes<br>Properties are different from their parts<br>Have a specific amount of each ingredient |
|---|---|
| Mixtures | Made up of two or more particles<br>Not formed by a chemical change<br>Can be separated by physical changes<br>Properties are the same as their parts<br>Do not have a definite amount of each ingredient. |

Common compounds are acids, bases, salts, and oxides. These are classified according to their characteristics.

## Atoms

The nucleus is the center of the atom. The positive particles inside the nucleus are called protons. The mass of a proton is about 2,000 times the mass of an electron. The number of protons in the nucleus of an atom is called the atomic number. All atoms of the same element have the same atomic number.

Neutrons are another type of particle in the nucleus. Neutrons and protons have about the same mass, but neutrons have no charge. Neutrons were discovered because scientists observed that not all atoms in neon gas have the same mass. They had identified isotopes. Isotopes of an element have the same number of protons in the nucleus, but have different masses. Neutrons explain the difference in mass.

The mass of matter is measured against a standard mass such as the gram. Scientists measure the mass of an atom by comparing it to that of a standard atom. The result is relative mass. The relative mass of an atom is its mass expressed in terms of the mass of the standard atom. The isotope of the element carbon is the standard atom. It has six (6) neutrons and is called carbon-12. It is assigned a mass of 12 atomic mass units (amu). Therefore, the ATOMIC MASS UNIT (AMU) is the standard unit for measuring the mass of an atom. It is equal to the mass of a carbon atom.

The mass number of an atom is the sum of its protons and neutrons. In any element, there is a mixture of isotopes, some having slightly more or slightly fewer protons and neutrons. The atomic mass of an element is an average of the mass numbers of its atoms.

> **ATOMIC MASS UNIT (AMU):** the standard unit for measuring the mass of an atom, equal to the mass of a carbon atom

The following table summarizes the terms used to describe atomic nuclei:

| TERM | EXAMPLE | MEANING | CHARACTERISTIC |
|------|---------|---------|----------------|
| Atomic Number | No. of protons (p) | Same for all atoms of a given element | Carbon (C) Atomic number = 6 (6p) |
| Mass Number | No. of protons + no. of neutrons (p + n) | Changes for different isotopes of an element | C-12 (6p + 6n) C-13 (6p + 7n) |
| Atomic Mass | Average mass of the atoms of the element | Usually not a whole number | Atomic mass of carbon equals 12.011 |

Each atom has an equal number of electrons (negative) and protons (positive). Therefore, atoms are neutral. Electrons orbiting the nucleus occupy energy levels that are arranged in order and the electrons tend to occupy the lowest energy level available. A **stable electron arrangement** is an atom that has all of its electrons in the lowest possible energy levels.

Each energy level holds a maximum number of electrons. However, an atom with more than one level does not hold more than eight electrons in its outermost shell.

| LEVEL | NAME | MAXIMUM NUMBER OF ELECTRONS |
|-------|------|------------------------------|
| First | K shell | 2 |
| Second | L shell | 8 |
| Third | M shell | 18 |
| Fourth | N shell | 32 |

This can help to explain why chemical reactions occur. Atoms react with each other when their outer levels are unfilled. When atoms either exchange or share electrons with each other, these energy levels become filled and the atom becomes more stable.

As an electron gains energy, it moves from one energy level to a higher energy level. The electron cannot leave one level until it has enough energy to reach the next level. **Excited electrons** are electrons that have absorbed energy and have moved farther from the nucleus.

Electrons can also lose energy. When they do, they fall to a lower level. However, they can only fall to the lowest level that has room for them. This explains why atoms do not collapse.

## SKILL 11.2 Understands forces and motions (e.g., types of motion, laws of motion, forces and equilibrium)

DYNAMICS is the study of the relationship between motion and the forces affecting motion. Force causes motion. Surfaces that touch each other have a certain resistance to motion. This resistance is friction. Some principles of friction include:

- The materials that make up the surfaces will determine the magnitude of the frictional force

- The frictional force is independent of the area of contact between the two surfaces

- The direction of the frictional force is opposite to the direction of motion

- The frictional force is proportional to the normal force between the two surfaces in contact

Static friction describes the force of friction of two surfaces that are in contact but do not have any motion relative to each other, such as a block sitting on an inclined plane. Kinetic friction describes the force of friction of two surfaces in contact with each other when there is relative motion between the surfaces.

When an object moves in a circular path, a force must be directed toward the center of the circle in order to keep the motion going. This constraining force is called centripetal force. Gravity is the centripetal force that keeps a satellite circling the Earth.

ELECTRICAL FORCE is the force between two charged objects and is described by Coulomb's law. Coulomb's law shows that like charges repel each other (for example, two positive charges) and unlike charges attract each other (for example, a positive and a negative charge) and that the size of the force varies inversely as a square of the distance between the 2 charged objects.

There is something of a mystery as to how objects affect each other when they are not in mechanical contact. Newton wrestled with the concept of "action-at-a-distance" (as electrical force is now classified) and eventually concluded that it was necessary for there to be some form of ether, or intermediate medium, which made it possible for one object to transfer force to another. We now know that no

> **DYNAMICS:** the study of the relationship between motion and the forces affecting motion

> **ELECTRICAL FORCE:** the force between two charged objects described by Coulomb's law: that like charges repel each other, unlike charges attract each other, and the size of the force varies inversely as a square of the distance between the two charged objects

ether exists. It is possible for objects to exert forces on one another without any medium to transfer the force. From our fluid notion of electrical forces, however, we still associate forces as being due to the exchange of something between the two objects. The electrical field force acts between two charges, in the same way that the gravitational field force acts between two masses.

Magnetic force occurs when magnetized items interact with other items in specific ways. If a magnet is brought close enough to a ferromagnetic material (that is not magnetized itself) the magnet will strongly attract the ferromagnetic material regardless of orientation. Both the north and south pole of the magnet will attract the other item with equal strength. In opposition, diamagnetic materials weakly repel a magnetic field. This occurs regardless of the north-south orientation of the field. Paramagnetic materials are weakly attracted to a magnetic field. This occurs regardless of the north-south orientation of the field. Calculating the attractive or repulsive magnetic force between two magnets is, in the general case, an extremely complex operation, as it depends on the shape, magnetization, orientation, and separation of the magnets.

In the nuclear force, the protons in the nucleus of an atom are positively charged. If protons interact, they are usually pushed apart by the electromagnetic force. However, when two or more nuclei come very close together, the nuclear force comes into play. The nuclear force is a hundred times stronger than the electromagnetic force, so the nuclear force may be able to "glue" the nuclei together to allow fusion to happen. The nuclear force is also known as the strong force. The nuclear force keeps together the most basic of elementary particles, the quarks. Quarks combine to form the protons and neutrons in the atomic nucleus.

> **FORCE OF GRAVITY:** the force at which the Earth, moon, or other massively large object attracts another object toward itself

The FORCE OF GRAVITY is the force by which the Earth, moon, or other massively large object attracts another object toward itself. By definition, this is the weight of the object. All objects on Earth experience a force of gravity that is directed "downward" toward the center of the Earth. The force of gravity on Earth is always equal to the weight of the object as found by the equation:

$\textbf{Fgrav} = \textbf{m} \times \textbf{g}$ where $g = 9.8\,\frac{m}{s^2}$ (on Earth) and m = mass (in kg)

## Newton's Laws of Motion

Newton's first law of motion is also called the law of inertia. It states that an object at rest will remain at rest, and an object in motion will remain in motion at a constant velocity unless acted upon by an external force.

**Newton's second law of motion** states that if a net force acts on an object, it will cause the acceleration of the object. The relationship between force and motion is force equals mass times acceleration ($F = ma$).

**Newton's third law of motion** states that for every action there is an equal and opposite reaction. Therefore, if an object exerts a force on another object, that second object exerts an equal and opposite force on the first.

> SKILL **Understands energy** (e.g., forms of energy, transfer and conservation of energy,
> 11.3 simple machines)

The kinetic theory states that matter consists of molecules that possess kinetic energies in continual random motion. The state of matter (solid, liquid, or gas) depends on the speed of the molecules and the amount of kinetic energy the molecules possess. The molecules of solid matter merely vibrate, allowing strong intermolecular forces to hold the molecules in place. The molecules of liquid matter move freely and quickly, and the molecules of gaseous matter move randomly and at high speeds.

Matter changes state when energy is added or taken away. The addition of energy, usually in the form of heat, increases the speed and kinetic energy of the component molecules. Faster-moving molecules more readily overcome the intermolecular attractions that maintain the form of solids and liquids. In conclusion, as the speed of molecules increases, matter changes state from solid to liquid to gas (melting and evaporation).

*Matter changes state when energy is added or taken away.*

As matter loses heat energy to the environment, the speed of the component molecules decreases. Intermolecular forces have greater impact on slower-moving molecules. Thus, as the speed of molecules decreases, matter changes from gas to liquid to solid (condensation and freezing).

## Heat and Temperature

Heat and temperature are different physical quantities. **Heat** is a measure of energy. **Temperature** is the measure of how hot (or cold) a body is with respect to a standard object.

Two concepts are important in the discussion of temperature changes. Objects are in thermal contact if they can affect each other's temperatures. Set a hot cup of coffee on a desktop. The two objects are in thermal contact with each other and will begin affecting each other's temperatures. The coffee will become cooler and the desktop warmer. Eventually, they will have the same temperature. When this happens, they are in **thermal equilibrium**.

We cannot rely on our sense of touch to determine temperature because the heat from a hand may be conducted more efficiently by certain objects than others, making them feel colder. **Thermometers** are used to measure temperature. In thermometers, a small amount of mercury in a capillary tube will expand when heated. The thermometer and the object whose temperature it is measuring are put in contact long enough for them to reach thermal equilibrium. The temperature can then be read from the thermometer scale.

Three temperature scales are used:

- **Celsius:** The freezing point of water is set at 0 and the steam (boiling) point is 100. The interval between the two is divided into 100 equal parts called degrees Celsius.

- **Fahrenheit:** The freezing point of water is 32 degrees and the boiling point is 212. The interval between is divided into 180 equal parts called degrees Fahrenheit.

- Temperature readings can be converted from one to the other as follows:

  **Fahrenheit to Celsius**    **Celsius to Fahrenheit**
  $$C = \frac{5}{9}(F - 32) \qquad F = \left(\frac{9}{5}\right)C + 32$$

- **Kelvin:** The Kelvin scale has degrees the same size as the Celsius scale, but the zero point is moved to the triple point of water. Water inside a closed vessel is in thermal equilibrium in all three states (ice, water, and vapor) at 273.15 degrees Kelvin. This temperature is equivalent to .01 degrees Celsius. Because the degrees are the same in the two scales, temperature changes are the same in Celsius and Kelvin.

- Temperature readings can be converted from Celsius to Kelvin:

  **Celsius to Kelvin**     **Kelvin to Celsius**
  $$K = C + 273.15 \qquad C = K - 273.15$$

The **heat capacity** of an object is the amount of heat energy it takes to raise the temperature of the object by one degree.

Heat capacity (C) per unit mass (m) is called **specific heat** (c):

$$c = \frac{C}{m} = \frac{Q}{m}$$

There are a number of ways that heat is measured. In each case, the measurement is dependent upon raising the temperature of a specific amount of water by a specific amount. These conversions of heat energy and work are called the **mechanical equivalent of heat**.

A **CALORIE** is the amount of energy it takes to raise one gram of water one degree Celsius.

A **KILOCALORIE** is the amount of energy it takes to raise one kilogram of water by one degree Celsius. Food calories are kilocalories.

In the International System of Units (SI), the calorie is equal to 4.184 joules.

A British thermal unit (BTU) = 252 calories = 1.054 kJ.

## Heat transfer

Heat energy that is transferred into or out of a system is **HEAT TRANSFER**. The temperature change is positive for a gain in heat energy and negative when heat is removed from the object or system.

The formula for heat transfer is $Q = mc\triangle T$ where Q is the amount of heat energy transferred, m is the amount of substance (in kilograms), c is the specific heat of the substance, and $\triangle T$ is the change in temperature of the substance. It is important to assume that the objects in thermal contact are isolated and insulated from their surroundings.

If a substance in a closed container loses heat, then another substance in the container must gain heat.

A calorimeter uses the transfer of heat from one substance to another to determine the specific heat of the substance. When an object undergoes a change of phase it goes from one physical state (solid, liquid, or gas) to another. For instance, water can go from liquid to solid (freezing) or from liquid to gas (boiling). The heat that is required to change from one state to the other is called latent heat.

The heat of fusion is the amount of heat it takes to change from a solid to a liquid or the amount of heat released during the change from liquid to solid.

The heat of vaporization is the amount of heat it takes to change from a liquid to a gaseous state.

Heat is transferred in three ways:

- Conduction: Heat travels through the heated solid. The transfer rate is the ratio of the amount of heat per amount of time it takes to transfer heat from one area of an object to another. For example, if you place an iron pan on a flame, the handle will eventually become hot. How fast the handle gets too hot to handle is a function of the amount of heat and how long it is applied. Because the change in time is in the denominator of the function, the shorter the amount of time it takes to heat the handle, the greater the transfer rate.

- **Convection:** Heat transported by the movement of a heated substance. Warmed air rising from a heat source such as a fire or electric heater is a common example of convection. Convection ovens make use of circulating air to more efficiently cook food.

- **Radiation:** Heat transfer as the result of electromagnetic waves. The Sun warms the Earth by emitting radiant energy.

An example of all three methods of heat transfer occurs in a thermos bottle or dewar flask. The bottle is constructed of double walls of Pyrex glass that have a space in between. Air is evacuated from the space between the walls and the inner wall is silvered. The lack of air between the walls lessens heat loss by convection and conduction. The heat inside is reflected by the silver, cutting down heat transfer by radiation. Hot liquids remain hotter and cold liquids remain colder for longer periods of time.

## Laws of thermodynamics

The relationship between heat, forms of energy, and work (mechanical, electrical, etc.) are the **laws of thermodynamics**. These laws deal strictly with systems in thermal equilibrium and not those within the process of rapid change or in a state of transition. Systems that are nearly always in a state of equilibrium are called **reversible systems**.

The **first law of thermodynamics** is a restatement of conservation of energy. The change in heat energy supplied to a system (Q) is equal to the sum of the change in the internal energy (U) and the change in the work done by the system against internal forces.

$$\triangle Q = \triangle U + \triangle W$$

The **second law of thermodynamics** is stated in two parts:

1. No machine is 100 percent efficient. It is impossible to construct a machine that only absorbs heat from a heat source and performs an equal amount of work because some heat will always be lost to the environment.

2. Heat cannot spontaneously pass from a colder to a hotter object. An ice cube sitting on a hot sidewalk will melt into a little puddle, but it will never spontaneously cool and form the same ice cube. Certain events have a preferred direction called the **arrow of time.**

**ENTROPY:** the measure of how much energy or heat is available for work

**ENTROPY** is the measure of how much energy or heat is available for work. Work occurs only when heat is transferred from hot to cooler objects. Once this is done, no more work can be extracted. The energy is still being conserved, but it is not available for work as long as the objects are the same temperature. Theory has it that, eventually, all things in the universe will reach the same temperature. If this happens, energy will no longer be usable.

## SKILL Understands interactions of energy and matter (e.g., electricity, 11.4 magnetism, sound)

The law of conservation of energy states that energy is neither created nor destroyed. Thus, energy changes form when energy transactions occur in nature. Because the total energy in the universe is constant, energy continually transitions between forms. For example, an engine burns gasoline, converting the chemical energy of the gasoline into mechanical energy; a plant converts radiant energy of the Sun into chemical energy found in glucose; and a battery converts chemical energy into electrical energy.

CHEMICAL REACTIONS are the interactions of substances that result in chemical changes and changes in energy. Chemical reactions involve changes in electron motion as well as the breaking and forming of chemical bonds. Reactants are the original substances that interact to form distinct products. Endothermic chemical reactions consume energy while exothermic chemical reactions release energy with product formation. Chemical reactions occur continually in nature and are also induced by humans for many purposes.

Nuclear reactions, or atomic reactions, are reactions that change the composition, energy, or structure of atomic nuclei. Nuclear reactions change the number of protons and neutrons in the nucleus. The two main types of nuclear reaction are fission (splitting of nuclei) and fusion (joining of nuclei). Fusion reactions are exothermic, releasing heat energy. Fission reactions are endothermic, absorbing heat energy. Fission of large nuclei (e.g., uranium) releases energy because the products of fission undergo further fusion reactions. Fission and fusion reactions can occur naturally, but are usually recognized as manufactured events. Particle acceleration and bombardment with neutrons are two methods of inducing nuclear reactions.

The law of conservation can also be applied to physical and biological processes. For example, when a rock is weathered, it does not just lose pieces. Instead it is broken down into its composite minerals, many of which enter the soil. Biology takes advantage of decomposers to recycle decaying material. Since energy is neither created nor destroyed, we know it must change form. An animal may die, but its body will be consumed by other animals or decay into the ecosystem. Either way, it enters another form and the matter still exists—it was not destroyed.

> **CHEMICAL REACTION:** the interactions of substances that result in chemical changes and changes in energy

### SKILL 11.5 Understands science as a human endeavor, process, and career

*See Skill 10.8*

### SKILL 11.6 Understands science as inquiry *(e.g., questioning, gathering data, drawing reasonable conclusions)*

*See Skill 10.9*

### SKILL 11.7 Understands how to use resource and research material in science

*See Skill 10.9*

### SKILL 11.8 Understands the unifying processes of science *(e.g., systems, order, and organization)*

*See Skill 10.11*

# SAMPLE TEST

## Questions

## Reading and Language Arts (5002)

*(Average) (Skill 1.1)*

1. Rhyming is the manipulation of sounds, which is indicative of:

   A. Phonological awareness

   B. Phonemic awareness

   C. Morphology

   D. Syntax

*(Average) (Skill 1.1)*

2. Foundation skills taught to develop a student's understanding and working knowledge of reading are:

   A. Print concepts, phonological awareness, phonics and word recognition, and fluency

   B. Print concepts, phonological awareness, syllabication, and fluency

   C. Print concepts, morphology, phonics and word recognition, and fluency

   D. Print concepts, phonological awareness, phonics and word recognition, and receptive language

*(Easy) (Skill 1.1)*

3. An example of a three-letter onset is:

   A. spr.

   B. spl.

   C. Neither

   D. Both A and B

*(Average) (Skill 1.1)*

4. Ryan is having difficulty developing his phonological awareness. Mrs. Debber has created a phoneme deletion activity for him to do each morning. An example of a phoneme deletion question she may ask is:

   A. What word do you have if you add /p/ to the beginning of *lay*?

   B. What is *smile* without the /s/?

   C. The word is *rug*. Change the /g/ to /t/. What is the new word?

   D. Can you tell me the three sounds in the word *fun*?

*(Average) (Skill 1.1)*

5. Which of the following is a question a teacher may ask a student when developing the student's ability to substitute phonemes in words?

   A. What is *kite* without the /e/?

   B. The word is *sub*. Change the /b/ to /n/. What's the new word?

   C. Can you separate the four sounds in the word *flag*?

   D. Which word does not belong in the group of words: *sun, cloud, boot, moon*?

*(Average) (Skill 1.2)*

6. What is sound–letter correspondence?

   A. It is the manner in which a student orally articulates letter sounds

   B. Is it composed of the sounds represented by the letters of the alphabet

   C. It includes the letters in multisyllabic words

   D. It is the manner in which a student transcribes a word

*(Challenging) (Skill 1.2)*

7. Sight words for third graders may include:

   A. Laugh and together

   B. Bicycle and classify

   C. Ambivalent and myriad

   D. Extraterrestrial and autobiography

*(Challenging) (Skill 1.2)*

8. The root word for *geographical* is:

   A. Graph

   B. Hical

   C. Al

   D. Geo

*(Average) (Skill 1.2)*

9. The suffix *–ology* or *–logy* means:

   A. The study of

   B. The condition of

   C. The reading of

   D. The state of

*(Challenging) (Skill 1.2)*

10. According to the WIDA taxonomy, when a student is identifying language that indicates narrative points of view (e.g., "I" vs. "he/she") from illustrated text using word/phrase banks with a partner, the student is at which level?

    A. Entering

    B. Emerging

    C. Developing

    D. Bridging

*(Challenging) (Skill 1.2)*

11. Stages of language acquisition involve levels of thinking and language functions. One can use Bloom's Taxonomy across the stages of second-language acquisition. The early production (level 2) is when:

    A. Students are nonverbal

    B. Students offer one-word responses

    C. Students use short phrases

    D. Students make longer, complex sentences

*(Average) (Skill 1.2)*

12. The most common rimes include:

    A. –ash, –ell, –ug

    B. –ote, –ank, –ell

    C. –ube, –ate, –ame

    D. –eat, –at, –ipe

*(Challenging) (Skill 1.2)*

13. In order to give an ELL student context when reading using phonics, a teacher may:

    A. Give background information

    B. Preview the words

    C. Use a picture or visual

    D. Review prefixes

*(Average) (Skill 1.2)*

14. A word with one syllable that ends in the letter *y* will have the same final *y* sound as the:

    A. /short i/

    B. /long i/

    C. /long y/

    D. /short u/

*(Easy) (Skill 1.2)*

15. The word lump follows which pattern?

    A. CCVCC

    B. CVC

    C. CVCC

    D. CCVC

*(Easy) (Skill 1.3)*

16. What is fluency also known as?

    A. Comprehension

    B. Decoding

    C. Automaticity

    D. Understanding

*(Challenging) (Skill 1.3)*

17. What is prosody?

    A. The rhythm and intonation of language

    B. The rise and fall of a person's voice

    C. Word recognition

    D. Decoding of multisyllabic words

*(Average) (Skill 1.3)*

18. In a reading fluency study, the National Center for Education Statistics (NCES) reported high-fluency fourth graders read with expression and grouped words into meaningful phrases, but low-fluency fourth graders:

    A. Read with prosody in a smooth manner

    B. Ignore sentence structure and read in one- or two-word phrases

    C. Ignore sentence structure and read multisyllabic words

    D. Ignore sentence structure and decode words

*(Easy) (Skill 1.4)*

19. Identifying the moral of a story (literary text) occurs within the development of the plot of a story, but can often be specifically located:

    A. At the beginning of a story

    B. In the middle of a story

    C. In the first sentence of a story

    D. In the last paragraph of a story

*(Average) (Skill 1.4)*

20. Grady is a second grader who has trouble making inferences from the text he reads. A strategy the teacher can demonstrate or model for Grady is:

    A. Rereading the topic and concluding sentences

    B. Using context clues to figure out what the author doesn't write explicitly

    C. Underlining boldface words

    D. Defining vocabulary

*(Easy) (Skill 1.4)*

21. An effective summary deletes:

    A. Minor and irrelevant details

    B. The author's name

    C. The main points

    D. Paraphrased portions of the text

*(Easy) (Skill 1.4)*

22. The plot of a literary text is:

    A. The main events presented by the writer in a specific manner

    B. The location in which a story takes place

    C. The foreshadowing of events to come

    D. The characters

*(Average) (Skill 1.4)*

23. Students in Mr. Klar's fifth-grade science class are analyzing the relationship between oxygen and carbon dioxide while studying the photosynthesis unit. Many members of his class have a visual learning style. The best way to teach them this relationship by using:

    A. An audio recording of the process

    B. A diagram on the board

    C. A worksheet

    D. A hands-on class activity

*(Challenging) (Skill 1.4)*

24. Lexical priming is a technique teachers use to encourage:

    A. Word parts

    B. Word recognition

    C. Word study

    D. Word definitions

*(Challenging) (Skill 1.5)*

25. What is cadence?

    A. A pattern of rhythm in speech or poetry without meter

    B. Repetitious speech in poetry

    C. Metered poetry technique

    D. Rhythm in speech

*(Easy) (Skill 1.5)*

26. What is a hyperlink?

    A. A sidebar in an internet link

    B. A link from a hypertext file or document to another location or file

    C. A link to an email message

    D. A link to a specific area of text

*(Average) (Skill 1.5)*

27. A piece of informational text presented to fourth-grade students discussed oil spills. The students identified the oil spill and understood it caused many deaths in wildlife. This type of text analysis is called:

    A. Problem/solution

    B. Narrative

    C. Cause and effect

    D. Prose fiction

*(Challenging) (Skill 1.5)*

28. The fifth graders in Mr. Deter's class are studying literary elements. What literary element can be derived from this passage he shared with the students?

    "The sun rose in the sky that morning. Donna felt she was ready for a new beginning. It shined brightly through her window. The sunbeams reached her face."

    A. Style

    B. Theme

    C. Conflict

    D. Symbolism

*(Challenging) (Skill 1.5)*

29. In literary terms, which elements characterize style?

    A. Syntax and diction

    B. Author's attitude and plot

    C. Conflicts that arise and plot

    D. Setting and tone

*(Easy) (Skill 1.6)*

30. Which pronoun is used in text to indicate possible first-person point of view?

    A. They

    B. Her

    C. I

    D. Him

*(Average) (Skill 1.6)*

31. The story of *Cinderella* is one that has been told by many cultures across the world. In order for students to assess the similarities and differences, a teacher may want to use a:

    A. Comparison matrix

    B. Flow chart

    C. T-chart

    D. KWL diagram

*(Easy) (Skill 1.7)*

32. Mr. Murphy uses a multimedia presentation in his third-grade class that shows only segments of the tale of *Icarus and Daedalus.* He is also reading the tale in class to the students. Why might he only show parts of the multimedia version?

    A. Time constraints

    B. To allow students to make their own mental imagery

    C. To provide visual support to comprehension

    D. All of the above

*(Average) (Skill 1.7)*

33. Hyla is a fifth grader who prefers to read graphic novels rather than traditional books. What is a graphic novel?

    A. Structured, sequential art used to tell a story

    B. A semi-structured story with arbitrary pictures

    C. A heavily designed comic book

    D. A series of short vignettes

*(Challenging) (Skill 1.7)*

34. Mr. Jessup's 20 first graders listened to him read a story in class. There are four characters in the story. How can the students most effectively replicate the story and produce a play?

    A. The class can be divided in half, and each can read sections of the dialogue

    B. The class can be divided into groups of five, and each student plays a role

    C. The class can be divided into 10 pair of students, and each acts out two pages

    D. The class can do a whole-group activity and take turns

*(Average) (Skill 1.7)*

35. Students are reading two texts about tigers in Mr. Franklin's fifth-grade class. The students are creating charts to describe characteristics tigers possess. What else can the students do to enhance their understanding of tigers?

    A. Draw a picture of a tiger

    B. Underline their favorite fact

    C. Read the charts again

    D. Enhance the charts with bigger letters and different fonts

*(Challenging) (Skill 1.7)*

36. A pie chart shows the fractional portion of brownies eaten. The pie chart is embedded in the story of Rebecca and Mary, who make a pan of brownies with their grandmother. Out of the eight brownie squares, Mary ate two. How can students understand this concept verbally?

    A. Students can color in the fractional part that represents the amount of brownies Mary ate

    B. Students can write a sentence that depicts the amount Mary ate

    C. Students can draw two brownies in the white space of the paper

    D. Students can cut the pie chart into segments

*(Challenging) (Skill 1.8)*

37. What is a qualitative evaluation of a text?

    A. Reader and task variables are used to match text to student

    B. Readability measures and other scores of text complexity

    C. Detailed information revealed in text-complexity measurements

    D. Levels of meaning, structure, language conventionality, and clarity

*(Average) (Skill 1.8)*

38. DRA text leveling is used for students in grades:

    A. K–5

    B. K–6

    C. K–12

    D. K–8

*(Challenging) (Skill 1.8)*

39. In the Lexile Framework for Reading, a book is labeled NC, or nonconforming, when it:

    A. Is best shared as a read-aloud

    B. Is a beginning reader

    C. Contains vocabulary and sentence length that are complex compared to subject matter

    D. Contains vocabulary and sentence length that are simplistic compared to subject matter

*(Easy) (Skill 2.1)*

40. Opinion writing can be both:

    A. Informative and explanatory

    B. Opinionated and argumentative

    C. Narrative and explanatory

    D. Opinionated and obvious

*(Easy) (Skill 2.1)*

41. Informative and explanatory genres of writing always contain:

    A. Characters

    B. A story arch

    C. Facts

    D. Lists

*(Easy) (Skill 2.1)*

42. The intent of a speech is to:

    A. Convey a message

    B. Be concise and effective

    C. Target an audience

    D. All of the above

*(Average) (Skill 2.2)*

43. **Student writing, on the elementary level, should have:**

    A. A specific purpose

    B. A clear audience

    C. A targeted task

    D. All of the above

*(Challenging) (Skill 2.2)*

44. **Edits are different from revisions. Edits:**

    A. Address problems with spelling, grammar, punctuation, or word choice

    B. Address problems with spelling, voice, organization, and cohesiveness

    C. Address problems of development, structure, coherence, and length

    D. Focus on the paper by asking questions and expanding ideas

*(Average) (Skill 2.2)*

45. **Prewriting strategies can include:**

    A. Brainstorming

    B. Clustering

    C. Listing

    D. All of the above

*(Challenging) (Skill 2.3)*

46. **According to Zaner Bloser, the stages of early writing development from ages 2 to 6 are:**

    A. Random scribbling, controlled scribbling, mock writing, writing words, writing letters

    B. Random scribbling, controlled scribbling, mock writing, writing letters, writing words

    C. Random scribbling, mock writing, controlled scribbling, writing letters, writing words

    D. Random scribbling, mock writing, writing letters, controlled scribbling, writing words

*(Challenging) (Skill 2.3)*

47. **In his book,** *Developmental Variation and Learning Disorders,* **Dr. Mel Levine identifies six stages of writing development. They are:**

    A. Imitation, graphic presentation, progressive incorporation, automatization, elaboration, and personalization-diversification

    B. Imitation, progressive incorporation, graphic presentation, automatization, elaboration, and personalization-diversification

    C. Graphic presentation, imitation, progressive incorporation, automatization, elaboration, and personalization-diversification

    D. Imitation, graphic presentation, progressive incorporation, automatization, elaboration, and diversification

*(Easy) (Skill2.4)*

48. Word processing programs can be used during writing portions of class time or during times when the students are in the computer lab in order to:

    A. Compose music

    B. Create graphic art

    C. Type drafts

    D. Practice with the mouse

*(Easy) (Skill 2.4)*

49. Using digital tools for sharing and working on writing pieces can be helpful for group projects because it fosters:

    A. Responses

    B. Pacing

    C. Writing

    D. Collaboration

*(Average) (Skill 2.4)*

50. Published writing in the classroom can be displayed or mounted on bulletin boards and classroom walls, but digital publishing allows for students to publish on a:

    A. School website

    B. Desktop

    C. Hardware

    D. Software

*(Challenging) (Skill 2.5)*

51. Collecting data for the research process in second grade is more elaborate than in kindergarten. When students are finding facts, they need to gain information from a variety of modalities, including:

    A. Listening

    B. Viewing

    C. Reading

    D. All of the above

*(Easy) (Skill 2.5)*

52. What is an example of a primary source?

    A. Census data

    B. Artifact

    C. Photo

    D. All of the above

*(Easy) (Skill 2.5)*

53. What is an example of a secondary source?

    A. Textbook

    B. Article

    C. Historical report

    D. All of the above

*(Challenging) (Skill 2.5)*

54. How can a student distinguish between a reliable and an unreliable source?

    A. Verify the organization who published the article

    B. Check the copyright date

    C. Identify the total number of pages

    D. Confirm the sources of the photographs

*(Average) (Skill 2.5)*

55. Paraphrasing and plagiarizing are two very different practices. Students must learn not to plagiarize from sources. How might a teacher describe what paraphrasing is to his or her students?

   A. Paraphrasing is when we use parts of someone else's text

   B. Paraphrasing is when we copy sentences word for word

   C. Paraphrasing is when we read text and write it in our own words

   D. Paraphrasing is when we read text and locate more information

*(Easy) (Skill 2.5)*

56. Which school staff member, who is not typically in the classroom, can help students locate reliable, credible information for research projects?

   A. Co-teacher

   B. Push-in reading consultant

   C. Paraprofessional

   D. Librarian

*(Average) (Skill 2.5)*

57. Students need to evaluate the following criteria when identifying credible website sources:

   A. Subject, author, audience, source, documentation

   B. Subject, audience, source, documentation

   C. Subject, audience, author, source

   D. Documentation, subject, author, publication date

*(Challenging) (Skill 2.6)*

58. Plural nouns always end in:

   A. /s/

   B. /es/

   C. /s/ or /es/

   D. None of the above

*(Challenging) (Skill 2.6)*

59. Miss Murphy is presenting possessive pronouns. Which words should she include in a presentation on Power Point?

   A. My, mine, you, your, hers, his

   B. Myself, yourself, himself, herself, itself

   C. You, me, my, I, they

   D. His, hers, he, she, it, its

*(Challenging) (Skill 2.6)*

60. There are seven coordinating conjunctions in the English language. Three of them are:

   A. In, on, upon

   B. And, but, or

   C. Rarely, always, often

   D. Me, he, I

*(Challenging) (Skill 2.6)*

61. What is an example of a compound sentence?

   A. Maya will go to the store and Maya will go to school.

   B. Maya and Greta will go to the playground.

   C. Maya and Murphy will get along very well.

   D. The new house is in the next town.

*(Average) (Skill 2.6)*

62. Identifying word derivatives is an excellent way for students to understand vocabulary they do not know. A derivative is:

   A. A word with multiple syllables

   B. A word formed from another word

   C. A word with two meanings

   D. A word that ends with /s/

*(Challenging) (Skill 2.7)*

63. An example of a metaphor is:

   A. The sun is like a giant flame in the sky

   B. The bird's wings made a fluttering sound

   C. Her hair was pure silk

   D. She was singing at the top of her lungs

*(Challenging) (Skill 2.7)*

64. An example of a personification is:

   A. The donuts were piled to the ceiling

   B. The bird's wings made a fluttering sound

   C. The teddy bear smiled as she hugged him tightly

   D. She was singing at the top of her lungs

*(Challenging) (Skill 2.7)*

65. An example of an idiom is:

   A. The donuts were piled to the ceiling

   B. The bird's wings made a fluttering sound

   C. Her hair was pure silk

   D. She was singing at the top of her lungs

*(Average) (Skill 2.7)*

66. How can Ms. Ritch define the meaning of the word *illuminate* to her class of fifth graders by using word part analysis?

   A. Related word parts: in (into), lumen (light), ate (to cause to)

   B. Related word parts: in (for), lumen (light), ate (to cause to)

   C. Related word parts: in (into), lumen (light), ate (to eat)

   D. Related word parts: in (for), lumen (light), ate (to be)

*(Average) (Skill 2.7)*

67. Which of the following words is an example of onomatopoeia?

   A. Fire

   B. Him

   C. Waste or waist

   D. Pop

*(Average) (Skill 2.7)*

68. The term *figurative* is the antonym to:

   A. Abstract

   B. Literal

   C. Substantial

   D. None of the above

*(Challenging) (Skill 2.6)*

69. The words *addition* and *edition* are:

   A. Homonyms

   B. Homophones

   C. Homographs

   D. None of the above

*(Challenging) (Skill 2.6)*

70. **Which spelling shows possession?**

    A. Whose

    B. Who's

    C. Whom

    D. Who

*(Average) (Skill 2.8)*

71. **In the Common Core State Standards, the second-tier vocabulary words are:**

    A. Everyday, common words

    B. High-utility words

    C. Domain-specific academic vocabulary words

    D. Abstract nouns and adjectives

*(Average) (Skill 2.8)*

72. **In order to teach the three tiers of words, teachers may want to consider:**

    A. Direct instruction

    B. Specific word lists

    C. District-wide vocabulary lists

    D. All of the above

*(Challenging) (Skill 2.8)*

73. **Another term for *word choice* is:**

    A. Diction

    B. Word decision

    C. Wordplay

    D. Tone

*(Challenging) (Skill 2.9)*

74. **Receptive language is:**

    A. The ability to understand or comprehend language heard or read

    B. The ability to say words and understand the meaning of them

    C. A facet of language pattern recognition

    D. A large study of psychological impacts of dialogue

*(Average) (Skill 2.9)*

75. **An example of a nonverbal cue is a:**

    A. Gesture

    B. Eye wink

    C. Wave

    D. All of the above

*(Average) (Skill 2.9)*

76. **Visual communication occurs when a teacher presents a:**

    A. Story to the class

    B. Lecture to the class

    C. Graph to the class

    D. Sound bite to the class

*(Challenging) (Skill 2.10)*

77. **Engaging oral presentations require:**

    A. Volume

    B. Articulation

    C. Awareness of the audience

    D. All of the above

*(Challenging) (Skill 2.10)*

78. Articulation is the act of:

   A. Expressing

   B. Presenting

   C. Noticing

   D. Nonverbally communicating

*(Average) (Skill 2.10)*

79. Engaging oral presentations may contain:

   A. Humor

   B. Sarcasm

   C. High-level vocabulary words

   D. Intonation

*(Average) (Skill 2.10)*

80. Engaging the audience may include:

   A. Asking for volunteers

   B. Providing a visual diagram

   C. Singing or performing

   D. All of the above

## Mathematics (5003)

*(Easy) (Skill 5.2)*

81. Which statement below expresses the number 4,308?

   A. $4 + 3 + 0 + 8$

   B. $400 + 30 + 8$

   C. $4,000 + 300 + 8$

   D. None of the above

*(Challenging) (Skill 3.3)*

82. The words "four hundred seven and three hundredths" are represented by which number below?

   A. 47.3

   B. 407.03

   C. 400.73

   D. 4,007.300

*(Average) (Skill 3.5)*

83. $3 \times 10^6$ is equivalent to which of the following?

   A. 36

   B. 306

   C. 3,000,000

   D. 30,000,000

*(Average) (Skill 3.6)*

84. Calculate the quotient of $299 \div 3$ to the nearest hundredth.

   A. 100

   B. 99

   C. 99.7

   D. 99.67

*(Challenging) (Skill 3.7)*

85. A group of 87 students and 10 adults is going on a class field trip. Each bus holds 30 passengers. How many busses must be reserved?

   A. 3

   B. 4

   C. 8.7

   D. 10

*(Challenging) (Skill 3.8)*

86. Given natural numbers a and b, which symbol inserted in the blank would make the following relation always true?

$$\frac{1}{a} + \frac{1}{b} \ \underline{\hspace{1.5cm}} \ \left(\frac{1}{a}\right)\left(\frac{1}{b}\right)$$

   A. $=$

   B. $\leq$

   C. $\geq$

   D. $\subseteq$

*(Average) (Skill 3.9)*

87. Which set of numbers is in order from least to greatest?

   A. 100, 40, 20, 10

   B. $\frac{1}{100}, \frac{1}{40}, \frac{1}{20}, \frac{1}{10}$

   C. –10, –20, –40, –100

   D. 0.1, 0.02, 0.003, 0.0004

*(Challenging) (Skill 3.11)*

88. Identify the false statement.

   A. Addition is a commutative operation.

   B. Subtraction is a commutative operation.

   C. Addition is an associative operation.

   D. Multiplication is an associative operation.

*(Average) (Skill 3.12)*

89. If $\frac{5}{3}$ representing point J, is to be placed on the number line below, between which two points will point J lie?

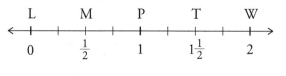

   A. T and W

   B. P and T

   C. M and P

   D. L and M

*(Easy) (Skill 3.13)*

90. Which of the following choices represent a rational number?

   A. $\frac{12}{5}$

   B. $\frac{1}{3}$

   C. $\sqrt{16}$

   D. All of the above

*(Average) (Skill 3.14)*

91. Which of the following values is equivalent to $\frac{2}{3}$?

   A. 0.67

   B. $\frac{200}{300}$

   C. $2\frac{1}{3}$

   D. None of the above

(Easy) (Skill 3.16)

92. Which value below does NOT represent 75%?

A. $\frac{7}{5}$

B. $\frac{3}{4}$

C. $\frac{75}{100}$

D. 0.75

(Average) (Skill 3.17)

93. If a 30 oz. jar of pickles costs $2.75, what is the price per ounce?

A. $0.09 per ounce

B. $0.11 per ounce

C. $0.83 per ounce

D. $0.90 per ounce

(Challenging) (Skill 3.18)

94. Solve the proportion $\frac{4}{x+1} = \frac{5}{22}$.

A. $x = 2$

B. $x = 4.25$

C. $x = 16.6$

D. $x = 20$

(Challenging) (Skill 3.19)

95. If two prime numbers are multiplied together, the result is always:

A. Prime

B. Composite

C. Zero

D. Even

(Average) (Skill 3.20)

96. Find the prime factorization of 24.

A. $4 \cdot 6$

B. $3 \cdot 8$

C. $2^3 \cdot 3$

D. $2^4$

(Easy) (Skill 3.22)

97. Find a reasonable estimate for the sum $298 + 988$.

A. 1,000

B. 1,100

C. 1,300

D. 2,000

(Challenging) (Skill 4.1)

98. Which of the choices below represents an expression?

A. $\frac{3}{x} = \frac{15}{11}$

B. $x^2 + 3x = x - 4$

C. $-8 < x - 2 < 7$

D. $4(x - 9)$

(Easy) (Skill 4.4)

99. Evaluate the expression $\frac{2x+1}{5}$ for $x = 12$.

A. 25

B. 12

C. 5

D. 3

*(Challenging) (Skill 4.6)*

100. Which choice below represents the phrase "3 less than 5 times a number"?

   A. $(5 - 3)n$

   B. $3 + 5n$

   C. $3 < 5n$

   D. $5n - 3$

*(Average) (Skill 4.7)*

101. Given the formula for the area of an isosceles trapezoid is $A = \frac{h}{2}(b_1 + b_2)$, find the area if the height is 10 cm and the bases are 12 cm and 9 cm.

   A. $210 \text{ cm}^2$

   B. $105 \text{ cm}^2$

   C. $57.5 \text{ cm}^2$

   D. $41 \text{ cm}^2$

*(Average) (Skill 4.9)*

102. Which of the following would NOT be a correct first step to solve the following equation?

   $3x - 7 = 5x + 13$

   A. Add -7 to both sides of the equation

   B. Add -13 to both sides of the equation

   C. Add -5x to both sides of the equation

   D. Subtract $3x$ from both sides of the equation

*(Challenging) (Skill 4.10)*

103. Which inequality statement below is equivalent to $3 < x$?

   A. $3 \leq x$

   B. $x > 3$

   C. $x < 3$

   D. $-3 < x < 3$

*(Challenging) (Skill 4.11)*

104. Which equation below represents the same set of ordered pairs as the equation $2x - 3y = 12$?

   A. $3x - 2y = 12$

   B. $x - y = 2$

   C. $y = -2x + 4$

   D. $y = \frac{2}{3}x - 4$

*(Easy) (Skill 4.12)*

105. Find the next term in the pattern: 3, 7, 11, 15, …

   A. 4

   B. 19

   C. 21

   D. 36

*(Challenging) (Skill 4.14)*

106. Find the rule that would generate the table of values given below.

| *x* | −1 | 0 | 2 | 7 |
|-----|-----|-----|-----|-----|
| *y* | 3 | −1 | −9 | −29 |

   A. $y = x + 4$

   B. $y = x - 11$

   C. $y = -3x$

   D. $y = -4x - 1$

*(Challenging) (Skill 5.3)*

107. Complete the analogy.
   circle: sphere :: square: _____

   A. ellipse

   B. cone

   C. cube

   D. hexagon

*(Average) (Skill 5.4)*

108. Which of the following shapes does NOT have at least one pair of parallel opposite sides?

   A. rectangle

   B. trapezoid

   C. rhombus

   D. triangle

*(Average) (Skill 5.6)*

109. A right square pyramid has a base with area 10 square units and triangular faces each with an area of 14 square units. Find the total surface area of the pyramid.

   A. 24

   B. 48

   C. 66

   D. 140

*(Challenging) (Skill 5.7)*

110. Find the perimeter of the polygon pictured below.

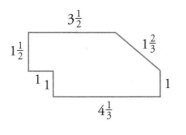

   A. 12

   B. $12\frac{5}{6}$

   C. 13

   D. 14

*(Challenging) (Skill 5.9)*

111. If the length of the side of a square is tripled, then the area of the square is increased by a factor of:

   A. 3

   B. 9

   C. 12

   D. 27

*(Average) (Skill 5.11)*

112. If the given triangle is shifted 3 units to the right, what are the new coordinates of point *S*?

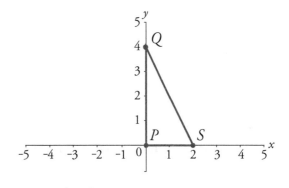

   A. (2, 3)

   B. (5, 0)

   C. (3, 0)

   D. (2, 4)

*(Easy) (Skill 5.12)*

113. A teacher shows students a price list for the school store. Pencils cost 25¢, erasers are 50¢, and a sheet of paper costs 10¢. Students are asked to come up with a purchase that totals exactly $1. Which answer below would NOT be correct?

   A. 4 pencils

   B. 2 pencils and 1 eraser

   C. 1 eraser and 5 sheets of paper

   D. 3 erasers

*(Average) (Skill 5.13)*

114. **Which is the most reasonable choice below for the length of a pencil?**

    A. 9 cm

    B. 9 mm

    C. 9 m

    D. 90 cm

*(Average) (Skill 5.17)*

115. **What is the range of the following set of data?**

    52, 86, 98, 74, 90

    A. 90

    B. 80

    C. 86

    D. 46

*(Challenging) (Skill 5.19)*

116. **Which of the following statements is false?**

    A. A set of data can have multiple modes

    B. The mean is always larger than the median

    C. The median can be the average of two numbers

    D. The mean is always equal to the average

*(Average) (Skill 5.20)*

117. **Which set of data below could be said to have outliers?**

    A. 5, 0, –3, –6, 2

    B. $\frac{1}{2}, \frac{1}{3}, \frac{1}{5}, \frac{1}{4}, \frac{1}{10,000}$

    C. 10, 20, 30, 40, 50

    D. None of the above

*(Challenging) (Skill 5.21)*

118. **What conclusion can be made based on the scatter plot below?**

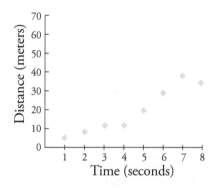

    A. Distance and time are not related

    B. Distance equals time

    C. Distance is decreasing with time

    D. Distance is increasing with time

*(Average) (Skill 5.22)*

119. **If a school has 170 employees, how many can be expected to buy their lunch at school, according to the graph below?**

**Faculty and Staff Lunch Choices**

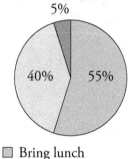

☐ Bring lunch
☐ Buy cafeteria food
☐ Go out for lunch

    A. 85

    B. 68

    C. 45

    D. 40

*(Easy) (Skill 5.24)*

120. What is the probability of rolling a 5 on a standard die?

   A. $\frac{1}{6}$

   B. $\frac{5}{6}$

   C. 50%

   D. It is impossible to quantify the probability.

*(Easy) (Skill 5.4)*

121. A cone is a figure that has which of the following characteristics?

   A. Two congruent circular bases that are parallel

   B. A circular base and a single vertex

   C. All points are the same distance from the center

   D. A square base and 4 triangle-shaped sides

*(Easy) (Skill 4.8)*

122. In the equation of the line, $3x + 2y = 14$, which term represents the independent variable?

   A. $3x$

   B. $x$

   C. $-\frac{3}{2}$

   D. $y$

*(Average) (Skill 4.10)*

123. Select the graph of the solution.

   $7 \leq 5 - 2x \leq 17$

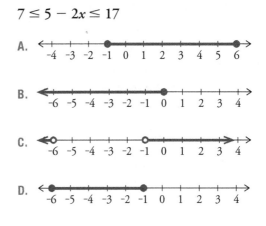

*(Average) (Skill 4.13)*

124. Identify the missing term in the following harmonic sequence: $\frac{1}{3}, \frac{1}{6}, \frac{1}{9}, \frac{1}{12}, \frac{1}{15} \cdots$

   A. $\frac{1}{16}$

   B. $\frac{1}{17}$

   C. $\frac{1}{18}$

   D. 18

*(Average) (Skill 5.1)*

125. These lines share a common point, and intersecting planes share a common set of points or a line. This describes:

   A. Parallel lines

   B. Perpendicular lines

   C. Intersecting lines

   D. Skew lines

*(Average) (Skill 5.3)*

126. A simple closed surface formed from planar polygonal regions is known as a:

   A. Vertex

   B. Polyhedron

   C. Edge

   D. Face

*(Challenging) (Skill 5.7)*

127. A car is driven north at 74 miles per hour from point A. Another car is driven due east at 65 miles per hour starting from the same point at the same time. How far are the cars away from each other after 2 hours?

A. 175.87 miles

B. 232.66 miles

C. 196.99 miles

D. 202.43 miles

*(Challenging) (Skill 5.7)*

128. Find the area of the figure.

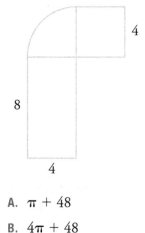

A. $\pi + 48$

B. $4\pi + 48$

C. $16\pi + 32$

D. $16\pi + 48$

*(Challenging) (Skill 5.17)*

129. Find the median of the test scores below:

| 70 | 80 | 86 |
|----|----|----|
| 90 | 91 | 90 |
| 87 | 70 | 98 |
| 54 | 63 | 62 |
| 98 | 76 | 70 |

A. 79

B. 80

C. 83

D. 84

*(Challenging) (Skill 5.24)*

130. Given a drawer with 5 black socks, 3 blue socks, and 2 red socks, what is the probability that you will draw 2 black socks in two draws in a dark room?

A. $\frac{2}{9}$

B. $\frac{1}{4}$

C. $\frac{17}{18}$

D. $\frac{1}{18}$

# Social Studies (5004)

*(Easy) (Skill 6.1)*

131. Which group of colonists were the most willing to work with the Native Americans?

   A. Spanish

   B. English

   C. Dutch

   D. French

*(Challenging) (Skill 6.1)*

132. Which of the following colonies was a New England colony?

   A. Maine

   B. New York

   C. Connecticut

   D. Vermont

*(Average) (Skill 6.1)*

133. Which colony was called "New Sweden?"

   A. Delaware

   B. Pennsylvania

   C. Maryland

   D. Massachusetts

*(Challenging) (Skill 6.2)*

134. Why was the Proclamation Act opposed?

   A. The act taxed the colonists to support British military defense

   B. The act placed a tax on tea

   C. The act prohibited English settlement beyond the Appalachian Mountains

   D. The act prohibited the colonial governments from issuing paper money

*(Challenging) (Skill 6.2)*

135. Which act placed the first "internal" tax placed on the colonists?

   A. Currency Act

   B. Stamp Act

   C. Townshend Acts

   D. Proclamation Act

*(Average) (Skill 6.2)*

136. Which statement about the "Sons of Liberty" is INCORRECT?

   A. The groups were formed to protest the Townshend Acts

   B. The groups were secret

   C. The groups staged riots against tax collectors

   D. The groups hanged British officials in effigy

*(Challenging) (Skill 6.3)*

137. Why did George Washington warn against the creation of "factions?"

   A. Factions were not political parties

   B. Factions had been popular in Great Britain

   C. Factions caused jealousies, false alarms, and could cause damage

   D. Factions were more interested in their own personal profits than in the public good

*(Easy) (Skill 6.3)*

138. Who spurred the formation of the first political parties in the newly created United States of America?

   A. Benjamin Franklin

   B. Alexander Hamilton

   C. Patrick Henry

   D. George Washington

*(Challenging) (Skill 6.3)*

139. What was Alexander Hamilton's attitude about the Constitution?

   A. He was a strict constructionist

   B. He believed the Constitution did not give Congress the power to collect taxes

   C. He strongly disfavored a national bank

   D. He believed Congress had power to make all laws "necessary and proper" to carry out its duties

*(Challenging) (Skill 6.3)*

140. During which election did political parties first play a role?

   A. 1792

   B. 1796

   C. 1800

   D. 1804

*(Average) (Skill 6.3)*

141. Which statement is INCORRECT about the Whigs?

   A. They favored strong national growth

   B. They united behind President John Quincy Adams

   C. Farmers supported the policies of the Whigs

   D. Northeast businesspeople supported the Whigs

*(Average) (Skill 6.3)*

142. What does the term "Manifest Destiny" mean in United States history?

   A. International expansion

   B. Imperialism

   C. Conquering territories

   D. Westward Expansion

*(Average) (Skill 6.3)*

143. Which statement about the settlement of Texas is INCORRECT?

   A. Many new settlers took slaves with them

   B. Slavery was outlawed in Mexico

   C. Slavery was legal in Texas

   D. Many of the new settlers were southerners

*(Easy) (Skill 6.3)*

144. **Which statement is INCORRECT about the tensions between the United States and Mexico in relation to the settlement of Texas?**

   A. The American influence permeated all parts of southwestern life

   B. The doctrine of Manifest Destiny was the motive for settling the Southwest

   C. The Mexican government owed debts to U.S. citizens for damages to property during the struggle for independence from Spain

   D. Mexico had not paid war debts

*(Challenging) (Skill 6.3)*

145. **Why were Northerners in Congress opposed to the admission of Texas as a state?**

   A. The slavery issue in Texas had not been decided

   B. Slavery was permitted in Texas

   C. Admission would disrupt the balance between free and slave states

   D. Northerners believed only free states should be admitted to the Union

*(Average) (Skill 6.3)*

146. **What is the significance of the Kansas-Nebraska Act of 1854?**

   A. It caused extreme violence

   B. It repealed some of the terms of the Missouri Compromise of 1820

   C. It maintained the balance of free and slave states

   D. It gave Southerners increased influence in Congress

*(Easy) (Skill 6.3)*

147. **In which state were the Lincoln-Douglas debates held?**

   A. Indiana

   B. Missouri

   C. Illinois

   D. Maryland

*(Challenging) (Skill 6.3)*

148. **Which of the following was an advantage the South possessed before the Civil War?**

   A. More industries

   B. More mineral resources

   C. More railroads

   D. More confidence

*(Average) (Skill 6.4)*

149. **Which statement about populism is correct?**

   A. It is a philosophy concerned with the lower classes

   B. It flourished in the late nineteenth and early twentieth centuries in the U.S.

   C. The Federalist Party was formed out of the populist philosophy

   D. The Industrial Revolution stifled the growth of the Populist Party

*(Challenging) (Skills 6.4, 6.5)*

150. **The Sherman Antitrust Act is an example of legislation passed during which period?**

   A. Populism

   B. Progressivism

   C. Imperialism

   D. World War II

*(Challenging) (Skill 6.6)*

151. Which is the political movement that believes in the elimination of all government and the replacement of government by a cooperative community of individuals?

A. Dictatorship

B. Anarchism

C. Fascism

D. Communism

*(Average) (Skill 6.6)*

152. What is another name for an oligarchy?

A. Socialism

B. Monarchy

C. Presidential System

D. Dictatorship

*(Average) (Skill 6.7)*

153. Which document was based on Greek ideas of democracy, individual rights, and ideas of the European Enlightenment and the Renaissance?

A. Articles of Confederation

B. Albany Plan of Union

C. U.S. Constitution

D. Declaration of Independence

*(Average) (Skill 6.7)*

154. How many states were required to ratify the Constitution?

A. 9

B. 7

C. 11

D. All 13

*(Easy) (Skill 6.8)*

155. Which Amendment to the U.S. Constitution guarantees freedom of religion?

A. Tenth

B. Sixth

C. Fourth

D. First

*(Easy) (Skill 7.1)*

156. What is 123 Main Street an example of?

A. Settlement pattern

B. Absolute location

C. Relative location

D. Topography

*(Average) (Skill 7.1)*

157. Which of the following is an example of a physical characteristic?

A. Canal

B. Road

C. River

D. Tunnel

*(Easy) (Skill 7.1)*

158. Humans adapting to the environment by wearing warm clothing in cold climates is an example of what theme of geography?

A. Human-environmental interaction

B. Location

C. Regions

D. Place

*(Challenging) (Skill 7.1)*

159. Relief units are examples of which type of landform?

   A. Formal region

   B. Elementary landform

   C. Functional region

   D. Vernacular region

*(Easy) (Skill 7.1)*

160. What percentage of the Earth's surface is made up of land?

   A. 70%

   B. 50%

   C. 45%

   D. 30%

*(Average) (Skill 7.1)*

161. Which of the following is NOT a characteristic of a delta?

   A. Lowlands area

   B. Steep slopes

   C. Fertile land

   D. Crop-growing area

*(Challenging) (Skill 7.1)*

162. Where are the Atlas Mountains located?

   A. Africa

   B. Europe

   C. North America

   D. South America

*(Challenging) (Skill 7.1)*

163. Which statement about a mesa is INCORRECT?

   A. It is the flat top of a hill

   B. It is the flat top of a mountain

   C. It usually has steep sides

   D. It is similar to a plateau but larger

*(Average) (Skill 7.1)*

164. What is a low area drained by rivers or low spots in mountains?

   A. Marsh

   B. Basin

   C. Swamp

   D. Delta

*(Challenging) (Skill 7.1)*

165. Which ocean covers almost one-third of the entire surface of the Earth and separates North and South America from Asia and Australia?

   A. Pacific

   B. Atlantic

   C. Arctic

   D. Indian

*(Average) (Skill 7.1)*

166. What is considered a nation's lifeblood?

   A. Lake

   B. Sea

   C. River

   D. Ocean

*(Average) (Skill 7.1)*

167. **Which oceans does the Panama Canal connect?**

   A. Arctic and Indian

   B. Indian and Atlantic

   C. Atlantic and Pacific

   D. Pacific and Arctic

*(Average) (Skill 7.1)*

168. **Which statement about a subtropical climate is correct?**

   A. It is characterized by low levels of moisture

   B. It is a humid climate

   C. It is found only north of the tropics

   D. It is found only south of the tropics

*(Challenging) (Skill 7.1)*

169. **Which of the following is a correct statement about vertical climates?**

   A. The temperatures remain constant

   B. They are found in high mountain areas

   C. The crops remain the same, regardless of level

   D. The economic activities are limited because of snow

*(Challenging) (Skill 7.2)*

170. **Which of the following is true about a grid as relating to pinpointing exact locations?**

   A. A grid is the intersection of parallels and meridians at right angles

   B. A grid is the intersection of longitudes and meridians at right angles

   C. A grid is the intersection of parallels and latitudes at right angles

   D. Parallels and meridians do not intersect

*(Average) (Skill 7.2)*

171. **Which of the following is a country in the "land bridge of Middle America?**

   A. Brazil

   B. Ecuador

   C. Bosnia

   D. Jamaica

*(Easy) (Skill 8.1)*

172. **Which ancient civilization created paper from papyrus?**

   A. Sumerians

   B. Chinese

   C. Egyptians

   D. Greeks

*(Challenging) (Skill 8.1)*

173. Which of the following statements about the Kush civilization is INCORRECT?

   A. They lived in Egypt

   B. Their civilization was characterized as an "unsettled way of life"

   C. The people subsisted on hunting and herding cattle

   D. Their civilization appears to be the second oldest in Egypt

*(Easy) (Skill 8.1)*

174. Which ancient civilization's attitude about sports, with an emphasis on a physically sound body, led to the tradition of the Olympic Games?

   A. Greece

   B. Rome

   C. Persia

   D. China

*(Average) (Skill 8.1)*

175. Which ancient civilization is remembered for its city-states?

   A. Rome

   B. Persia

   C. Greece

   D. China

*(Challenging) (Skill 8.1)*

176. Approximately how long did the ancient civilization of Rome last?

   A. 100 years

   B. 500 years

   C. 1000 years

   D. 1500 years

*(Challenging) (Skill 8.1)*

177. Which statement about the Pax Romana is INCORRECT?

   A. The Pax Romana was an accomplishment of the Greeks

   B. The Pax Romana allowed for free travel

   C. The Pax Romana affected a vast area

   D. The Pax Romana was an accomplishment of the Romans

*(Average) (Skill 8.1)*

178. Who unified Greece?

   A. Julius Caesar

   B. Alexander

   C. Pythagoras

   D. Homer

*(Easy) (Skill 8.1)*

179. Which ancient civilization served as a model for modern government, especially in federal systems such as that found in the United States?

   A. Egyptian

   B. Greek

   C. Chinese

   D. Roman

*(Challenging) (Skill 8.2)*

180. Which decade marked the fall of the Soviet Union?

   A. 1990s

   B. 1980s

   C. 1970s

   D. 1960s

*(Average) (Skill 8.2)*

181. Saddam Hussein was ousted as dictator of which country?

A. Iraq

B. Afghanistan

C. Iran

D. Palestine

*(Challenging) (Skill 8.4)*

182. Which statement about a market is INCORRECT?

A. Markets exist in both the input and output sides of the economy

B. Buyers and sellers must meet face to face

C. An output market refers to the market in which goods and services are sold

D. In a market-oriented economy, markets function on the basis of supply and demand

*(Average) (Skill 8.4)*

183. Which of the following is NOT a category of factors of production?

A. Land

B. Labor

C. Markets

D. Capital

*(Challenging) (Skill 8.4)*

184. Which of the following terms is determined as the overlap of the buying decisions of buyers with the selling decisions of the sellers?

A. Supply and demand

B. Factor of production

C. Input market

D. Equilibrium price

*(Average) (Skill 8.6)*

185. Which type of economic system is characterized by both markets and planning?

A. Market economy

B. Centrally planned economy

C. Market socialism

D. Non-market economy

# Science (5005)

*(Average) (Skill 9.1)*

186. The earth's core is _____ its mantle.

A. less dense than

B. denser than

C. just as dense as

D. the core and mantle are the same

*(Average) (Skill 9.1)*

187. Which of the following is NOT located in the upper mantle?

A. Sial

B. Asthenosphere

C. Troposphere

D. Mesosphere

*(Easy) (Skill 9.1)*

188. _____ is the second-most abundant gas in the earth's atmosphere.

A. Nitrogen

B. Argon

C. Oxygen

D. Chlorine

*(Average) (Skill 9.1)*

189. The _____ is the coldest layer in the atmosphere.

    A. mesosphere

    B. thermosphere

    C. troposphere

    D. stratosphere

*(Challenging) (Skill 9.1)*

190. When gases in the _____ emit light energy after being excited by solar radiation, the Aurora Borealis occurs in the northern hemisphere.

    A. exosphere

    B. stratosphere

    C. ionosphere

    D. troposphere

*(Average) (Skill 9.2)*

191. _____ is natural mountain building.

    A. Orogeny

    B. Dig slip

    C. Folding

    D. Faulting

*(Average) (Skill 9.2)*

192. When lava cools, _____ rock is formed.

    A. sedimentary

    B. igneous

    C. metamorphic

    D. flint

*(Challenging) (Skill 9.2)*

193. Which of the following is true about the three rock types?

    A. Igneous rock is formed from the cementation of sediments

    B. Sedimentary rock is formed from molten rock

    C. Metamorphic rock is formed at low temperatures and high pressures

    D. Metamorphic rock results from its parent rock undergoing chemical change

*(Easy) (Skill 9.3)*

194. We are currently living in the _____ era.

    A. Cenozoic

    B. Mesozoic

    C. Jurassic

    D. Permian

*(Challenging) (Skill 9.3)*

195. Which of the following is NOT true about fossils?

    A. A fossilized cast of a bone is composed of bone

    B. Some organisms are embedded in amber (tree sap)

    C. Fossils of footprints are possible

    D. The heat of magma would inhibit fossilization

*(Challenging) (Skill 9.3)*

196. The _____ the time period an index fossil could have been deposited the more precise geologic dating will be.

  A. longer

  B. shorter

  C. it depends

  D. the timing does not matter

*(Easy) (Skill 9.4)*

197. There are _____ established planets in the solar system.

  A. ten

  B. nine

  C. eight

  D. seven

*(Average) (Skill 9.4)*

198. Earth's galaxy is called the _____.

  A. Big Dipper

  B. Ursa Minor

  C. Milky Way

  D. Great Bear

*(Average) (Skill 9.4)*

199. When the sun and moon are on opposite sides of the earth, observers on Earth perceive a _____.

  A. gibbous moon

  B. new moon

  C. full moon

  D. crescent moon

*(Challenging) (Skill 9.5)*

200. Which of the following is NOT true about the sun?

  A. The sun is a star

  B. The chromosphere produces sunspots

  C. The photosphere is the surface of the sun

  D. The corona is only visible during total solar eclipses

*(Challenging) (Skill 9.5)*

201. Which of the following is NOT true about the earth's seasons?

  A. The earth's tilted rotation axis influences the amount of sunlight the northern and southern hemispheres receive

  B. The solstices occur when the sun reaches its highest or lower point of the day at noon

  C. During the summer solstice the southern hemisphere leans toward the sun

  D. During the winter solstice the northern hemisphere leans away from the sun

*(Average) (Skill 10.1)*

202. Mitochondria are on the _____ scale in size while the animal cell that contains them is on the _____ scale in size.

  A. micron; nanometer

  B. millimeter; nanometer

  C. nanometer; micron

  D. micron; millimeter

*(Challenging) (Skill 10.2)*

203. The mitotic division of one somatic cell results in what number of diploid/haploid (choose one) cells?

A. 4 cells; haploid

B. 4 cells; diploid

C. 2 cells; haploid

D. 2 cells; diploid

*(Average) (Skill 10.2)*

204. View the monohybrid cross below for having blue or brown eyes. B is the dominant allele and b is the recessive allele. Having the B allele results in brown eyes and not having it will result in blue eyes. What percentage of children are heterozygotes?

|   | B | B |
|---|---|---|
| B | BB | Bb |
| b | Bb | bb |

A. 25%

B. 0%

C. 50%

D. 75%

*(Easy) (Skill 10.2)*

205. What is a heterozygote?

A. A person having two dominant alleles for a gene

B. A person having two recessive alleles for a gene

C. A person having one dominant and one recessive allele for a gene

D. A person having codominant alleles for a gene

*(Easy) (Skill 10.3)*

206. _____ is the change in a population's heritable traits over time.

A. Biological evolution

B. Natural selection

C. Reproduction

D. Convergence

*(Average) (Skill 10.4)*

207. Which of the following does NOT reproduce sexually?

A. Fungi

B. Animals

C. Protists

D. Plants

*(Easy) (Skill 10.5)*

208. Which of the following is NOT one of the five kingdoms of living organisms?

A. Animalia

B. Chordata

C. Plantae

D. Monera

*(Average) (Skill 10.5)*

209. Which of the following is NOT the correct match of an Animalia phylum with examples of organisms found within the phylum?

A. Arthropoda – spiders and insects

B. Echinodermata – sea urchins and starfish

C. Mollusca – clams and octopi

D. Annelida – crustaceans

*(Average) (Skill 10.6)*

210. Which of the following shows the levels of biomes in increasing complexity from left-to-right?

   A. Biomes – community – population – species

   B. Biomes – population – community – species

   C. Species – population – community – biomes

   D. Species – community – population – biomes

*(Challenging) (Skill 10.6)*

211. Which of the following is NOT a characteristic of an environment's carrying capacity?

   A. The carrying capacity is the maximum life that can be supported in an environment

   B. The carrying capacity of an environment increases as populations of species increase

   C. The rate of population growth stops when resources are exhausted

   D. The rate of population growth slows as resources become scarcer

*(Easy) (Skill 10.7)*

212. Which of the following is NOT a communicable disease?

   A. Influenza

   B. Diabetes Mellitus

   C. Tuberculosis

   D. Measles

*(Average) (Skill 10.8)*

213. Which of the following is NOT a characteristic of science as an endeavor?

   A. Scientific experiments and undertakings are limited by current technology

   B. Scientific knowledge changes over time

   C. The scientific enterprise consists of various people and activities in many locations

   D. Scientific knowledge is based on individuals' feelings and biases

*(Average) (Skill 10.8)*

214. All of the following are primary sources of funding for scientific research in the United States except _____?

   A. the federal government

   B. state governments

   C. private or public corporations

   D. private citizens

*(Challenging) (Skill 10.9)*

215. Which of the following is true when a new theory is developed regarding a topic?

   A. The existing theories on the topic could be altered/adjusted upon proof

   B. The new theory should just be accepted

   C. The new theory should not be even considered

   D. Both the new and old theories should be debated and a vote taken on which one to accept

*(Average) (Skill 10.9)*

216. In which stage of the scientific inquiry process can a researcher be required to include graphical representations of the information he has gathered?

   A. Observation

   B. Hypothesis generation

   C. Data analysis

   D. Conclusion

*(Challenging) (Skill 10.10)*

217. Which of the following are online databases that scientists use to search for journal articles?

   A. Web of Science

   B. PubMed and PubChem

   C. Google Scholar

   D. All of the above

*(Challenging) (Skill 10.11)*

218. Which of the following is NOT a type of equilibrium?

   A. Biological evolution

   B. Genetic (population) equilibrium

   C. Thermal equilibrium

   D. Chemical equilibrium

*(Average) (Skill 11.1)*

219. Which property of matter is NOT matched with its correct unit of measurement?

   A. Velocity – meter/second

   B. Electrical potential – volt

   C. Power – joule/second

   D. Specific gravity – gram/cubic centimeter

*(Average) (Skill 11.1)*

220. _____ properties cannot be observed without changing the identity of a substance.

   A. Chemical

   B. Intensive

   C. Physical

   D. Extensive

*(Challenging) (Skill 11.1)*

221. Which process is NOT matched with its correct state of matter conversion?

   A. Condensation – gas to liquid

   B. Melting – solid to liquid

   C. Sublimation – gas to solid

   D. Evaporation – liquid to gas

*(Easy) (Skill 11.1)*

222. Which particle is correctly matched with its charge?

   A. Proton – negative

   B. Neutron – positive

   C. Electron – no charge

   D. None of the above

*(Challenging) (Skill 11.1)*

223. Which of the following terms is NOT correctly matched with its definition?

   A. Atomic mass – average mass of an element's isotopes

   B. Mass number – number of protons and electrons

   C. Atomic number – number of protons

   D. Atomic mass unit – standard unit of measurement for atomic mass

*(Challenging) (Skill 11.1)*

224. Which of the following is NOT an example of a mixture?

   A. Soil

   B. Air

   C. Ocean water

   D. $H_2O$

*(Challenging) (Skill 11.2)*

225. If an object is moving it can be said to have _____.

   A. velocity

   B. acceleration

   C. kinetic energy

   D. All of the above

*(Average) (Skill 11.2)*

226. Force is measured in _____.

   A. watts

   B. amperes

   C. newtons

   D. meters/second

*(Challenging) (Skill 11.2)*

227. Car 1 is traveling on a highway has mass 1800 kg and velocity 30 m/s. Another car (Car 2) on the highway also has mass 1800 kg, but is traveling at a velocity of 50 m/s. Which car has greater momentum?

   A. Car 1

   B. Car 2

   C. The cars have the same momentum

   D. It's impossible to tell

*(Challenging) (Skill 11.2)*

228. Which of the following laws is incorrectly matched with its description?

   A. Newton's 3rd Law: For every action there is just an equal reaction

   B. Law of Gravity: Two bodies in the universe attract each other with a force that is directly proportional to the product of their masses

   C. Newton's 2nd Law: If a force acts on an object it will cause the object to accelerate

   D. Newton's 1st Law: An object in motion will remain in motion unless acted upon by an external force

*(Easy) (Skill 11.3)*

229. The law of the conservation of energy states that _____.

   A. energy is neither created nor destroyed

   B. energy changes form

   C. energy is conserved over time

   D. All of the above

*(Challenging) (Skill 11.3)*

230. What are the units of measurement for work?

   A. N/m

   B. N·m

   C. J

   D. B and C

*(Average) (Skill 11.3)*

231. If a gas is expanding in a container, then _____.

   A. the gas is doing work on the walls of the container

   B. the container is doing work on the container

   C. neither the gas nor container is doing work

   D. both the gas and container are doing work

*(Challenging) (Skill 11.3)*

232. Which of the following terms is NOT true about the laws of thermodynamics?

   A. The laws cover systems in thermal equilibrium

   B. The 1st law of thermodynamics states that the heat energy supplied to the system is equal to the energy used by the system to do work externally

   C. The 2nd law of thermodynamics states that a machine can be 100% efficient—all the energy it uses goes towards its work and is not lost passively

   D. The 2nd law of thermodynamics states that heat cannot spontaneously move from a colder to warmer object

*(Easy) (Skill 11.4)*

233. _____ are the atomic particles primarily responsible for electricity.

   A. Electrons

   B. Protons

   C. Neutrons

   D. Quarks

*(Average) (Skill 11.4)*

234. Which of the following does NOT describe chemical reactions?

   A. Chemical reactions involve the breaking of chemical bonds

   B. Chemical reactions result in chemical changes of the starting substances

   C. Chemical reactions involve changes in the structure of atomic nuclei

   D. Chemical reactions involve the activity of electrons

*(Challenging) (Skill 11.4)*

235. Which of the following is true about magnets?

   A. Magnets produce electric fields

   B. All metals are attracted to magnets

   C. Magnets only attract magnetic objects

   D. Magnetic fields are invisible to the human eye

## Answer Key

| | | | | | | | | |
|---|---|---|---|---|---|---|---|---|
| 1. A | 29. A | 57. A | 85. B | 113. D | 141. C | 169. B | 197. C | 225. D |
| 2. A | 30. C | 58. C | 86. C | 114. A | 142. D | 170. A | 198. C | 226. C |
| 3. D | 31. A | 59. A | 87. B | 115. D | 143. C | 171. D | 199. C | 227. B |
| 4. B | 32. D | 60. B | 88. B | 116. B | 144. A | 172. C | 200. B | 228. A |
| 5. B | 33. A | 61. A | 89. A | 117. B | 145. C | 173. B | 201. C | 229. D |
| 6. B | 34. B | 62. B | 90. D | 118. D | 146. B | 174. A | 202. C | 230. D |
| 7. A | 35. A | 63. C | 91. B | 119. B | 147. C | 175. C | 203. D | 231. A |
| 8. D | 36. B | 64. C | 92. A | 120. A | 148. D | 176. C | 204. C | 232. C |
| 9. A | 37. D | 65. D | 93. A | 121. B | 149. B | 177. A | 205. C | 233. A |
| 10. A | 38. D | 66. A | 94. C | 122. B | 150. B | 178. B | 206. A | 234. C |
| 11. B | 39. C | 67. D | 95. B | 123. D | 151. B | 179. D | 207. C | 235. D |
| 12. A | 40. B | 68. B | 96. C | 124. C | 152. D | 180. A | 208. B | |
| 13. C | 41. C | 69. B | 97. C | 125. C | 153. D | 181. A | 209. D | |
| 14. B | 42. D | 70. A | 98. D | 126. B | 154. A | 182. B | 210. C | |
| 15. C | 43. D | 71. B | 99. C | 127. C | 155. D | 183. C | 211. A | |
| 16. C | 44. A | 72. D | 100. D | 128. A | 156. B | 184. D | 212. B | |
| 17. A | 45. D | 73. A | 101. B | 129. D | 157. C | 185. C | 213. D | |
| 18. B | 46. B | 74. A | 102. A | 130. A | 158. A | 186. B | 214. D | |
| 19. D | 47. A | 75. D | 103. B | 131. D | 159. B | 187. A | 215. A | |
| 20. B | 48. C | 76. C | 104. D | 132. C | 160. D | 188. C | 216. C | |
| 21. A | 49. D | 77. D | 105. B | 133. A | 161. B | 189. A | 217. D | |
| 22. A | 50. A | 78. A | 106. D | 134. C | 162. A | 190. C. | 218. A | |
| 23. B | 51. D | 79. A | 107. C | 135. B | 163. D | 191. A | 219. D | |
| 24. B | 52. D | 80. D | 108. D | 136. A | 164. B | 192. B | 220. A | |
| 25. A | 53. D | 81. C | 109. B | 137. C | 165. A | 193. D | 221. C | |
| 26. B | 54. A | 82. B | 110. D | 138. B | 166. C | 194. A | 222. D | |
| 27. C | 55. C | 83. C | 111. B | 139. D | 167. C | 195. A | 223. B | |
| 28. D | 56. D | 84. D | 112. B | 140. B | 168. B | 196. B | 224. D | |

# Rigor Table

| RIGOR | QUESTIONS |
|-------|-----------|
| Easy | 3, 15, 16, 19, 21, 22, 26, 30, 32, 40, 41,42, 48, 49, 52, 53, 56, 81, 90, 92, 97, 99, 105, 113, 120, 121, 122, 131, 138, 144, 147, 155, 156, 158, 160, 172, 174, 179, 188, 194, 197, 205, 206, 208, 212, 222, 229, 233 |
| Average | 1, 2, 4, 5, 6, 9, 12, 14, 18, 20, 23, 27, 31, 33, 35, 38, 43, 45, 50, 55, 57, 62, 66, 67, 68, 71, 72, 75, 76, 79, 80, 83, 84, 87, 89, 91, 93, 96, 101, 102, 108, 109, 112, 114, 115, 117, 119, 123, 124, 125, 126, 133, 136, 141, 142, 143, 146, 149, 152, 153, 154, 157, 161, 164, 166, 167, 168, 171, 175, 178, 181, 183, 185, 186, 187, 189, 191, 192, 198, 199, 202, 204, 207, 209, 210, 213, 214, 216, 219, 220, 226, 231, 234 |
| Challenging | 7, 8, 10, 11, 13, 17, 24, 25, 28, 29, 34, 36, 37, 39, 44, 46, 47, 51, 54, 58, 59, 60, 61, 63, 64, 65, 69, 70, 73, 74, 77, 78, 82, 85, 86, 88, 94, 95, 98, 100, 103, 104, 106, 107, 110, 111, 116, 118, 127, 128, 129, 130, 132, 134, 135, 137, 139, 140, 145, 148, 150, 151, 159, 162, 163, 165, 169, 170, 173, 176, 177, 180, 182, 184, 190, 193, 195, 196, 200, 201, 203, 211, 215, 217, 218, 221, 223, 224, 225, 227, 228, 230, 232, 235 |

# Questions with Rationales

## Reading and Language Arts (5002)

*(Average) (Skill 1.1)*

1. **Rhyming is the manipulation of sounds, which is indicative of:**

    A. Phonological awareness

    B. Phonemic awareness

    C. Morphology

    D. Syntax

    **Answer: A. Phonological awareness**

    Students who have strong phonological awareness are able to rhyme well and understand how words sound alike and are spelled similarly.

*(Average) (Skill 1.1)*

2. **Foundation skills taught to develop a student's understanding and working knowledge of reading are:**

    A. Print concepts, phonological awareness, phonics and word recognition, and fluency

    B. Print concepts, phonological awareness, syllabication, and fluency

    C. Print concepts, morphology, phonics and word recognition, and fluency

    D. Print concepts, phonological awareness, phonics and word recognition, and receptive language

    **Answer: A. Print concepts, phonological awareness, phonics and word recognition, and fluency**

    These foundation skills allow for the basic underpinnings of reading ability to be solidified and refined.

*(Easy) (Skill 1.1)*

3. **An example of a three-letter onset is:**

    A. spr.

    B. spl.

    C. Neither

    D. Both A and B

    **Answer: D. Both A and B**

    The onset is the beginning sound of the word, which also may be referred to as an initial blend.

*(Average) (Skill 1.1)*

4. **Ryan is having difficulty developing his phonological awareness. Mrs. Debber has created a phoneme deletion activity for him to do each morning. An example of a phoneme deletion question she may ask is:**

    A. What word do you have if you add /p/ to the beginning of *lay*?

    B. What is *smile* without the /s/?

    C. The word is *rug*. Change the /g/ to /t/. What is the new word?

    D. Can you tell me the three sounds in the word *fun*?

    **Answer: B. What is *smile* without the /s/?**

    This type of phoneme deletion question helps Ryan develop and strengthen his phonological awareness.

*(Average) (Skill 1.1)*

5. Which of the following is a question a teacher may ask a student when developing the student's ability to substitute phonemes in words?

   A. What is *kite* without the /e/?

   B. The word is *sub*. Change the /b/ to /n/. What's the new word?

   C. Can you separate the four sounds in the word *flag*?

   D. Which word does not belong in the group of words: *sun, cloud, boot, moon*?

   **Answer: B. The word is *sub*. Change the /b/ to /n/. What's the new word?**

   This substitution method is useful for developing phonological awareness so the student may understand words more deeply.

*(Average) (Skill 1.2)*

6. **What is sound–letter correspondence?**

   A. It is the manner in which a student orally articulates letter sounds

   B. Is it composed of the sounds represented by the letters of the alphabet

   C. It includes the letters in multisyllabic words

   D. It is the manner in which a student transcribes a word

   **Answer: B. Is it composed of the sounds represented by the letters of the alphabet**

   Sound–letter correspondence is a term that relates to sounds represented by a particular letter of the alphabet.

*(Challenging) (Skill 1.2)*

7. **Sight words for third graders may include:**

   A. Laugh and together

   B. Bicycle and classify

   C. Ambivalent and myriad

   D. Extraterrestrial and autobiography

   **Answer: A. Laugh and together**

   These words are indicative of sight words that may be found on third-grade-level sight word lists.

*(Challenging) (Skill 1.2)*

8. **The root word for *geographical* is:**

   A. Graph

   B. Hical

   C. Al

   D. Geo

   **Answer: D. Geo**

   The root gives information pertaining to the meaning of the word.

*(Average) (Skill 1.2)*

9. **The suffix *–ology* or *–logy* means:**

   A. The study of

   B. The condition of

   C. The reading of

   D. The state of

   **Answer: A. The study of**

   The suffix is a word part that gives the reader a hint as to what the definition of a word may be.

*(Challenging) (Skill 1.2)*

10. **According to the WIDA taxonomy, when a student is identifying language that indicates narrative points of view (e.g., "I" vs. "he/she") from illustrated text using word/phrase banks with a partner, the student is at which level?**

    A. Entering

    B. Emerging

    C. Developing

    D. Bridging

    **Answer: A. Entering**

    The WIDA taxonomy is a useful tool for educators to consult when understanding the reading and linguistic developmental levels of students in the classroom.

*(Challenging) (Skill 1.2)*

11. **Stages of language acquisition involve levels of thinking and language functions. One can use Bloom's Taxonomy across the stages of second-language acquisition. The early production (level 2) is when:**

    A. Students are nonverbal

    B. Students offer one-word responses

    C. Students use short phrases

    D. Students make longer, complex sentences

    **Answer: B. Students offer one-word responses**

    Second-language acquisition involves layers of thinking and language recognition. The early production level is when students are truly interpreting what is being communicated to them, and in turn, they are expressing one-word responses.

*(Average) (Skill 1.2)*

12. **The most common rimes include:**

    A. –ash, –ell, –ug

    B. –ote, –ank, –ell

    C. –ube, –ate, –ame

    D. –eat, –at, –ipe

    **Answer: A. –ash, –ell, –ug**

    All of these rimes have short vowels in them, and they are the most common rimes.

*(Challenging) (Skill 1.2)*

13. **In order to give an ELL student context when reading using phonics, a teacher may:**

    A. Give background information

    B. Preview the words

    C. Use a picture or visual

    D. Review prefixes

    **Answer: C. Use a picture or visual**

    The picture and visual stimuli gives students a reference point that is pictorial and can support the context when reading words.

*(Average) (Skill 1.2)*

14. **A word with one syllable that ends in the letter *y* will have the same final *y* sound as the:**

    A. /short i/

    B. /long i/

    C. /long y/

    D. /short u/

    **Answer: B. /long i/**

Words such as *fly* and *sky* have a final ending of a /long i/ sound.

*(Easy) (Skill 1.2)*

15. The word lump follows which pattern?

A. CCVCC

B. CVC

C. CVCC

D. CCVC

**Answer: C. CVCC**

The consonant-vowel-consonant-consonant pattern works for the word lump.

*(Easy) (Skill 1.3)*

16. What is fluency also known as?

A. Comprehension

B. Decoding

C. Automaticity

D. Understanding

**Answer: C. Automaticity**

Fluency is the automatic recognition of words, and the words are spoken fluently.

*(Challenging) (Skill 1.3)*

17. What is prosody?

A. The rhythm and intonation of language

B. The rise and fall of a person's voice

C. Word recognition

D. Decoding of multisyllabic words

**Answer: A. The rhythm and intonation of language**

Prosody involves the rhythm of language and how words are expressed with intonation.

*(Average) (Skill 1.3)*

18. In a reading fluency study, the National Center for Education Statistics (NCES) reported high-fluency fourth graders read with expression and grouped words into meaningful phrases, but low-fluency fourth graders:

A. Read with prosody in a smooth manner

B. Ignore sentence structure and read in one- or two-word phrases

C. Ignore sentence structure and read multisyllabic words

D. Ignore sentence structure and decode words

**Answer: B. Ignore sentence structure and read in one- or two-word phrases**

The low-fluency groups exhibit impaired reading capabilities and they are at a higher risk for not developing the skills needed.

*(Easy) (Skill 1.4)*

19. Identifying the moral of a story (literary text) occurs within the development of the plot of a story, but can often be specifically located:

A. At the beginning of a story

B. In the middle of a story

C. In the first sentence of a story

D. In the last paragraph of a story

**Answer: D. In the last paragraph of a story**

The moral is often embedded in the ending of a story or tale.

*(Average) (Skill 1.4)*

20. **Grady is a second grader who has trouble making inferences from the text he reads. A strategy the teacher can demonstrate or model for Grady is:**

    A. Rereading the topic and concluding sentences

    B. Using context clues to figure out what the author doesn't write explicitly

    C. Underlining boldface words

    D. Defining vocabulary

    **Answer: B. Using context clues to figure out what the author doesn't write explicitly**

    Grady can use context clues to understand inferential information in the text.

*(Easy) (Skill 1.4)*

21. **An effective summary deletes:**

    A. Minor and irrelevant details

    B. The author's name

    C. The main points

    D. Paraphrased portions of the text

    **Answer: A. Minor and irrelevant details**

    An effective summary focuses on the main points at hand and does not touch upon superfluous details, which detract from the main idea.

*(Easy) (Skill 1.4)*

22. **The plot of a literary text is:**

    A. The main events presented by the writer in a specific manner

    B. The location in which a story takes place

    C. The foreshadowing of events to come

    D. The characters

    **Answer: A. The main events presented by the writer in a specific manner**

    The plot is an overview of the main events. The main events characterize what occurs in the story.

*(Average) (Skill 1.4)*

23. **Students in Mr. Klar's fifth-grade science class are analyzing the relationship between oxygen and carbon dioxide while studying the photosynthesis unit. Many members of his class have a visual learning style. The best way to teach them this relationship by using:**

    A. An audio recording of the process

    B. A diagram on the board

    C. A worksheet

    D. A hands-on class activity

    **Answer: B. A diagram on the board**

    The diagram is a visual representation, which helps visual learners process the information from the lesson.

*(Challenging) (Skill 1.4)*

24. Lexical priming is a technique teachers use to encourage:

    A. Word parts

    B. Word recognition

    C. Word study

    D. Word definitions

**Answer: B. Word recognition**

Priming gives a basis for students to recognize words.

*(Challenging) (Skill 1.5)*

25. What is cadence?

    A. A pattern of rhythm in speech or poetry without meter

    B. Repetitious speech in poetry

    C. Metered poetry technique

    D. Rhythm in speech

**Answer: A. A pattern of rhythm in speech or poetry without meter**

Cadence gives a rhythm to words, which allows the words to feel poetic in a sense.

*(Easy) (Skill 1.5)*

26. What is a hyperlink?

    A. A sidebar in an internet link

    B. A link from a hypertext file or document to another location or file

    C. A link to an email message

    D. A link to a specific area of text

**Answer: B. A link from a hypertext file or document to another location or file**

A hyperlink is a link that directs students and teachers to other files and locations on websites.

*(Average) (Skill 1.5)*

27. A piece of informational text presented to fourth-grade students discussed oil spills. The students identified the oil spill and understood it caused many deaths in wildlife. This type of text analysis is called:

    A. Problem/solution

    B. Narrative

    C. Cause and effect

    D. Prose fiction

**Answer: C. Cause and effect**

This relationship of cause and effect is essential for students to develop reading comprehension skills, while adhering to the Common Core State Standards.

*(Challenging) (Skill 1.5)*

28. The fifth graders in Mr. Deter's class are studying literary elements. What literary element can be derived from this passage he shared with the students?

    "The sun rose in the sky that morning. Donna felt she was ready for a new beginning. It shined brightly through her window. The sunbeams reached her face."

    A. Style

    B. Theme

    C. Conflict

    D. Symbolism

**Answer: D. Symbolism**

The symbol is the sun. It represents a new beginning for Donna.

*(Challenging) (Skill 1.5)*

29. **In literary terms, which elements characterize style?**

    A. Syntax and diction

    B. Author's attitude and plot

    C. Conflicts that arise and plot

    D. Setting and tone

    **Answer: A. Syntax and diction**

    Syntax and diction are essentially word choices the author makes and this characterizes the style of a passage.

*(Easy) (Skill 1.6)*

30. **Which pronoun is used in text to indicate possible first-person point of view?**

    A. They

    B. Her

    C. I

    D. Him

    **Answer: C. I**

    The first-person point of view is a first-person narration and can include the personal pronoun "I."

*(Average) (Skill 1.6)*

31. **The story of *Cinderella* is one that has been told by many cultures across the world. In order for students to assess the similarities and differences, a teacher may want to use a:**

    A. Comparison matrix

    B. Flow chart

    C. T-chart

    D. KWL diagram

    **Answer: A. Comparison matrix**

Assessing the similarities and differences can be done with many graphic organizers, but a comparison matrix is highly effective.

*(Easy) (Skill 1.7)*

32. **Mr. Murphy uses a multimedia presentation in his third-grade class that shows only segments of the tale of *Icarus and Daedalus*. He is also reading the tale in class to the students. Why might he only show parts of the multimedia version?**

    A. Time constraints

    B. To allow students to make their own mental imagery

    C. To provide visual support to comprehension

    D. All of the above

    **Answer: D. All of the above**

    He is only showing parts of the film so students can derive their own ideas and create their own mental images of what is occurring in the story he is reading in the classroom.

*(Average) (Skill 1.7)*

33. **Hyla is a fifth grader who prefers to read graphic novels rather than traditional books. What is a graphic novel?**

    A. Structured, sequential art used to tell a story

    B. A semi-structured story with arbitrary pictures

    C. A heavily designed comic book

    D. A series of short vignettes

    **Answer: A. Structured, sequential art used to tell a story**

Graphic novels have become more popular over the years. Students often find the artwork to be helpful when determining information pertaining to the storyline.

*(Challenging) (Skill 1.7)*

34. Mr. Jessup's 20 first graders listened to him read a story in class. There are four characters in the story. How can the students most effectively replicate the story and produce a play?

   A. The class can be divided in half, and each can read sections of the dialogue

   B. The class can be divided into groups of five, and each student plays a role

   C. The class can be divided into 10 pair of students, and each acts out two pages

   D. The class can do a whole-group activity and take turns

   **Answer: B. The class can be divided into groups of five, and each student plays a role**

   When working in smaller groups, teachers can assess what is occurring on the small group level and identify individual students and their progress.

*(Average) (Skill 1.7)*

35. Students are reading two texts about tigers in Mr. Franklin's fifth-grade class. The students are creating charts to describe characteristics tigers possess. What else can the students do to enhance their understanding of tigers?

   A. Draw a picture of a tiger

   B. Underline their favorite fact

   C. Read the charts again

   D. Enhance the charts with bigger letters and different fonts

**Answer: A. Draw a picture of a tiger**

They can draw a picture to understand various aspects and characteristics of a tiger, as well as physical attributes.

*(Challenging) (Skill 1.7)*

36. A pie chart shows the fractional portion of brownies eaten. The pie chart is embedded in the story of Rebecca and Mary, who make a pan of brownies with their grandmother. Out of the eight brownie squares, Mary ate two. How can students understand this concept verbally?

   A. Students can color in the fractional part that represents the amount of brownies Mary ate

   B. Students can write a sentence that depicts the amount Mary ate

   C. Students can draw two brownies in the white space of the paper

   D. Students can cut the pie chart into segments

**Answer: B. Students can write a sentence that depicts the amount Mary ate**

The sentence gives verbal weight to the concept and allows students to translate the numerical process into words.

*(Challenging) (Skill 1.8)*

37. **What is a qualitative evaluation of a text?**

    A. Reader and task variables are used to match text to student

    B. Readability measures and other scores of text complexity

    C. Detailed information revealed in text-complexity measurements

    D. Levels of meaning, structure, language conventionality, and clarity

    **Answer: D. Levels of meaning, structure, language conventionality, and clarity**

    Qualitative evaluations measure elements of text, which are non-numerical in nature.

*(Average) (Skill 1.8)*

38. **DRA text leveling is used for students in grades:**

    A. K–5

    B. K–6

    C. K–12

    D. K–8

    **Answer: D. K–8**

    The DRA level is a data collection point that allows teachers to identify a student's reading level in grades K–8.

*(Challenging) (Skill 1.8)*

39. **In the Lexile Framework for Reading, a book is labeled NC, or nonconforming, when it:**

    A. Is best shared as a read-aloud

    B. Is a beginning reader

    C. Contains vocabulary and sentence length that are complex compared to subject matter

    D. Contains vocabulary and sentence length that are simplistic compared to subject matter

    **Answer: C. Contains vocabulary and sentence length that are complex compared to subject matter**

    The label NC means it is nonconforming and does not fit the normal pattern for the grade level.

*(Easy) (Skill 2.1)*

40. **Opinion writing can be both:**

    A. Informative and explanatory

    B. Opinionated and argumentative

    C. Narrative and explanatory

    D. Opinionated and obvious

    **Answer: B. Opinionated and argumentative**

    Opinion writing can be argumentative and perhaps even persuasive because the author is conveying his or her opinion on a subject.

*(Easy) (Skill 2.1)*

41. **Informative and explanatory genres of writing always contain:**

    A. Characters

    B. A story arch

    C. Facts

    D. Lists

    **Answer: C. Facts**

    Informative text gives the factual information on a topic.

*(Easy) (Skill 2.1)*

42. **The intent of a speech is to:**

    A. Convey a message

    B. Be concise and effective

    C. Target an audience

    D. All of the above

    **Answer: D. All of the above**

    Speeches are verbal deliveries of information to an audience. These aspects attribute to the flow of the speech and how effective it is.

*(Average) (Skill 2.2)*

43. **Student writing, on the elementary level, should have:**

    A. A specific purpose

    B. A clear audience

    C. A targeted task

    D. All of the above

    **Answer: D. All of the above**

    Student writing should be targeted for a specific purpose and the audience should be clear. This is essential for the foundational aspects of elementary writing.

*(Challenging) (Skill 2.2)*

44. **Edits are different from revisions. Edits:**

    A. Address problems with spelling, grammar, punctuation, or word choice

    B. Address problems with spelling, voice, organization, and cohesiveness

    C. Address problems of development, structure, coherence, and length

    D. Focus on the paper by asking questions and expanding ideas

    **Answer: A. Address problems with spelling, grammar, punctuation, or word choice.**

    Edits pertain to the surface mistakes that may occur in a paper; revisions are very different because they address the structural and organizational framework of the paper.

*(Average) (Skill 2.2)*

45. **Prewriting strategies can include:**

    A. Brainstorming

    B. Clustering

    C. Listing

    D. All of the above

    **Answer: D. All of the above**

    Prewriting can come in many forms, but the choices above are very common and effective.

*(Challenging) (Skill 2.3)*

46. According to Zaner Bloser, the stages of early writing development from ages 2 to 6 are:

   A. Random scribbling, controlled scribbling, mock writing, writing words, writing letters

   B. Random scribbling, controlled scribbling, mock writing, writing letters, writing words

   C. Random scribbling, mock writing, controlled scribbling, writing letters, writing words

   D. Random scribbling, mock writing, writing letters, controlled scribbling, writing words

   **Answer: B. Random scribbling, controlled scribbling, mock writing, writing letters, writing words**

   Early stages of writing development occur before school age. For some developing students it may occur during kindergarten, and sometimes even first grade.

*(Challenging) (Skill 2.3)*

47. In his book, *Developmental Variation and Learning Disorders,* Dr. Mel Levine identifies six stages of writing development. They are:

   A. Imitation, graphic presentation, progressive incorporation, automatization, elaboration, and personalization-diversification

   B. Imitation, progressive incorporation, graphic presentation, automatization, elaboration, and personalization-diversification

   C. Graphic presentation, imitation, progressive incorporation, automatization, elaboration, and personalization-diversification

   D. Imitation, graphic presentation, progressive incorporation, automatization, elaboration, and diversification

   **Answer: A. Imitation, graphic presentation, progressive incorporation, automatization, elaboration, and personalization-diversification**

   These are the six stages according to Dr. Mel Levine.

*(Easy) (Skill2.4)*

48. Word processing programs can be used during writing portions of class time or during times when the students are in the computer lab in order to:

   A. Compose music

   B. Create graphic art

   C. Type drafts

   D. Practice with the mouse

   **Answer: C. Type drafts**

By typing drafts, students can reread and reword their work in order to get it ready for the final stage of publication.

*(Easy) (Skill 2.4)*

49. **Using digital tools for sharing and working on writing pieces can be helpful for group projects because it fosters:**

    A. Responses

    B. Pacing

    C. Writing

    D. Collaboration

    **Answer: D. Collaboration**

    Collaboration can occur digitally in many ways, including apps, software, and websites such as Google Classroom.

*(Average) (Skill 2.4)*

50. **Published writing in the classroom can be displayed or mounted on bulletin boards and classroom walls, but digital publishing allows for students to publish on a:**

    A. School website

    B. Desktop

    C. Hardware

    D. Software

    **Answer: A. School website**

    The school website serves as a digital forum for parents, teachers, and students to view student work.

*(Challenging) (Skill 2.5)*

51. **Collecting data for the research process in second grade is more elaborate than in kindergarten. When students are finding facts, they need to gain information from a variety of modalities, including:**

    A. Listening

    B. Viewing

    C. Reading

    D. All of the above

    **Answer: D. All of the above**

    Using these modes enhances the learning process and makes it easier for students to identify facts while gaining information.

*(Easy) (Skill 2.5)*

52. **What is an example of a primary source?**

    A. Census data

    B. Artifact

    C. Photo

    D. All of the above

    **Answer: D. All of the above**

    These three primary sources are only a few of the many primary sources available to students while they are researching.

*(Easy) (Skill 2.5)*

53. **What is an example of a secondary source?**

    A. Textbook

    B. Article

    C. Historical report

    D. All of the above

    **Answer: D. All of the above**

    Secondary sources are not directly from the person who experienced the event firsthand, but a secondary source is still viable and useful when researching and writing.

*(Challenging) (Skill 2.5)*

54. **How can a student distinguish between a reliable and an unreliable source?**

    A. Verify the organization who published the article

    B. Check the copyright date

    C. Identify the total number of pages

    D. Confirm the sources of the photographs

    **Answer: A. Verify the organization who published the article**

    By understanding who wrote the piece, students can verify if the source is reliable and usable for research.

*(Average) (Skill 2.5)*

55. **Paraphrasing and plagiarizing are two very different practices. Students must learn not to plagiarize from sources. How might a teacher describe what paraphrasing is to his or her students?**

    A. Paraphrasing is when we use parts of someone else's text

    B. Paraphrasing is when we copy sentences word for word

    C. Paraphrasing is when we read text and write it in our own words

    D. Paraphrasing is when we read text and locate more information

    **Answer: C. Paraphrasing is when we read text and write it in our own words**

    After reading a text we can interpret the information and translate it into our own words so it becomes authentic and usable.

*(Easy) (Skill 2.5)*

56. **Which school staff member, who is not typically in the classroom, can help students locate reliable, credible information for research projects?**

    A. Co-teacher

    B. Push-in reading consultant

    C. Paraprofessional

    D. Librarian

    **Answer: D. Librarian**

    The librarian is a resourceful individual who can always guide students in the right direction when researching.

(Average) (Skill 2.5)

57. Students need to evaluate the following criteria when identifying credible website sources:

A. Subject, author, audience, source, documentation

B. Subject, audience, source, documentation

C. Subject, audience, author, source

D. Documentation, subject, author, publication date

**Answer: A. Subject, author, audience, source, documentation**

These criteria are critical to understanding whether or not a website is credible and reliable.

(Challenging) (Skill 2.6)

58. Plural nouns always end in:

A. /s/

B. /es/

C. /s/ or /es/

D. None of the above

**Answer: C. /s/ or /es/**

Plural nouns are nouns that represent more than one item. For example, *apple* is a singular noun but *apples* is a plural noun.

(Challenging) (Skill 2.6)

59. Miss Murphy is presenting possessive pronouns. Which words should she include in a presentation on Power Point?

A. My, mine, you, your, hers, his

B. Myself, yourself, himself, herself, itself

C. You, me, my, I, they

D. His, hers, he, she, it, its

**Answer: A. My, mine, you, your, hers, his**

Possessive pronouns as stated are helpful for students to understand which part of speech they are utilizing in their writing.

(Challenging) (Skill 2.6)

60. There are seven coordinating conjunctions in the English language. Three of them are:

A. In, on, upon

B. And, but, or

C. Rarely, always, often

D. Me, he, I

**Answer: B. And, but, or**

Coordinating conjunctions link two parts of a sentence together.

*(Challenging) (Skill 2.6)*

**61. What is an example of a compound sentence?**

A. Maya will go to the store and Maya will go to school.

B. Maya and Greta will go to the playground.

C. Maya and Murphy will get along very well.

D. The new house is in the next town.

**Answer: A. Maya will go to the store and Maya will go to school.**

The compound sentence has two independent clauses and is linked by the word *and,* which is a conjunction.

*(Average) (Skill 2.6)*

**62. Identifying word derivatives is an excellent way for students to understand vocabulary they do not know. A derivative is:**

A. A word with multiple syllables

B. A word formed from another word

C. A word with two meanings

D. A word that ends with /s/

**Answer: B. A word formed from another word**

A derivative is a word related to another because it is formed from another word.

*(Challenging) (Skill 2.7)*

**63. An example of a metaphor is:**

A. The sun is like a giant flame in the sky

B. The bird's wings made a fluttering sound

C. Her hair was pure silk

D. She was singing at the top of her lungs

**Answer: C. Her hair was pure silk**

The metaphor for the hair is pure silk. The hair must be incredibly soft as it is being compared to silk.

*(Challenging) (Skill 2.7)*

**64. An example of a personification is:**

A. The donuts were piled to the ceiling

B. The bird's wings made a fluttering sound

C. The teddy bear smiled as she hugged him tightly

D. She was singing at the top of her lungs

**Answer: C. The teddy bear smiled as she hugged him tightly**

The teddy bear is personified, or given human attributes.

*(Challenging) (Skill 2.7)*

**65. An example of an idiom is:**

A. The donuts were piled to the ceiling

B. The bird's wings made a fluttering sound

C. Her hair was pure silk

D. She was singing at the top of her lungs

**Answer: D. She was singing at the top of her lungs**

This idiom is an expression used in the English language.

*(Average) (Skill 2.7)*

66. **How can Ms. Ritch define the meaning of the word *illuminate* to her class of fifth graders by using word part analysis?**

    A. Related word parts: in (into), lumen (light), ate (to cause to)

    B. Related word parts: in (for), lumen (light), ate (to cause to)

    C. Related word parts: in (into), lumen (light), ate (to eat)

    D. Related word parts: in (for), lumen (light), ate (to be)

    **Answer: A. Related word parts: in (into), lumen (light), ate (to cause to)**

    By breaking the words into parts, the students can see how the parts come together to make the whole word and the definition.

*(Average) (Skill 2.7)*

67. **Which of the following words is an example of onomatopoeia?**

    A. Fire

    B. Him

    C. Waste or waist

    D. Pop

    **Answer: D. Pop**

    The word *pop* indicates a sound and perhaps also an action.

*(Average) (Skill 2.7)*

68. **The term *figurative* is the antonym to:**

    A. Abstract

    B. Literal

    C. Substantial

    D. None of the above

    **Answer: B. Literal**

    Literal is the opposite of figurative; literal is highly concrete.

*(Challenging) (Skill 2.6)*

69. **The words *addition* and *edition* are:**

    A. Homonyms

    B. Homophones

    C. Homographs

    D. None of the above

    **Answer: B. Homophones**

    The two words are spelled differently, even though they sound very much alike.

*(Challenging) (Skill 2.6)*

70. **Which spelling shows possession?**

    A. Whose

    B. Who's

    C. Whom

    D. Who

    **Answer: A. Whose**

    Whose indicates possession without the use of an apostrophe.

*(Average) (Skill 2.8)*

71. **In the Common Core State Standards, the second-tier vocabulary words are:**

    A. Everyday, common words

    B. High-utility words

    C. Domain-specific academic vocabulary words

    D. Abstract nouns and adjectives

    **Answer: B. High-utility words**

    Second-tier words are the genre, according to the Common Core State Standards.

*(Average) (Skill 2.8)*

72. **In order to teach the three tiers of words, teachers may want to consider:**

    A. Direct instruction

    B. Specific word lists

    C. District-wide vocabulary lists

    D. All of the above

    **Answer: D. All of the above**

    These words are third tier because they are content specific and may be definitive to the grade level or assessment at hand.

*(Challenging) (Skill 2.8)*

73. **Another term for *word choice* is:**

    A. Diction

    B. Word decision

    C. Wordplay

    D. Tone

**Answer: A. Diction**

Diction is another term for word choice. This is important for an author because word choice indicates the information he or she wants to convey as well as the tone.

*(Challenging) (Skill 2.9)*

74. **Receptive language is:**

    A. The ability to understand or comprehend language heard or read

    B. The ability to say words and understand the meaning of them

    C. A facet of language pattern recognition

    D. A large study of psychological impacts of dialogue

    **Answer: A. The ability to understand or comprehend language heard or read**

    Receptive language is the language received and interpreted by the listener.

*(Average) (Skill 2.9)*

75. **An example of a nonverbal cue is a:**

    A. Gesture

    B. Eye wink

    C. Wave

    D. All of the above

    **Answer: D. All of the above**

    These nonverbal cues are essential to getting a point across without words. Nonverbal cues are different for each culture, but there are universal cues as well.

*(Average) (Skill 2.9)*

76. **Visual communication occurs when a teacher presents a:**

   A. Story to the class

   B. Lecture to the class

   C. Graph to the class

   D. Sound bite to the class

   **Answer: C. Graph to the class**

   The graph is a visual depiction of information the teacher may want to teach or convey to the class.

*(Challenging) (Skill 2.10)*

77. **Engaging oral presentations require:**

   A. Volume

   B. Articulation

   C. Awareness of the audience

   D. All of the above

   **Answer: D. All of the above**

   Oral presentations need all of these elements in order to be successful.

*(Challenging) (Skill 2.10)*

78. **Articulation is the act of:**

   A. Expressing

   B. Presenting

   C. Noticing

   D. Nonverbally communicating

   **Answer: A. Expressing**

   When one articulates, they convey ideas and express themselves to others.

*(Average) (Skill 2.10)*

79. **Engaging oral presentations may contain:**

   A. Humor

   B. Sarcasm

   C. High-level vocabulary words

   D. Intonation

   **Answer: A. Humor**

   Humor can be included in a presentation in order to make it engaging so the audience will receive the information more efficiently.

*(Average) (Skill 2.10)*

80. **Engaging the audience may include:**

   A. Asking for volunteers

   B. Providing a visual diagram

   C. Singing or performing

   D. All of the above

   **Answer: D. All of the above**

   In order to engage an audience, teachers and students must appeal to various levels of engagement using many senses.

## Mathematics (5003)

*(Easy) (Skill 5.2)*

81. **Which statement below expresses the number 4,308?**

    A. $4 + 3 + 0 + 8$

    B. $400 + 30 + 8$

    C. $4,000 + 300 + 8$

    D. None of the above

    **Answer: C. 4000 + 300 + 8**

    Choice C shows the expansion starting with four thousand, continuing with three hundred, and ending with eight.

*(Challenging) (Skill 3.3)*

82. **The words "four hundred seven and three hundredths" are represented by which number below?**

    A. 47.3

    B. 407.03

    C. 400.73

    D. 4,007.300

    **Answer: B. 407.03**

    The place values described represent the number as shown.

*(Average) (Skill 3.5)*

83. **$3 \times 10^6$ is equivalent to which of the following?**

    A. 36

    B. 306

    C. 3,000,000

    D. 30,000,000

    **Answer: C. 3,000,000**

    The expression presented in scientific notation represents the product of three times one million.

*(Average) (Skill 3.6)*

84. **Calculate the quotient of $299 \div 3$ to the nearest hundredth.**

    A. 100

    B. 99

    C. 99.7

    D. 99.67

    **Answer: D. 99.67**

    The nearest hundredth is two places after the decimal point.

*(Challenging) (Skill 3.7)*

85. **A group of 87 students and 10 adults is going on a class field trip. Each bus holds 30 passengers. How many busses must be reserved?**

    A. 3

    B. 4

    C. 8.7

    D. 10

    **Answer: B. 4**

    The total number of passengers is 97. Dividing 97 by 30 results in 3 with a remainder of 7. In this situation, the answer needs to be rounded up to the next whole number. Four busses will be needed to transport all passengers.

*(Challenging) (Skill 3.8)*

86. Given natural numbers a and b, which symbol inserted in the blank would make the following relation always true?

$$\frac{1}{a} + \frac{1}{b} \underline{\hspace{1.5cm}} \left(\frac{1}{a}\right)\left(\frac{1}{b}\right)$$

   A. $=$

   B. $\leq$

   C. $\geq$

   D. $\subseteq$

**Answer: C.** $\geq$

Choice A would be true only if $a$ and $b$ both equaled 1. C is the correct choice because the addition side of the statement increases (adding two positive numbers), while the multiplication side will decrease in value, since each fraction represents a value less than one.

*(Average) (Skill 3.9)*

87. Which set of numbers is in order from least to greatest?

   A. 100, 40, 20, 10

   B. $\frac{1}{100}, \frac{1}{40}, \frac{1}{20}, \frac{1}{10}$

   C. −10, −20, −40, −100

   D. 0.1, 0.02, 0.003, 0.0004

**Answer: B.** $\frac{1}{100}, \frac{1}{40}, \frac{1}{20}, \frac{1}{10}$

As the denominator of a unit fraction decreases, the value of the fraction increases.

*(Challenging) (Skill 3.11)*

88. Identify the false statement.

   A. Addition is a commutative operation.

   B. Subtraction is a commutative operation.

   C. Addition is an associative operation.

   D. Multiplication is an associative operation.

**Answer: B. Subtraction is a commutative operation.**

Subtraction is not commutative.
(Example: $3 - 8 \neq 8 - 3$)

*(Average) (Skill 3.12)*

89. If $\frac{5}{3}$ representing point J, is to be placed on the number line below, between which two points will point J lie?

| L | M | P | T | W |
|---|---|---|---|---|
| 0 | $\frac{1}{2}$ | 1 | $1\frac{1}{2}$ | 2 |

   A. T and W

   B. P and T

   C. M and P

   D. L and M

**Answer: A. T and W**

The value $\frac{5}{3}$ is equal to $1\frac{2}{3}$ and is greater than $1\frac{1}{2}$ and less than 2.

*(Easy) (Skill 3.13)*

90. Which of the following choices represent a rational number?

    A. $\frac{12}{5}$

    B. $\frac{1}{3}$

    C. $\sqrt{16}$

    D. All of the above

**Answer: D. All of the above**

A rational number is any number that can be written as a ratio. If the radicand of choice C were not a perfect square, then C would not be a rational number.

*(Average) (Skill 3.14)*

91. Which of the following values is equivalent to $\frac{2}{3}$?

    A. 0.67

    B. $\frac{200}{300}$

    C. $2\frac{1}{3}$

    D. None of the above

**Answer: B. $\frac{200}{300}$**

Choice A is an estimate of the fraction $\frac{2}{3}$ (rounded to the nearest hundredth), while choice B is an unreduced form of the fraction but is an equivalent value.

*(Easy) (Skill 3.16)*

92. Which value below does NOT represent 75%?

    A. $\frac{7}{5}$

    B. $\frac{3}{4}$

    C. $\frac{75}{100}$

    D. 0.75

**Answer: A. $\frac{7}{5}$**

A percent can be expressed as a fraction over 100 or any rational equivalent.

*(Average) (Skill 3.17)*

93. If a 30 oz. jar of pickles costs $2.75, what is the price per ounce?

    A. $0.09 per ounce

    B. $0.11 per ounce

    C. $0.83 per ounce

    D. $0.90 per ounce

**Answer: A. $0.09 per ounce**

To calculate price per ounce, create a fraction $\frac{price}{ounce}$ and divide: $\frac{275 \text{ cents}}{9 \text{ ounces}}$. It is reasonable in this case to round to the nearest cent.

*(Challenging) (Skill 3.18)*

94. Solve the proportion $\frac{4}{x+1} = \frac{5}{22}$.

    A. $x = 2$

    B. $x = 4.25$

    C. $x = 16.6$

    D. $x = 20$

**Answer: C. $x = 16.6$**

The first step to solve the proportion is to cross-multiply:

$$5(x+1) = 4 \cdot 22$$
$$5x + 5 = 88$$
$$5x = 83$$
$$x = \frac{83}{5} = 16.6$$

*(Challenging) (Skill 3.19)*

95. **If two prime numbers are multiplied together, the result is always:**

    A. Prime

    B. Composite

    C. Zero

    D. Even

    **Answer: B. Composite**

    The product of two primes is a result with two factors, so it will be composite. Additionally, zero is not prime so the product of two primes could never be zero.

*(Average) (Skill 3.20)*

96. **Find the prime factorization of 24.**

    A. $4 \cdot 6$

    B. $3 \cdot 8$

    C. $2^3 \cdot 3$

    D. $2^4$

    **Answer: C. $2^3 \cdot 3$**

    While choices A, B, and C all represent factors of 24, only choice C has been factored all the way to the prime numbers.

*(Easy) (Skill 3.22)*

97. **Find a reasonable estimate for the sum 298 + 988.**

    A. 1,000

    B. 1,100

    C. 1,300

    D. 2,000

    **Answer: C. 1,300**

The best way to estimate this problem is to round the values to 300 and 1,000, resulting in a sum of 1,300.

*(Challenging) (Skill 4.1)*

98. **Which of the choices below represents an expression?**

    A. $\frac{3}{x} = \frac{15}{11}$

    B. $x^2 + 3x = x - 4$

    C. $-8 < x - 2 < 7$

    D. $4(x - 9)$

    **Answer: D. $4(x - 9)$**

    Choice D is an expression because it lacks an equals sign. Choice A is a proportion, a form of an equation. Choice B is a quadratic equation. Choice C is a compound inequality.

*(Easy) (Skill 4.4)*

99. **Evaluate the expression $\frac{2x + 1}{5}$ for $x = 12$.**

    A. 25

    B. 12

    C. 5

    D. 3

    **Answer: C. 5**

    Replace $x$ with 12: $\frac{2 \cdot 12 + 1}{5} = \frac{25}{5} = 5$.

*(Challenging) (Skill 4.6)*

100. **Which choice below represents the phrase "3 less than 5 times a number"?**

 A. $(5 - 3)n$

 B. $3 + 5n$

 C. $3 < 5n$

 D. $5n - 3$

**Answer: D. $5n - 3$**

Choice D shows the product of 5 and a number made less by the subtraction of 3. For choice C to be correct, the phrase would have to state "3 IS less than 5 times a number."

*(Average) (Skill 4.7)*

101. **Given the formula for the area of an isosceles trapezoid is $A = \frac{h}{2}(b_1 + b_2)$, find the area if the height is 10 cm and the bases are 12 cm and 9 cm.**

 A. 210 cm$^2$

 B. 105 cm$^2$

 C. 57.5 cm$^2$

 D. 41 cm$^2$

**Answer: B. 105 cm$^2$**

Simplify:
$A = \frac{10}{2}(12 + 9) = 5(21) = 105$

*(Average) (Skill 4.9)*

102. **Which of the following would NOT be a correct first step to solve the following equation?**

$3x - 7 = 5x + 13$

 A. Add -7 to both sides of the equation

 B. Add -13 to both sides of the equation

 C. Add -5x to both sides of the equation

 D. Subtract 3x from both sides of the equation

**Answer: A. Add -7 to both sides of the equation**

The first goal in solving the given equation should be to put the variable terms on one side of the equation and the constant terms on the other. Choice A is not correct because addition of a positive 7 is needed, rather than a negative, to put the constant terms on the right side of the equation.

*(Challenging) (Skill 4.10)*

103. **Which inequality statement below is equivalent to $3 < x$?**

 A. $3 \le x$

 B. $x > 3$

 C. $x < 3$

 D. $-3 < x < 3$

**Answer: B. $x > 3$**

The given inequality and choice B both indicate that $x$ is the greater value. Choice C shows 3 as the greater value.

*(Challenging) (Skill 4.11)*

**104.** **Which equation below represents the same set of ordered pairs as the equation $2x - 3y = 12$?**

A.  $3x - 2y = 12$

B.  $x - y = 2$

C.  $y = -2x + 4$

D.  $y = \frac{2}{3}x - 4$

**Answer: D. $y = \frac{2}{3}x - 4$**

All of the equations in this question represent lines with ordered pairs $(x, y)$. Choice D is the same as the given line, as it is created by algebraic manipulation as follows:

$$2x - 3y = 12$$
$$-3y = -2x + 12$$
$$y = \frac{-2}{-3}x + \frac{12}{-3}$$
$$y = \frac{2}{3}x - 4$$

Since they are the same line, they represent the same set of ordered pairs.

*(Easy) (Skill 4.12)*

**105.** **Find the next term in the pattern: 3, 7, 11, 15, …**

A.  4

B.  19

C.  21

D.  36

**Answer: B. 19**

The given terms are increasing by 4 each time. Therefore, the next term would be $15 + 4$, or 19.

*(Challenging) (Skill 4.14)*

**106.** **Find the rule that would generate the table of values given below.**

| x | −1 | 0 | 2 | 7 |
|---|----|----|----|----|
| y | 3 | −1 | −9 | −29 |

A.  $y = x + 4$

B.  $y = x - 11$

C.  $y = -3x$

D.  $y = -4x - 1$

**Answer: D. $y = -4x - 1$**

Each $y$ value in the table is 1 less than $(-4)$ times the given $x$ value.

*(Challenging) (Skill 5.3)*

**107.** **Complete the analogy.**
**circle: sphere :: square: _____**

A.  ellipse

B.  cone

C.  cube

D.  hexagon

**Answer: C. cube**

The cross-section of a sphere is a circle, just as the cross section of a cube is a square.

*(Average) (Skill 5.4)*

**108.** **Which of the following shapes does NOT have at least one pair of parallel opposite sides?**

A.  rectangle

B.  trapezoid

C.  rhombus

D.  triangle

**Answer: D. triangle**

A rectangle and rhombus have two pairs of parallel opposite sides; the trapezoid, one. With only three sides, the triangle has no parallel opposite sides.

*(Average) (Skill 5.6)*

109. **A right square pyramid has a base with area 10 square units and triangular faces each with an area of 14 square units. Find the total surface area of the pyramid.**

    A. 24

    B. 48

    C. 66

    D. 140

**Answer: B. 48**

A right square pyramid has one base and four faces. Therefore, the total surface area for this problem can be found by:
$10 + 4(14) = 10 + 46 = 66$

*(Challenging) (Skill 5.7)*

110. **Find the perimeter of the polygon pictured below.**

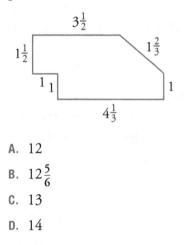

    A. 12

    B. $12\frac{5}{6}$

    C. 13

    D. 14

**Answer: D. 14**

The perimeter is found by adding the length of all sides.

$$P = 1\frac{1}{2} + 3\frac{1}{2} + 1\frac{2}{3} + 1 + 4\frac{1}{3} + 1 + 1$$
$$= 1\frac{1}{2} + 3\frac{1}{2} + 1\frac{2}{3} + 4\frac{1}{3} + 1 + 1 + 1$$
$$= 5 + 6 + 3$$
$$= 14$$

*(Challenging) (Skill 5.9)*

111. **If the length of the side of a square is tripled, then the area of the square is increased by a factor of:**

    A. 3

    B. 9

    C. 12

    D. 27

**Answer: B. 9**

A square with side $n$ has an area of $n^2$, since area is calculated by length times width. The tripled side is represented by $3n$. Then the new area is $(3n)(3n)$ or $9n^2$. The increase in area from $n^2$ to $9n^2$ is by a factor of 9.

*(Average) (Skill 5.11)*

112. If the given triangle is shifted 3 units to the right, what are the new coordinates of point *S*?

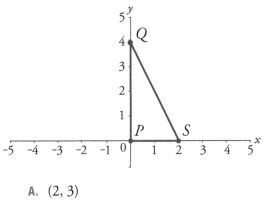

A. (2, 3)

B. (5, 0)

C. (3, 0)

D. (2, 4)

Answer: B. (5, 0)

The original location of point *S* is (2, 0). When moved to the right 3 units, the new point becomes (2 + 3, 0) or (5, 0).

*(Easy) (Skill 5.12)*

113. A teacher shows students a price list for the school store. Pencils cost 25¢, erasers are 50¢, and a sheet of paper costs 10¢. Students are asked to come up with a purchase that totals exactly $1. Which answer below would NOT be correct?

A. 4 pencils

B. 2 pencils and 1 eraser

C. 1 eraser and 5 sheets of paper

D. 3 erasers

Answer: D. 3 erasers

Three erasers cost $1.50, which does not equal the requested amount.

*(Average) (Skill 5.13)*

114. Which is the most reasonable choice below for the length of a pencil?

A. 9 cm

B. 9 mm

C. 9 m

D. 90 cm

Answer: A. 9 cm

A pencil could be 9 cm long. Choice B is too short, and choices C and D are too long.

*(Average) (Skill 5.17)*

115. What is the range of the following set of data?

52, 86, 98, 74, 90

A. 90

B. 80

C. 86

D. 46

Answer: D. 46

The range is the difference between the greatest and smallest pieces of data. In this case, $98 - 52 = 46$.

*(Challenging) (Skill 5.19)*

116. Which of the following statements is false?

A. A set of data can have multiple modes

B. The mean is always larger than the median

C. The median can be the average of two numbers

D. The mean is always equal to the average

**Answer: B. The mean is always larger than the median**

The mean is the average of a set of data. The median is the number representing the exact middle of the pieces of data, or the average between two data values when there is an even number of data pieces. Therefore, the mean can be equal to, greater than, or less than the median. It depends on other data values in the set.

*(Average) (Skill 5.20)*

**117.** **Which set of data below could be said to have outliers?**

A. 5, 0, –3, –6, 2

B. $\frac{1}{2}, \frac{1}{3}, \frac{1}{5}, \frac{1}{4}, \frac{1}{10,000}$

C. 10, 20, 30, 40, 50

D. None of the above

**Answer: B.** $\frac{1}{2}, \frac{1}{3}, \frac{1}{5}, \frac{1}{4}, \frac{1}{10,000}$

While all the values in choice B are smaller than one, the last number, $\frac{1}{10,000}$, is much smaller than the others listed, causing it to be considered an outlier.

*(Challenging) (Skill 5.21)*

**118.** **What conclusion can be made based on the scatter plot below?**

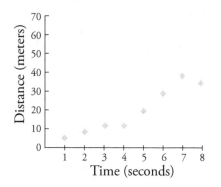

A. Distance and time are not related

B. Distance equals time

C. Distance is decreasing with time

D. Distance is increasing with time

**Answer: D. Distance is increasing with time**

A reasonable line of best fit can be drawn through the points and would have a positive slope. This indicates that there is a relationship between distance and time and the distance increases as the time increases.

(Average) (Skill 5.22)

119. If a school has 170 employees, how many can be expected to buy their lunch at school, according to the graph below?

Faculty and Staff Lunch Choices

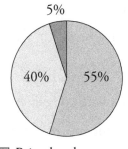

☐ Bring lunch
☐ Buy cafeteria food
☐ Go out for lunch

A. 85

B. 68

C. 45

D. 40

Answer: B. 68

The pie chart indicates that 40% of the employees buy the school cafeteria lunch.

40% of 170 = 0.40(170) = 68

(Easy) (Skill 5.24)

120. What is the probability of rolling a 5 on a standard die?

A. $\frac{1}{6}$

B. $\frac{5}{6}$

C. 50%

D. It is impossible to quantify the probability.

Answer: A. $\frac{1}{6}$

A standard die has 6 sides, and the desired number 5 occurs once on the die.

Therefore, the chances of rolling a 5 are 1 out of 6 or $\frac{1}{6}$.

(Easy) (Skill 5.4)

121. A cone is a figure that has which of the following characteristics?

A. Two congruent circular bases that are parallel

B. A circular base and a single vertex

C. All points are the same distance from the center

D. A square base and 4 triangle-shaped sides

Answer: B. A circular base and a single vertex

Choice A describes a cylinder; choice C describes a sphere; and choice D describes a pyramid.

(Easy) (Skill 4.8)

122. In the equation of the line, $3x + 2y = 14$, which term represents the independent variable?

A. $3x$

B. $x$

C. $-\frac{3}{2}$

D. $y$

Answer: B. $x$

$x$ is the independent variable because when different values are substituted for $x$, $y$ changes; $x$ can be changed independently.

*(Average) (Skill 4.10)*

**123. Select the graph of the solution.**

$$7 \le 5 - 2x \le 17$$

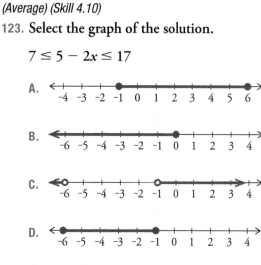

A.
B.
C.
D.

**Answer: D**

Solve by subtracting 5 from each side of the inequality. Divide by -2 on each side, which causes a reversal in the inequality signs. The end points are included so the circles on the graph are solid.

*(Average) (Skill 4.13)*

**124. Identify the missing term in the following harmonic sequence: $\frac{1}{3}, \frac{1}{6}, \frac{1}{9}, \frac{1}{12}, \frac{1}{15} \cdots$**

A. $\frac{1}{16}$

B. $\frac{1}{17}$

C. $\frac{1}{18}$

D. 18

**Answer: C. $\frac{1}{18}$**

The difference between the denominators is 3, so the next term in the progression is $\frac{1}{18}$.

*(Average) (Skill 5.1)*

**125. These lines share a common point, and intersecting planes share a common set of points or a line. This describes:**

A. Parallel lines

B. Perpendicular lines

C. Intersecting lines

D. Skew lines

**Answer: C. Intersecting lines**

Intersecting lines share a common point, and intersecting planes share a common set of points (a line).

*(Average) (Skill 5.3)*

**126. A simple closed surface formed from planar polygonal regions is known as a:**

A. Vertex

B. Polyhedron

C. Edge

D. Face

**Answer: B. Polyhedron**

A 3-dimensional figure is a solid, and solids are the union of all points on a simple closed surface, including points in its interior. A polyhedron is a simple closed surface formed from planar polygonal regions.

*(Challenging) (Skill 5.7)*

**127.** A car is driven north at 74 miles per hour from point A. Another car is driven due east at 65 miles per hour starting from the same point at the same time. How far are the cars away from each other after 2 hours?

A. 175.87 miles

B. 232.66 miles

C. 196.99 miles

D. 202.43 miles

**Answer: C. 196.99 miles**

The route the cars take form a right triangle with edges 74 × 2 and 65 × 2. This gives two sides of a right triangle of 148 and 130. Using the Pythagorean Theorem, we get $148^2 + 130^2 = $ distance$^2$. Therefore, the distance between the cars is 196.99 miles.

*(Challenging) (Skill 5.7)*

**128.** Find the area of the figure.

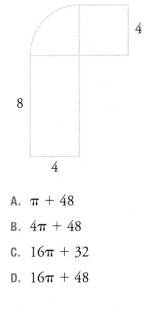

A. $\pi + 48$

B. $4\pi + 48$

C. $16\pi + 32$

D. $16\pi + 48$

**Answer: A. $\pi + 48$**

The total area is the sum of the areas of the square, quarter circle, and rectangle.

$$A_{square} = 4 \times 4 = 16.$$
$$A_{rectangle} = 8 \times 4 = 32.$$
$$A_{quarter\ circle} = \frac{1}{4} \cdot \pi \cdot 2^2 = \pi.$$

The sum, or total area is $\pi + 48$.

*(Challenging) (Skill 5.17)*

**129.** Find the median of the test scores below:

| 70 | 80 | 86 |
|----|----|----|
| 90 | 91 | 90 |
| 87 | 70 | 98 |
| 54 | 63 | 62 |
| 98 | 76 | 70 |

A. 79

B. 80

C. 83

D. 84

**Answer: D. 84**

To find the median, put the numbers in order from least to greatest. The median is the middle number. If there are two numbers in the middle, find the average of the two. The middle number of the test scores is 84.

*(Challenging) (Skill 5.24)*

130. **Given a drawer with 5 black socks, 3 blue socks, and 2 red socks, what is the probability that you will draw 2 black socks in two draws in a dark room?**

    A. $\frac{2}{9}$

    B. $\frac{1}{4}$

    C. $\frac{17}{18}$

    D. $\frac{1}{18}$

**Answer: A. $\frac{2}{9}$**

In this example of conditional probability, the probability of drawing a black sock on the first draw is $\frac{5}{10}$. The sock is not replaced, so the probability of drawing a black sock on the second draw is $\frac{4}{9}$.

## Social Studies (5004)

*(Easy) (Skill 6.1)*

131. **Which group of colonists were the most willing to work with the Native Americans?**

    A. Spanish

    B. English

    C. Dutch

    D. French

**Answer: D. French**

The Dutch colonists were mostly interested in surviving in their new homes. The English and Spanish colonists did not have good working relations with the Native Americas because Europeans had a habit of taking land, breaking treaties, and massacring. The French colonists

found ways to maintain a relative peace and fought on the same side in the war against England.

*(Challenging) (Skill 6.1)*

132. **Which of the following colonies was a New England colony?**

    A. Maine

    B. New York

    C. Connecticut

    D. Vermont

**Answer: C. Connecticut**

Maine and Vermont were not colonies. New York was a Middle Atlantic colony. Connecticut was a New England colony.

*(Average) (Skill 6.1)*

133. **Which colony was called "New Sweden?"**

    A. Delaware

    B. Pennsylvania

    C. Maryland

    D. Massachusetts

**Answer: A. Delaware**

Pennsylvania was settled by Quakers; Maryland was settled by Catholics. Massachusetts was settled by the English. New Jersey and Delaware were settled by Dutch and Swedish people. Delaware was called New Sweden.

*(Challenging) (Skill 6.2)*

**134. Why was the Proclamation Act opposed?**

A. The act taxed the colonists to support British military defense

B. The act placed a tax on tea

C. The act prohibited English settlement beyond the Appalachian Mountains

D. The act prohibited the colonial governments from issuing paper money

**Answer: C. The act prohibited English settlement beyond the Appalachian Mountains**

The British government passed several acts that imposed taxes on the colonists. The Currency Act prohibited the colonists from issuing paper money. The Proclamation Act prohibited English settlement beyond the Appalachian Mountains. The purpose of the act was to appease Native Americans.

*(Challenging) (Skill 6.2)*

**135. Which act placed the first "internal" tax placed on the colonists?**

A. Currency Act

B. Stamp Act

C. Townshend Acts

D. Proclamation Act

**Answer: B. Stamp Act**

The Currency Act prohibited the colonists from issuing paper money. The Townshend Acts placed taxes on the colonists and were passed in 1767. The Proclamation Act prohibited settlement beyond the Appalachian Mountains. The Stamp Act was the first instance of an "internal" tax on the colonists. The Stamp Act was passed in 1765.

*(Average) (Skill 6.2)*

**136. Which statement about the "Sons of Liberty" is INCORRECT?**

A. The groups were formed to protest the Townshend Acts

B. The groups were secret

C. The groups staged riots against tax collectors

D. The groups hanged British officials in effigy

**Answer: A. The groups were formed to protest the Townshend Acts**

The Sons of Liberty protested the Stamp Act. The groups were made up of colonists and were secret groups that staged riots against tax collectors and hanged British officials in effigy. The INCORRECT answer is Choice A because the groups were not formed to protest the Townshend Acts.

*(Challenging) (Skill 6.3)*

**137. Why did George Washington warn against the creation of "factions?"**

A. Factions were not political parties

B. Factions had been popular in Great Britain

C. Factions caused jealousies, false alarms, and could cause damage

D. Factions were more interested in their own personal profits than in the public good

**Answer: C. Factions caused jealousies, false alarms, and could cause damage**

Factions were political parties in Great Britain and were made up of a few people who schemed to win favors from the government. George Washington feared they would harm politics in America. He believed they caused jealousies and false alarms and that they had the potential to damage government.

*(Easy) (Skill 6.3)*

**138. Who spurred the formation of the first political parties in the newly created United States of America?**

A. Benjamin Franklin

B. Alexander Hamilton

C. Patrick Henry

D. George Washington

**Answer: B. Alexander Hamilton**

George Washington feared the damage political parties could cause. Patrick Henry was a colonial leader. Benjamin Franklin was a Founding Father but died in 1790. The political parties began in the early 1790s and were spurred by Thomas Jefferson and Alexander Hamilton who were two of President Washington's chief advisors.

*(Challenging) (Skill 6.3)*

**139. What was Alexander Hamilton's attitude about the Constitution?**

A. He was a strict constructionist

B. He believed the Constitution did not give Congress the power to collect taxes

C. He strongly disfavored a national bank

D. He believed Congress had power to make all laws "necessary and proper" to carry out its duties

**Answer: D. He believed Congress had power to make all laws "necessary and proper" to carry out its duties**

Alexander Hamilton believed the Constitution should be interpreted loosely and that Congress did have the power to collect taxes. He favored the creation of a national bank and believed Congress had the power to make all laws "necessary and proper" to carry out its duties.

*(Challenging) (Skill 6.3)*

**140. During which election did political parties first play a role?**

A. 1792

B. 1796

C. 1800

D. 1804

**Answer: B. 1796**

President Washington retired from office in 1796. Political parties played an important role in choosing his successor. The election of 1796 was the first one in which political parties played a role.

(Average) (Skill 6.3)

**141. Which statement is INCORRECT about the Whigs?**

A. They favored strong national growth

B. They united behind President John Quincy Adams

C. Farmers supported the policies of the Whigs

D. Northeast businesspeople supported the Whigs

**Answer: C. Farmers supported the policies of the Whigs**

Northeast business people and some wealthy southern planters supported the Whigs. The Whigs favored a strong national growth policy and were united behind President John Quincy Adams. Generally, farmers did not support the policies of the Whigs.

(Average) (Skill 6.3)

**142. What does the term "Manifest Destiny" mean in United States history?**

A. International expansion

B. Imperialism

C. Conquering territories

D. Westward Expansion

**Answer: D. Westward Expansion**

International expansion and imperialism involved obtaining territories and areas outside the continental United States. Conquering territories as the result of wars, such as the war against Mexico and the Spanish-American War involved the concept of imperialism. Manifest Destiny involved the territorial and westward expansion within the United States.

(Average) (Skill 6.3)

**143. Which statement about the settlement of Texas is INCORRECT?**

A. Many new settlers took slaves with them

B. Slavery was outlawed in Mexico

C. Slavery was legal in Texas

D. Many of the new settlers were southerners

**Answer: C. Slavery was legal in Texas**

Many new settlers in Texas were southerners who took their slaves with them. Slavery was outlawed in Mexico and technically illegal in Texas. However, the Mexican government often "looked the other way." Therefore, Choice C is correct because it is an INCORRECT answer.

(Easy) (Skill 6.3)

**144. Which statement is INCORRECT about the tensions between the United States and Mexico in relation to the settlement of Texas?**

A. The American influence permeated all parts of southwestern life

B. The doctrine of Manifest Destiny was the motive for settling the Southwest

C. The Mexican government owed debts to U.S. citizens for damages to property during the struggle for independence from Spain

D. Mexico had not paid war debts

**Answer: A. The American influence permeated all parts of southwestern life**

Mexico had not paid war debts and owed money to U.S. citizens for property damages. The doctrine of Manifest Destiny was the impetus for expansion into the

Southwest. However, it was Spanish, not American, influence that permeated all parts of southwestern life.

*(Challenging) (Skill 6.3)*

145. **Why were Northerners in Congress opposed to the admission of Texas as a state?**

   A. The slavery issue in Texas had not been decided

   B. Slavery was permitted in Texas

   C. Admission would disrupt the balance between free and slave states

   D. Northerners believed only free states should be admitted to the Union

**Answer: C. Admission would disrupt the balance between free and slave states**

The slavery issue in Texas had been decided, and although slavery was permitted in the state, that was not the reason for the Northerners' objections. Northerners did not believe that only free states should be admitted to the Union but they believed that the admission of Texas would disrupt the balance between slave and free states.

*(Average) (Skill 6.3)*

146. **What is the significance of the Kansas-Nebraska Act of 1854?**

   A. It caused extreme violence

   B. It repealed some of the terms of the Missouri Compromise of 1820

   C. It maintained the balance of free and slave states

   D. It gave Southerners increased influence in Congress

**Answer: B. It repealed some of the terms of the Missouri Compromise of 1820**

The Missouri Compromise admitted Maine as a free state and Missouri as a slave state. The Compromise also drew an imaginary line across the Louisiana Territory to divide the parts that would be free from the parts that would be slave. The Kansas-Nebraska Act of 1854 "erased" the imaginary line and provided that the people of those two territories could decide for themselves whether or not to permit slavery. As a result, violence and bloodshed erupted and two governments existed, one pro-slavery and one anti-slavery.

*(Easy) (Skill 6.3)*

147. **In which state were the Lincoln-Douglas debates held?**

   A. Indiana

   B. Missouri

   C. Illinois

   D. Maryland

**Answer: C. Illinois**

Abraham Lincoln and Stephen Douglas were running for the U.S. Senate from Illinois. They debated in several cities throughout Illinois. The debates directly affected the presidential election of 1860.

*(Challenging) (Skill 6.3)*

148. **Which of the following was an advantage the South possessed before the Civil War?**

    A. More industries

    B. More mineral resources

    C. More railroads

    D. More confidence

**Answer: D. More confidence**

The North had a greater population and more industries and mineral resources. The North also had a better and more extensive transportation system. However, the South was completely confident they would be victorious. Their area was larger and the North would need to invade it. The South also had excellent military officers and men from the south were more familiar with living and working in outdoor environments.

*(Average) (Skill 6.4)*

149. **Which statement about populism is correct?**

    A. It is a philosophy concerned with the lower classes

    B. It flourished in the late nineteenth and early twentieth centuries in the U.S.

    C. The Federalist Party was formed out of the populist philosophy

    D. The Industrial Revolution stifled the growth of the Populist Party

**Answer: B. It flourished in the late nineteenth and early twentieth centuries in the U.S.**

The philosophy of populism was concerned with the common-sense needs of average people. Many parties were formed out of this philosophy but the Federalist Party was an earlier political party. The Industrial Revolution led to a demand for reform, and the philosophy of populism attempted to meet this demand. It was a philosophy that flourished in the late nineteenth and early twentieth centuries in the United States.

*(Challenging) (Skills 6.4, 6.5)*

150. **The Sherman Antitrust Act is an example of legislation passed during which period?**

    A. Populism

    B. Progressivism

    C. Imperialism

    D. World War II

**Answer: B. Progressivism**

Populism was concerned with the common-sense needs of the average person. Imperialism was the era in which countries obtained colonies throughout the world to bolster the nation's economies. The Sherman Antitrust Act was passed by Congress in 1890 and had as its purpose the curtailment of trusts and the creation of monopolies. It was the first "trust-busting" legislation to pass Congress.

*(Challenging) (Skill 6.6)*

**151.** **Which is the political movement that believes in the elimination of all government and the replacement of government by a cooperative community of individuals?**

- A. Dictatorship
- B. Anarchism
- C. Fascism
- D. Communism

**Answer: B. Anarchism**

A dictatorship centralizes all political control in itself and enforces its will with a strong police force. Fascism's basic structure is a one-party state with centralized political control. Communism is characterized by a classless, stateless social organization. Anarchism is a political movement believing in the elimination of all government and its replacement by a cooperative community of individuals.

*(Average) (Skill 6.6)*

**152.** **What is another name for an oligarchy?**

- A. Socialism
- B. Monarchy
- C. Presidential System
- D. Dictatorship

**Answer: D. Dictatorship**

In socialism, the state takes a guiding role in the national economy and provides extensive social services to its population. In a presidential system, the president is elected by direct or indirect election. A monarchy is ruled by a nonelected, usually heredity leader. A dictatorship is also called an oligarchy and rule may be by an individual or small group of individuals.

*(Average) (Skill 6.7)*

**153.** **Which document was based on Greek ideas of democracy, individual rights, and ideas of the European Enlightenment and the Renaissance?**

- A. Articles of Confederation
- B. Albany Plan of Union
- C. U.S. Constitution
- D. Declaration of Independence

**Answer: D. Declaration of Independence**

The Articles of Confederation was the result of the first attempt of the newly independent states to reach a new understanding among themselves. The Albany Plan of Union was proposed as a peaceful resolution with Great Britain by establishing a unified form of government within the colonies. The plan was proposed by Benjamin Franklin. The U.S. Constitution describes and defines the organization of government for the United States. The Declaration of Independence was based on Greek ideas of democracy, individual rights, the philosophy of John Locke and ideas of the Enlightenment and Renaissance.

*(Average) (Skill 6.7)*

**154.** **How many states were required to ratify the Constitution?**

- A. 9
- B. 7
- C. 11
- D. All 13

**Answer: A. 9**

Nine of the original thirteen states were required to ratify the Constitution before it officially became the law of the land. The ratification was completed on June 21, 1788.

*(Easy) (Skill 6.8)*

155. **Which Amendment to the U.S. Constitution guarantees freedom of religion?**

    A. Tenth

    B. Sixth

    C. Fourth

    D. First

**Answer: D. First**

The Tenth Amendment provides that powers not mentioned in the Constitution shall be retained by the states or the people. The Sixth Amendment guarantees the right to a trial by jury. The Fourth Amendment protects people from unreasonable searches and seizures. The First Amendment guarantees freedom of religion.

*(Easy) (Skill 7.1)*

156. **What is 123 Main Street an example of?**

    A. Settlement pattern

    B. Absolute location

    C. Relative location

    D. Topography

**Answer: B. Absolute location**

Settlement patterns relate to distances between cities, town, and villages. A relative location refers to the surrounding geography, such as on the banks of the Mississippi River. Topography refers to the natural and artificial features of an area. Absolute location refers to a specific point, such as 123 Main Street.

*(Average) (Skill 7.1)*

157. **Which of the following is an example of a physical characteristic?**

    A. Canal

    B. Road

    C. River

    D. Tunnel

**Answer: C. River**

Canals, roads, and tunnels are examples of human characters because they are features created by human interaction with the environment. Physical characteristics include features such as rivers, mountains, and deserts.

*(Easy) (Skill 7.1)*

158. **Humans adapting to the environment by wearing warm clothing in cold climates is an example of what theme of geography?**

    A. Human-environmental interaction

    B. Location

    C. Regions

    D. Place

**Answer: A. Human-environmental interaction**

Location refers to geography and is divided into relative and absolute location. Movement covers how humans interact with one another through trade, communications, emigration, and other forms of contact. Regions are areas that have some kind of unifying characteristic, such as a common language. Place has to do with human and physical characteristics. Human-environmental interaction has three main concepts: humans adapting to the environment, modifying the environment, and depending upon the environment.

*(Challenging) (Skill 7.1)*

159. **Relief units are examples of which type of landform?**

A. Formal region

B. Elementary landform

C. Functional region

D. Vernacular region

**Answer: B. Elementary landform**

A formal region is an area defined by actual boundaries. A functional region is defined by a common function, such as telephone service. A vernacular region is a region formed by people's perception, such as the South. A relief unit is an elementary landform. An elementary landform is the smallest homogeneous division of land surface at a given scale or resolution.

*(Easy) (Skill 7.1)*

160. **What percentage of the Earth's surface is made up of land?**

A. 70%

B. 50%

C. 45%

D. 30%

**Answer: D. 30%**

Seventy percent of the Earth's surface is made up of water. Thirty percent is made up of land.

*(Average) (Skill 7.1)*

161. **Which of the following is NOT a characteristic of a delta?**

A. Lowlands area

B. Steep slopes

C. Fertile land

D. Crop-growing area

**Answer: B. Steep slopes**

A delta is an area of lowlands formed by soil and sediment deposited at the mouths of rivers. The soil is generally very fertile and most fertile river deltas are important crop-growing areas. Mountains are landforms with rather steep slopes at least 2,000 feet or more above sea level.

*(Challenging) (Skill 7.1)*

162. **Where are the Atlas Mountains located?**

A. Africa

B. Europe

C. North America

D. South America

**Answer: A. Africa**

The Atlas Mountains are located in North Africa in the country of Morocco.

*(Challenging) (Skill 7.1)*

163. **Which statement about a mesa is INCORRECT?**

    A. It is the flat top of a hill

    B. It is the flat top of a mountain

    C. It usually has steep sides

    D. It is similar to a plateau but larger

    **Answer: D. It is similar to a plateau but larger**

    A mesa is the flat top of a hill or mountain, usually has steep sides, and is similar to a plateau but smaller.

*(Average) (Skill 7.1)*

164. **What is a low area drained by rivers or low spots in mountains?**

    A. Marsh

    B. Basin

    C. Swamp

    D. Delta

    **Answer: B. Basin**

    Marshes and swamps are wet lowlands providing growth of such plants as rushes and reeds. Deltas are areas of lowlands formed by soil and sediment deposited at the mouths of rivers. The soil is generally very fertile and most fertile river deltas are important crop-growing areas. A basin is a low area drained by rivers or low spots in mountains.

*(Challenging) (Skill 7.1)*

165. **Which ocean covers almost one-third of the entire surface of the Earth and separates North and South America from Asia and Australia?**

    A. Pacific

    B. Atlantic

    C. Arctic

    D. Indian

    **Answer: A. Pacific**

    The Atlantic Ocean is one-half the size of the Pacific Ocean and separates North and South America from Africa and Europe. The Indian Ocean touches Africa, Asia, and Australia. The Arctic Ocean extends from North America and Europe to the North Pole.

*(Average) (Skill 7.1)*

166. **What is considered a nation's lifeblood?**

    A. Lake

    B. Sea

    C. River

    D. Ocean

    **Answer: C. River**

    Rivers are considered a nation's lifeblood because they begin as small streams, flow into larger bodies of water, serve as transportation systems, and have many tributaries.

*(Average) (Skill 7.1)*

167. **Which oceans does the Panama Canal connect?**

    A. Arctic and Indian

    B. Indian and Atlantic

    C. Atlantic and Pacific

    D. Pacific and Arctic

    **Answer: C. Atlantic and Pacific**

    The Panama Canal is a man-made passage that crosses Panama's isthmus and connects the Atlantic and Pacific oceans.

*(Average) (Skill 7.1)*

168. **Which statement about a subtropical climate is correct?**

    A. It is characterized by low levels of moisture

    B. It is a humid climate

    C. It is found only north of the tropics

    D. It is found only south of the tropics

    **Answer: B. It is a humid climate**

    Subtropical climates are found north and south of the tropics and have high levels of moisture. These climates have high humidity and are considered humid climates.

*(Challenging) (Skill 7.1)*

169. **Which of the following is a correct statement about vertical climates?**

    A. The temperatures remain constant

    B. They are found in high mountain areas

    C. The crops remain the same, regardless of level

    D. The economic activities are limited because of snow

**Answer: B. They are found in high mountain areas**

Vertical climates are found in high mountain areas. Temperatures, crops, vegetation, and human activities change as one ascends through the different levels of elevation. Economic activities change from things such as grazing sheep and growing corn. Snow is found year round at the top of many mountains.

*(Challenging) (Skill 7.2)*

170. **Which of the following is true about a grid as relating to pinpointing exact locations?**

    A. A grid is the intersection of parallels and meridians at right angles

    B. A grid is the intersection of longitudes and meridians at right angles

    C. A grid is the intersection of parallels and latitudes at right angles

    D. Parallels and meridians do not intersect

**Answer: A. A grid is the intersection of parallels and meridians at right angles**

Lines of latitude are called parallels. Lines of longitude are called meridians. The intersections of these lines at right angles form a grid, making it possible to pinpoint an exact location of any place using any two grid coordinates.

*(Average) (Skill 7.2)*

171. **Which of the following is a country in the "land bridge of Middle America?**

    A. Brazil

    B. Ecuador

    C. Bosnia

    D. Jamaica

**Answer: D. Jamaica**

Brazil and Ecuador are located in South America. Bosnia is located in Europe. Jamaica is an island nation of the West Indies and part of the "land bridge" of Middle America.

*(Easy) (Skill 8.1)*

172. **Which ancient civilization created paper from papyrus?**

    A. Sumerians

    B. Chinese

    C. Egyptians

    D. Greeks

    **Answer: C. Egyptians**

    The Sumerians devised the system of cuneiform writing and the Chinese invented printing. The Greeks contributed the alphabet that was derived from Phoenicians, which formed the basis for the Roman alphabet. The Egyptians created paper from papyrus.

*(Challenging) (Skill 8.1)*

173. **Which of the following statements about the Kush civilization is INCORRECT?**

    A. They lived in Egypt

    B. Their civilization was characterized as an "unsettled way of life"

    C. The people subsisted on hunting and herding cattle

    D. Their civilization appears to be the second oldest in Egypt

    **Answer: B. Their civilization was characterized as an "unsettled way of life"**

The Kush civilization lived in a region upstream from the first cataract of the Nile River in Egypt. They were hunters and fishers, herded cattle, and gathered grain. Their civilization appears to be the second oldest in Africa, after Egypt.

*(Easy) (Skill 8.1)*

174. **Which ancient civilization's attitude about sports, with an emphasis on a physically sound body, led to the tradition of the Olympic Games?**

    A. Greece

    B. Rome

    C. Persia

    D. China

    **Answer: A. Greece**

    The Greeks' attitude about sports, with an emphasis on a physically sound body, led to the tradition of the Olympic Games.

*(Average) (Skill 8.1)*

175. **Which ancient civilization is remembered for its city-states?**

    A. Rome

    B. Persia

    C. Greece

    D. China

    **Answer: C. Greece**

    Greece was responsible for the rise of independent, strong city-states. Athens and Sparta are two examples.

*(Challenging) (Skill 8.1)*

**176. Approximately how long did the ancient civilization of Rome last?**

A.  100 years

B.  500 years

C.  1000 years

D.  1500 years

**Answer: C. 1000 years**

The ancient civilization of Rome lasted approximately one thousand years. That period includes the periods of the Roman Republic and the Roman Empire. Rome's influence on Europe and its history was felt for a much longer period.

*(Challenging) (Skill 8.1)*

**177. Which statement about the Pax Romana is INCORRECT?**

A.  The Pax Romana was an accomplishment of the Greeks

B.  The Pax Romana allowed for free travel

C.  The Pax Romana affected a vast area

D.  The Pax Romana was an accomplishment of the Romans

**Answer: A. The Pax Romana was an accomplishment of the Greeks**

The Pax Romana was one of the greatest accomplishments of the Romans. The term means "Roman peace" and it was the long period of peace that allowed free travel and trade, which spread people, culture, goods, and ideas all over a vast area of the known world.

*(Average) (Skill 8.1)*

**178. Who unified Greece?**

A.  Julius Caesar

B.  Alexander

C.  Pythagoras

D.  Homer

**Answer: B. Alexander**

Homer was the Greek epic poet who wrote the Illiad and the Odyssey. Pythagoras laid the foundations of geometry. Julius Caesar was named consul of Rome during the first century BCE and later became dictator. He was the transitional leader between the Roman Republic and what would become the Roman Empire. Alexander was a Macedonian and he conquered Greece. He unified Greece and introduced the culture throughout the eastern world. He also provided many Roman emperors with a role model.

*(Easy) (Skill 8.1)*

**179. Which ancient civilization served as a model for modern government, especially in federal systems such as that found in the United States?**

A.  Egyptian

B.  Greek

C.  Chinese

D.  Roman

**Answer: D. Roman**

The ancient Roman civilization served as a model for modern government, especially in federal systems such as that found in the United States. The Greek civilization served as an inspiration to the Roman Republic, which followed in its tradition of democracy.

(Challenging) (Skill 8.2)

180. **Which decade marked the fall of the Soviet Union?**

    A. 1990s

    B. 1980s

    C. 1970s

    D. 1960s

**Answer: A. 1990s**

The Cold War began after World War II when the United States attempted to control the spread of Communism throughout the world. The threat of nuclear war increased as the Soviet Union and the United States produced more and more weapons in an extended arms race. The threat of the spread of nuclear weapons largely diminished after the fall of the Soviet Union in the early 1990s, which ended the Cold War.

(Average) (Skill 8.2)

181. **Saddam Hussein was ousted as dictator of which country?**

    A. Iraq

    B. Afghanistan

    C. Iran

    D. Palestine

**Answer: A. Iraq**

The United States invaded Afghanistan after the terrorist attack on New York City on September 11, 2001. The United States, England, and several smaller

countries addressed instability in the Middle East by ousting Iraqi dictator Saddam Hussein in a military campaign. Palestine is located in the eastern Mediterranean.

(Challenging) (Skill 8.4)

182. **Which statement about a market is INCORRECT?**

    A. Markets exist in both the input and output sides of the economy

    B. Buyers and sellers must meet face to face

    C. An output market refers to the market in which goods and services are sold

    D. In a market-oriented economy, markets function on the basis of supply and demand

**Answer: B. Buyers and sellers must meet face to face**

A market is defined as the mechanism that brings buyers and sellers in contact with each other so they can buy and sell. Markets exist in both the input and output sides of the economy. Output markets refer to the markets in which goods and services are sold. In a market-oriented economy, markets function on the basis of supply and demand. Buyers and sellers do not have to meet face to face. Purchasing items from a catalog or through the Internet are examples of parts of a bona fide market where buyers and sellers never come face to face.

*(Average) (Skill 8.4)*

183. **Which of the following is NOT a category of factors of production?**

    A. Land

    B. Labor

    C. Markets

    D. Capital

    **Answer: C. Markets**

    Land, labor, and capital are examples of factors of production. Factors of production exist in the market and are bought and sold in the market. A market is defined as the mechanism that brings buyers and sellers together so they can buy and sell.

*(Challenging) (Skill 8.4)*

184. **Which of the following terms is determined as the overlap of the buying decisions of buyers with the selling decisions of the sellers?**

    A. Supply and demand

    B. Factor of production

    C. Input market

    D. Equilibrium price

    **Answer: D. Equilibrium price**

    Supply refers to what sellers produce. Demand refers to what buyers will purchase. A factor of production is a resource that is bought and sold. An input market is the market where factors of production are bought and sold. Equilibrium prices are determined as the overlap of the buying decisions of buyers with the selling decisions of sellers.

*(Average) (Skill 8.6)*

185. **Which type of economic system is characterized by both markets and planning?**

    A. Market economy

    B. Centrally planned economy

    C. Market socialism

    D. Non-market economy

    **Answer: C. Market socialism**

    A non-market economy would not use markets. A market economy uses supply and demand to answer economic questions. A centrally planned economy means there is little, if any, private ownership. The planning authority makes the decisions. Market socialism is between the two extremes of market economies and planning. Planning is usually used to direct resources at the upper levels of the economy, with markets used to determine the prices of consumer goods and wages. A market socialism economy uses planning and markets.

## Science (5005)

*(Average) (Skill 9.1)*

186. The earth's core is _____ its mantle.

    A. less dense than

    B. denser than

    C. just as dense as

    D. the core and mantle are the same

    **Answer: B. denser than**

    The earth's core is denser as the heaviest matter is found at the Earth's center.

*(Average) (Skill 9.1)*

187. Which of the following is NOT located in the upper mantle?

    A. Sial

    B. Asthenosphere

    C. Troposphere

    D. Mesosphere

    **Answer: A. Sial**

    The troposphere is located in the earth's atmosphere. The sial is the layer of the lithosphere that is above water.

*(Easy) (Skill 9.1)*

188. _____ is the second-most abundant gas in the earth's atmosphere.

    A. Nitrogen

    B. Argon

    C. Oxygen

    D. Chlorine

    **Answer: C. Oxygen**

Oxygen is the second most abundant gas, behind nitrogen.

*(Average) (Skill 9.1)*

189. The _____ is the coldest layer in the atmosphere.

    A. mesosphere

    B. thermosphere

    C. troposphere

    D. stratosphere

    **Answer: A. mesosphere**

    The mesosphere is the coldest layer in the atmosphere, with average temperatures reaching close to −100°C at its top.

*(Challenging) (Skill 9.1)*

190. When gases in the _____ emit light energy after being excited by solar radiation, the Aurora Borealis occurs in the northern hemisphere.

    A. exosphere

    B. stratosphere

    C. ionosphere

    D. troposphere

    **Answer: C. ionosphere**

    Auroras can occur around 80 kilometers or more above the earth's surface. This distance demarcates the ionosphere, which is the lower layer of the thermosphere. The exosphere is the upper layer of the thermosphere.

*(Average) (Skill 9.2)*

191. _____ is natural mountain building.

    A. Orogeny

    B. Dig slip

    C. Folding

    D. Faulting

**Answer: A. Orogeny**

Orogeny is the process of natural mountain building. Folding, dig slip, and faulting are ways in which different shaped mountains can form.

*(Average) (Skill 9.2)*

192. When lava cools, _____ rock is formed.

    A. sedimentary

    B. igneous

    C. metamorphic

    D. flint

**Answer: B. igneous**

Igneous rocks forms as lava cools, and this can happen above or below ground.

*(Challenging) (Skill 9.2)*

193. Which of the following is true about the three rock types?

    A. Igneous rock is formed from the cementation of sediments

    B. Sedimentary rock is formed from molten rock

    C. Metamorphic rock is formed at low temperatures and high pressures

    D. Metamorphic rock results from its parent rock undergoing chemical change

**Answer: D. Metamorphic rock results from its parent rock undergoing chemical change**

Metamorphic rock is formed at *high* temperatures and high pressures, which cause deformation, compaction, and chemical change (through reactions with water and other compounds) of the parent rock.

*(Easy) (Skill 9.3)*

194. We are currently living in the _____ era.

    A. Cenozoic

    B. Mesozoic

    C. Jurassic

    D. Permian

**Answer: A. Cenozoic**

We are currently living in the quaternary period of the Cenozoic era in the paleontological record.

*(Challenging) (Skill 9.3)*

195. Which of the following is NOT true about fossils?

    A. A fossilized cast of a bone is composed of bone

    B. Some organisms are embedded in amber (tree sap)

    C. Fossils of footprints are possible

    D. The heat of magma would inhibit fossilization

**Answer: A. A fossilized cast of a bone is composed of bone**

When the original organism or parts of an organisms are completely destroyed or decayed and are replaced with the components of sedimentary rock, then the resulting fossil is more of an outline or impression of the organism rather than the actual organism.

*(Challenging) (Skill 9.3)*

196. The _____ the time period an index fossil could have been deposited the more precise geologic dating will be.

A. longer

B. shorter

C. it depends

D. the timing does not matter

**Answer: B. shorter**

An index fossil is known to have lived in a specific time period. The shorter the time period then the more precise geologic dating will be because the range of possible times is narrower.

*(Easy) (Skill 9.4)*

197. There are _____ established planets in the solar system.

A. ten

B. nine

C. eight

D. seven

**Answer: C. eight**

As of 2006 Pluto's status as a planet has been reconsidered, and it is no longer considered an *established* planet.

*(Average) (Skill 9.4)*

198. Earth's galaxy is called the _____.

A. Big Dipper

B. Ursa Minor

C. Milky Way

D. Great Bear

**Answer: C. Milky Way**

A galaxy is a spiral or elliptical collection of stars. Earth's galaxy is called the Milky Way and it is a spiral galaxy. The Big Dipper, Usra Minor, and Great Bear are all constellations, not galaxies.

*(Average) (Skill 9.4)*

199. When the sun and moon are on opposite sides of the earth, observers on Earth perceive a _____.

A. gibbous moon

B. new moon

C. full moon

D. crescent moon

**Answer: C. full moon**

Because the sun and moon are on opposite sides, the full face of one side of the moon is illuminated by the sun.

*(Challenging) (Skill 9.5)*

200. Which of the following is NOT true about the sun?

A. The sun is a star

B. The chromosphere produces sunspots

C. The photosphere is the surface of the sun

D. The corona is only visible during total solar eclipses

**Answer: B. The chromosphere produces sunspots**

The sun's photosphere produces sunspots. Its chromosphere, composed of hydrogen gas, produces solar flares and gases that are emitted outward into space.

*(Challenging) (Skill 9.5)*

201. **Which of the following is NOT true about the earth's seasons?**

  A. The earth's tilted rotation axis influences the amount of sunlight the northern and southern hemispheres receive

  B. The solstices occur when the sun reaches its highest or lower point of the day at noon

  C. During the summer solstice the southern hemisphere leans toward the sun

  D. During the winter solstice the northern hemisphere leans away from the sun

**Answer: C. During the summer solstice the southern hemisphere leans toward the sun**

During the summer solstice in June the northern hemisphere leans toward the sun, and that part of the world experiences the summer season.

*(Average) (Skill 10.1)*

202. **Mitochondria are on the _____ scale in size while the animal cell that contains them is on the _____ scale in size.**

  A. micron; nanometer

  B. millimeter; nanometer

  C. nanometer; micron

  D. micron; millimeter

**Answer: C. nanometer; micron**

Mitochondria are nanometer-sized organelles that produce a cell's energy. Animal cells typically range from ten to one hundred microns in diameter.

*(Challenging) (Skill 10.2)*

203. **The mitotic division of one somatic cell results in what number of diploid/haploid (choose one) cells?**

  A. 4 cells; haploid

  B. 4 cells; diploid

  C. 2 cells; haploid

  D. 2 cells; diploid

**Answer: D. 2 cells; diploid**

Mitosis is the division of somatic cells. Somatic cells are diploid meaning that they have two copies of each chromosome. For each cell that undergoes mitosis two diploid cells result.

*(Average) (Skill 10.2)*

204. View the monohybrid cross below for having blue or brown eyes. B is the dominant allele and b is the recessive allele. Having the B allele results in brown eyes and not having it will result in blue eyes. What percentage of children are heterozygotes?

|   | B  | B  |
|---|----|----|
| B | BB | Bb |
| b | Bb | bb |

A. 25%

B. 0%

C. 50%

D. 75%

**Answer: C. 50%**

Heterozygotes have one dominant allele and one recessive allele. In the monohybrid cross $\frac{2}{4}$ are Bb, which equals 50%.

*(Easy) (Skill 10.2)*

205. **What is a heterozygote?**

A. A person having two dominant alleles for a gene

B. A person having two recessive alleles for a gene

C. A person having one dominant and one recessive allele for a gene

D. A person having codominant alleles for a gene

**Answer: C. A person having one dominant and one recessive allele for a gene**

Heterozygotes have one dominant allele and one recessive allele for a gene.

*(Easy) (Skill 10.3)*

206. _____ is the change in a population's heritable traits over time.

A. Biological evolution

B. Natural selection

C. Reproduction

D. Convergence

**Answer: A. Biological evolution**

Biological evolution is the change in a population's genes over time as a result of different processes like natural selection, sexual selection, or mutation.

*(Average) (Skill 10.4)*

207. **Which of the following does NOT reproduce sexually?**

A. Fungi

B. Animals

C. Protists

D. Plants

**Answer: C. Protists**

All protists reproduce asexually. Fungi, animals and plants can reproduce either asexually or sexually.

*(Easy) (Skill 10.5)*

208. **Which of the following is NOT one of the five kingdoms of living organisms?**

A. Animalia

B. Chordata

C. Plantae

D. Monera

**Answer: B. Chordata**

Chordata is a classification for a phylum, the taxonomy level immediately below kingdom.

*(Average) (Skill 10.5)*

209. **Which of the following is NOT the correct match of an Animalia phylum with examples of organisms found within the phylum?**

    A. Arthropoda – spiders and insects

    B. Echinodermata – sea urchins and starfish

    C. Mollusca – clams and octopi

    D. Annelida – crustaceans

    **Answer: D. Annelida – crustaceans**

    Annelida is the phylum of animals that includes segmented worms.

*(Average) (Skill 10.6)*

210. **Which of the following shows the levels of biomes in increasing complexity from left-to-right?**

    A. Biomes – community – population – species

    B. Biomes – population – community – species

    C. Species – population – community – biomes

    D. Species – community – population – biomes

    **Answer: C. Species – population – community – biomes**

    A population is a group of the same species in an area, a community is the composite of multiple populations in the same area, and a biome is the composite of multiple communities.

*(Challenging) (Skill 10.6)*

211. **Which of the following is NOT a characteristic of an environment's carrying capacity?**

    A. The carrying capacity is the maximum life that can be supported in an environment

    B. The carrying capacity of an environment increases as populations of species increase

    C. The rate of population growth stops when resources are exhausted

    D. The rate of population growth slows as resources become scarcer

    **Answer: B. The carrying capacity of an environment increases as populations of species increase**

    The carrying capacity moderates population growth within an environment and is fixed. As population growth increases and resources are depleted more, the carrying capacity limits the rate at which populations can continue to grow until populations can no longer grow.

*(Easy) (Skill 10.7)*

212. **Which of the following is NOT a communicable disease?**

    A. Influenza

    B. Diabetes Mellitus

    C. Tuberculosis

    D. Measles

    **Answer: B. Diabetes Mellitus**

    Diabetes cannot be spread from person to person so it is a non-communicable disease.

*(Average) (Skill 10.8)*

213. **Which of the following is NOT a characteristic of science as an endeavor?**

    A. Scientific experiments and undertakings are limited by current technology

    B. Scientific knowledge changes over time

    C. The scientific enterprise consists of various people and activities in many locations

    D. Scientific knowledge is based on individuals' feelings and biases

    **Answer: D. Scientific knowledge is based on individuals' feelings and biases**

    Scientific knowledge is validated by extensive testing and review before accepted as fact.

*(Average) (Skill 10.8)*

214. **All of the following are primary sources of funding for scientific research in the United States except _____?**

    A. the federal government

    B. state governments

    C. private or public corporations

    D. private citizens

    **Answer: D. private citizens**

    The science enterprise is so complex and expensive that the smallest scientific research projects costs tens of thousands of dollars to conduct after taking into account salaries, supplies, equipment, and facilities. Such a cost is the reason that federal and state governments support scientific research.

*(Challenging) (Skill 10.9)*

215. **Which of the following is true when a new theory is developed regarding a topic?**

    A. The existing theories on the topic could be altered/adjusted upon proof

    B. The new theory should just be accepted

    C. The new theory should not be even considered

    D. Both the new and old theories should be debated and a vote taken on which one to accept

    **Answer: A. The existing theories on the topic could be altered/adjusted upon proof**

    The nature of science is such that it is always changing. Therefore, new theories, upon proof, can help adjust or alter currently existing theories. New data and new technologies contribute to different interpretations of observations.

*(Average) (Skill 10.9)*

216. **In which stage of the scientific inquiry process can a researcher be required to include graphical representations of the information he has gathered?**

    A. Observation

    B. Hypothesis generation

    C. Data analysis

    D. Conclusion

    **Answer: C. Data analysis**

    The data analysis stage is when the researcher incorporates mathematical operations and graphical representation to critically explain trends in his/her study. In the hypothesis stage he would not have collected the data yet to present it graphically, and the conclusion would summarize his findings.

*(Challenging) (Skill 10.10)*

217. **Which of the following are online databases that scientists use to search for journal articles?**

    A. Web of Science

    B. PubMed and PubChem

    C. Google Scholar

    D. All of the above

    **Answer: D. All of the above**

    All of the databases are popular within the scientific community. They all provide articles (behind a paywall) for reading across a wide range of scientific disciplines, and some include research articles that focus on teaching science at the elementary level.

*(Challenging) (Skill 10.11)*

218. **Which of the following is NOT a type of equilibrium?**

    A. Biological evolution

    B. Genetic (population) equilibrium

    C. Thermal equilibrium

    D. Chemical equilibrium

    **Answer: A. Biological evolution**

    Biological evolution is by definition a state in which equilibrium is not met because genes are evolving and the net change is not zero. Conversely, genetic equilibrium is the theoretical and rare occurrence in which a population is not evolving.

*(Average) (Skill 11.1)*

219. **Which property of matter is NOT matched with its correct unit of measurement?**

    A. Velocity – meter/second

    B. Electrical potential – volt

    C. Power – joule/second

    D. Specific gravity – gram/cubic centimeter

    **Answer: D. Specific gravity – gram/cubic centimeter**

    An object's specific gravity does not have units since it is the ratio of a substance's density to the density of water.

*(Average) (Skill 11.1)*

220. **_____ properties cannot be observed without changing the identity of a substance.**

    A. Chemical

    B. Intensive

    C. Physical

    D. Extensive

    **Answer: A. Chemical**

    Chemical properties describe how a substance's composition can be changed, resulting in a new substance. Extensive and intensive properties are both types of physical properties.

*(Challenging) (Skill 11.1)*

221. **Which process is NOT matched with its correct state of matter conversion?**

    A. Condensation – gas to liquid

    B. Melting – solid to liquid

    C. Sublimation – gas to solid

    D. Evaporation – liquid to gas

    **Answer: C. Sublimation – gas to solid**

    Sublimation is the process by which a substance changes from a solid to a gaseous state.

*(Easy) (Skill 11.1)*

222. **Which particle is correctly matched with its charge?**

    A. Proton – negative

    B. Neutron – positive

    C. Electron – no charge

    D. None of the above

    **Answer: D. None of the above**

    None of the particles in the answer choices are matched with their correct charges. Protons are positively charged, electrons are negatively charged, and neutrons have no charge.

*(Challenging) (Skill 11.1)*

223. **Which of the following terms is NOT correctly matched with its definition?**

    A. Atomic mass – average mass of an element's isotopes

    B. Mass number – number of protons and electrons

    C. Atomic number – number of protons

    D. Atomic mass unit – standard unit of measurement for atomic mass

**Answer: B. Mass number – number of protons and electrons**

An element's mass number is its number of protons and *neutrons,* not electrons.

*(Challenging) (Skill 11.1)*

224. **Which of the following is NOT an example of a mixture?**

    A. Soil

    B. Air

    C. Ocean water

    D. $H_2O$

**Answer: D. $H_2O$**

$H_2O$ is not a mixture but is instead a compound because the two elements, hydrogen and oxygen, are chemically bound.

*(Challenging) (Skill 11.2)*

225. **If an object is moving it can be said to have _____.**

    A. velocity

    B. acceleration

    C. kinetic energy

    D. All of the above

**Answer: D. All of the above**

If an object is moving then it will have a velocity, a rate at which the velocity is changing (acceleration), and the energy associated with its velocity (kinetic energy).

*(Average) (Skill 11.2)*

226. Force is measured in _____.

   A. watts

   B. amperes

   C. newtons

   D. meters/second

**Answer: C. newtons**

The unit of measurement for force is the newton, named after Sir Isaac Newton.

*(Challenging) (Skill 11.2)*

227. Car 1 is traveling on a highway has mass 1800 kg and velocity 30 m/s. Another car (Car 2) on the highway also has mass 1800 kg, but is traveling at a velocity of 50 m/s. Which car has greater momentum?

   A. Car 1

   B. Car 2

   C. The cars have the same momentum

   D. It's impossible to tell

**Answer: B. Car 2**

No calculations are necessary for this problem. An object's momentum is its mass multiplied by its velocity. Since both cars have the same mass and Car 2's velocity is 50 m/s (a value greater than 30m/s) then the resulting momentum for Car 2 will be higher.

*(Challenging) (Skill 11.2)*

228. Which of the following laws is incorrectly matched with its description?

   A. Newton's 3rd Law: For every action there is just an equal reaction

   B. Law of Gravity: Two bodies in the universe attract each other with a force that is directly proportional to the product of their masses

   C. Newton's 2nd Law: If a force acts on an object it will cause the object to accelerate

   D. Newton's 1st Law: An object in motion will remain in motion unless acted upon by an external force

**Answer: A. Newton's 3rd Law – For every action there is just an equal reaction**

Newton's 3rd Law states that for every action there is an equal and *opposite* reaction.

*(Easy) (Skill 11.3)*

229. The law of the conservation of energy states that _____.

   A. energy is neither created nor destroyed

   B. energy changes form

   C. energy is conserved over time

   D. All of the above

**Answer: D. All of the above**

The law of the conservation of energy states that because energy is neither created nor destroyed it must change form and be conserved over time within a system.

*(Challenging) (Skill 11.3)*

230. **What are the units of measurement for work?**

    A. N/m

    B. N·m

    C. J

    D. B and C

**Answer: D. B and C**

Work is form of energy so it is measured in joules. Similarly the equation for work is force multiplied by the distance the object that the force is applied to moves. A newton-meter (N·m) is the same as a joule.

*(Average) (Skill 11.3)*

231. **If a gas is expanding in a container, then _____.**

    A. the gas is doing work on the walls of the container

    B. the container is doing work on the container

    C. neither the gas nor container is doing work

    D. both the gas and container are doing work

**Answer: A. the gas is doing work on the walls of the container**

When a gas expands in a closed volume, it applies a force on the surface of the container, which must respond to its expansion.

*(Challenging) (Skill 11.3)*

232. **Which of the following terms is NOT true about the laws of thermodynamics?**

    A. The laws cover systems in thermal equilibrium

    B. The 1st law of thermodynamics states that the heat energy supplied to the system is equal to the energy used by the system to do work externally

    C. The 2nd law of thermodynamics states that a machine can be 100% efficient—all the energy it uses goes towards its work and is not lost passively

    D. The 2nd law of thermodynamics states that heat cannot spontaneously move from a colder to warmer object

**Answer: C. The 2nd law of thermodynamics states that a machine can be 100% efficient—all the energy it uses goes towards its work and is not lost passively**

The 2nd law of thermodynamics states that no machine can be 100% efficient because there will always be some amount of heat lost to the environment as the machine does its work.

*(Easy) (Skill 11.4)*

233. **_____ are the atomic particles primarily responsible for electricity.**

    A. Electrons

    B. Protons

    C. Neutrons

    D. Quarks

**Answer: A. Electrons**

Moving electrons that surround the atomic nucleus in orbitals are primarily responsible for the interaction of atoms with other atoms and/or compounds.

*(Average) (Skill 11.4)*

234. **Which of the following does NOT describe chemical reactions?**

    A. Chemical reactions involve the breaking of chemical bonds

    B. Chemical reactions result in chemical changes of the starting substances

    C. Chemical reactions involve changes in the structure of atomic nuclei

    D. Chemical reactions involve the activity of electrons

    **Answer: C. Chemical reactions involve changes in the structure of atomic nuclei**

    Chemical reactions do not change the structure, energy, or composition of atomic nuclei.

*(Challenging) (Skill 11.4)*

235. **Which of the following is true about magnets?**

    A. Magnets produce electric fields

    B. All metals are attracted to magnets

    C. Magnets only attract magnetic objects

    D. Magnetic fields are invisible to the human eye

    **Answer: D. Magnetic fields are invisible to the human eye**

    Magnetic fields are invisible—we cannot see them but know that they exist when we use magnets. Magnets do not produce magnetic fields, only metals like iron and nickel are attracted to magnets, and magnets can attract or repel magnetic objects.

CPSIA information can be obtained
at www.ICGtesting.com
Printed in the USA
BVHW011103120419
545355BV00013B/795/P

9 781607 873594